12.99. ZP 9/03

075288

MANCHE

Dinard St-Malo Mont-
St-Michel

St-Brieuc

CÔTES D'ARMOR
Pages 86–111

Dinan

CÔTES D'ARMOR

ILLE-ET-VILAINE

Loudéac

Rennes

Pontivy

Ploërmel

ILLE-ET-VILAINE
Pages 52–85

MORBIHAN

MAYENNE

Vannes

Châteaubriant

LOIRE-
ATLANTIQUE

St-Nazaire

MAINE-
ET-LOIRE

Nantes

D1407097

**LOIRE-
ATLANTIQUE**
Pages 196–211

VENDÉE

BRITTANY

DK EYEWITNESS *TRAVEL GUIDES*

BRITTANY

DORLING KINDERSLEY
LONDON • NEW YORK • MUNICH
MELBOURNE • DELHI
www.dk.com

DK

A DORLING KINDERSLEY BOOK

www.dk.com

Produced by Hachette Tourisme, Paris, France

EDITORIAL DIRECTOR Cécile Boyer
PROJECT EDITOR Catherine Laussucq
ART DIRECTOR JAD-Hersienne
DESIGNERS Maogani
CARTOGRAPHY Fabrice Le Goff

CONTRIBUTORS
Gaëtan du Chatenet, Jean-Philippe Follet,
Jean-Yves Gendillard, Éric Gibory, Renée Grimaud,
Georges Minois

Dorling Kindersley Limited
PUBLISHING MANAGERS Jane Ewart, Fay Franklin
ENGLISH TRANSLATION & EDITOR Lucilla Watson
DTP Jason Little, Conrad van Dyke
PRODUCTION Sarah Dodd

Reproduced in Singapore by Colourscan
Printed and bound in Italy by Graphicom s.r.l.

First published in Great Britain in 2003
by Dorling Kindersley Limited
80 Strand, London WC2R 0RL

◁ **A beach at Brignogan, on the Pointe de Pontusval, Finistère**

CONTENTS

**Santig Du, Cathédrale
St-Corentin, Quimper**

INTRODUCING
BRITTANY

**Detail of traditional costume,
pardon of St-Anne-d'Auray**

The Jaudy estuary at Plougrescant, Côtes d'Armor

BRITTANY REGION BY REGION

The lighthouse on the Île Vierge, Côtes d'Armor

TRAVELLERS' NEEDS

Detail of a stained-glass window,
Cathédrale St-Corentin, Quimper

Château de Traonjoly, near
Plouescat, northern Finistère

Château de Josselin, in the Morbihan *(pp192–3)*

INTRODUCING
BRITTANY

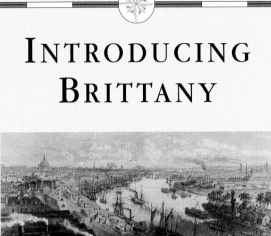

Putting Brittany on the Map

Surrounded by 2,863 km (1,779 miles) of coastline, Brittany covers an area of 34,000 sq km (13,125 sq miles), or 6 per cent of French territory. It has over 4 million inhabitants (7 per cent of the French population), and a population density of 119 per sq km (308 per sq mile). Over the last 25 years, Brittany's population has increased faster than the national average. The westernmost point in Europe, Brittany has become an economic hub of international importance. Its growing prosperity is paralleled by a strong cultural identity.

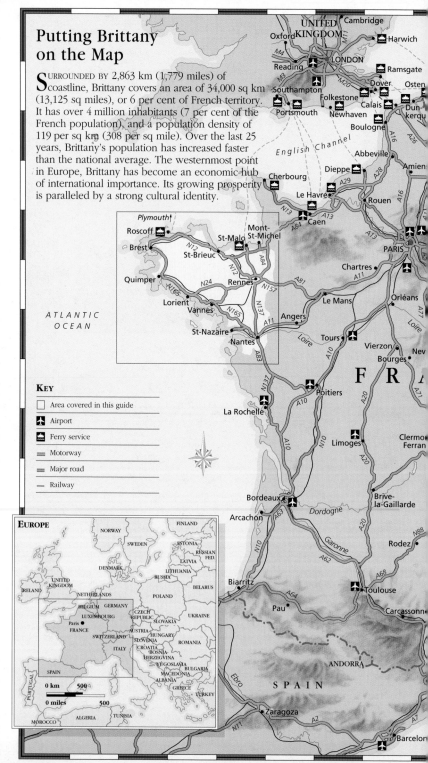

KEY

☐	Area covered in this guide
✈	Airport
⛴	Ferry service
▬	Motorway
▬	Major road
—	Railway

EUROPE

◁ **Port Breton**, by Paul Bellanger-Adhémar

Aerial view of the town of Quimper

0 km 100
0 miles 100

MEDITERRANEAN SEA

A PORTRAIT OF BRITTANY

ITH ITS EVENTFUL *history, contrasting landscapes, diverse economy and exceptionally rich cultural heritage, Brittany is a multifaceted region. While Breton traditions are very much alive, and while the region is famous for its menhirs, Brittany has also embraced the technological revolutions of the modern age. It is, for example, a major centre of the electronics industry.*

Brittany consists of two distinct areas: a coastal region and an inland area. This is reflected in the Celtic names Armor, meaning "country by the sea", and Argoat, "wooded country". The coastline consists of a succession of cliffs, dunes, estuaries, mud flats and marsh land. The westernmost point in Europe, Brittany sinks beneath the sea, extended by a continental shelf. To the north, this shelf rises to form the British Isles. To the south, it extends along the coast of Brittany.

Since ancient times, this maritime region has provided rich fishing grounds. Today, the abundant fish stocks here are still a mainstay of the Breton economy. Another is the seaweed that grows along the coast and that is used by the food, pharmaceuticals and cosmetics industries.

Bordered by the English Channel and the Atlantic Ocean, Brittany is closely associated with seafaring. From the monks that sailed from Britain in their makeshift boats to evangelize Armorica (the old name for western Brittany), to the international yachtsmen of today, and including some great explorers and notorious privateers, Brittany's seamen have an illustrious place in the annals of European seafaring.

Young woman from Fouesnant

Stately ships at the Fête Internationale de la Mer et des Marins, a major annual event held in Brest

◁ Procession, with parish banners and traditional costume, at the Grand Pardon in Quimper

Breton lace for sale at a market in Ste-Anne-d'Auray, in the Morbihan

It was shipbuilding and metalworking that stripped the Argoat region of most of its trees, which had already been heavily exploited since Roman times. Only 10 per cent of Brittany's primeval forest remains today.

A DIVERSE ECONOMY

Bretons have never been daunted by harsh natural elements. They went as far as Newfoundland and Iceland during the peak deep-sea fishing years of the 19th century, then, following the collapse of that trade, turned to factory ships,

Old advertising poster for Béghin-Say sugar

which concentrated on the Atlantic coastlines of Africa, Morocco,

Mauritania, Senegal and South America. Local coastal fishing, by contrast, has proved more resistant to economic instability. However, while the industry still involves three-quarters of Breton fishing vessels, it has to contend with foreign imports, falling prices, dwindling fish stocks, industrial pollution, periodic oil spillages and competition from fish farming. The industry is now undergoing reorganization in order to strengthen its infrastructure.

While fishing has been under threat for some 50 years, agriculture, food crops and tourism underpin the region's economy. Brittany is the foremost milk producer in France. It also provides a quarter of the country's livestock and is a prime producer of fruit and vegetables. Breton produce is marketed under such well-known brand names as Saupiquet, Béghin-Say, Petit Navire, Paysans Bretons, Père Dodu and Hénaff (a famous pâté). Manufacturing and the service industry are also well developed. One Breton in three works in manufacturing or the

Plage du Casino, one of the beautiful beaches at St-Quay-Portrieux, on the Côtes d'Armor building trade, while one in two works in retailing, the service industry or administration. High-tech industries have multiplied and many technological innovations have been developed in the region. Brittany is also one of the most popular tourist destinations in France.

A CULTURE REVIVED

Traditional Breton music underwent a major revival in the 1960s

Breton woman at the Festival Interceltique in Lorient

thanks to Alan Stivell, Kristen Noguès, Gilles Servat and Tri Yann, who, with others, have been prominent among the *bagadou*, as Breton musical groups are known. For several years now, a second wave in the revival of Breton music has turned certain recordings into bestsellers. Denez Prigent, the pioneer of this generation, has also played a major role in the revival of traditional Breton dance and *festou-noz*, or popular Breton dance festivals.

Street sign in Quimper

However, the music scene in Brittany goes well beyond traditional forms. In terms of their importance, rock festivals such as the Transmusicales in Rennes, the Route du Rock in St-Malo, and the Festival des Vieilles Charrues in Carhaix, are on a par with the great Festival Interceltique in Lorient.

In parallel with the Breton cultural revival of the 1960s and 1970s, the Breton language has also been reinvigorated, thanks most notably to the establishment of bilingual schools (known as Diwan). Although only a minority of Bretons support this revival, the whole population is aware of Armorica's great literary heritage.

The growth of high-tech establishments can seem incongruous in this land of menhirs, Romanesque chapels, Gothic churches, fortified castles, coastal forts and 18th-century manor houses. Since Neolithic times, when menhirs were raised, and cairns, megalithic monuments and other passage graves were built, religion has imbued local culture. Romanesque churches appeared in the 11th and 12th centuries, but the golden age of religious architecture came in the 13th century, with the Gothic period.

If religion has left its mark on the landscape of Brittany, so has secular life. Throughout the Middle Ages, local noblemen, engaged in wars with France and England, built fortresses and citadels. Indeed, Brittany is one of the regions of France with the greatest number of historic monuments. These, with the local traditions of furniture-making, textiles, gastronomy and painting, contribute to Brittany's fabulously rich cultural heritage.

The Roche aux Fées, one of Brittany's finest megalithic monuments, in the Ille-et-Vilaine

Landscape and Birds of Brittany

Montagu's harrier

Brittany attracts more sea birds than any other coastal region of France. At the end of the summer, birds that have nested in northern Europe begin to appear on the coast of Brittany. While some species continue on their southern migrations to spend the winter in warmer climates, many stay in Brittany until the early spring, when, together with birds newly returned from the south, they fly north once again to breed.

Male and female razorbills

FLAT, SANDY COASTLINE

Plants growing on beaches and dunes can withstand saline conditions. Sea rocket and several species of orach grow on the beaches. Among the grasses that take root on the dunes and prevent them from being eroded by wind, are spurge, sea holly, convolvulus and gillyflowers.

BAYS AND MARSHY COASTS

Sandy, muddy coastal areas are covered with greyish, low-growing vegetation such as glasswort, salt-wort and obione, and sometimes with the purple-flowering sea lavender. These plants thrive in saline, waterlogged ground, which is washed by the tide twice a day.

The ringed plover *patrols sandy beaches, where it feeds on marine worms, sandhoppers and small molluscs.*

Sandpipers *move about in large flocks, constantly probing the mud with their beaks.*

The European bee-eater *is seen in Brittany from April to September. It overwinters south of the Sahara.*

Herring gulls *nest in northern Europe. At the end of August, they arrive in Brittany, where they spend the winter.*

The sanderling*, which breeds in northern Europe, arrives in Brittany in August. It will either spend the winter there or fly south to Africa.*

The pied oystercatcher *can be seen in Brittany all year round. It feeds mostly on mussels, cockles and winkles.*

THE GUILLEMOT

This diving sea bird, with black and white plumage, a short neck and slender wings, spends the winter on the coasts of the English Channel and Atlantic Ocean. It nests in colonies on cliffs at Cap Fréhel and Cap Sizun, at Camaret and on the Sept-Îles, laying a single egg on a rocky ledge. It can also be seen on isolated rocks, often with penguins and kittiwakes. During the breeding season, its cry is a strident cawing. The young bird takes to the water 20 days after hatching, but begins to fly only at two months of age. It feeds mainly on fish, which it catches out at sea by diving to depths of more than 50 m (165 ft).

A colony of guillemots

CLIFFS AND ROCKY COASTS

Particular types of plants grow on the cliffs. They include sea pinks, the pink-flowering campion, golden rod and the yellow-flowering broom, as well as sea squill, small species of fern and many varieties of different-coloured lichen.

HEATHLANDS OF THE INTERIOR

For much of the year, various species of heathers cover Brittany's heathlands with a carpet of pink, which contrasts with the yellow flowers of the gorse and broom. The heathlands are also dotted with thickets of bramble and dog-rose.

The fulmar spends most of its time at sea. It nests on the ledges of sheer cliffs.

The puffin feeds on fish that it catches far out at sea. In spring, it excavates deep burrows where the female lays a single white egg.

The sheerwater's only nesting grounds in France are in Brittany – on the Sept-Îles and in the archipelagos of Ouessant and Houat.

The hen-harrier preys on voles and small birds, which it finds in open land.

The curlew migrates from June onwards to the Atlantic coast, where large numbers spend the winter.

The warbler feeds all year round on small insects and spiders.

Rural Architecture

Finial on gateway pillar

T HE SCENIC APPEAL of the Breton countryside owes much to its picturesque old houses, which seem to be fixed in time. Their appearance varies markedly according to topography, available materials and local traditions. In Upper Brittany, houses were built in rows, standing gable to gable so as to form rectangular groups *(longères)*. Typical of Lower Brittany is the *pennti*, a more compact house, with contiguous outbuildings, such as byres and coach houses surrounding the yard and providing shelter from the prevailing wind. Until the mid-19th century, these modest houses rarely had an upper floor. Thatched and asymmetrical, they blend harmoniously with the surrounding fields, heath and woodland.

***Windows**, which are narrow and relatively few, are usually framed by dressed stones. They were once closed from within by wooden shutters.*

Chimneys are built into the gable wall.

The coping stone, sometimes decoratively carved, crowns the apex of the gable.

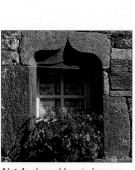

***Lintels** above older windows are bevelled and sometimes have an ogee arch, a legacy of the Gothic style. Such windows are typical of manor houses.*

EXTERIOR STAIRWAYS

Steps parallel to the façade

Several types of exterior staircase can be seen on Breton country houses. Many houses in the Léon and Vannes areas have a stairway parallel to the façade. The stairway, covered with an awning, led up to the loft, where hay and other provisions might be stored. The space beneath the steps was sometimes occupied by a pigsty. In plainer houses, the stairway, which often had no awning, was set in the angle of two buildings.

Steps set between buildings, with no awning

AROUND THE HOUSE

Certain integral features of the rural Breton house are to be found not inside its walls but outside. One is the bread oven, the style of which has remained almost unchanged since the Middle Ages. Because of the danger of fire, the oven was often located away from the house. The granite trough, a traditional piece of equipment in Lower Brittany, served as a drinking trough for animals and was also used as a mortar in which fodder was ground before it was given to horses.

Granite drinking-trough or mortar

Bread oven with small recess

The ridge of the roof was sometimes finished with a row of slates – known as kribenn *in Breton. The slates may be carved into shapes such as cats or birds, or into dates or initials.*

HOUSES WITH EXTENSIONS

Many houses in Finistère have an extension – known as *apoteiz* or *kuz taol* in Breton – that protrudes 4 to 5 m (13 to 16 ft) from the façade. This additional space was used to store the table, benches and sometimes a box-bed, so as to create more space around the hearth.

Blocks of hewn stone were used as cornerstones in both houses and enclosure walls.

The granite doorway, with a lintel consisting of three voussoirs (blocks of curved stone), is one of the most typical of Brittany.

***Dormer windows** are a relatively late feature of rural Breton houses. They did not appear until the 1870s.*

Religious Architecture

Detail of a choir stall

Brittany boasts several abbeys, nine cathedrals, some 20 large churches, about 100 parish closes and thousands of country chapels. This rich heritage is proof not only of the strength of religious faith but also of the skill of local builders. The golden age of religious architecture in Brittany occurred in the 16th and 17th centuries, when buildings were profusely decorated. Porches and rood screens sprouted motifs carved in oak, limestone or *kersanton*, a fine-grained granite that is almost impervious to the passage of time.

Calvary at Notre-Dame-de Tronoën *(see p154)*

PRE-ROMANESQUE AND ROMANESQUE (6TH–8TH C.)

The Romanesque style reached Brittany after it had become established in Anjou and Normandy, reaching its peak in about 1100 with the building of abbeys, priories and modest churches. A distinctive feature of these buildings is the stylized carvings on the capitals of columns.

Crypt of the Église St-Mélar in Lanmeur

Capital with carved leaf motif.

The cloister of the Abbaye de Daoulas, restored in 1880, is one of the finest examples of Romanesque architecture in Brittany.

Capital with plain abacus

Volute carved in *kersanton*, with various motifs.

Paired columns

EARLY GOTHIC (13TH–14TH C.)

At a time when new buildings in the Romanesque style were still being constructed, the Gothic style and the art of the stained-glass window took root in Brittany. Buildings in this new, restrained style, shaped by Norman and English influences, were based on a rectangular or T-shaped plan, and had a tall steeple.

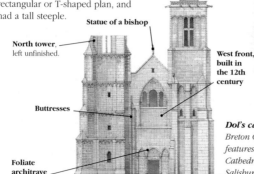

Statue of a bishop

North tower, left unfinished.

West front, built in the 12th century

Buttresses

Foliate architrave

Stained-glass, Cathédrale St-Samson, Dol-de-Bretagne

Dol's cathedral, a fine example of Breton Gothic architecture, shares features in common with Coutances Cathedral in Normandy and with Salisbury Cathedral in England.

FLAMBOYANT GOTHIC (14TH–15TH C.)

As an expression of their political power, the dukes and noblemen of Brittany funded the decoration of Gothic churches. These buildings thus acquired elegant chapels and finial belfries, carved doorways, wall paintings and beautiful rose windows.

Trefoil window

Rood screen in the Basilique du Folgoët

The Porche du Peuple of the Cathédrale St-Tugdual in Tréguier features some fine examples of 14th-century decorative carving.

Quatrefoil tracery framed by two trefoils.

Tierce-point arch divided into two trilobe arches.

BRETON RENAISSANCE (16TH C.)

The Flamboyant Gothic style was gradually superseded by a new, markedly purer style. Adopted by architects, metalworkers and sculptors, the Breton Renaissance style combined that of the Loire and that of Italy. In Lower Brittany, the fashion for parish closes and open belfries became established.

Figures of the 12 apostles.

Arches decorated with secular motifs.

Bust of Francis I set within a scallop shell.

Pilaster with lozenge decoration.

West door of the Basilique Notre-Dame-du-Bon-Secours in Guingamp (1537–90).

Pediment, in the Baroque style, over the archway.

Stone wall, designed to prevent farm animals from entering the sacred enclosure.

Entrance used at christenings, weddings, funerals and other great occasions.

Detail of the rood screen of the church at La Roche Maurice

The ceremonial entrance to the parish close of the Église St-Miliau in Guimiliau, one of the most important in northern Finistère.

BAROQUE (17TH C.)

The Counter-Reformation brought out a taste for extravagant church decora-tion. This took the form of statues of apostles, dramatic depictions of the Pietà, highly ornate pulpits, Baroque altarpieces and garlanded columns. There are around 1,300 churches with such Baroque decoration in Brittany.

Finials

Broken pediment

Fluted columns

Statue of St Derrien flanked by the heads of two angels.

The great porch (1645–55) of the church at Commana, whose interior furnishings are in an extravagant Baroque style, still has many Renaissance features.

Breton Music

As it continues to grow in popularity, Breton music goes from strength to strength. In the 1990s, *L'Héritage des Celtes* and *Again*, two of Alan Stivell's albums, sold in their thousands, the instrumentalist Dan Ar Braz has twice been awarded the prestigious Victoire de la Musique, and the techno specialist Denez Prigent has won critical acclaim. In Brittany, music is a central aspect of popular culture. Almost 70 per cent of French traditional musicians are Bretons, and in Brittany new music venues open at a faster rate than anywhere else in France. Celtic heritage lives on.

BREST

FESTIVAL-CONCOURS NATIONAL DE MUSIQUE

4.5.6 JUIN 1932

Poster advertising a music festival in Brest in 1932.

TRADITIONAL INSTRUMENTS

The bagpipes and the bombard are the only two specifically Breton musical instruments. Although others are played by Breton musicians, the bagpipes and bombard, sometimes accompanied by a drum or tambourine, are the traditional combination.

Drum

The bombard, a wind instrument similar to the oboe, is made of ebony or fruitwood.

The Breton bagpipe is increasingly neglected in favour of the larger Scottish bagpipes.

Bagpipes are known as biniou *in Brittany. In the Guérande region and in the Breton fenlands of the Vendée they are known as* veuze.

Irish transverse flute

The Celtic harp, sacred instrument of bards and Druids, captivated audiences throughout antiquity and the Middle Ages.

The diatonic accordion, known as bouëze *in Brittany, has gradually replaced the old concertina that was once seen mostly in rural areas.*

Sonneurs *are players of Breton and Scottish bagpipes who traditionally perform together. In the early 20th century, some sonneurs learned to play the clarinet – popularly known as "tronc de choux" (cabbage stalk) – the accordion and later the saxophone. Sonneurs once made their living from music.*

Tri Yann, a band that celebrated its 30th anniversary in 2001, practises the Breton musical tradition of extemporization. For the second time since the band came into existence, a woman has replaced one of its founders.

Gilles Servat gave a fresh boost to Breton music during the 1970s.

Alan Stivell *has recorded over 20 albums since his* Reflets *was released in 1970.*

Scottish bagpipes

Dan Ar Braz, from Quimper, has twice won the Victoire de la Musique. He has represented France at the Eurovision Song Contest and he now attracts a large audience. Describing the music that he plays, he prefers to call it the music of Brittany rather than traditional Breton music.

BRETON ORCHESTRAS

Bagadou, or Breton orchestras, feature bombards, bagpipes and drums. It is these orchestras that are responsible for keeping alive Breton musical tradition. Among the most famous *bagadou* are those of Landerneau and Lann Bihoué.

THE CONTEMPORARY SCENE

The young generation understands that it is new kinds of music that will help Breton traditions survive. Erik Marchand, who was born in Paris, learned Breton songs and then went on to join forces with gipsy and Oriental musicians. Kristen Nikolas gives Breton music a techno flavour. His band, Angel IK, freely mixes wild guitar-playing with Breton songs. Yann-Fanch Kemener, who began his career as a singer of Breton songs, now performs with jazz musicians. One of the most outstanding young talents is Denez Prigent. After specializing in *gwerzou* (ballads) and *kan ha diskan* (songs with descant), he is now exploring techno.

Denez Prigent

Breton Literature

Emgann Kergidu

PERHAPS BECAUSE OF its melancholy mists and secret woodlands, or because of the peculiar light that bathes its windswept coastline, Brittany is a strangely inspirational land. How else to account for the unique alchemy that encourages the imagination to take wing and that instills an innate penchant for the mystical, the mysterious and the marvellous? All those Bretons who figure in the history of regional as well as French literature, have this characteristic, the inevitable consequence of life lived on the edge of the world.

The Life of St Nonne, a popular Breton mystery play

LITERATURE IN BRETON

RELATIVELY LITTLE is known about medieval Breton literature. Besides a few glimpses gained from the charters compiled in abbeys and a single page from an obscure treatise on medicine dating from the late 8th century, no single Breton text survives to this day.

There is every evidence, however, that Armorican poets enjoyed a certain prestige in courtly circles and that their lays – ballads or poems set to music and accompanied on the harp – played an important part in the development of the chivalrous epics of the Middle Ages. It was, indeed, this Breton tradition that provided French minstrels with tales of the valour of Lancelot, the adventures of Merlin and other wonders of the Forêt de Paimpont *(see p62)*, the legendary Forêt de Brocéliande.

MYSTERY PLAYS

THE EARLIEST surviving evidence of a true literary tradition dates from the 15th century, in the manuscripts of mystery plays. In these

Barzhaz Breizh

plays, religious scenes, such as *Buez Santez Nonn*, which tells the story of the life of a saint, were enacted. Performed in the open air, they were extremely popular, especially in the Trégor. The actors, who might be clog-makers or weavers by trade, knew by heart entire tracts of the most dramatic plays, such as *Ar pevar mab Hemon (The Four Sons of Aymon)*, which was still being performed in about 1880.

Contemporary with this popular repertoire, a handful of long, erudite poems with sophisticated internal rhyming has survived, as well as a considerable body of literature (such as missals and books of hours) written by clergy-men in imperfect Breton. For hundreds of years, the latter was ordinary people's only reading matter.

STORIES AND LEGENDS

THE LITERARY GENRE in which Bretons excelled was that of stories and legends. During long winter evenings and at country gatherings, woodcutters, beggars and spinners would weave stories of make-believe filled with fairytale princesses and such legendary figures as giants in glass castles. It was by listening to these imaginative storytellers that Théodore Hersart de la Villemarqué (1815–95), whose Breton name was Kervarker, and François-Marie Luzel, or Fañch An Uhel, (1821–95) compiled collections of Breton literature. The stories are, however, too good to be true: it is now known that neither man set them down as he heard them but that they polished and rounded off the stories.

At the end of the 19th century, Lan Inizan (1826–91) published *Emgann Kergidu*, an

Théodore Hersart de la Villemarqué, a great 19th-century recorder of Breton tales and legends

Per-Jakez Hélias, author of the novel *Le Cheval d'Orgueil*

historic account of events that occurred in the Léon district during the Terror (*see p46*). Anatole Le Braz (1859–1926), meanwhile, explored Breton legends that are concerned with death.

BRETON CLASSICS

DURING THE 1930s, three accomplished novelists – Youenn Drezen, Yeun ar Gow and Jakez Riou – demonstrated that Breton literature was not limited to the description of life in the countryside in times gone by. While their novels had only a small readership, those of Tanguy Malmanche enjoyed wider renown. Two poets also emerged: Yann-Ber Kalloc'h (1888–1917), a native of Vannes, with his moving *Ar en deulin (Kneeling)*, and Anjela Duval (1905–81), of the Trégor.

The most widely read Breton writer is Per-Jakez Hélias, who came to the notice of the general public in 1975 with *Le Cheval d'Orgueil (Horse of Pride)*, later translated into 20 languages.

LITERATURE IN FRENCH

ALTHOUGH THEY did not belong to the canon of Breton writers, three of the greatest 19th-century French authors were, in fact, of

THE BRETON LANGUAGE

Brezoneg, an ancient Celtic language that is related to Welsh, is spoken west of a line running from Plouha to Vannes. Although this linguistic frontier has hardly changed since the 12th century, over recent generations Brezoneg has become much less widely spoken. In 1914, 90 per cent of the population of that part of Brittany spoke Brezoneg. After 1945, parents were encouraged to have their children speak French and, until 1951, Brezoneg was suppressed in schools. It was thus no longer passed down from parent to child. Today, although it is increasingly rare to hear Brezoneg spoken (only 240,000 Bretons over 60 know it well), it is attracting new interest. There are now bilingual schools (Diwan), an official Breton institute, and a Breton television channel (TV Breizh), all of which contribute to keeping Brezoneg alive.

Breton grammar books used in Diwan schools

Ernest Renan, noted for his writing on science and religion

Breton stock. Two were natives of St-Malo. One of these was the statesman, traveller and memoir-writer François René de Chateaubriand (*see p69*), author of *Génie du Christianisme* and *Mémoires d'Outre-Tombe*. Describing his attachment to the region, he once said "It was in the woods near Combourg that I became what I am". The other was Félicité de Lamennais, whose social ideals included harnessing political liberalism to Roman Catholicism. At his manor house at St-Pierre-de-Plesguen, near Dinan, he

entertained a coterie of disciples. The third, Ernest Renan, author of *Vie de Jésus (Life of Jesus)*, often returned to his native Trégor, where, he said, "you can feel a strong opposition to all that is dull and flat".

In the 20th century, too, Breton soil spawned many writers of renown: they include the poets René-Guy Cadou, Eugène Guillevic and Xavier Grall, the essayist Jean Guéhenno, of Fougères, and the novelist Louis Guilloux, of St-Brieuc, whose *Le Sang Noir (Black Blood*, 1935) was hailed by critics as a work of major importance.

Louis Guilloux, author of *Le Sang Noir* and an active anarchist

Seafaring Traditions

THE WESTERNMOST POINT in Europe, Brittany has over 2,700 km (1,680 miles) of coastline. From the 11th and 12th centuries, Breton seafarers distinguished themselves on the high seas. They were also prominent in the 15th and 16th centuries, when sea trade brought Brittany great prosperity. In the 17th century, Bretons accounted for one third of personnel in the French navy and one third of French merchant seamen. Bretons are also skilled and enterprising fishermen. Today, in Brest and Douarnenez, lobster boats, schooners, luggers and other commercial craft, together with old warships, gather for major reunions, some of international importance.

Almanach du Marin Breton, dating from 1899

Fishermen, warmly dressed against cold and wet conditions, worked their nets from the safety of barrels attached to the outside of the hull.

COD FISHING
In the 19th century, when cod fishing was at its height, hundreds of vessels sailed from the northern coasts of Brittany for Newfoundland or Iceland. For six months, these fishermen endured harsh and dangerous conditions. Apart from that still undertaken by vessels based in St-Malo, deep-sea fishing died out after World War II.

Jacques Cartier, in a masted ship like this one, set sail from his native St-Malo in 1534 for Newfoundland and Labrador and discovered the estuary of the St Lawrence river. Following the river upstream, he discovered Canada. The territory was named New France.

PRIVATEERS AND PIRATES

In the 17th and 18th centuries, St-Malo, described as "a wasps' nest", was the acknowledged capital of privateers. In November 1693, English forces tried to take the port by means of an infernal machine – a booby-trapped vessel filled with gunpowder, bombs and grenades. The attempt failed, and St-Malo remained in the hands of privateers, most notorious of whom were Duguay-Trouin, Surcouf and La Moinerie-Trochon. A captain at the age of 18, Duguay-Trouin (1673–1736) terrorized the seas around Iceland but was captured by the English. His greatest achievement was the capture of Rio de Janeiro, in 1711. Having won many sea battles, Surcouf (1773–1827) grew rich by fitting out privateers and merchantmen.

The privateer Surcouf boarding an English vessel, the *Kent*

Pardons and processions, *held to ward off the perils of deep-sea fishing, became more frequent as the industry expanded. Le Pardon des Terre-Neuves (1928), by Paul Signac, illustrates such an event.*

The exploits of Duguay-Trouin *of St-Malo resulted in his being ennobled by Louis XIV, who said of the privateer: "Courage has bestowed nobility on him." Here, assisted by the Chevalier Forbin, he overcomes five English warships.*

Seamen wore a fur-lined bonnet or a polished leather cap, typical headwear of fishermen in the 19th century.

Fire launches *are operated by a non-mobile division of the French navy. The fire service is staffed by an organization based in Brest.*

Brest 2000 *drew 2,500 tall ships and 20,000 sailors from 620 home-ports in 20 different countries. Every four years, when the festival takes place, Brest becomes the tall ships capital of the world.*

Luggers *were used for coastal fishing. This type of vessel was built at Cancale and Granville in the 19th and early 20th centuries.*

Michel Desjoyaux, *winner of the Vendée Globe round-the-world yacht race, is one of an illustrious succession of Breton yachtsmen. Having crewed with the great Éric Tabarly (see p181) from 1984 to 1985, he went on to win some of the most prestigious international yacht races.*

Olivier de Kersauson, *well-known through his media appearances, is another successful Breton yachtsman. Behind the outgoing character with a ready sense of humour lies a skilled and determined seaman.*

Traditional Breton Costume

Tʜᴇʀᴇ ᴡᴇʀᴇ ᴏɴᴄᴇ 66 different types of traditional Breton costume and around 1,200 variations. Breton clothing differed from one small area to the next. In the 19th century, it was possible to tell at a glance the precise geographical origins of any Breton. Colours also indicated an individual's age and status: in Plougastel-Daoulas, young women wore a small flowery shawl, married women a shawl with squares, widows a white shawl, and, when they had lost a close relative, a winged headdress. Unmarried men wore green waistcoats, and married men, blue jackets.

Femmes de Plougastel au Pardon de Sainte-Anne by Charles Cottet (1903)

Bɪɢᴏᴜᴅᴇɴ Cᴏsᴛᴜᴍᴇ
In the area of Pont-l'Abbé, capital of the Bigouden region, traditional costume is very uniform. Women were still wearing it as everyday dress in the early 20th century. According to their wealth, they either wore richly decorated, layered bodices or modest embroidered cuffs.

Lace gloves

Embroidered sleeve

Shirt

Chupenn, a man's coat

Embroidered waistcoat

Child's bonnet

Jewellery
In Cornouaille and western Brittany, the most popular pieces of jewellery were "pardon pins", brooches made of silver, copper or blown glass.

Lᴀᴄᴇ ᴀɴᴅ Eᴍʙʀᴏɪᴅᴇʀʏ

Aprons worn on feast days, women's bodices and men's waistcoats are richly embroidered with silk, metallic thread, and steel or glass beads. Executed in chain stitch, motifs include floral patterns featuring palmettes and fleur-de-lys, and stylized elements such as sun discs and concentric circles. They are always very bright, like the orange and yellow *plum paon* motifs that are typical of the Bigouden.

Lace-makers from Tréboul, in Finistère

Embroidery from Pont-l'Abbé

Embroidery from Quimper

Detail of a beaded costume

Newborn children, represented here by dolls, were once all customarily dressed in a bonnet, gown and apron. Not until the age of five or six did boys swap their infant clothes for adult male clothing. Girls would start to wear a headdress from the time of their first communion.

HEADWEAR

Traditional Breton headwear is extraordinarily diverse. This can be appreciated today only thanks to René-Yves Creston (1898–1964), an ethnologist who recorded its range before it ceased to be worn on a daily basis.

Small lace coiffe

Some headdresses had back-swept wings, others were tied at the chin with ribbons, and still others had "aircraft" or "lobster-tail" wings. Many women possessed two *koef*, or, in French, *coiffes* (headdresses), a small one made of lace netting that covered the hair, and a tall one, which was worn over the smaller one, though only on ceremonial occasions. The most spectacular headdresses are those of the Bigouden, which are almost 33 cm (13 in) high and which older women wear on Sundays. Men's hats are decorated with long velvet ribbons and sometimes with an oval buckle.

Women's headdress

Apron

Brooch

Chain

Belt buckles, like this heart-shaped example, were part of a man's costume. The waistcoat and trousers, which replaced the traditional baggy trousers in the mid-19th century, are tied at the waist by a belt.

The back of the bodice *was decorated with flowers whose size indicated the wearer's status. A married woman's bodice featured gold thread, spangles and tinsel.*

Men's waistcoats were eye-catchingly sumptuous. In Plougastel, young men wore a green waistcoat under a purple jacket, and adult men a blue waistcoat, the hue being darker or paler according to their age. Men wore a purple waistcoat on their wedding day and at the christening of their first child.

Aprons, worn to keep a woman's skirt clean, were originally plain rather than decorated. These voluminous working garments were made of ordinary fabric and were tied at the waist with a ribbon. Aprons were usually worn with a bib – a rectangular piece of fabric that covered the chest.

BRITTANY THROUGH THE YEAR

IN BRITTANY, every season has something to offer. In spring, towns and villages reawaken from their winter slumber: feast days in honour of patron saints and popular festivals mark this renewal. As the sun shines more brightly, heath and woodland come to life. Through the summer, the tourist season is in full swing,

Musician Festival Interceltique, Lorient

and every community holds its own *fest-noz* or pardon. The high point is the Festival Interceltique de Lorient, the greatest Celtic festival in France. By the autumn, the number of tourists begins to dwindle and festivals are fewer. Bretons ward off the rigours of winter by meeting in bistros or holding such events as the Transmusicales de Rennes.

SPRING

IN BRITTANY, spring is a time of joyfulness. From March, watered by gentle showers, gorse blooms cover the landscape in a carpet of golden yellow. In May, broom comes into flower, with its lighter yellow blooms. Fruit and vegetables – including Brittany's famous artichokes – are piled high in the markets. The region is reborn, and welcomes the return of warm, sunny days.

APRIL

Salon du Livre *(mid-April)*, Bécherel, Ille-et-Vilaine. An antiquarian book festival held in a medieval town. Bookbinders, booksellers and second-hand dealers hold open house.

MAY

Festival En Arwen *(early May)*, Cléguérec, Morbihan. A festival of traditional Breton music, drawing many performers and enthusiasts.

Fields of gorse, thickly carpeted in flowers from March

Advertisement for Étonnants Voyageurs, a festival held in St-Malo

Festival Étonnants Voyageurs *(first two weeks in May)*, St-Malo. The focus of this festival *(Amazing Explorers)*, held in the historic corsair port of St-Malo, is travel writing and accounts of exploration. It features exhibitions, lectures and signing sessions. Organized by a group of enthusiasts, it has become a major cultural event, and is now taken to other countries.

SUMMER

AS ONE OF THE most popular tourist regions of France, Brittany receives a large number of visitors during the summer. Coastal resorts are busy, and bars and nightclubs are filled to capacity. Besides swimming in the sea or relaxing on the beach, going hiking or cycling, or taking a boat trip round the coast, there are many other activities for visitors to enjoy *(see pp248–51)*.

JUNE

Festival Art Rock *(mid-June)*, St-Brieuc, Côtes d'Armor. Concerts, exhibitions, shows and contemporary dance.

JULY

Festival Tombées de la Nuit *(early July)*, Rennes, Ille-et-Vilaine. Filled with musicians, comedians, mime artists and storytellers from all over the world, Rennes, the capital of Brittany, becomes a gigantic stage.
Contes et Légendes de Bretagne *(July–August)*, Carnac, Morbihan. Every Wednesday, against the backdrop of the menhir known as the Giant of Manio, a storyteller weaves beguiling Celtic tales.
Art dans les Chapelles *(early July to mid-September)*, Pontivy and environs, Morbihan. About 15 chapels in and around Pontivy, and dating from the 15th and 16th centuries, host

AVERAGE DAILY HOURS OF SUNSHINE

Hours: 12, 10, 8, 6, 4, 2, 0

Jan Feb Mar Apr May Jun Jul Aug Sep Oct Nov Dec

Sunshine Chart
High pressure from the Azores gives southern Brittany more than 2,200 hours of sunshine per year. The north, by contrast, has only 1,700 hours per year. Coastal areas, where rainfall is lighter than in the interior, sometimes suffer from drought during the summer.

exhibitions of contemporary painting, sculpture and photography.
Troménie *(second Sunday in July)*, Locronan, southern Finistère. One of the largest and most elaborate pardons in Brittany.
Festival Médiéval *(14 July)*, Josselin, Morbihan. A day of medieval entertainment centred around the old market square, with troubadours and tumblers.
Festival des Vieilles Charrues *(mid-July)*, Carhaix-Plouguer, southern Finistère. Rock festival featuring both international stars and local bands. James Brown, Massive Attack and numerous others have performed in front of large audiences here.
Fête Internationale de la Mer et des Marins *(mid-July, every four years)*, Brest, northern Finistère. The largest tall ships regatta in the world, first held in 1992.
Fête de la Crêpe *(third week-end in July)*, Tronjoly-Gourin, southern Finistère. Pancake-tastings and lessons in how to made pancakes, held in the municipal park.

Fête des Remparts *(third weekend in July, every two years)*, Dinan, Côtes d'Armor. Historical reconstructions, theatrical farce, dancing, games, concerts, jousts and a procession in costume.
Grand Pardon *(26 July)*, Ste-Anne-d'Auray, Morbihan. The greatest Breton pilgrimage, with a following of a million.
Festival de Jazz *(last week of July)*, Vannes, Morbihan. Blues and jazz played by professional and amateur musicians are the festival's main attractions.

AUGUST

Fête des Fleurs d'Ajoncs *(first Sunday in August)*, Pont-Aven, southern Finistère. A picturesque procession in honour of flowering gorse, dating back to 1905.
Festival Interceltique *(first two weeks in August)*, Lorient, Morbihan. Musicians and other performers from Scotland, Ireland, the Isle of Man, Wales and Cornwall, Galicia and Asturia (in Spain), and, of course, Brittany gather for the largest Celtic festival in the world.

Fête internationale de la Mer et des Marins in Brest

Route du Rock *(mid-August)*, St-Malo, Ille-et-Vilaine. Held in the Fort de St-Père, a rock festival at the cutting edge of the genre.
Festival des Hortensias *(mid-August)*, Perros-Guirec, Côtes d'Armor. Accompanied by traditional music, festivities in honour of the hydrangea, whose deep blue flowers are prized and which thrives in Brittany's acid soil.
Fête des Filets Bleus *(mid-August)*, Concarneau, southern Finistère. Traditional Breton bands parade through the streets of the town, and a festival queen is chosen. The programme also includes concerts, shows and fishing competitions.
Fête de l'Andouille *(fourth Sunday in August)*, Guéméné-sur-Scorff, Morbihan. The Confrérie des Goustiers de l'Andouille (sausage-makers' guild) celebrate this prized Breton delicacy.

Rock group at the Festival des Vieilles Charrues at Carhaix-Plouguer

AVERAGE RAINFALL

AUTUMN

THOSE OF A romantic disposition who love open spaces will find this season particularly appealing. There are still many fine days. The equinox on 21/22 September marks the beginning of the great autumn tides, when large expanses of the sea bed are exposed. Rapidly changing weather and the dramatic ebb and flow of the sea also make for a landscape whose appearance alters by the hour. Inland, the leaves on the trees start to turn, catching the sunlight between scudding clouds. As tourists become fewer, Bretons return to their daily lives, anticipating winter.

SEPTEMBER

Championnat de Bretagne de Musique Traditionelle
(first weekend in September), Gourin, southern Finistère. The finest performers of traditional Breton music gather at the Domaine de Tronjoly to take part in marching, music and dancing competitions; these are held in two categories: *kozh* (with Breton pipes and bombards) and *bras* (with Scottish bagpipes and bombards). A *fest-noz* also takes place.

OCTOBER

Festival du Film Britannique
(early October), Dinard, Ille-et-Vilaine. The British film industry's producers and distributors come here to promote British cinema in France. The event attracts around 15,000 people.

Festival de Lanvallec
(second half of October), in the Trégor, Côtes d'Armor. The leading exponents of Baroque music perform in various churches in the region, particularly in Lanvallec, which has one of the oldest organs in Brittany.

Fête du Marron
(end of October), Redon, Ille-et-Vilaine. The town hosts a chestnut festival with a traditional fair, chestnut tastings and, most prominently, the largest *fest-noz* in Brittany. The Bogue d'Or, a musical contest in which the best traditional Breton musicians compete, takes place in the morning. In the evening, the winners give a performance, along with other traditional Breton music groups.

Quai des Bulles
(last weekend in October), St-Malo, Ille-et-Vilaine. An annual gathering attended by over 100 strip-cartoonists and animated cartoon producers, together with a following of enthusiasts. Showings of cartoon films and exhibitions also form part of the event. In the year 2000, when the festival marked its 20th year, the world's leading cartoonists and animators attended.

NOVEMBER

Festival des Chanteurs de Rue et Foire and St-Martin
(early November), Quintin, Côtes d'Armor. Since 1993, the St Martin's Fair, which dates back to the 15th century, has been held at the same time as this festival of street singers. Hawkers, entertainers and comedians re-enact historical scenes of daily life and singers perform time-honoured songs, with the audience joining in the chorus. Traditional Breton food is also on offer.

A signing session during the Quai des Bulles in St-Malo

AVERAGE TEMPERATURES

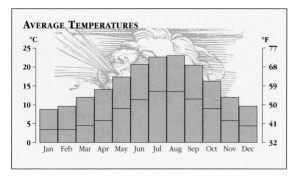

Temperatures
Although winters in Brittany are cold, temperatures rarely fall below 0° C (32° F). Average winter temperatures are between 6 and 8° C (43 and 46° F). Average summer temperatures are between 16 and 18° C (61 to 64° F).

WINTER

WINTER BRINGS periods of inclement weather, which become progressively more severe as the season advances. However, warm, moist air from the tropics can cause temperatures to rise to as much as 12° C (54° F), even in mid-January. Warm rainfall allows camellias to thrive, flowering in sheltered areas. In winter, the prevailing wind is from the northwest. Cold and strong, it batters the region in squally gusts. As an antidote to such tempestuous weather, Bretons hold rumbustuous weekend festivals.

DECEMBER

Les Transmusicales *(early December)*, Rennes, Ille-et-Vilaine). The buzzing rock scene has spawned such artistes as Étienne Daho, Niagara, Marquis de Sade and a long list of bands that are well-known in France.

A still winter seascape in Brittany

For almost 25 years, this key festival has launched the careers of many British and American bands, as well as that of other musicians, such as the Icelandic singer Björk, who has performed in France since the start of her career.

Villages de Lumières *(mid-December)*, Quessoy, Côtes d'Armor. A Christmas market, with such attractions as rides in horse-drawn carriages and displays of Christmas cribs, is held in the colourfully lit and decorated streets. Over

50,000 people come to enjoy this temporary fairyland.

FEBRUARY

Panoramas *(mid-February)*, Morlaix, northern Finistère. A festival introducing to the general public unknown singers and new talent in the field of rap and electronic music. Some established musicians also perform.

PUBLIC HOLIDAYS

New Year's Day
(1 January)
Easter Sunday and Easter Monday
Ascension (sixth Thursday after Easter)
Pentecost (second Monday after Ascension)
Labour Day (1 May)
Victory Day (8 May)
Bastille Day (14 July)
Assumption (15 August)
All Saints' Day (1 Nov)
Armistice Day (11 Nov)
Christmas Day (25 Dec)

A stall at the Christmas market in Brest

Pardons and Festou-noz

THE TERM *pardon* dates from the Middle Ages, when popes granted indulgences (remissions of punishment for sin) to worshippers who came to church. The annual pardon later became a day of worship honouring a local patron saint, with a procession and pilgrimage. In rural areas, a large number of saints were venerated, and here, minor pardons have evolved into occasions when communities join together to celebrate. After mass, the confession of penitents and procession of banners, the secular *fest-noz*, with singing and dancing, begins.

Celtic cultural clubs, *which give displays at pardons, still perform dances that are specific to particular areas of Brittany.*

Gwenn ha du,
the Breton flag

The bagad
Playing bombards, bagpipes and drums, this group of musicians – the bagad *– tours the streets. They provide dance music for the fest-noz.*

Sonneurs, *bagpipe and bombard players, have always been an integral part of Breton festivities. Seated on a table or a large barrel, they took it in turns to play popular tunes both to accompany dancing and as entertainment during the outdoor banquet that traditionally followed a pardon.*

GOUEL AN EOST

In several parishes, pardons are also occasions when older people can relive the sights and sounds of a traditional harvest. Activities include threshing by traditional methods: threshers, truss-carriers and sheaf-binders set up the chaff-cutter and the winnowing machine, which separates the grain from the chaff, and harness horses to the circular enclosure where the grain is milled. A hearty buffet rounds off this *gouel an eost*.

Harvest festival

Traditional dancing *is not the exclusive preserve of Celtic cultural clubs. Far from sitting on the sidelines, local people and holiday-makers both eagerly join in, accompanied by the* sonneurs *and singers of* kan ha diskan *(songs with descant).*

Banners, *made of embroidered silk, are carried in procession during pardons. Each parish has its own banner, behind which the parishioners walk. This one belongs to the Chapelle Notre-Dame de Lambader, in Haut-Léon.*

The Troménie *at Locronan is not only a major pilgrimage but also a test of physical endurance for those who carry the banners. Dressed in traditional costume, for five hours they continuously circle a hill in the heat of July, holding aloft banners, statues and relics.*

A banner with the image of the patron saint of a parish.

TRO BREIZ

Held in honour of the seven saints – Samson, Malo, Brieuc, Paul Aurélien, Patern, Corentin and Tugdual – who established Christianity in Brittany, the *Tro Breiz* is not a modest parish pardon but a lengthy pilgrimage covering about 650 km (400 miles) and linking the seven Breton sees. Pilgrims from all over the world have attended this event.

Modern banner, carried in honour of the well-known preacher Mikael an Nobletz (see p127).

Blessing the Sea
In villages around the coast of the Golfe du Morbihan, when a pardon takes place, the clergy boards a boat and blesses all the vessels in the harbour. This custom dates from the 19th century.

The pardon of Ste-Anne-d'Auray *has become a spectacular event over the centuries, with a long procession of priests and pilgrims. After mass, they fervently sing Hail Marys and Breton hymns.*

THE HISTORY OF BRITTANY

BRITTANY'S LONG HISTORY, *no less than its geography, has made it one of the most distinctive regions of France. It has a strong cultural identity, and, at the westernmost point in Europe, it has benefited from its location at the centre of Europe's Atlantic seaboard – between land and sea, and between Britain and France.*

The borders of Brittany have altered often since ancient times. During the prehistoric period, the coastline was very different from what it is today. Many sites of human occupation, some of which date back 500,000 years, have been discovered in places that are now beneath the sea. During the glaciations of the early Quaternary period, the sea level was about 100 m (30 ft) lower than it is today.

When the glaciers melted, about 10,000 years ago, the sea level rose dramatically. Large areas of land were flooded, creating the present coastline, which is indented by long narrow inlets – or rias – ancient river valleys flooded by the sea. It may be some remote memory of this cataclysmic event that gave rise to legends about submerged cities, like the town of Ys.

Stone necklace, c. 4000-3500 BC

were traded in the Rhône valley, in southeastern France, and in Britain. This was also a time of stable social organization, when impressive megalithic monuments were built. Skeletons and pottery were placed in megalithic tombs (menhirs), some in the form of burial chambers approached by a long corridor, consisting of huge blocks of stone covered by an earth mound. The oldest and most impressive of these megalithic monuments, the cairn at Barnenez *(see p119)*, dates from 4600 BC. No less spectacular are the menhirs, standing stones that were probably connected to a religion involving astronomy. The most important dolmens are those at Carnac *(see pp178–9)*. Some, like the Giant of Locmariaquer *(see p180)*, are as much as 20 m (65 ft) high.

MEGALITH-BUILDERS

Traces of human occupation become more numerous at the beginning of the Neolithic period, around 5000 BC, when local populations adopted agriculture and a settled way of life. They made axes of polished granite, which

THE CELTS

In about 500 BC, the peninsula, which was then known as Armorica, or "country near the sea", was invaded by Celts. Five tribes settled there: the Osismes (in present-day Finistère), the Veneti (in the Morbihan), the Coriosolites (in the Côtes d'Armor), the Riedones (in the Ille-et-Vilaine),

TIMELINE

10,000 BC Sea levels begin to rise, flooding sites of human habitation

4000 BC–2000 BC Polished stone axes are made, at Plussulien and other sites

Polished jadeite axe

10,000 BC	5000 BC	4000 BC	3000 BC	2000 BC	1000 BC

5000 BC Start of the Neolithic period. The great megalithic tombs (dolmens) are built and menhirs erected

4600 BC The great burial mound at Barnenez is built

◁ **The mythical origins of the kingdom of Armorica, from Le Baud's *Chroniques de Bretagne* (1480–82)**

and the Namnetes (in the Loire-Atlantique). The Celts, who lived in villages and fortified settlements, were agriculturalists who also worked iron, minted coins and engaged in overseas trade. They were ruled by a warrior aristocracy and a priesthood, the Druids, at the head of a religion whose deities represented the forces of nature. Bards (poet-musicians) sang of the exploits of mythical heroes. Armorica gradually entered the annals of recorded history. Explorers from the Mediterranean, among them the Carthaginian Himilco (c. 500 BC) and the Greek merchant-explorer Pytheas (c. 320 BC), arrived on its shores.

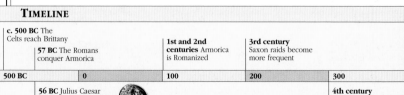

Bronze figure of an ox, from a Roman villa at Carnac

ROMAN ARMORICA

In 57 BC, the Romans occupied Armorica, as well as the rest of Gaul. However, in 56 BC, the Veneti rebelled and held the Romans at bay by taking refuge on the rocky promontories of the Atlantic coast. With difficulty, Julius Caesar routed them in a sea battle outside the Golfe du Morbihan.

For 400 years, Armorica, incorporated into the province of Lugdunensis, was under Roman domination. The province was divided into five areas *(pagi),* corresponding to Celtic tribal territory. A network of roads was built and a few small towns established, which aided the process

Roman Venus from Crucuny, Carnac

of Romanization. Among them were Condate (now Rennes), Fanum Martis (Corseul), Condevincum (Nantes) and Darioritum (Vannes). While baths, amphitheatres and villas marked the influence of Roman civilization, Celtic and Roman gods were amalgamated. Rural areas, however, were less affected by the Roman presence. From AD 250–300, as the Roman Empire began to decline, instability set in. Raids by Frankish and Saxon pirates led to the desertion of towns. The coastline was ineffectually defended by forts, such as Alet (near St-Malo) and Le Yaudet (in Ploulec'h). As the 5th century dawned, Armorica was abandoned to its fate.

ARRIVAL OF THE BRITONS

During the 6th century, large numbers of Britons from Wales and Cornwall crossed the English Channel to settle in Armorica, which they named "Little Britain", or "Brittany". This peaceful invasion continued for 200 years. Among the newcomers were many Christian monks, who introduced a Celtic variant of Christianity, distinct from Roman Christianity. Many isolated hermitages were built on small offshore islands, and monasteries were headed by an abbot who also acted as itinerant bishop. Among them were Brieuc, Malo, Tugdual (in Tréguier) and Samson (in Dol); with Gildas, Guénolé, Méen and Jacut, whose lives and miracles became the subject of hagiographies from the 8th century onwards, they inspired the religious traditions that survive today, marked by pilgrimages and pardons, such as the Troménie in Locronan *(see p153).*

TIMELINE

500 BC	0	100	200	300
c. 500 BC The Celts reach Brittany		**1st and 2nd centuries** Armorica is Romanized	**3rd century** Saxon raids become more frequent	
	57 BC The Romans conquer Armorica			
	56 BC Julius Caesar defeats the Veneti in a naval battle			**4th century** The Romans withdraw from Armorica

Coins minted by the Veneti

St Corentin laying the foundation stone of Quimper Cathedral, before King Gradlon

It was these immigrants from Britain who introduced the typically Breton place names consisting of the prefix *plou*, or its derivatives *plo, plu, plé*, followed by a proper name or other word (as in Plougastel and Ploufragan). *Plou*, from the Latin *plebs* (the common people), refers to a community of Christians. *Lan* (as in Lannion and Lannilis) refers to a monastery. *Tré* (as in Trégastel), from the ancient British word *treb*, refers to a place of habitation. The concentration of these place names in western Brittany, and the frequency of those ending in *ac* in the eastern part of the region, from the Latin *acum* (as in Trignac and Sévignac), indicates a cultural duality. This is backed up by the coexistence of two languages: French, which is derived from Latin, east of a line running from La Baule to Plouha, and Breton to the west.

THE BRETON KINGDOM

From the 6th to the 10th century, the peninsula, now known as Britannia, fought off the attempts of Frankish kings who now controlled Gaul to dominate the region. Several times, Brittany was invaded by the Merovingians. Their influence was short-lived, however, and the Bretons kept their independence – ruled by warlike local chiefs or petty kings.

The powerful Carolingian dynasty could do no more than establish a buffer zone, the Marches, which extended from the Baie du Mont-St-Michel to the Loire estuary. From about 770, this was controlled by Roland, "nephew" of Charlemagne. In the 9th century, the Bretons established an independent kingdom, whose frontiers stretched to Angers in the east, Laval in the south and Cherbourg in the northwest. The kingdom was founded by Nominoë, who overcame Charles the Bald at the Battle of Ballon in 845. His son, Erispoë, succeeded him but was murdered in 857 by his cousin Salomon, whose reign, until 874, marked the peak of the short-lived Breton monarchy.

Brittany's political independence was strengthened by the clergy, who resisted the jurisdiction of the see of Tours. This was the great age of the Benedictine abbeys, rich centres of culture. Fine illuminated manuscripts were produced *(see p147)*, and the historic Cartulaire de Redon compiled.

The Cartulaire de Redon, a charter in which statutes were recorded from the 9th century

c. 480 The first wave of Britons reaches Brittany	630 Judicaël, the Breton leader, meets King Dagobert	832 The monastery of Redon is founded	843 The Normans sack Nantes	

500	600	700	800	900
Altarpiece from St-Méliau	7th & 8th centuries Armorica becomes Brittany	753 Pepin the Short launches an expedition to Brittany	845 King Nominoë is victorious at Ballon	857–874 Reign of Salomon, king of Brittany

William the Conqueror takes Dinan, a scene from the Bayeux Tapestry

THE NORMAN INVASIONS

From the end of the 8th century, the raids led by the Normans, from Scandinavia, became more frequent. Sailing up Brittany's coastal inlets and estuaries, they ransacked towns and monasteries, bringing terror to the land. Nantes was sacked in 843. Entire monastic communuties fled east, taking with them the relics of saints. After the murder of Salomon in 874, Brittany descended into chaos. From around 930–40, a semblance of order returned when King Alain Barbetorte regained Nantes in 937 and defeated the Normans at Trans in 939. Settling in neighbouring Normandy, the invaders gradually ceased their raiding activities, although they remained a dangerous presence.

FEUDAL BRITTANY

From the mid-10th century to the mid-14th, Brittany slowly evolved into a feudal state, maintaining a fragile independence from the

Henry II Plantagenet

kings of France and of England, both of whom had designs on Brittany.

In the 12th century, Brittany, now a county, narrowly avoided being absorbed into the Anglo-Angevin kingdom of the Plantagenets. Victorious at the Battle of Hastings in 1066, William the Conqueror had unified Normandy and England. His successor, Henry Plantagenet, was also Count of Anjou. In 1156, he took Conan IV, Count of Brittany, under his protection; Conan's daughter Constance was to marry Geoffrey, son of the king of England and brother of Richard the Lionheart and John Lackland. In 1203, the latter murdered Geoffrey's son, Arthur, and Brittany fell under the rule of the king of England. Philippe Auguste, king of France, then forced Alix, Arthur's half-sister, to marry a French prince, Pierre de Dreux, (Pierre Mauclerc). As a royal fiefdom, Brittany then came under the

TIMELINE

c. 900 The Norman invasion. Monks flee Brittany		**c. 1000** The feudal system is established	**1066** Led by William the Conqueror, many Bretons take part in the Norman Conquest of England
900	950	1000	1050
	937 Alain Barbetorte reconquers Brittany, expelling the Normans		**11th century** Many castles are built and small towns established

Château de Vitré

direct control of the French Crown. The Count of Brittany paid obeisance to the king of France, pledging his loyalty and aid.

Despite these vicissitudes, a Breton state was forming. In 1297, Philip the Fair, king of France, made the fiefdom a vassal-duchy, and a ducal government was set up. Although tied to the king of France through his vassal status, by the 13th century the count (then the duke) of Brittany was in a sufficiently strong position to move towards independence. As Count of Richmond, in Yorkshire, he was also a vassal of the Plantagenet king, and was thus able to steer a political course between the two monarchs.

In Brittany, however, his authority was limited by the power of his vassals, who controlled extensive fiefdoms from the safety of impregnable castles. These included the barons of Vitré and Fougères, on the border with Normandy; the Viscount of Porhoët, who ruled over 140 parishes and 400,000 ha (990,000 acres) of land from the Château de Josselin; and the Viscount of Léon, who, with the Count of Penthièvre, controlled part of the northern coast around Lamballe.

LIFE IN TOWN AND COUNTRY DURING THE MIDDLE AGES

Breton country-dwellers seem to have led more peaceful lives than those of their counterparts in France. In the west of the peninsula, there existed an unusual type of land tenure that persisted until the French Revolution. Every piece of farmland was owned by two people, one owning the land and the other the buildings and crops. Neither could be forced out without being paid for the value of what he owned. The towns, all of them small,

The seven saints who founded the Breton sees

enjoyed no administrative autonomy. Almost all were fortified, and many stood at the head of an inlet. Towndwellers lived from the linen trade.

Feudal Brittany was intensely religious. In areas of population growth, the number of parishes increased as new hamlets sprung up, their names prefixed with *loc* (as in Locmaria) or *ker* (as in Kermaria). Ancient pagan beliefs melded with the cult of old Breton saints, whose relics were the focus of pardons and pilgrimages. The best-known is the Tro Breiz, a tour of Brittany, about 650 km (400 miles) long, taking in shrines in St-Malo, Dol, Vannes, Quimper, St-Pol, Tréguier and St-Brieuc.

ST YVES

St Yves, between a rich and a poor man

Born at the Manoir de Kermartin, near Tréguier, in 1248, St Yves was a magistrate at the bishop's tribunal in Rennes, then in Tréguier. He was also the parish priest at Trédrez and then at Louannec, in the Trégor. He preached, led an ascetic life, and ensured justice for the poor, all of which brought him favourable renown. He died in 1303 and was canonized in 1347. He is the patron saint of Bretons and barristers. His skull is paraded in a procession at Tréguier that takes place on 19 May *(see pp100–01)*.

	1166 With Henry Plantagenet, Brittany is under English rule	1203 Arthur, Count of Brittany, is murdered by John Lackland	c. 1250 Dominican and Franciscan monasteries are founded	1297 Brittany becom a vassal-duchy
William the Conqueror				
	1150	**1200**	**1250**	**1300**
12th century Cistercian abbeys are founded	1185 Geoffrey Plantagenet gives Brittany its own government	1203 With Pierre de Dreux, Brittany comes under the control of France *St Louis*	1270 John I sets off on a Crusade with St Louis	1303 Death of St Yves

The Battle of Thirty, 1351, in which 30 Bretons, led by Beaumanoir, fought 30 Englishmen

WAR OF THE BRETON SUCCESSION

From 1341 to 1364, Brittany was ravaged by the warring of two families who claimed the dukedom. This conflict became part of the Hundred Years' War (1337–1453) fought between the kings of France and England. While the former supported Charles of Blois and his wife, Joan of Penthièvre, the latter aided John of Montfort and his wife, Joan of Flanders. This war, in which both women were closely involved, gave rise to such isolated incidents as the Battle of Thirty (1351).

The war ended in victory for the Montforts and their English allies: Charles of Blois was killed at the Battle of Auray (1364) and Bertrand du Guesclin was taken prisoner. John IV of Montfort's victory was ratified by the Treaty of Guérande and, for over a century, his dynasty held power in an almost independent Brittany, which could rely on English support to foil the ambitions of the king of France.

The Battle of Auray (1364), at which the Montforts and their English allies overcame the French

APOGEE OF THE BRETON STATE

The Breton state reached the peak of its power in the 15th century. The Duke of Brittany, who enjoyed the status of ruler and who was crowned in Rennes Cathedral, took up residence in Nantes. Surrounded by courtiers, he inaugurated a new age, patronizing artists and encouraging an interpretation of history that exalted Breton culture.

Government (the council, chancellery, court of exchequer, parliament and law court) was shared between Nantes, Vannes and Rennes. Every year, the States of Brittany held a meeting at which they voted on taxes. Complex and burdensome, these taxes were not sufficient to finance the duke's ever more extravagant tastes, nor to cover the upkeep of fortresses and the maintenance of an army. But, raising the necessary funds himself, the duke managed to keep his distance from the king of France.

From the reign of John V (1399–1442), Brittany remained relatively neutral in the Hundred Years' War. This allowed Bretons to enjoy a certain prosperity:

TIMELINE

1341 Start of the War of the Breton Succession	**1364** Death of Charles of Blois at the Battle of Auray	**1378** Charles V attempts to secure the dukedom of Brittany	**15th century** The duch of Brittany reaches its peak. Flowering of the Breton Gothic style
1340	**1360**	**1380**	**1400** **1420**
1351 Battle of Thirty	**1365** Treaty of Guérande: the Montforts are victorious	**1380** Death of Bertrand du Guesclin	**1399–1442** Reign of John V. Shifting allegiance between France and England

Equestrian statue of Olivier de Clisson

maritime trade developed, Breton seamen acting as middlemen between Bordeaux and England, and exporting salt from Guérande and linen cloth from Vitré, Locronan and Léon. The population of Brittany, less seriously affected by the great plagues than that of France, reached 800,000. Refugees from Normandy settled in the east, while many impoverished petty noblemen left to seek their fortune in France. During the Hundred Years' War, Breton mercenaries fighting on both sides won renown for their prowess. Three of them – Bertrand du Guesclin, Olivier de Clisson and Arthur de Richemont – became constables (chief military officers) of France.

Noblemen enlarged their castles, turning them into impressive residences. There was a lack of morality, however, and this reached its nadir in the depraved treatment of children and their cruel murder, in a satanic ritual, committed by Gilles de Rais, companion-at-arms of Joan of Arc, at the Château de Tiffauges, near Nantes.

In the 15th century, a typically Breton variant of the Gothic architectural style

BERTRAND DU GUESCLIN

A minor nobleman born in about 1320 near Broons, Bertrand du Guesclin showed his prowess as a warrior during the War of the Breton Succession.

Du Guesclin kneeling before Charles V

He was also victorious at some famous jousts and duels, such as the one he fought in Dinan with Sir Thomas Canterbury. In the service of Charles V, he retook part of France from the English, and defeated the king of Navarre at Cocherel in 1364. He led *compagnies* (bands of mercenaries) to Spain. He was taken prisoner by the Black Prince at Najera in 1367, but returned to the battlefield. He was made a constable of France, and died during a siege in 1380.

developed, combining the delicacy of the Flamboyant Gothic with the austerity of granite. The first texts in Breton appeared and, with the advent of printing in 1484, printed books were produced; one of the first was *Catholicon*, a Breton-French-Latin lexicon. A university was founded in Nantes in 1460.

THE END OF INDEPENDENCE

Francis II (1458–88), the incapable and debauched Duke of Brittany, was powerless to prevent the increasing use of royal power in France, where Louis XI abolished the last great vassals in 1477. The king then turned his attention to Brittany, the only major fiefdom that still remained to be subjugated. Forced into a war, Francis II was defeated in 1488. By the Treaty of Le Verger, the duke was forced to submit to the king if his successor was to rule Brittany. He died soon after. His daughter and successor, Anne of Brittany, was not yet 12 years old.

The execution of Gilles de Rais in 1440

Dance of Death (late 15th century)

1460 Foundation of the University of Nantes

1488 Battle of St-Aubin-du-Cormier. Treaty of Le Verger

1514 Death of Anne of Brittany

1440	1460	1480	1500	1520

1440 Execution of Gilles de Rais

1491 Anne of Brittany marries Charles VIII

1499 Anne of Brittany marries Louis XII

Anne of Brittany

Anne of Brittany

Anne of Brittany

A CENTRAL FIGURE in the history of Brittany, Anne stood both for the duchy's independence and, through her marriage first to Charles VIII and then to Louis XII – both of them kings of France – for its integration with France. The vissicitudes of her short and eventful life also made her popular. She became a duchess at the age of 11, a queen at 13, a mother at 16, and a widow at 21. She died at the age of 37, having lost seven of her nine children. Even today, some Bretons revere her almost as a saint. A patron of the arts, she aided the development of Breton culture by supporting historians.

***Anne of Brittany's coat of arms** feature a Franciscan nun, an ermine and the motto To my Life.*

Jean de Rely, bishop of Angers.

THE MARRIAGE OF CHARLES VIII AND ANNE OF BRITTANY

On the death of Francis II, Duke of Brittany, Charles VIII, the young king of France, resumed war with his successor Anne and forced her to marry him. The ceremony took place in Langeais on 6 December 1491. This early 19th-century painting shows the couple making their marriage vows.

***Pierre de Baud**, canon of Vitré, wrote a* History of Brittany *in 1505, at Anne's behest. The first account of its kind, it gave Breton identity a historical perspective.*

Anne of Brittany at the age of 15.

ANNE OF BRITTANY'S RESIDENCES

The castle in Nantes *(see pp208–9)* was Anne's main residence. She was born there, in the part known as the "old building", and she undertook the work that gives the castle its present appearance. As a young girl, she regularly stayed in Vannes, in the Château de l'Hermine and the Manoir de Plaisance, which now no longer exists, and in the Château de Suscinio, in the Morbihan, and the Château de Clisson, in the Loire-Atlantique. In Rennes, she lived in what is known as the Logis des Ducs, in the old town. During her tour of Brittany in 1505, she stayed in private houses, many of which are difficult to identify today. In Hennebont, Quimper, Locronan, Morlaix, Guingamp, St-Brieuc and Dinan, houses reverently known as "the Duchess Anne's houses" keep alive the memory of her visit. She also stayed for a few days in the castles at Hunaudaye, Vitré and Blain.

Château des Ducs de Bretagne, Nantes, Anne of Brittany's main residence

Louis XII, *who succeeded Charles VIII, married Anne according to an agreement made at the time of her marriage to Charles.*

As patroness of the arts *and a woman of the Renaissance, Anne supported artists and writers. Here, the Dominican friar Antoine Dufour presents to her his* Lives of Illustrious Women.

Charles VIII

Claude of Brittany, *Anne's daughter, was born in 1499 and married Francis of Angoulême, the future Francis I. As king, he acquired through Claude the duchy of Brittany. Their son became Francis III, Duke of Brittany.*

Burial of Anne of Brittany *took place at the Château de Blois, on 9 January 1514. She was 37 years old.*

This gold reliquary *contains the heart of Anne of Brittany. According to her last wish, Anne's heart was brought from Blois to her native land, "the place that she loved more than any other in the world, so that it might be interred there". It was placed in the tomb that she had built for her parents in Nantes.*

Map of Brittany in 1595, at the time of the wars of
the Holy League

played the most prominent role. Every year, the delegates agreed with the king the level of taxation to be levied on the province. Brittany paid lower taxes than the rest of the kingdom and was exempt from the salt tax.

Parliament, restored in 1554, was housed in a suitably imposing building in Rennes dating from 1618–55 *(see pp60–61)*. Parliament was the supreme court of Breton law and was also a court in which royal decrees became statute. Brittany was thus able to retain its own legal system.

In the 16th century, Brittany was largely unaffected by the Wars of Religion fought between Catholics and Protestants. Strongly Catholic, it contained only a small number of Calvinists. However, under Henry IV, king of France and governor of Brittany, was the ambitious Philippe-Emmanuel de Lorraine, Duke of Mercœur. One of the mainstays of the Holy League – a group of Catholic extremists – he attempted to harness the loyalty of Bretons to Rome so as to draw them into a war against the heretical king, and lured them with thoughts of independence. After ten years of conflict, from 1589 to 1598, Mercœur was forced to withdraw, and, in Nantes, Henry IV signed the Edict of Nantes, ending the Wars of Religion.

BRITTANY JOINS FRANCE

Brittany's integration into the kingdom of France made no fundamental difference to the lives of Bretons. The Treaty of Union of 1532 ensured that their "rights, freedoms and privileges" would be respected. The province was ruled on behalf of the king by a governor, who usually had connections with the great Breton families. The interests of the population were, in principle, defended by the States of Brittany, an assembly that was, however, unrepresentative, since the rural population had no delegate. The nobility and high clergy

François d'Argouges, who became first
Speaker of the Breton parliament, in 1669

RESISTANCE TO THE MONARCHY

In the 17th century, royal power became absolute, and the monarchy in France developed centralized rule. Local autonomy was curtailed and taxes rose. New taxes on tobacco and

TIMELINE

1532 Treaty of Union signed by Brittany and France

1554 Creation of the Breton parliament

1589–1598 Wars of Religion

Parish close at La Martyre

| 1530 | 1550 | 1570 | 1590 | 1610 | 1630 | 1650 |

1534–1542 Jacques Cartier explores Canada

1598 Edict of Nantes

c. 1600–1650 Parish closes are built

Jacques Cartier

on printed paper used for legal documents caused a revolt in Lower Brittany in 1675. The harsh repression that followed was described by Madame de Sévigné *(see p67)*.

In 1689, so that his decisions might be more effectively implemented, Louis XIV placed the province under the control of an intendant,whose remit was to impose law and order and collect taxes. These measures caused a resurgence of Breton nationalism, most strongly among the petty nobility, that continued until the end of the Ancien Régime.

Henry IV on a military campaign against partisans of the Holy League, a group of Catholic extremists, in Brittany in 1598

Much more troublesome for royal rule was legal opposition mounted against the intendant and the governor led by the States of Brittany and the Breton parliament. While the States claimed to defend Breton autonomy, they in fact supported the interests of the nobility. From 1759 to 1770, tensions ran high, reaching a climax in the conflict between Louis-René de Caradeuc de La Chalotais, the Breton parliament's ambitious and popular procurator-general, and the Duke of Aiguillon, the authoritarian and effi-cient commander-in-chief of Brittany. The "Breton question" enflamed the province and did not die down until the death of Louis XV, in 1774.

BRITTANY'S THRIVING PORTS

Under the Ancien Régime, Brittany experienced vigorous economic growth. Port activity prospered as a result both of Brittany's integration with France and of the opening of sea routes across the Atlantic. Brittany played its part in voyages of discovery with the expedition to Canada undertaken by Jacques Cartier, of St-Malo, (1534–42). The three busiest French seaports were St-Malo, Nantes and Lorient, built in 1666 as a base for the French East India Company. Conflict between France and England interfered with economic activity on the coasts, as the English launched attacks on St-Malo, Belle-Île and St-Cast. Naval warfare also led to Colbert's building an arsenal at Brest (c. 1680), while Vauban increased coastal defences.

St-Malo, France's major port at the end of the 17th century, used for trade and for fitting out the ships of privateers

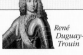

René Duguay-Trouin

1670	1690	1710	1730	1750	1770

1675 Revolt against taxes on tobacco and printed paper; the Bonnets Rouges

1689 The administration of Brittany is set up

1693 The English attack St-Malo

1711 Rio de Janeiro taken by Duguay-Trouin

1720 Pontcallec's conspiracy

1758 The Duke of Aiguillon repulses an attempted English invasion at St-Cast

1764–74 The Breton Question (La Chalotais and the Duke d'Aiguillon)

THE CHOUANS AND THE REVOLUTION

During the French Revolution, Brittany was divided between *"les bleus"*, who were in favour of new ideas, and *"les blancs"*, supporters of the Ancien Régime. *"Les bleus"* consisted of the liberal bourgeoisie and of country-dwellers of those cantons of Lower Brittany that were opposed to the clergy and nobility; *"les blancs"*, consisting mostly of nobility and unruly clergy, predominated in southern and eastern Brittany.

Jean Cottereau, known as Jean Chouan

In 1792, a few aristocrats led by La Rouërie hatched an unsuccessful counter-revolutionary plot, but in 1793, when the National Convention ordered that 300,000 men should be levied to fight in the war, the Loire-Atlantique, Morbihan and Ille- et-Vilaine rebelled. The Chouans, led by Cadoudal, Guillemot, Boishardy and Jean Chouan, fought a guerrilla war in the country-side. The Republicans responded by launching the Terror: in Nantes, 10,000 people were beheaded or drowned.

"Les blancs" had been dealt a blow. The army of Catholics and royalists was defeated at Savenay in 1793; attempts by émigré nobles to land in Brittany, with British aid, were quashed. At Quiberon, in June 1795, 6,000 of them were taken prisoner by Hoche's republican army and 750 executed.

Stability was not restored until the advent of Napoleon Bonaparte, who reconciled Church and State, appointed prefects, and ensured military control by building roads and establishing garrison towns, such as Napoléonville in Pontivy. Because of the Napoleonic Wars, during which the British ruled the seas, Brittany's fortunes were in decline, despite the exploits of privateers such as Robert Surcouf of St-Malo.

THE 19TH CENTURY

During the 19th century and until the 1950s, Brittany, isolated from the centres of the industrial revolution, became a rural backwater, although it supported a thriving canning industry. Fishing off Iceland and Newfoundland was another key activity.

Awareness of Brittany's Celtic heritage gathered strength as poets, ethnologists and folklorists documented and recorded Breton traditions and ancient tales. The Breton language,

Mass drownings in the Loire at Nantes, ordered by Jean-Baptiste Carrier during the French Revolution

TIMELINE

	Nantes is attacked by the Vendéens				**1865** The Paris-Brest railway is completed		**1886** Paul Gauguin arrives in Pont-Aven		**1898** The URB is founded
1789 Riots in Rennes	**1793–1802** Chouan uprising								
1780	**1800**	**1820**	**1840**	**1860**	**1880**				
1792 La Rouërie's plot	**1795** The landing of royalist émigrés in Quiberon ends in failure		**1839** La Villemarqué publishes *Barzaz Breiz*	**1848** F. de Lamennais is elected people's delegate at the Constituent Assembly		**1896** La Borderie starts his *History of Brittany*			

De Lamennais

strongly discouraged in undenominational schools during the Third Republic (1870–1940), found ardent supporters among the clergy, while regional history became the object of renewed interest, culminating in La Borderie's monumental *History of Brittany*. Strong cultural regionalism asserted itself around 1900, with the Union Régionaliste Bretonne, followed by the formation of the Parti National Breton, which was supported by the occupying Germans in 1940–44.

In the 19th century, continuing high birth rates and the absence of industry caused large-scale rural emigration to Paris, where a vigorous Breton community became established.

Poster for the inauguration of the Paris-Brest railway

Bretons became prominent on the national stage. Among them were Chateaubriand, politician and writer of the Romantic age; René Pléven, a minister during the Fourth Republic; Félicité de Lamennais, a founder of social Catholicism; and the religious sceptic Ernest Renan. With the arrival of the railway in the mid-19th century, Brittany began to attract writers and artists, drawn by the wild beauty of its countryside and the exotic nature of its Celtic traditions.

Brittany suffered greatly during the two world wars: in 1914–18, the proportion of Breton soldiers killed was twice the national average. In 1939–45, the region was occupied, and several ports, including St-Nazaire, Lorient, Brest and St-Malo, were razed by fighting during the Liberation.

BRITTANY IN THE MODERN WORLD

Brittany made a remarkable recovery after World War II. Since 1950, the Comité d'Étude et de Liaison des Intérêts Bretons has attracted investment and such decentralized operations as that of Citroën in Rennes and telecommunications in Lannion. Toll-free highways, high-speed train services and the installation of airports have ended Brittany's isolation. Cross-Channel links and a strong hotel industry make it the second-most popular tourist destination in France.

Brittany is also France's foremost producer of fruit and vegetables, and a leading producer of pigs and chickens. Such success has its price: farmers are crippled by the cost of modern equipment and soil is overloaded with nitrate. The region's problems are now being addressed: the need to preserve places of historic interest and natural beauty is seen as a priority, as is the importance of keeping alive Brittany's links with other Celtic regions in Europe.

Naval dockyards at St-Nazaire, where cruise liners are now built

	1925 Morvan Marchal designs the *Gwenn-ha-du*, the Breton flag	**1944** End of the German occupation. Many ports are destroyed	**1978** Oil spill from the *Amoco Cadiz*		**1992** The terms of the Maastricht Treaty concerning the European Union are supported by 60 per cent of Bretons

Breton flag

00	1920	1940	1960	1980	2000	2010

	1932 The PNB is founded	**1950** The CELIB is founded	**1989** High-speed-train link to Rennes	**2000** The aircraft carrier *Charles de Gaulle* is launched at Brest naval arsenal

BRITTANY
REGION
by REGION

Brittany at a Glance

BRITTANY'S BEACHES, like those on the Côte d'Émeraude and Côte de Granit Rose, the Golfe du Morbihan and Belle-Île, are very popular with holiday-makers. Brittany is also a land of history, with a rich heritage of ancient monuments. The timber-framed houses in Vannes and Dinan conjure up the Middle Ages, while in Nantes and St-Malo the town houses of shipowners reflect the fortunes that were made in the 17th and 18th centuries. Coastal forts such as that in St-Malo and castles in the Breton marches have fiercely defended Brittany from attack from land and sea throughout the centuries.

The Château de Kerouzéré is one of many fortified castles in the region (see p122).

The Logis de Rohan, a tower in Quimper, houses the Musée Départemental Breton (see pp160–61).

Île d'Ouessant

Lannion

Morlaix

Guingamp

Brest

Saint-Brieu

NORTHERN FINISTÈRE

CÔTES D'ARMOR

Châteaulin

Loudéac

SOUTHERN FINISTÈRE

Pontivy

Quimper

Concarneau

MORBIHAN

Lorient

Île de Groix

Vannes

Atlantic Ocean

Belle-Île

The postern gate in Vannes, not far from the Château de l'Hermine, leads through to pleasant gardens beneath the city walls (see pp186–9).

0 km	20
0 miles	20

The famous Mont-St-Michel is one of the most remarkable sights on the coast of Brittany (see pp72–5).

The timber-framed houses in St-Brieuc (see pp102–3) surround the city's impressive cathedral.

English Channel

Dinard   St-Malo

Mont-St-Michel

Dinan

Ploërmel

Rennes

ILLE-ET-VILAINE

Châteaubriant

LOIRE-ATLANTIQUE

La Baule   St-Nazaire

Nantes

The Cathédrale St-Pierre in Rennes (see pp56–9) has a magnificent 19th-century interior.

The Théâtre de Nantes is notable for its Neo-Classical interior (see pp204–8).

ILLE-ET-VILAINE

···

I N THE NORTH, *the Côte d'Émeraude and Mont-St-Michel face onto the English Channel. Further south, at the confluence of the Ille and the Vilaine rivers, lies Rennes, the regional capital, which is famous for its elegant parliament building. To the east, the proud fortresses of the Breton marches, which once protected the duchy of Brittany, face neighbouring Normandy.*

The beaches of the Côte d'Émeraude are lined by a succession of resorts. But well before this part of Brittany was discovered by tourists, Pierre-Auguste Renoir, Paul Signac and other artists had already been struck by its beauty when they came to paint in St-Briac.

Whether they are drawn to the megalithic Roche-aux-Fées or to the fortified castle in Fougères, lovers of ancient monuments will be spoiled for choice. On the coast, Mont-St-Michel stands as a jewel of Gothic religious architecture, while the citadel in St-Malo encloses within its ramparts several luxury hotels. Inland, noblemen built a multitude of manor houses, symbols of social standing, during the 16th and 17th centuries.

In the towns, a prosperous and influential middle class developed; the medieval houses in Vitré and Dol, as well as the town houses in Rennes, are proof of this opulence. As acts of piety, tradesmen's guilds commissioned the artists of Laval to create rich altarpieces.

From Celtic mythology to French Romanticism, the *département* of the Ille-et-Vilaine also has two emblems of Breton literary heritage: one is the the Forêt de Paimpont, the legendary Forêt de Brocéliande where Merlin fell under the spell of the fairy Vivian; the other is the lugubrious Château de Combourg, haunted by the ghost of the 19th-century writer and statesman the Vicomte de Chateaubriand.

The Château de La Bourbansais, near Tinténiac

◁ **The Promenade des Onze-Écluses, a path along a canal famous for its 11 locks, at Hédé**

Exploring the Ille-et-Vilaine

THIS *DÉPARTEMENT*, which covers an area of 6,758 sq km (2,608 sq miles), is named after the two rivers that flow through it: the Ille and the Vilaine. In the north, a hilly area culminating in Mont Dol overlooks the coast. East of Cancale, the marshlands of Dol have been converted into polders, sunken areas of land reclaimed from the sea. The coastline then descends to trace a bay out of which rises Mont-St-Michel. From the Pointe du Grouin, the Côte d'Émeraude (Emerald Coast) is marked by alternating jagged cliffs and soft sandy beaches. Rennes, in the centre of the *département*, is the administrative capital. On the eastern border of the Ille-et-Vilaine, the fortresses of Fougères and Vitré face neighbouring Normandy. Occupying a corner of the Morbihan and of the Ille-et-Vilaine, the Forêt de Paimpont is a vestige of Argoat, woodland that once covered the whole of inland Brittany.

THE REGION AT A GLANCE

Baie du Mont-St-Michel 18
Bécherel 12
Cancale 21
Château du Bos 24
Château des Rochers-Sévigné 9
Combourg 14
Dinard 25
Dol-de-Bretagne 15
Forêt de Paimpont 3
Fougères 10
Grand-Fougeray 6
Hédé 11
La Guerche-de-Bretagne 7
Langon 5
Mont-St-Michel pp72–5 19
Menhir du Champ-Dolent 16
Mont-Dol 17
Paimpont 2
Pointe du Grouin 22
Redon 4
Rennes pp56–61 1
St-Briac 27
St-Lunaire 26
St-Malo pp78–83 23
Tinténiac 13
Vitré 8

Hike
Sentier des Douaniers 20

SENTIER DES DOUANIERS 20
POINTE DU GROUIN 22
CANCALE 21
ST-LUNAIRE 26
ST-BRIAC 27
DINARD 25
ST-MALO 23
CHÂTEAU DU BOS 24
CHÂTEAUNEUF-D'ILLE-ET-VILAINE
MONT-DOL 17
N 176 E
DOL-DE-BRETAGNE 15
MENHIR DU CHAMP-DOLE 16
Dinan
N 137
Dinan
COMBOU 14
Canal
D 795
TINTÉNIAC 13
HÉDÉ 11
d'Ille
et
Rance
BÉCHEREL 12
St-Brieuc
D 71
N 137
Loudéac
MONTAUBAN-DE-BRETAGNE
N 12 E 50
D 27
D 29
D 15
RENNI 1
FORÊT DE PAIMPONT
PAIMPONT 2 3
N 24
D
PLÉLAN-LE-GRAND
D 177
Vilaine
N 137 E 3
Ploërmel, Vannes
PIPRIAC
D 777
BAIN BRETA
GRAND-FOUGERAY 6
N 137 E 3
LANGON 5
D 59
D 777
D 177
Nantes
REDON 4

0 km   20
0 miles   20

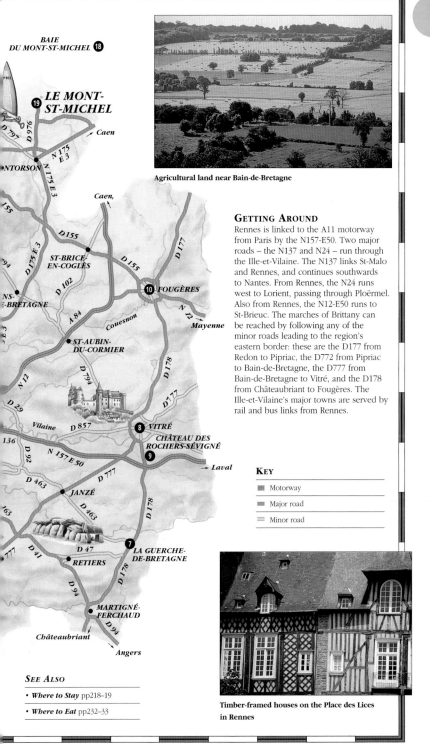

Agricultural land near Bain-de-Bretagne

GETTING AROUND

Rennes is linked to the A11 motorway from Paris by the N157-E50. Two major roads – the N137 and N24 – run through the Ille-et-Vilaine. The N137 links St-Malo and Rennes, and continues southwards to Nantes. From Rennes, the N24 runs west to Lorient, passing through Ploërmel. Also from Rennes, the N12-E50 runs to St-Brieuc. The marches of Brittany can be reached by following any of the minor roads leading to the region's eastern border: these are the D177 from Redon to Pipriac, the D772 from Pipriac to Bain-de-Bretagne, the D777 from Bain-de-Bretagne to Vitré, and the D178 from Châteaubriant to Fougères. The Ille-et-Vilaine's major towns are served by rail and bus links from Rennes.

KEY

▬	Motorway
▬	Major road
▭	Minor road

Timber-framed houses on the Place des Lices in Rennes

SEE ALSO

Street-by-Street: Rennes ❶

AROUND THE CATHEDRAL, narrow streets wind between timber-framed houses that conceal courtyards. On Saturdays, the Place des Lices throngs with the colourful stalls of one of the liveliest markets in Brittany. During the week, the district's many bars and restaurants are filled with the animated babble of students. Neo-Classical buildings by the architect Jacques Gabriel (1698–1782) line Place de la Mairie. Rue Le Bastard, leading off the square, is a pedestrianized zone and the main link between the Vilaine and the northern part of the city.

★ Rue du Champ-Jacquet
Tall timber-framed houses dating from the 17th century back onto the old city walls.

Hôtel de Robien

★ Hôtel de Blossac
This is one of the finest mansions in Rennes. The building, in the Neo-Classical style, was designed by a follower of Jacques Gabriel.

Hôtel Hayo de Tizé

Basilique St-Sauveur

RUE LE BAST...

RUE DU CHAMP JAQUET

RUE RALLIER DU-BATY

RUE DE TOULOUSE

RUE DE CLISSON

RUE DE LA MONNAIE

R. ST GUILLAUME

RUE ST SAUV...

R. DE LA PSALETTE

PLACE DES LICES

RUE DE JUILLET

CARREFOUR DE LA CATHÉDRALE

RUE DU GRIFFON

RUE D...

★ Cathédrale St-Pierre
The building stands on the site of an ancient place of worship. Although it retains its 16th-century façade, the cathedral was rebuilt from 1784.

Pavillons des Halles

Portes Mordelaises were the ceremonial gates used by kings, dukes and bishops.

Rue de la Psalette is lined with medieval houses.

STAR SIGHTS

★ Cathédrale St-Pierre

★ Hôtel de Blossac

★ Rue du Champ-Jacquet

KEY

– – – Suggested route

0 ─────────── 100 m
0 yards ─────── 100

Parlement de Bretagne
Now housing the law courts, this building's sumptuous decoration and paintings have been restored to their original splendour following a fire in 1994 (see pp60–61).

TIPS FOR VISITORS

Road map E3. 197,540. St-Jacques-de-la-Lande. Sat am; Place des Lices. 11 Rue St-Yves, (02) 99 67 11 11. Les Tombées de la Nuit (theatre & concerts; Jul), Transmusicales (rock; first week in Dec), Film Festival (Jan.)
W www.ville-rennes.fr

Église St-Germain reflects the opulence of the haberdashers' parish in the 16th century.

Theatre
In designing the theatre, which consists of a rotunda with arcades and covered alleyways, the architect Millardet wished to create a meeting place and centre of trade. He also designed the neighbouring residential buildings.

Hôtel de Ville
Built by Jacques Gabriel after the great fire of 1720, the town hall consists of two wings framing the clock tower, with a belfry in the Italian style. Sculptures by Jacques Verberckt decorate the main entrance.

Chapelle St-Yves houses the tourist office.

Head of an Angel by Botticelli, in the Robien Collection

ROBIEN'S CABINET OF CURIOSITIES

Built at the beginning of the 17th century, the mansion known as the Hôtel de Robien was acquired in 1699 by Christophe Paul de Robien. Filled not only with paintings and statues but also with plants and minerals, it became a true cabinet of curiosities. Robien bequeathed the collection to his son in 1756, but it was confiscated by the Revolutionaries in 1792. It was stored in the Church of the Visitation, then in the Carmelite convent in Rennes. The Robien Collection now forms part of the city's Musée des Beaux Arts.

Exploring Rennes

D ESPITE THE FIRE that devastated the city centre in
1720, Rennes still has some fine medieval houses.
It also has many delightful mansions and a remarkable
17th-century palace. The city has stood at a strategic
crossroads since Roman times. In the 10th century,
it withstood Norman invaders and became a symbol
of Breton resistance. In the 15th century, new
fortifications were built to strengthen the existing
Gallo-Roman ramparts. When Brittany became part
of France in 1532 and the parliament of Brittany was
created *(see pp60–61)*, Rennes became the regional
capital. After the fire of 1720, a Neo-Classical city
centre with rigidly straight streets was built. This
layout, and the buildings dating from the same
period, give Rennes a somewhat austere appearance.
A university town, Rennes has a conspicuously
lively population of students.

**Timber-framed houses around
Place des Lices**

🏛 Old Town

Between the Vilaine in the
south and Place des Lices
in the north, the medieval
centre of Rennes is full of
timber-framed houses.
Place des Lices (Square
of the Lists) takes its
name from the lists
where jousting tourna-
ments where once held. It
was here that Bertrand
du Guesclin *(see p41)*
first entered the lists.
Around the square,
three mansions – the
Hôtel du Molant, Hôtel
de la Noue and Hôtel
Racapée de la Feuillée
– all built after the fire
of 1720 – stand as
symbols of the power of the
Breton parliamentary nobility.

The **Portes Mordelaises**, at
the end of Rue de la Monnaie,
were the main gateway through
which kings entered the city.
Behind the **Cathédrale St-
Pierre**, in Rue du Chapitre,
the Hôtel de Brie and **Hôtel
de Blossac**, with a monumental stairway, are among
the finest residences.

Place de la Mairie is a large
Neo-Classical square designed
by Jacques Gabriel. The most
prominent feature of the
Hôtel de Ville, overlooking
the square, is the clocktower,
which replaced the old belfry.
The sculptures on the doors
are by Jacques Verberckt, who
worked on the decoration of
Versailles for Louis XV. The
theatre and arcaded

**Wooden statue in
Impasse de
la Psalette**

residential buildings opposite were designed by
Millardet in 1836.

The 17th–18th century
Basilique St-Sauveur,
in Rue de Clisson, is
associated with the
composer Gabriel Fauré,
who was organist there.
Rue St-Georges, lined with
old houses, leads to the
Église St-Germain,
whose transept is a
fine example of Breton
Romanesque archi-
tecture. Behind the Église
Notre-Dame is the **Jardin
du Thabor**, a master-
piece by the Bülher
brothers *(see p59)*.

🔒 Cathédrale St-Pierre

*Between the Portes Mordelaises
and Rue de la Poterne.*
The cathedral stands on the
site of an ancient shrine in
front of which a trove of
Gallo-Roman artifacts was
discovered. Work on the
building began in the 15th
century, and the façade was
completed in 1560. The rest
was built from 1784 to plans
by the architect Crucy. The
19th-century stuccowork and
gilding within give the
interior an opulence worthy
of Roman basilicas. The gilt
wood altarpiece, dating from
1520 and by the Flemish
School, is of particular note.

Marine Bleue, by G. Lacombe, in the Musée des Beaux-Arts, Rennes

The Bülher Brothers

Although little-known today, Denis (1811–90) and Eugène (1822–1907) Bülher revolutionized the art of garden design. Giving imagination free reign, they rejected the strictures of the classic formal gardens in the French style.

The Bülher brothers designed some 100 gardens. About 20 of these are in Brittany, and they include the gardens of the Château de Kervenez in St-Pol-de-Léon and of the Château de la Briantais in St-Malo. But it was in Rennes that they designed their finest garden, the Jardin du Thabor. Laid out in the style of a 19th-century park, the garden follows the contours of the land and incorporates greenhouses, pavilions and an aviary. Exotic and indigenous trees frame the garden's perspectives.

The Jardin du Thabor, laid out by the Bülher brothers

🏛 Musée des Beaux-Arts

20 Quai Émile-Zola. 【 (02) 99 28 55 85. ● Tue & public holidays. 📷 The works on display here cover the main periods in the history of art. The Robien Collection (see p57) contains drawings by Leonardo da Vinci, Botticelli, Donatello and Dürer. Besides early Italian painting, the most interesting part of the museum's display is that devoted to the 17th century, with works by Le Brun and Philippe de Champaigne, as well as Rubens' Tiger Hunt and Nouveau-né by Georges de La Tour, the museum's star painting. Modern art is represented by such painters as Lacombe, Corot, Gauguin, Sisley, Denis and Caillebotte. One of Picasso's Baigneuses, which he painted in Dinard, can be seen alongside works by Kupka and Juan Gris. The contemporary collection includes works by Poliakoff, Nicolas de Staël, Raymond Hains and Dufrêne.

🏛 Écomusée de la Bintinais

On the road to Châtillon-sur-Seiche, via the D82, 4 km (3 miles) south of Rennes. 【 (02) 99 51 38 15. ● Tue and public holidays. 📷 La Bintinais is one of the largest old farms in the countryside around Rennes. Converted into a living museum, it illustrates the history of rural life, through the themes of everyday activities, domestic life and costumes.

Fields have been planted to show various farming practices of the past, and a conservation orchard has been created to preserve varieties of cider apples that have become rare. Local strains that were at risk of dying out are cultivated on the farmland.

Rennes City Centre

Basilique St-Sauveur ③
Cathédrale St-Pierre ②
Église St-Germain ⑧
Hôtel de Ville ④
Jardin du Thabor ⑦
Musée des Beaux-Arts ⑨
Parlement de Bretagne ⑥
Portes Mordelaises ①
Theatre ⑤

Key

■ See pp56–7
🄿 Parking
ℹ Tourist information
Ⓜ Metro station
⊠ Post office
✝ Church

Parlement de Bretagne

THE BRETON PARLIAMENT, dating from 1618–55, is a major landmark in the city of Rennes. Salomon de la Brosse, the architect of the Palais du Luxembourg in Paris, designed the façade in the Italian style. The interior courtyard, by contrast, is built in brick and stone in the French style. The interior decoration of the building emphasizes the hallowed importance of Brittany's independent political power: the sumptuous Salle des Pas-Perdus, with the coat of arms of Brittany and France, and the ceiling of the Grand'Chambre, designed by Louis XIV's foremost painter, amply express this. Gutted by fire in February 1994, the building took five years to restore.

★ Court of Assises
The tables and benches in the audience chambers are made of oak. The room is lit by antique and modern chandeliers.

Former Court of Criminal Justice

★ Salle des Pas-Perdus
The door to the Salle des Pas-Perdus (the lobby) features windows decorated with metalwork. The room has an ornate wooden coffered ceiling.

Salle Jobbé-Duval
The allegories painted by Félix Jobbé-Duval in 1866 were the last decorative elements to be added. The allegory seen here is Eloquence.

Pediment

STAR FEATURES

★ Court of Assises

★ Grand'Chambre

★ Salle des Pas-Perdus

Salle des Piliers
This is the grand entrance hall to the parliament building. Like the rest of the interior, it consists of stone and brick, a traditionally French combination that contrasts with Jacques Gabriel's Italianate façade.

Upper Gallery
The audience chambers on the upper level are arranged in a gallery running around the court.

Slate roof, covering 5,200 sq m (18, 660 sq ft)

VISITORS' CHECKLIST

Place du Parlement-de-Bretagne.
(02) 99 67 11 11. W www.parlement-bretagne.com
Compulsory. Information from the tourist office;
(02) 99 67 11 11.

★ Grand'Chambre
Charles Errard, in charge of the building's decoration, experimented here before starting the decoration of Versailles. For the Grand'Chambre, he called on his pupil Noël Coypel, and, for the First Chamber, on Jean-Baptiste Jouvenet. Both decorated the rooms with allegorical paintings.

Allegorical Figures
Four allegorical figures, representing Eloquence, Fortitude, Law and Justice, once decorated the roof of the south lodges. Cast in lead and covered in gold leaf, the figures were made by Dolivet in the 19th century and restored by Jean-Loup Bouvier.

The ground-floor rooms were used for religious and official ceremonies.

PARLEMENT DE BRETAGNE

1 Salle des Pas-Perdus (lobby)
2 Salle Jobbé-Duval
3 Chapel
4 Court of Assises
5 Presiding judge's office
6 Second Chamber
7 First Chamber
8 Grand'Chambre (upper house)
9 Library
10 Courtyard and galleries

The Château de Trécesson, built in the late 14th century and surrounded by a moat

Paimpont ❷

Road map E3. 30 km (18.5 miles) south of Rennes via the N24 then the D38. 🚆 *Rennes*. 🚶 *1,385*. 🗏 *Pays de Brocéliande, 37 Avenue de la Libération, Plélan-le-Gran; (02) 99 06 86 07*. 🎪 *Pardon (Whitsun)*.

THE VILLAGE grew up around an abbey founded in the 7th century. Of this, only the 13th-century abbey church and a 17th-century building, now the village hall, survive. The abbey church features Romanesque elements, a Gothic rose window and some notable 17th-century woodcarvings. The village is the starting point for hikes in the Forêt de Brocéliande.

ENVIRONS: Industrial buildings at **Forges-de-Paimpont**, 6 km (4 miles) southeast of

Forêt de Paimpont, vestige of the legendary Forêt de Brocéliande

Paimpont on the D773, are vestiges of the village's former iron and steel industry. The first metal foundries were built there in 1663. The rise of the iron and steel industry in northern and eastern France caused their decline.

Forêt de Paimpont ❸

Road map E3. Around Paimpont. 🗏 *Pays de Brocéliande, 37 Avenue de la Libération, Plélan-le-Grand; (02) 99 06 86 07*.

THIS WOODLAND, the Forêt de Brocéliande of Celtic legend, was originally the extensive forest that once covered almost all of inland Brittany. Today, the woodland around Paimpont is all that remains and it is peppered with sites that have kept Arthurian legends alive. The Château de Comper, where the fairy Vivian is supposed to have lived, houses the **Centre de l'Imaginaire Arthurien**, where exhibitions and shows take place, and from which walks are organized. Rebuilt in the 18th century in Renaissance style, the building features three 14th-century towers.

The D31 leads northeast to Merlin's Tomb and the Fountain of Youth. The tree above the tomb is filled with strange offerings. From the hamlet of Folle Pensée, a short walk leads to the

Fontaine de Barenton, into which young women once cast pins in order to find a husband. Here, druids are supposed to have nursed people suffering from foolish thoughts *(folles pensées)*.

ENVIRONS: At Coëtquidan is the École de St-Cyr, a military academy. The **Musée de l'Armée** here displays gifts from prominent alumni, such as the statesman General de Gaulle (1890–1970). It is at Coëtquidan that Merlin is said to have met the fairy Vivian. The unusual Chapelle de Tréhorenteuc, 14 km (9 miles) west of Paimpont, contains mosaics and stained-glass windows on the theme of the Round Table. This is the starting point for the Promenade du Val-sans-Retour (Valley of No Return), dwelling place of Morgan le Fay, Arthur's half-sister, who trapped unfaithful men here. Passing the lake known as the Étang du Miroir-aux-Fées, the path leads up onto moorland and then on through the valley. Further south is the 14th-century red schist **Château de Trécesson**.

♣ **Centre de l'Imaginaire Arthurien**
Château de Comper. 📞 *(02) 97 22 79 96*. 🕐 *Apr–Oct; Wed–Mon. Shows on Sun in Jul & Aug*.
♣ **Château de Trécesson**
🚫 *to visitors*.
🏛 **Musée de l'Armée**
Coëtquidan. 📞 *(02) 97 73 52 99*. 🕐 *Tue–Sun*. 🚫 *Jan*.

Romances of the Round Table

A LARGE NUMBER of romances (medieval vernacular tales) make up the cycle of Arthurian literature. From that of Chrétien de Troyes, writing in the 12th century, to that of Sir Thomas Malory, in the 15th, there are almost 100 separate accounts. While

The knight Tristan carries away Queen Iseult

the earliest are in verse, later ones are in prose, and they are written either in French, English or German. They tell of the adventures of Gawain, of the love of Tristan and Iseult (the queen with the milk-white hands), of Arthur's unstoppable rise, of Merlin's tragic fate, of the creation of the Round

Table, of magic and sorcery in Brittany, of the quest for the Holy Grail and of the epic Battle of Salesbières. A conflation of several different ideologies, Arthurian literature contains pagan Celtic and Indo-European elements, and Christian dialectic, giving an insight into the multifaceted culture of the late Middle Ages. Long neglected, Arthurian literature was rediscovered at the beginning of the 20th century. It has inspired not only literature but also music (Wagner's *Parsifal*, for example), and film (John Borman's *Excalibur*, for instance).

The conception of Merlin *the wizard took place between the Devil and a pious mortal.*

Angels support the Holy Grail, an aspect of Christianity incorporated into Arthurian legend.

The Holy Grail, symbol of the mystery of the Eucharist.

Sir Galahad, destined to find the Holy Grail.

THE HOLY GRAIL
The vessel used by Christ and his disciples at the Last Supper appeared before the Knights of the Round Table. In *The Quest of the Holy Grail*, it is said to have floated in mid-air, giving the knights divine sustenance while a heavenly voice invited them to go in search of it.

King Arthur and the Knights of the Round Table *are shown in this fresco by Eugène Viollet-le-Duc. The knights are dressed in their familiar colours.*

Merlin's passion for Vivian *led the wizard to reveal to his pupil the secrets that were to lead him to his unhappy fate. He was imprisoned forever in a tree.*

The cloister of the Abbaye de St-Sauveur in Redon, dating from the 17th century

Redon ❹

Road map E3. 🏛 *10,500.*
🚉 🛈 *Place de la République,*
(02) 99 71 06 04. 🚌 *Mon, Fri & Sat.*
🎭 *Nocturiales (Baroque and Celtic music), Jul–Aug.*

Tᴴɪꜱ ᴛᴏᴡɴ is located on the borders of three *départements*: the Ille-et-Vilaine, the Loire-Atlantique and the Morbihan. From the 9th century, it was renowned for its Benedictine abbey, which was the most important in Brittany. The Cartulaire de Redon (*see p37*), the earliest document in the history of Brittany, was written here. At the hub of roads and railways, and near the con-

fluence of two rivers, Redon developed a diverse economy and has become an industrial centre. In the 20th century, several important companies chose it as their base.

In the historic centre, timber-framed houses dating from the 15th, 16th and 17th centuries can be seen around Grande-Rue. In the harbour, houses with over-hanging upper storeys alternate with 17th- and 18th-century shipowners' mansions. In Rue du Port, three 17th-century salt ware-houses, now restored, can be seen at Nos. 32, 36 and 40. The **Musée de la Batellerie**, on Quai Jean-Bart, illustrates the history of river navigation in Brittany through models and documents.

The **Abbaye de St-Sauveur**, the most important abbey in Brittany during the Middle Ages, is a monument to the power of the Benedictine order. Its Romanesque belfry, built in limestone and granite and set apart from the abbey itself, rises in three open tiers. It is unique in Brittany. The Romanesque nave with wooden ceiling contrasts with the choir, which has quatrefoil columns and Gothic chapels. The cloister was rebuilt in the 17th century. In 1622, Richelieu was an abbot here.

Environs: Some 10 km (6 miles) north of Redon, the perfume manufacturer Yves Rocher and the Muséum National d'Histoire Naturelle have joined forces to create the **Végétarium de La Gacilly,** Here, aromatic and medicinal plants are grown in their appropriate habitat (such as desert and tropical) and their uses explained.

St Just, 20 km (12 miles) north of Redon, is at the centre of an area rich in megaliths, including the galleried grave at **Tréal** and the **Landes de Coujoux**, a long narrow ridge with many megaliths. At Lohéac, 15 km (9 miles) north of St Just, the **Manoir de l'Automobile** contains a display of over 200 collectors' cars, including Rolls-Royces, Ferraris, Lamborghinis, Cadillacs and pre-war models. There is also a go-karting circuit.

Exhibits at the Manoir de l'Automobile in Lohéac

🏛 **Musée de la Batellerie**
Quai Jean-Bart. 🕿 *(02) 99 72 30 95.*
◯ *mid-Jun–mid-Sep: daily.* 🈳
⛪ **Abbaye de St-Sauveur**
Place St-Sauveur. 🕿 *(02) 99 71 06 04.* 🈳 *8 Jul–Aug; Mon & Wed.*
🌿 **Végétarium de La Gacilly**
La Croix-des-Archers
🕿 *(02) 99 08 35 84.* ◯ *end Apr–mid-Jun & mid-Sep–mid-Oct: Sat–Sun & public holidays; mid-Jun–end Sep: daily.* ● *Nov–Mar.* 🈳
⛩ **Tréal Archaeological Site and Landes de Coujoux**
◯ *all year.* 🕿 *(02) 99 72 61 02.* 🈳 *end-Jun–mid-Sep.*
🏛 **Manoir de l'Automobile**
Lohéac, on the D177.
🕿 *(02) 99 34 02 32.* ◯ *Jul–Aug: daily.* ● *Mon & Sep–Jun.*

CHURCH ALTARPIECES

Reacting against Protestant austerity, the Counter-Reformation in Brittany extolled the Catholic faith through magnificent church ornament. Altarpieces carved in wood or stone in an extravagant Baroque style graced the region's churches. The town of La Guerche-de-Bretagne is located in the heart of a region in which artists from Laval excelled in this field. Working with marble from Laval and Le Mans, and with tufa from the Loire, the sculptors Houdault, Corbineau and Langlois created consoles, pyramids, putti, foliate scrolls and garlands of fruit.

Detail of altarpiece at Domalain

The Chapelle Ste-Agathe, dedicated to Venus, in Langon

Langon 5

Road map E3. 20 km (13 miles) northeast of Redon via the D177 then the D55. 1,260.

THIS SMALL TOWN is separated from the Vilaine river by marshland known as the Marais de l'Étier. The **Chapelle Ste-Agathe** is a rare survival from the Gallo-Roman period. It is dedicated to Venus and, behind the altar, there is a fresco depicting Venus rising from the waves and Eros astride a dolphin. The Église St-Pierre is worth a visit for its unusual bell tower, which features 12 bell-turrets.

On the Lande du Moulin stands an alignment of menhirs known as the Demoiselles de Langon. According to legend, young girls who chose to dance on the heath rather than attend vespers were punished by being turned to stone.

Grand-Fougeray 6

Road map E3. 30 km (18.5 miles) northeast of Redon, via the D177 then the D54. 4,125.

THE TOUR DU GUESCLIN is all that remains of the medieval castle that once stood in Grand-Fougeray. The fortress belonged to the Rieux family, allies of John IV, Duke of Brittany, against the constable (chief military officer) Olivier de Clisson. In 1350, an English sea captain took the castle. Bertrand du Guesclin (see p41) and his men later recaptured it for France and ever since it has borne his name.

La Guerche-de-Bretagne 7

Road map F3. 20 km (12.5 miles) south of Vitré via the D178. 4,090. Place Charles-de-Gaulle; (02) 99 96 30 78. Tue.

ON THE BORDER with Normandy, La Guerche-de-Bretagne is one of the fortified towns that once defended the borders of Brittany. Its geographical location also made it a centre of commerce, and it was especially renowned for its linen trade (see p104). The market that takes place here was first held in 1121 and is one of the oldest in France.

Half-timbered houses dating from the 16th and 17th centuries line the main square. The many gables on the **Collégiale Notre-Dame** are fine examples of the Flamboyant Gothic style of Upper Brittany (see p19).

The church, built in the 15th and 16th centuries, has unusual Renaissance choir stalls (1525) with carvings depicting the Seven Deadly Sins. The dark blue barrel-vaulted ceiling and 15th-century stained-glass windows are also notable.

ENVIRONS: La Roche-aux-Fées stands 15 km (9 miles) west of La Guerche-de-Bretagne. It was built during the third millenium BC and is one of the most important dolmens in France. It consists of 41 stones, some of which weigh 45 tonnes, and is 19.5 m (64 ft) long and 4 m (13 ft) high. The interior contains four chambers. How and why it was built has still not been determined.

The ponds and wood around Martigné-Ferchaud, 15 km (9 miles) south of La Roche-aux-Fées, have become a sanctuary for migratory birds. The Étang de la Forge is a haven for ducks, coots and small waders. The pond is named after the ironworks, dating from 1672, that are to be found nearby.

 Collégiale Notre-Dame
Place Charles-de-Gaulle. (02) 99 96 30 78. daily. Summer: Mon–Fri; out of season: by request.
 La Roche-aux-Fées
From La Guerche-de-Bretagne, take the D178 towards Chateaubriant then the D47 towards Retiers and the D41 towards Janzé. The site is 2 km (1 mile) from Retiers. daily. Open access.

La Roche-aux-Fées, one of Brittany's mysterious megalithic monuments

Vitré ❽

Road map F3. 🏰 *15,910.* 🚉
ℹ️ *Place St-Yves; (02) 99 75 04 46.*
🚌 *Mon & Sat.*

U NUSUALLY WELL preserved, this fortified town has a wealth of picturesque houses. Until the end of the 17th century, it owed its prosperity to the trade in linen cloth, which was exported all over Europe and as far away as South America. In 1472, the Brotherhood of the Annunciation became the organizational force behind this international trade.

A succession of powerful lords – Laval, Montmorency and Montfort – were prominent in the region's history. In the 16th century, Guy XVI established what amounted to a court in Vitré. The **Château**, perched on a rocky outcrop, is one of the great fortresses that defended the marches of Brittany. It was enlarged from the 13th century onwards. The entrance is defended by a small castle flanked by machicolated towers. A triangular wall set with towers encloses the complex.

The museum within the castle contains a remarkable 16th-century triptych decorated with 32 Limoges enamels. Also on display are medieval and Renaissance sculpture, 16th- and 17th-century tapestries, and

Breton paintings. The top of the Tour Montafilant commands a superb panorama over the town.

The **Église Notre-Dame**, in Rue Montafilant, was rebuilt from 1420 to 1550, and is in the Flamboyant Gothic style; this can be seen clearly on its southern side, which bristles with finials. Inside are altarpieces *(see p64)* and a beautiful Renaissance stained-glass window. A plaque commemorates Field-marshal Gilles de Rais *(see p41)*, lord of Vitré and companion-at-arms of Joan of Arc. He was, however, executed for having murdered children.

Around the church, in Rue d'Embas, Rue Baudrairie, Rue St-Louis and Rue de Paris, the finest medieval and Renaissance houses in Vitré can be seen.

ENVIRONS: The 15th-century **Collégiale de Champeaux**, 9 km (6 miles) west of Vitré, recalls the former power of the lords of Espinay. It contains canopied Renaissance choir stalls with notable carvings, as well as 16th-century stained glass by the Fleming Jehan Adrian.

🏰 **Château de Vitré**
Place du Château. 📞 *(02) 99 75 04 54.* 🕐 *Apr–Sep: daily.* ⬤ *Mar–Oct: Tue & Sat, Sun & Mon am.* 📷
🏠 **Collégiale de Champeaux**
On the D29. 📞 *(02) 99 49 82 99* (information from the mairie).
🕐 *daily.*

The Breton coat of arms in the Eglise Notre-Dame in Vitré

Château des Rochers-Sévigné ❾

Road map F3. 8 km (5 miles) southeast of Vitré via the D88.
📞 *(02) 99 75 04 54.* 🕐 *daily Apr–Sep.* ⬤ *Tue, Oct–Mar & Sun & Mon am.* 📷

T HIS CASTLE, located 8 km (5 miles) southeast of Vitré, was built in the 15th century and later remodelled. It consists of two wings set at right angles. At the intersection is a polygonal turret, which contains a staircase. The circular tower on the opposite side predates the 15th century. The 17th-century chapel has a hull-shaped roof and is crowned by a lantern.

On the ground floor of the north tower, visitors can see a plan of the castle as it was in 1763, and, on the first floor, a portrait of Madame de Sévigné *(see p67)*. The castle overlooks an elegant formal garden, laid out in the 17th century by Charles de Sévigné, son of the *marquise.*

The Château de Vitré, once defending the marches of Brittany and now containing a museum

Timber-framed houses in the Marchix quarter of Fougères

Fougères ❿

Road map F2. 🎒 22,800.
🚌 🚏 Place de la République.
ℹ️ Place Aristide-Briand; (02) 99 94
12 20. 🍴 Sat; cattle market 5–9am
Fri. 🎻 Voix des Pays (Breton and
other folk music; Jul). Fêtes des
Angevines (early Sep).

A MAJOR TOWN in the marches
of Brittany, Fougères has
had a chequered history over
the centuries. The French
invasion of 1488 *(see p41)*
began here, and the defeat
of the Bretons at the Battle of
St-Aubin-du-Cormier sounded
the death-knell for their
independence.

The imposing **Château
de Fougères** is a superb
example of medieval military
architecture. It was built
between the 12th and 15th
centuries, and its ramparts, set
with 13 towers, enclose an
area of 2 ha (5 acres).

It is built to a concentric plan
that is typical of 12th-century
fortresses. In the 15th century,
with the development of
artillery, the walls were
strengthened and the
embrasures widened so as to
accommodate the barrels of
canons. The five towers that
defend the walls – the
Châtelet de l'Avancée, de
Coëtlogon, du Cadran, de
Guibé and de Coigny – also
date from this period. The
rampart walk offers a fine
view over the town.

The Église St-Sulpice,
with a slender spire, was built
between the 15th and 18th
centuries in the Flamboyant
Gothic style. The two 15th-
century granite altarpieces in
the transept contrast with the
monumental 18th-century
altarpiece in the choir. Also
of note is a fine 14th-century
Virgin and Child in painted
limestone.

The old town (Bourg Vieil), at
the foot of the castle, is filled
with old timber-framed
houses, particularly in **Place
du Marchix** and Rue de
Lusignan. The new town
(Bourg Neuf) overlooks the
castle. Gutted by fire on
several occasions, it was rebuilt in the 18th century.

A timber-framed building in
Rue Nationale, with a porch
and corbelling typical of
15th–16th-century houses in
Upper Brittany, contains the
**Musée Emmanuel-de-La-
Villéon**. As well as 70 paintings
dating from the 17th and 18th
centuries, the museum contains
18 works by Emmanuel de La
Villéon (1858–1944), an
Impressionist who was born
in Fougères, and whose work
depicts Breton landscapes
and scenes of daily life.

**Château de Fougères, a masterpiece
of military architecture**

ENVIRONS: The **Parc Floral
de Haute-Bretagne**, 20 km
(13 miles) northwest of
Fougères was laid out in the
19th century in the style of an
English landscaped park.

♣ **Château de Fougères**
Place Pierre-Symon. 📞 (02) 99 99 79
59. 🔲 daily. 🔴 Jan.
🏛 **Musée Emmanuel-
de-La-Villéon**
Rue Nationale. 🔲 mid-Jun–mid-Sep:
daily; mid-Sep–mid-Jun: Wed–Sun.
🔴 Jan.
🌿 **Parc Floral
de Haute-Bretagne**
La Foltière, Le Châtellier. 📞 (02) 99
95 48 32. 🔲 Mar–Nov: daily. 📷

LETTERS OF THE MARQUISE DE SÉVIGNÉ

The walls of the Château des Rochers-
Sévigné seem still to breathe the
finely honed prose of Madame de
Sévigné. In 1644, Marie de Rabutin-
Chantal married the Marquis Henri
de Sévigné, a spendthrift and
libertine. After his death in a duel,
the *marquise* withdrew to the
chateau. She filled her days by
writing long and frequent letters to
her daughter – to whom she addressed
almost 300 – as well as to the
Countess of Grignan, who was living
in the Drôme, in southern France.
The immediacy of this correspon-
dence is still compelling today.

**Marie de Rabutin-
Chantal, Marquise
de Sévigné**

The locks at Hédé, still manually operated

Hédé ⓫

Road map E2. 14 km (9 miles) south of Combourg on the D795. 🏛 *1,930.* ℹ *(02) 99 45 46 18.* 🛒 *Tue & Sun.*

Gustave Flaubert described the valley in which Hédé is located as "wide, beautiful and fertile, broad vista of greenery and trees". Of Hédé's castle, only a part of the walls and one side of the keep remain. The church, built in the 11th century and remodelled in the 12th, is in the early Romanesque style.

La Madeleine, 1 km (0.5 mile) north of Hédé, is the starting point of the **Promenade des Onze-Écluses**, a delectably bucolic walk along the Ille-et-Rance canal, which has a flight of 11 locks with a 27-m (88-ft) rise.

Bécherel ⓬

Road map E2. 17 km (10.5 miles) north of Monfort via the D72, D70 and D20. 🏛 *660.* ℹ *9 Rue Alexandre-Jehanin; (02) 99 66 75 23.* 🎭 *Fête du Livre Ancien (Easter weekend).*

With a wealth of antiquarian booksellers, second-hand book dealers, bookbinders and bookshops, Bécherel has both a literary and a medieval atmosphere. The castle, built in 1124 and now in ruins, was wrested from the English by Bertrand du Guesclin in 1374 after a 15-month siege. In the 17th and 18th centuries, the town prospered from the linen and hemp trade, exporting cloth throughout Europe. This former wealth can be seen in the houses of the town's historical middle class – handsome granite buildings of uniform design.

Environs: The **Château de Caradeuc**, 1 km (0.5 mile) west of Bécherel, once belonged to L. R. de Caradeuc La Chalotais (1701–85), Attorney-General of the Breton parliament and a heroic figure in Breton resistance to centralized French government. Built in the 18th century, the chateau has an elegant Regency façade and is set in a lovely park.

Les Iffs, 6 km (4 miles) east of Bécherel, is named after the 100-year-old yew trees (*ifs*) in its parish close. The church here, built in Flamboyant Gothic style, has nine beautiful stained-glass windows. The Fontaine St-Fiacre, just outside Les Iffs on its northern side, is a spring that was enclosed in the 15th century. In time of drought, pilgrims would come here to pray for rain.

The **Château de Montmuran**, on the road to Tinténiac, has associations with Bertrand du Guesclin, who was knighted in its chapel in 1354. The gatehouse, with original portcullis, is 14th-century, while the main building is mostly 18th-century, with 13th-century towers.

🏰 **Château de Caradeuc**
🗝 *(02) 99 66 77 76.*
⭘ *Park only: Apr–Oct: daily; Nov–Mar: Sat–Sun pm.*

🏰 **Château de Montmuran**
🗝 *(02) 99 45 88 88.* ⭘ *daily for groups by prior arrangement.* 📷 *Jun–Sep: Sun–Fri pm.* ♿

Tinténiac ⓭

Road map E2. 30 km (19 miles) north of Rennes via the N137 then the D20. 🏛 *2,434.* 🛒 *Wed.*

Clogs, Musée de l'Outil et des Métiers, Tinténiac

This small town is associated with the Chevalier de Tinténiac, who fought alongside the Chouans (*see p46*). The **Musée de l'Outil et des Métiers**, located on the canalside, contains collections of tools used for rope-making, harness-making, blacksmithing, barrel-making and other rural crafts. The church was completely rebuilt in the Byzantine style at the beginning of the 20th century.

Environs: The Château de La Motte-Beaumanoir, 12 km (8 miles) north of Tinténiac, has been rebuilt many times and is now a hotel. The façade, looking onto a courtyard, gives an idea of its appearance in the 15th century: the main part of the castle is a two-storey building with a corner tower containing a staircase. In 1776, the naval captain Jean Thomas de Lorgeril, who had prospered

Le Seanachi, one of many antiquarian bookshops in Bécherel

The Château de Combourg, now inhabited by a descendant of Chateaubriand's elder brother

as a privateer, acquired the manor, adding two wings to it.

About 12 km (8 miles) north of Tinténiac, in the direction of Dinan, is the **Château de la Bourbansais**, built in the 16th century and enlarged in the 18th. On the ground floor are 18th-century furniture, Aubusson tapestries and Oriental porcelain imported by the French East India Company. The park now contains a zoo.

🏛 **Musée de l'Outil et des Métiers**
Quai de la Donac. 🎫 (02) 99 23 09 30. ⭕ Jul–Sep: daily except Sun am.
♣ **Château de la Bourbansais and Zoo**
Pleugueneuc. 🎫 (02) 99 69 40 07.

Chateau 📷 Apr–Sep: daily; Oct–Mar: Sat–Sun & public holidays. 🌿 **Zoo** ⭕ Apr–Sep: daily; Oct–Mar: daily, pm.

Combourg ⑭

Road map E2. 🏘 4,843. 🚉 🛈
Maison de la Lanterne, Place Albert-Parent; (02) 99 73 13 93. 🔄 Mon.
🎪 Foire de l'Angevine, first Mon in Sep.

THIS TOWN is closely associated with the French Romantic writer François René de Chateaubriand, who lived in the **Château de Combourg**, an imposing building with pepperpot towers. The castle, whose origins go back to the 11th century, was rebuilt in the late Gothic style in the 14th and 15th centuries.

In 1761, it was acquired by Chateaubriand's father, a rich shipowner from St-Malo. As a child, Chateaubriand spent long periods of time here, and he described this in *Mémoires d'Outre-Tombe*.

Inside the castle, the writer's desk, armchair and deathbed, and a bust of him by David d'Angers, can be seen in the archive room. The rest of the interior was entirely restored in 1875. The landscaped park was designed by the Bülher brothers *(see p59)*.

ENVIRONS: The **Château de Landal**, 15 km (9 miles) northeast of Combourg, stands in an impressive location, within ramparts. Before it was acquired by Joseph de France, in 1696, it belonged to some of the greatest Breton families. Two of its corner towers date from the 15th century. Impressive displays of falconry take place in the castle's courtyard.

♣ **Château de Combourg**
🎫 (02) 99 73 22 95. **Park** ⭕ Jul–Aug: daily; Apr–Jun & Sep: Wed–Mon. **Chateau** ⭕ Jul–Aug: daily; Apr–Jun & Sept: Wed–Mon, pm. ● Nov–Feb.
♣ **Château de Landal**
3 km (2 miles) north of Broualan, on the Aigles de Bretagne route.
🎫 (02) 99 80 10 15. ⭕ Apr–Nov: Wed–Mon.

FRANÇOIS RENÉ DE CHATEAUBRIAND

"It was in the woods around Combourg that I became what I am," stated Chateaubriand (1768–1848) in his *Mémoires d'Outre-Tombe (Memoirs from Beyond the Grave*; 1830-41). Born in St-Malo, this great Romantic writer spent periods of time in the family castle. He later studied in Dol-de-Bretagne, Rennes, then Dinan, and regularly stayed with his sisters in Fougères until 1791. He came to fame with *Atala* (1801). *Le Génie du Christianisme (The Genius of Christianity*; 1802) established his reputation. The biographical *Mémoires* are considered to be his masterpiece.

François René de Chateaubriand

Dol-de-Bretagne ⑮

Road map E2. 👥 5,020. 🚉
ℹ️ *3 Grande-Rue-des-Stuarts;
(02) 99 48 15 37).* 🚌 *Sat.*
🎪 *Folk festival (last Sun in Jul);
Christmas market.*

THE RELIGIOUS CAPITAL of
Nominoë, king of Brittany
during the 9th century, Dol
owes its prestige and prosperity
to its cathedral, which is one
of the finest examples of
Gothic architecture in Brittany.

In about 548, St Samson,
one of the seven monks who
established Christianity in
Brittany, arrived from England
and founded a monastery. A
town grew up around it and,
despite suffering repeated
attacks by English-controlled
Normandy and from the kings
of France, it flourished and
enjoyed great prestige until
the abolition of its see in
1801. In 1793, it was the
scene of bloody conflict
between Chouan royalists and
Republicans *(see p46)*.

The **Cathédrale St-Samson**
stands on the site of a
Romanesque church that was
burned down by Jean sans
Terre in 1203. The great 14th-
century doorway on the south
side is finely decorated. The
north side, by contrast, faces
the open countryside and has
the appearance of a fortified
wall. The interior is impressive
through its sheer size. In the
nave, 93 m (305 ft) long,
seven spans of arches rise
through three tiers (an arcade,
triforium arches and a
clerestory), and the crossing
is crowned by a 20-m (65-ft)
high dome. The columns,
arches and stylized motifs
with which they are
decorated are in

the Anglo-Norman Gothic
style, and are similar to those
in Salisbury Cathedral.

A very expressive
Scourging of Christ can be
seen in the north aisle, and in
the north transept lies the
splendid tomb of Thomas
James, bishop of Dol from
1482 to 1504. Dating from the
16th century, with figures of
classical inspiration, this tomb
is one of the earliest signs of
the Renaissance in Brittany. It
was carved in the workshop
of the Florentine sculptor Jean
Juste, who also made the
tomb of Louis XII in St-Denis,
near Paris. The 77 choir stalls
are lit by an outstanding 13th-
century stained-glass window
with medallion-shaped
panels. Some of the stained-
glass windows here are
among the oldest in Brittany.

By means of modern tech-
niques, **Cathédraloscope**, in
the former bishop's palace on
Place de la Cathédrale, tells
the history of cathedral-
building, from methods of
construction and the various
crafts involved, to the
symbolism of the decoration
on the façade and the making
of stained-glass windows.

The Promenade des Douves
(Moat Walk), which passes
behind the cathedral's apse,
follows the ramparts on the
northern side of the town,
from where there is a view of
the marshes and of Mont Dol.
Grande-Rue-des-Stuart, with
houses with pillared porches,
offers a glimpse of Dol as it
appeared in the Middle Ages.
At No. 17, the Maison des
Petits-Palets, with carved
Romanesque arcades, is a rare
example of French 12th-
century town
architecture.

Opposite, a porch leads to
the Cour aux Chartiers, a
15th-century courtyard.

The Logis de la Croix Verte,
at No. 18, also dating from
the 12th century, was once
an inn run by the Knights
Templar. The Maison de
la Guillotière, at No. 27,
has a porch supported on
polygonal columns with
carved capitals.

🔒 **Cathédrale St-Samson**
Place de la Cathédrale.
📷 *Jul–Aug: Mon–Sat; Sep–Jun:
by prior arrangement.* **Concerts**
Thu eves. in Jul–Aug.
🏛️ **Cathédraloscope**
Place de la Cathédrale.
📞 *(02) 99 48 35 30.* ⭕ *daily.*
⚫ *Jan.*

**The Menhir du Champ-Dolent,
in the "Field of Sorrow"**

Menhir du Champ-Dolent ⑯

Road map E2. About 2 km (1 mile)
south of Dol-de-Bretagne on the
D795. ⭕ *daily. Open access.*

CONSISTING OF a single block
of granite 9.5 m (31 ft)
high, the Menhir du Champ-
Dolent is the tallest – and
some would say also the
finest – of Brittany's standing
stones. According to legend, it
fell from the sky, separating
two warring brothers who
were locked in deadly battle.
It is this legend that accounts
for the name "Champ Dolent",
meaning "Field of Sorrow".

Arch of the porch of the Cathédrale St-Samson in Dol-de-Bretagne

Sand yachts on wide, flat beaches near Cherrueix

Mont Dol ⓱

Road map E2. 2 km (1 mile) north of Dol-de-Bretagne on the D155.

THIS OUTCROP of granite, 65 m (213 ft) high, commands a breathtaking view over an expanse of polders (reclaimed land). Like neighbouring Mont-St-Michel and Mont Tombelaine, Mont Dol was once an island. During the Palaeolithic period, the region was covered in steppe and fenland. Finds of animal bones and stone tools prove that hunter-gatherers lived on the meat of reindeer, mammoth, lion, woolly rhino, horse, aurochs, bear and wolf. Much later, Mont Dol became a sacred place where druids worshipped.

A legend tells how St Michael and the Devil fought a battle on Mont Dol. Supposed traces of this can be seen on the rock: the Devil's claw marks, a hole for the Devil dug by St Michael, and footprints left by the Archangel Michael when he leaped across to Mont-St-Michel.

South of Mont Dol lies the small town of the same name. Frescoes dating from the 12th and 14th centuries, depicting scenes from the life of Christ, have been discovered in the nave of the church here.

Baie du Mont St-Michel ⓲

Road map E-F1. ⓘ *Dol-de-Bretagne; (02) 99 48 34 53.* ⚓ *Fête des Moules (Jul); Pardon de Ste-Anne in Roz-sur-Couesnon (Aug).*

THE COASTLINE HERE flattens out into a wide expanse of sand from which, almost magically, Mont-St-Michel

rises. The appearance of its silhouette subtly changes with atmospheric conditions. It is, apparently, possible to predict the weather accordingly, and every bit as accurately as the official forecast.

Oak stakes, known as *bouchots*, can be seen all along the bay. Driven into the sea bed, they are used for mussel-breeding, a practice that goes back as far as the 13th century. A quarter of all mussels farmed in France are raised in this bay, where the yield reaches 10,000 tonnes per year.

Windmills and low thatched houses line the coast as far as Cancale. At Le Vivier-sur-Mer, the **Maison de la Baie** houses a exhibition on mussel-farming and on the area's plants and animals. Visits to the *bouchots*, which are reachable on foot or by tractor-drawn transport, also start from here. Beware of fast-rising tides and quicksand. At Cherrueix, there is a sand-yachting centre, where this sport (*see p251*) is taught on the beaches.

⚓ Maison de la Baie
Le Vivier-sur-Mer. ⓒ *(02) 99 48 84 38.* ◐ *Easter–Oct: daily.* ● *Nov–Easter: Sun.*

POLDERS – LAND RECLAIMED FROM THE SEA

As glaciers began to melt at the end of the Ice Age, 10,000 years ago, the sea level rose, flooding coastal Brittany. The marshland around Mont Dol was eventually invaded by the sea. Work to reclaim the land began in the Middle Ages, when dykes were built. Crops were grown on these areas of fertile land, known as polders. However, since a dyke was built between Mont Dol and the mainland, sediment is no longer flushed out to sea on the ebbing tides, so that the bay is silting up. A solution under consideration is to remove part of the dyke, allowing Mont Dol to become an island again.

Cultivation on the polders in Baie du Mont-St-Michel

Mont-St-Michel ⑲

The abbey in the 10th century

WREATHED IN MIST and surrounded by the sea, Mont-St-Michel is one of the most extraordinary sights on the coast of France. Rising proudly from the bright waters of the bay, it stands at the Couesnon estuary, between Brittany and Normandy. It was known originally as Mont-Tombe, and a small oratory was built here in the 8th century. Work on the abbey began in the 10th century; by the 16th century, it increased the height of the mount almost two-fold. A place of pilgrimage, particularly during the 12th and 13th centuries, the mount drew large numbers of pilgrims, some of whom travelled great distances. "Mont-Michel", as it was known in the anti-religious climate of the French Revolution, became a prison. In 1874, its upkeep was entrusted to the Service des Monuments Historiques. It has been linked to the mainland by a causeway since 1879.

St Michael

The abbey in the 11th century

The abbey in the mid-17th century

Chapelle St-Aubert
Built on the rock in the 15th century, the chapel is dedicated to St Aubert, who founded Mont-St-Michel in AD 708.

Tour Gabriel

★ Ramparts
The town was fortified during the Hundred Years' War, to protect it from attack by the English.

Entrance

TIMELINE

966 A Benedictine abbey is founded	**1211–1228** Gothic buildings of La Merveille are completed	**1434** Final attack by the English. Ramparts are built	**1789** During the Revolution, the mount is used as a prison for political dissidents	**1874** Upkeep of the mount is entrusted to Monuments Historiques	
				1922 Church services resume	
700	**1000**	**1300**	**1600**	**1900**	
1017 Work starts on the building of the abbey	**1516** The abbey declines		**1877–1879** The dyke is built	**1895–1897** The tower, spire and statue of St Michael Archangel are added	
708 St Aubert builds an oratory on Mont-Tombe	**1067-1070** Mont-St-Michel is depicted in the Bayeux Tapestry *Detail of the Bayeux Tapestry*			**1969** Benedictine monks return to the mount	

Tides in Baie de Mont St-Michel
The bay is washed by unusually long tides, which flow unimpeded over the smooth quicksand. The strong spring tides can move at speeds of up to 10 kmh (6 mph).

VISITORS' CHECKLIST

🚃 *as far as Pontorson, then by bus.* ℹ️ *Boulevard de l'Avancée; (02) 33 60 14 30.*
🎪 *St-Michel de Printemps (May).*
Abbey 📞 *(02) 33 89 80 00.*
🕐 *Oct–Apr: 9:30am–4:30pm daily; May–Sep: 9am– 5:30pm; Oct–Apr during school holidays: 9:30am–5pm.* ⬤ *1 Jan, 1 May, 1 Nov, 11 Nov, 25 Dec.* 🎟️
✝️ *12:15 pm daily.*
📷 ♿ 🎁

★ Abbey
Enclosed within high walls, the abbey and its church occupy an impregnable position.

Saut Gauthier
This vantage point at the top of the Grand Degré commands a magnificent view over the south side of the bay.

Église St-Pierre

Tour de la Liberté

Tour de l'Arcade,
where the guards were accommodated

Tour du Roi

STAR FEATURES

★ Abbey

★ Grande-Rue

★ Ramparts

★ Grande-Rue
The route once taken by pilgrims as they made their way to the abbey, but now filled with tourists and souvenir shops, passes the Église St-Pierre.

Abbaye du Mont-St-Michel

THE HISTORY OF Mont-St-Michel can be read in its architecture. The abbey, the most prominent building, has served several different purposes; once attached to the Benedictine monastery, it later became a prison for political dissidents. The original abbey church, Notre-Dame-sous-Terre, was built in 1017, on the site of a 10th-century, pre-Romanesque building. In the early 13th century, La Merveille, an imposing three-storey monastery, was added to the north side of the church, built directly onto the rockface.

Cross in the choir

★ **Abbey Church**
Only four of the original seven spans in the nave survive. The other three were removed in 1776.

★ **La Merveille**
This masterpiece of Gothic architecture took 16 years to complete.

Monks' Refectory
This large room is bathed in soft light entering through windows in the end wall and through high, narrow niches.

Salle des Chevaliers
The vaulting and capitals in the Knight's Hall are in a pure Gothic style.

Upper Level (Church)

Intermediate Level

Lower Level

Crypte Notre-Dame-des-Trente-Cierges (Our Lady of the Thirty Candles) is one of two crypts beneath the transept.

★ **Cloisters**
With slender pudding-stone columns in an off-set alignment, the cloister is a perfect example of Anglo-Norman Gothic.

ABBEY GUIDE

The three levels on which the abbey is built reflect the hierarchy of the monastery. The monks' cells were on the upper level, where the church, cloister and refectory were also located. Important guests were entertained by the abbot on the intermediate level. On the lower level was accommodation for the guards, as well as for humbler pilgrims. The customary route for pilgrims was from the west platform to the almshouse, where the poor were given alms. This building is now a shop.

CHURCH

- Cloister
- Refectory
- Abbey church
- West platform
- Saut Gauthier
- Interior stairway

INTERMEDIATE LEVEL

- Salle des Chevaliers
- Salle des Hôtes
- Crypte Notre-Dame-des-Trente-Cierges
- Notre-Dame-sous-Terre
- Chapelle St-Étienne
- Crypte St-Martin
- Abbatial buildings

LOWER LEVEL

- Cellar
- Almshouse
- Abbey gardens
- Abbatial buildings
- Gatehouse

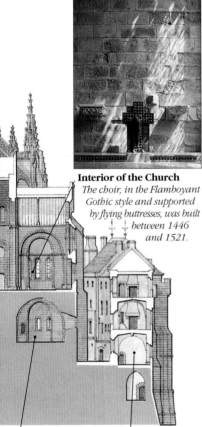

Interior of the Church
The choir, in the Flamboyant Gothic style and supported by flying buttresses, was built between 1446 and 1521.

Crypte St-Martin, a barrel-vaulted chapel, gives an idea of the austere appearance of the original abbey church.

The abbatial buildings, near the square in front of the church, allowed the abbot to entertain important visitors in suitable comfort. Lesser pilgrims were received at the almshouse.

Benedictines
A small community of Benedictine monks once again inhabits the abbey, continuing a tradition that goes back 1,000 years.

STAR FEATURES

★ **Abbey Church**

★ **Cloisters**

★ **La Merveille**

Sentier des Douaniers 🄳

THIS STRETCH of the GR34 (a *grande randonnée*, or long-distance path) starts at Cancale, follows the Pointe du Grouin along the edge of cliffs 40 m (130 ft) high, and ends at Les Daules. On one side is the English Channel and on the other a residential area with well-designed modern houses.

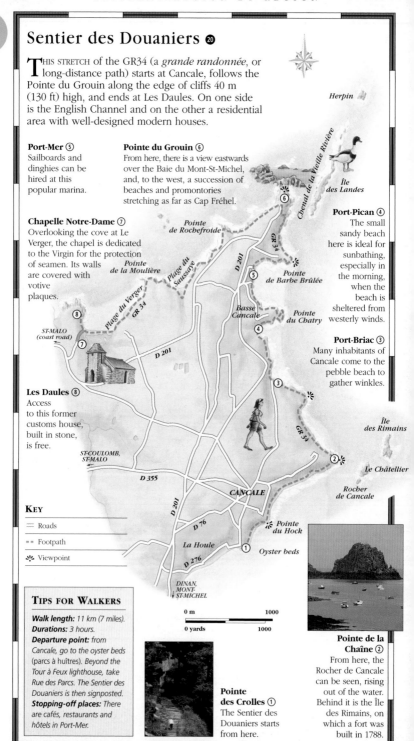

Port-Mer ⑤
Sailboards and dinghies can be hired at this popular marina.

Pointe du Grouin ⑥
From here, there is a view eastwards over the Baie du Mont-St-Michel, and, to the west, a succession of beaches and promontories stretching as far as Cap Fréhel.

Chapelle Notre-Dame ⑦
Overlooking the cove at Le Verger, the chapel is dedicated to the Virgin for the protection of seamen. Its walls are covered with votive plaques.

Port-Pican ④
The small sandy beach here is ideal for sunbathing, especially in the morning, when the beach is sheltered from westerly winds.

Port-Briac ③
Many inhabitants of Cancale come to the pebble beach to gather winkles.

Les Daules ⑧
Access to this former customs house, built in stone, is free.

Herpin

Île des Landes

Pointe de Rochefroide

Pointe de la Moulière

Plage du Saussaye

Pointe de Barbe Brûlée

Basse Cancale

Pointe du Chatry

Plage du Verger

ST-MALO (coast road)

D 201

Île des Rimains

Le Châtellier

Rocher de Cancale

ST-COULOMB, ST-MALO

D 355

CANCALE

Pointe du Hock

La Houle

Oyster beds

D 76

D 201

D 276

DINAN, MONT-ST-MICHEL

KEY

- ═ Roads
- ▪▪ Footpath
- ✳ Viewpoint

TIPS FOR WALKERS

Walk length: 11 km (7 miles).
Durations: 3 hours.
Departure point: from Cancale, go to the oyster beds (parcs à huîtres). Beyond the Tour à Feux lighthouse, take Rue des Parcs. The Sentier des Douaniers is then signposted.
Stopping-off places: There are cafés, restaurants and hôtels in Port-Mer.

0 m   1000

0 yards   1000

Pointe des Crolles ①
The Sentier des Douaniers starts from here.

Pointe de la Chaîne ②
From here, the Rocher de Cancale can be seen, rising out of the water. Behind it is the Île des Rimains, on which a fort was built in 1788.

Cancale ㉑

Road map E1. 🏘 5,350. ⚓
i 44 Rue du Port; (02) 99 89 63 72.
🚢 Voile-Aviron, tall ships festival
(Jun); Fêtes des Reposoirs (15 Aug);
Fête de la Confrérie des Huîtres (third
Sat in Sep). ⚓ Sun.

THIS CENTRE OF oyster-farming has kept its distinctive identity. The flat oysters *(belons)* that are farmed here today are famed for their large size. Along the harbour at La Houle, fishermen's houses have been converted into restaurants, cafés and shops.

When the cod-fishing industry collapsed in the 19th century, Cancale's fishermen turned to oyster-farming, using their boats – the *bisquines* – to harvest the oysters in the bay. Visitors can take a trip out to sea in one of them, ***La Cancalaise***.

The **Musée des Arts et Traditions Populaires**, laid out in a deconsecrated church, the 18th-century Église St-Méen, describes the history of oyster-farming, the lives of the seamen who once sailed to Newfoundland to fish for cod *(see pp24–5)* and those of their wives, whose legendary outspokenness goes back to the time when they would hawk fish on the quayside.

Port-Mer, Cancale's residential quarter, has an excellent sailing school. The terraces above the beach are an inviting place to stop and rest before walking around the Pointe du Grouin on the coast path, the Sentier des Douaniers *(see p76)*.

🏛 Musée des Arts et Traditions Populaires

2 Rue Vaujoyeux. **[** (02) 99 89 71 26. ◯ Jul–Aug: daily except Mon am; Jun & Sep: Thu–Sun, pm only. 🖾
⚓ **La Cancalaise**
Boat trips. **[** (02) 99 89 77 87. ◯ Apr–Oct: daily. 🖾

ÎLE DES LANDES BIRD SANCTUARY

Declared a bird sanctuary in 1961, the Île des Landes is separated from the Pointe du Grouin by a narrow channel, the Chenal de la Vieille Rivière. The island attracts the largest colony of cormorants in Brittany. Other species include the crested cormorant, herring gull and various other species of gull, and pied oystercatchers as well as the Belon sheldrake, the only sea duck native to Brittany. From August through to October, puffins, gannets and other sea birds flock to the island. Visitors can watch the birds through a fixed telescope and, every day throughout the summer, Bretagne Vivante (Living Brittany) organizes interesting nature walks on the island.

Pied oystercatchers on the Île des Landes

Pointe du Grouin, halfway along the Sentier des Douaniers

Pointe du Grouin ㉒

Road map E1. **[** (02) 98 49 07 18.
Events Jul–Aug: Tue–Sun in the Blockhaus.

THE LONGEST promontory in the Ille-et-Vilaine, Pointe du Grouin is covered with heath and coastal grassland that are typical of Brittany's rocky coast.

Having suffered degradation caused by excessive numbers of visitors, the area, which covers 21 ha (52 acres), is now under environmental protection. Soil erosion, the degradation of the chalky grassland and damage to protected species of plants by walkers have led the local council to lay out official paths and close off areas in order to allow grasses and wildflowers to recover. This plan of action has borne fruit, although the area is still vulnerable.

During World War II, German forces built *blockhausen (*blockhouses, or fortified gun positions) here to defend the strategically important headland. Most have survived intact, and one has been converted into a visitor centre. The greater horseshoe bat, one of the most endangered animals in France, nests in the abandoned blockhouses.

The lighthouse west of the promontory, built in 1861 and modernized in 1972, was decommissioned in 1999.

ENVIRONS: The Chapelle du Verger, which has been rebuilt on several occasions, nestles in an inlet known as the Cul-du-Chien (Dog's Bottom Cove). The belfry, at the foot of which many votive offerings have been laid, overlooks Cancale's largest sandy beach.

Flat-bottomed boats like these are used to harvest the oysters in the bay at Cancale

Street-by-Street: St-Malo's Walled City ㉓

A T THE END OF THE 17th century, St-Malo was France's foremost port, and shipowners who held a monopoly over trade with the East Indies amassed huge fortunes. Following attacks by the English in 1693 and 1695, plans were made to build a new fortified town, and the architect was Siméon de Garangeau. From 1708 to 1742, St-Malo grew rapidly, expanding by over one third. Tragically, during fighting at the end of World War II, in August 1944, 80 per cent of the port city was destroyed. It was, however, rebuilt in a style in keeping with its historic character, using granite-clad concrete. Immediately after the war, some buildings were reconstructed using their original stones.

The best view of St-Malo, from Dinard

Grande Porte
A niche inside the gate contains a 15th-century statue of Notre-Dame-de-Bon-Secours.

Cathédrale St-Vincent

Porte St-Vincent
The main entrance to the city is through a gateway in the walls, which are 7 m (23 ft) thick. From the gateway, a stairway leads up to the rampart walk.

The castle's four towers were built by Francis II and Anne of Brittany.

Rue du Pélicot

★ Château
Built by John V, Duke of Brittany, and enlarged by Anne of Brittany, the castle now houses the local council offices and two museums: the Musée d'Histoire de St-Malo and the Musée du Pays Malouin.

Église St-Benoît
The doorway of the former Église St-Benoît was built by the architect Jean Poulier in 1705, to a design by Garangeau. It consists of a pair of granite columns supporting a curved pediment.

★ **Hôtel d'Asfeld**
This mansion, once the residence of
Auguste Magon de La Lande, head
of the French East India Company
in 1715, is fronted by a courtyard
and a gateway. It was used as a
prison during the Revolution.
Chateaubriand's mother was
incarcerated here.

Hôtel André-Désilles

Porte de Dinan

Bastion St-Philippe

VISITORS' CHECKLIST

Road map E1. 🏠 48,057.
✈ Dinard-Pleurtuit-St-Malo.
🚌 (02) 23 18 15 15. 🚏 Square
Jean-Coquelin. 🛈 Esplanade
St-Vincent; (02) 99 56 64 48.
🗓 Mon–Sat in the old town.
🎭 Étonnants Voyageurs (Book
Fair, Whitsun); Folklore
du Monde (Jul); Festival de
Musique Sacrée (Jul–mid-Aug);
Route du Rock (mid-Aug), Quai
des Bulles (Oct), Route du Rhum
(transatlantic race; Nov, every
four years, the next in 2006).
W www.ville-saint-malo.fr

Église St-Sauveur
Completed in 1743 by the
architect Michel Marion to
plans by Garangeau, the
church is now used as a venue
for temporary exhibitions.
The west front, which faces
the street, is plain to the point
of being austere.

0 m   100
0 yards   100

KEY

– – – Suggested route

Statue of Jacques Cartier

★ **Ramparts**
Many stages of the city's
history can be seen from
the rampart walk. Among
the oldest parts are the
Cavalier des Champs-
Vauverts and the Tour
Bidouane, built around the
late 16th-century arsenal
that predates the 17th-
century fortified town.

STAR SIGHTS

★ **Château**

★ **Hôtel d'Asfeld**

★ **Ramparts**

Exploring St-Malo

T HROUGHOUT ITS HISTORY, this port city, sheltered from battering winds by its ramparts, has maintained a fierce spirit of independence. This is reflected in the motto "Foremost a native of St-Malo, a Breton perhaps, and a Frenchman last". Its indomitable seamen have sailed the high seas in search of undiscovered lands and of exotic goods that could be traded for a high return in Europe. Both privateers and shipowners made their fortunes here, and, in the 17th and 18th centuries, the kings of France as well as St-Malo itself also profited handsomely. The private residences and *malouinières* (grand country residences) that can be seen today are proof of this fabulous success.

An eventful history

As early as 1308, the inhabitants of St-Malo showed their mettle by establishing the first free town in Brittany, and, in 1395, rebelling against the Duke of Brittany, they obtained leave to answer only to Charles VI, king of France. St-Malo was then granted the status of an independent port, and for the next 300 years its economic success was assured. In 1415, John V, Duke of Brittany, attempted to regain authority over St-Malo and began to build the castle here. In 1436, the English described the seamen of St-Malo in these terms: "The people of St-Malo are the greatest thieves ...that ever sailed the seas... These pilferers who sail under false colours ... have no respect for their dukes." Neither did they have respect for France, as, in 1590, they formed an

Cathedral gargoyle

independent, albeit shortlived, republic in defiance of Henry IV's royal authority. By the end of the 15th century, having grown prosperous through trade and from fishing off Newfoundland, St-Malo had become a port of international renown. From 1698 to 1720, cargo ships sailing from St-Malo exported linen cloth, lace and other everyday goods to America, returning laden with gold and precious stones. The immensely rich shipowners were "invited" to lend the king half of the cargo brought back by their ships, thus saving France from bankruptcy.

⚓ **St-Malo's Walled City**
The main entrance into the walled city of St-Malo is **Porte St-Vincent**, built in 1709 and standing on its northeastern side. Inside the pedestrians' entrance is a map of the city showing the main stages in its construction and identifying the most important

GARANGEAU

The civil and naval architect Siméon de Garangeau (1647–1741) had worked in Marseille and in Brest before he took charge of building St-Malo's fortifications. The great military engineer Vauban considered that the coastal fort of La Conchée, which Garangeau built, was the best building in France. As a civil architect, Garangeau was also responsible for much of St-Malo's unique architectural character.

Fortifications of St-Malo

buildings. A stairway leads up to the rampart walk, which offers a wide view of the city. Further north, in front of Place du Poids-du-Roi, is **Grande Porte**, a 15th-century gateway with machicolated towers.

Cathédrale St-Vincent, on Place de Châtillon, was begun in the 12th century and completed in the 18th. Grimacing gargoyles stare down from the heights of the outer walls. Inside, the high, delicate Gothic choir contrasts with the nave, in the Angevin

The Quai St-Louis and Quai St-Vincent, on the western side of St-Malo

Romanesque style. It is an example of the influence of Anglo-Norman architecture on the design of churches in northern Brittany. The great rose window is filled with modern, brightly coloured glass. The tomb of the 16th-century explorer Jacques Cartier *(see p24)* can be seen in the north chapel.

At No. 3 Cour de la Houssaye, near Rue Chateaubriand, is the **Maison de la Duchesse Anne** *(see p42)*. With its outer tower, it is a typical example of a late Medieval urban manor house. Destroyed during World War II, it was rebuilt on the basis of old engravings.

Rue du Pélicot, which runs across Rue Chateaubriand, has some unusual "glass houses" – early 16th-century wooden houses with glazed galleries. At the end of Rue Mac-Law stands the Chapelle St-Aaron (1621), perched on the summit of the rock and

facing the law courts. The evangelizing monk Aaron, St-Malo's original inhabitant, chose this spot for his hermitage.

The rampart walk on the eastern side of the walled city, near Porte de Dinan, offers a bird's-eye view of several 18th-century shipowners' houses that either escaped war damage or were reconstructed. Built in a restrained and uniform style, they have an aristocratic elegance, and reflect both the personal wealth and social standing of their owners, who used them as a base for various trading activities. The ramparts also afford fine views as far as Dinard and the Côte d'Emeraude.

🏨 Hôtel d'Asfeld

5 Rue d'Asfeld. ((02) 99 56 09 40. 📅 *Jul–Aug: daily; Feb–Jun & Sep–Nov: Tue–Sun.* ⬤ *Dec–Jan.* 🚫 This fine building was once the residence of Auguste

Maison de la Duchesse Anne, a typical urban manor house

Magon de La Lande, one of the wealthiest shipowners in St-Malo and the head of the French East India Company in 1715. Open to visitors, it offers the opportunity to see inside one of these aristocratic houses, with their vaulted cellars.

ST-MALO CITY CENTRE

Château ②
Corniche d'Aleth ⑥
Fort National ③
Grand Aquarium ⑧
Musée du Long Cours
  Cap-Hornier ⑤
Paramé ⑦
St-Malo Walled City ①
St-Servan ④

KEY

🚉 Railway station
🚢 Boat boarding point
🚌 Bus station
🅿 Parking
ℹ Tourist information
▨ See pp78–9
⊠ Post office
✚ Hospital
🏠 Church

0 m   400
0 yards   400

♣ Château

Place Chateaubriand, near the marina.
Built in the 15th and 16th
centuries, the castle was used
by Jean V, Duke of Brittany
(1399–1442) mainly as a base
from which to keep watch
over the infamously rebellious
people of St-Malo. John's
daughter Anne *(see pp42–3)*,
who became queen of France
through her marriage to
Charles VIII, enlarged the castle,
with the same purpose in
mind. Knowing the dissenting
character of the townspeople,
she had these words engraved
in the wall of a tower in the
castle's east wing: "*Quic en
groigne, ainsi sera, car tel est
mon plaisir*" (Thus will it be,
whoever complains, for this
is my will.) The people of
St-Malo defiantly christened
the castle Quic-en-Groigne.

⑪ Musée d'Histoire de St-Malo

In the castle keep. ☎ *(02) 99 40 71
57.* ☐ *Apr–Sep: daily.* ● *Nov–Mar:
Mon and public holidays.* 🖼
This museum, dedicated to
the history of St-Malo, occupies
the keep, which stands at the
entrance to the castle. With
granite walls and high chimneypieces, it provides a sumptuous
setting for the exhibits.

The collection consists of
paintings, sculpture, figureheads, models of ships and
topographical models illustrating the city's history and its
seafaring traditions. Prominent
citizens of St-Malo, such as
Surcouf and Jacques Cartier
(see p24), Chateaubriand *(see
p69)* and Lamennais *(see p23)*
are also honoured.

The Fort National, designed by Vauban and built by Garangeau

LEE MILLER'S WARTIME SCOOP

In October 1944, an eight-page report on the siege of
St-Malo appeared in the pages of American *Vogue*. The
report and accompanying photographs were by-lined
Lee Miller, Man Ray's companion, a friend of Paul
Éluard and Pablo Picasso, and a model and fashion
photographer. The only journalist in the city during the
bombings, she recorded the destruction of St-Malo. "My
heel sank into a disembodied hand, and I cursed the
Germans for the horrible
destruction that they had
inflicted on this once-
splendid city," she wrote
at the time. Antony
Penrose, Lee Miller's son
and the author of her
biography, relates that
the photographs taken
by his mother were such
a scoop that they were
confiscated by the British
censors: it was during
the liberation of St-Malo
that napalm had first
been used.

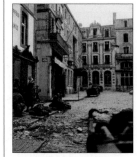

Place Chateaubriand in 1944

⑪ Musée du Pays Malouin

In the castle's Tour Générale.
☐ *Apr–Sep: daily.* ● *Nov–Mar:
Mon and public holidays.* 🖼
Housed in one of the castle's
towers, this museum comple-
ments the Musée d'Histoire
de St-Malo.

It illustrates daily life in the
city in historical times, as well
as local commercial activities
– particularly deep-sea fishing
off Newfoundland – and
major events in the history
of St-Malo and its environs.
Of particular interest are the
navigational instruments,
coiffes (Breton headdresses),
traditional costume, furniture
and paintings.

♣ Fort National

Northeast of the castle. ☎ *(02) 99
56 64 48. Accessible on foot at low
tide. When the French flag flies over
the fort, it is open to the public.*
🏳 *Jun–Sep: Sat–Sun.* 🖼
In the 18th century, five
coastal forts – La Varde,
Le Petit-Bé, La Conchée,
Harbourg and the Fort
National – defended the Baie
de St-Malo. The Fort National
was designed by the military
engineer Vauban in 1689. It
was built by Garangeau *(see
p80)* on the Rocher de l'Islet,
where criminals were once
executed. From here, there is
a splendid view of the
ramparts, the Rance estuary
and the Îles Chausey.

⊞ St-Servan

This residential district to the
south of the walled city of
St-Malo contains some fine
houses. Numerous sailing
ships are berthed in the Les
Bas-Sablons harbour. From
here, a road leads to Aleth.

⑪ Musée du Long Cours Cap-Hornier

In the Tour Solidor. ☎ *(02) 99 40 71
58.* ☐ *Apr–Sep: daily.* ● *Nov–Mar:
Mon & public holidays.* 🖼
The tower now houses a
museum devoted to those
who, following trade routes,

Notre-Dame-des-Flots, an oratory on the cliffs near Rothéneuf

sailed round Cape Horn in the 19th and 20th centuries. Items on display include navigational instruments, models of ships, sails, sperm whales' teeth and canoe paddles from New Caledonia. The tower, which is some 30 m (33 ft) high, was built on the orders of John IV, Duke of Brittany, between 1364 and 1382. It commands a fine view of the estuary.

Corniche d'Aleth

Aleth, inhabited by Celts in 80–70 BC, was settled before St-Malo was founded. Around 270, the peninsula was enclosed by walls and then, in about 350, a *castellum* (small fort) was built here, on a site now covered by the gardens of the Château de Solidor. In about 380, Aleth became the capital of the Coriosolites, a Gaulish tribe inhabiting what is now the Côtes d'Armor. In the mid-12th century, the see of St-Malo was transferred to Aleth, causing the city to decline. The walls, cathedral and castle were razed on the orders of St Louis, although a few ruins can still be seen.

The coast walk offers a breathtaking view of the walled city, the Île du Petit-Bé and Île du Grand-Bé, where Chateaubriand was laid to rest.

Paramé

On the road north out of St-Malo. Paramé and Rothéneuf have formed part of St-Malo since 1967. The coastal resort of Paramé was established at the end of the 19th century, when

developers built the dyke and the eclectic-style holiday villas here. Two beaches, the Plage du Casino and Plage Rochebonne, stretch for 2 km (1 mile).

Rothéneuf

Northeast of Paramé, via the D201.
A long-distance footpath (GR34) follows the coast to Rothéneuf from Pointe de la Varde, from where the view stretches from the Baie de St-Malo right round to Cap Fréhel *(see p107)*. This is a quiet village with two beaches, one of which lines a cove.

Grand Aquarium

La Ville-Jouan, Avenue du Général-Patton. *(02) 99 21 19 00.* daily.
This fascinating modern aquarium offers the opportunity to view almost 500 different species of cold-water and warm-water marine life. The route through the aquarium corresponds to that taken by the great navigators, from the North Atlantic to the Caribbean Sea. With a circular tank containing sharks, a tropical room, tanks where visitors can touch the fish, and the reconstruction of the wreck of a galleon, the aquarium has much to interest people of all ages.

Havre du Lupin

On the road north out of Rothéneuf. Also known as Havre de Rothéneuf, this cove is a saltwater lake at high tide and an expanse of sand at low tide. It is connected to the sea by a 300-m (985-ft) wide channel running between the coast and a peninsula, the Presqu'île Benard.

Carved Rocks

Chemin des Rochers-Sculptés. *From the walled city of St-Malo, take the track in the direction of Rothéneuf.* *(02) 99 56 23 95.* daily. Open access.
Between 1870 and 1895, the Abbé Fourré, a partly paralysed country priest, produced a masterpiece of naive art. He carved about 300 figures – a fantastic assemblage of grimacing monsters, animals and humans – out of the granite rockface.

From here, a path leads to the **Oratoire Notre-Dame-des-Flots**, in a converted coastguard's house. The simplicity of this chapel, on the cliff edge, gives the spot a special atmosphere.

One of the figures carved out of the living rock by the Abbé Fourré

Musée Jacques-Cartier

Manoir du Limoëlou. *Accessible via Rue David-Mac-Donald-Stewart.* *(02) 99 40 97 73.* *Jul–Aug: daily.* *May–Jun & Sep–Oct: Sat–Sun & public holidays.*
The museum is housed in a farmstead built in the 15th and 16th centuries and enlarged in the 19th century. It is devoted mainly to Jacques Cartier *(see p24)*, who discovered Canada in 1534. There is also a section illustrating daily life in the region during the 16th century.

The Manoir de Limoëlou, housing the Musée Jacques-Cartier

The Château du Bos, country residence of the Magons, built in 1717

Château du Bos ㉔

Road map E1-2. 5 km (3 miles) south of St-Malo via the N137, turning off to the right onto the road to La Passagère, Quelmer. ☎ (02) 99 81 40 11. 🕒 Jul–Aug: daily pm.

THIS IS A FINE example of the fully-fledged *malouinière*, a residence characteristic of the environs of St-Malo. It was built in 1717 for the Magons, an important shipowning family, whose prominence is reflected in a local saying of the time: "In Paris, the Bourbons, in St-Malo the Magons".

Through its sheer size, this chateau is similar to the type of grand country house where a shipowner would stay only occasionally, living for most of the time in his town house in St-Malo. The architect was

Bulet de Chamblain, who worked for the French and Swedish royal courts, and who also designed the Château de Champ-sur-Marne and the Château de la Chipaudière.

The formal garden, decorated with white marble busts in the Italian style, slopes down towards the River Rance. The façade overlooking the garden features a semicircular bay, built in Chausey granite, that contains the main reception room.

The oval drawing room, the *boiseries* (decorative woodwork) and the interior decoration are in the style that was fashionable during the reign of Louis XVI. The Regency *boiseries* in the dining room are similar to those in private residences in the walled city of St-Malo (*see pp78–81*).

MALOUINIÈRES

Part of the façade of a *malouinière* in Puits-Sauvage

Second residences of the wealthy shipowners of St-Malo, *malouinières* were built in the 17th and 18th centuries, a time when this port city of privateers was expanding. Their design being influenced by military architecture, *malouinières* typically have simple outlines, harmonious proportions and a certain austerity. Further characteristics are a steeply pitched roof and high chimneys with lead or terracotta stacks, emblems of the new élite. Bands of dressed Chausey granite surround window frames and mark the angles of the walls. The emphasis on symmetry and ordered perspective is in keeping with the Neo-Classical style of the period.

Dinard ㉕

Road map E1. 👥 11,000. 🚄 Dinard-Pleurtuit-St-Malo; (02) 99 46 18 46. 🚢 Emeraude Lines; (02) 99 46 10 45. 🏛 🏢 🛈 2 Boulevard Féart; (02) 99 46 94 12. 🛒 Tue, Thu & Sat. 🎭 Salon des Bateaux de Caractère (May); Festival de Musique Classique (Aug); Festival du Film Britannique (end Sep–beginning Oct).

AT THE BEGINNING of the 19th century, Dinard was no more than a small fishing village. This was before a small group of British and Americans created the fashion for comfortable mansions in coastal resorts. Dinard remains a high-class resort with a certain old-world appeal.

In 1873, the Lebanese aristocrat Joseph Rochaïd Dahda purchased land on which to build. English-style manor houses then appeared, along with Louis XIII-style chateaux, colonial houses and mock-Breton villas. British and European aristocrats flocked to Dinard's palatial residences. The attraction, albeit slightly antiquated, is still alive today, and the smart young set continues to come here.

Dinard, a fashionable and elegant resort since the 19th century

Walks in either direction along the coastal promenade pass various ostentatious villas typical of Dinard in its fashionable heyday. While the **Promenade de la Malouine**, leads westwards, the **Promenade Robert-Surcouf** leads eastwards to the Pointe du Moulinet, from where there is a spectacular view.

While the **Aquarium**, on Avenue Georges-V, is devoted to the marine plants and animals of the region, the **Musée de la Mer**, next door, documents the polar expeditions undertaken by Jean-Baptiste Charcot in the early 20th century. The **Musée du Site Balnéaire**, not far from Plage du Prieuré, is housed in a villa built for Empress Eugénie in 1867. It documents upper-class life in the resort at the height of its popularity with the British, a time when over 400 stately villas were built. As well as photographs and models, the exhibits include swimming costumes and sculpture.

ENVIRONS: A **tidal power station** *(usine marémotrice)* is located on the bridge over the Rance estuary, on the Dinard side. Harnessing the energy of the tides, which are among the strongest in the world here, the power station generates enough electricity to supply a town of 250,000 inhabitants for a year, or a quarter of what a nuclear power station would produce. It has no negative environmental impact. Built on the principle of tidal mills, it was inaugurated in 1966, after 25 years' research and six years' building work. It consists of a dam, a lock and an embankment, which contains the power station.

⚓ **Aquarium and Musée de la Mer**
17 Avenue Georges-V. 📞 *(02) 99 46 13 90.* ⬤ *for rebuilding.*
🏛 **Musée du Site Balnéaire**
Villa Eugénie, 12 Rue des Français-Libres. 📞 *(02) 99 46 81 05.*
⬜ *Easter–Nov: daily.* ⬤ *for rebuilding.*

The harbour at St-Briac, depicted by many 19th-century painters

St-Lunaire ㉖

Road map E1. 2 km (1 mile) west of Dinard, via the D786. 🏘 *2,163.* 🚉 ℹ *Place de la République; (02) 99 71 06 04.*

THIS SMALL RESORT, which, like Dinard, came into being at the end of the 19th century, is named after an Irish monk who settled here in the 6th century. The 11th-century **church** is one of the oldest in Brittany. It contains the tomb of St Lunaire, with a 14th-century recumbent figure.
Pointe du Décollé, north of St-Lunaire, is worth the detour for the panorama of the Côte d'Émeraude that it commands. The point is connected to the mainland by a natural bridge spanning a chasm known as the Trou du Chat (Cat's Hole).

St-Briac ㉗

Road map E1. 5 km (3 miles) southwest of Dinard, via the D786. 🏘 *1,825.* 🚉 ℹ *49 Grande-Rue; (02) 99 88 32 47.*

LIKE PONT-AVEN, in Finistère, this former fishing village, located on the right bank of the Frémur, attracted many painters at the end of the 19th century, among them Auguste Renoir, Henri Rivière, Émile Bernard and Paul Signac. The **Chemin des Peintres**, a former customs' officers' path that leads out of the village, has been especially arranged for art-lovers. The walk is lined with reproductions of paintings placed at spots where various artists set up their easels to paint the landscape.

The stained-glass windows in the 19th-century church show scenes from the life of St Briac, who, it is said, looked after the insane. Certain members of the Habsburg and Hohenzollern families used to visit the resort. The Grand Duke of Russia himself, pretender to the Russian throne, would come to stay in the family residence here.

The pleasingly simple 11th-century church in St-Lunaire

CÔTES D'ARMOR

T IS ON THE *Côtes d'Armor that the most timeless aspects of Brittany are preserved. While jewel-like churches and chapels hidden in remote hamlets express a profound piety, a wealth of fine buildings stands as ample proof of material riches derived from the linen trade. Here, also, are gentle landscapes and thriving crops, as well as fishing harbours and pirates' nests that are now picturesque holiday resorts.*

Majestic Cap Fréhel, on the Côte d'Émeraude, marks the eastern boundary of the Côtes d'Armor, where the coast is lined with beaches and where pink limestone cliffs and windswept heathland create an impressive landscape.

The hinterland south of St-Brieuc is the border between the Celtic, western part of Brittany and Lower Brittany. Lamballe, east of St-Brieuc, marks a later boundary. It was once the capital of the duchy of Penthièvre, enemy of the house of Brittany, and several fortresses were built near here.

While the historic towns of Quintin and Moncontour owe their rich heritage to the manufacture of linen cloth in the 17th and 18th centuries, Paimpol, on the Côte du Goëlo, looks back to an illustrious past, when courageous seamen left from here to sail for Iceland: 2,000 of Paimpol's fishermen never returned.

For nature-lovers, the Île de Bréhat, which has an almost Mediterranean microclimate, offers the opportunity to enjoy scenic walks, while the Sept-Îles archipelago is home to 15 species of sea birds. On the Côte de Granit Rose, outcrops of warm-toned granite eroded by wind and rain create a striking sight.

With their attractive settings and many beaches, resorts such as Perros-Guirec and Trégastel throng with holiday-makers during the summer. Inland, the heaths of the Trégor give way to the fields and wooded valleys of ancient Argoat. Churches and calvaries here reflect centuries of religious faith. Tréguier, with a delicately ornamented Gothic cathedral, is one of the finest cities in Brittany.

The Léguer estuary, winding for almost 6 km (4 miles) between Lannion and the English Channel

◁ **Pink granite boulders at the Pointe de Squewel, near the resort of Ploumanac'h**

Exploring the Côtes d'Armor

T HE NAME "CÔTES D'ARMOR", meaning "coasts of the sea country", comes from the area's deeply indented coastline formed by rias (ancient river valleys flooded by the sea). Jutting headlands, like the Trégor, alternate with wide inlets, such as the Baie de St-Brieuc. The highest point of the Côtes d'Armor are the Monts d'Arrée and the heathland of Le Méné, in the south. Coastal resorts such as Val-André, St-Cast and Perros-Guirec are the region's main tourist spots, and fishing harbours and islands, particularly the Sept-Îles archipelago and Île de Bréhat, are popular with holiday-makers. Inland are such picturesque medieval towns as Dinan, Quintin and Moncontour, and many impressive religious buildings, such as Tréguier's great Gothic cathedral.

Cloister of the Cathédrale St-Tugdual, Tréguier

SEE ALSO

- *Where to Stay* pp220–21
- *Where to Eat* pp234–5

THE REGION AT A GLANCE

GETTING AROUND

The N12, a major road, runs through the heart of the Côtes d'Armor. St-Brieuc is the hub of the region's road network. From here, the D786 runs along the Côte de Granit Rose to Plestin, and, heading southwards, the D790 and D700 link St-Brieuc with the heart of the region. From Rennes, the N12 leads to Montauban and the N164 to Loudéac, Mûr-de-Bretagne, Gouarec and Rostrenen. There is a bus service from St-Brieuc to Vannes every two hours. From Guingamp, a train service runs five times a day both to Carhaix and to Paimpol.

The coast path between Perros-Guirec and Ploumanac'h

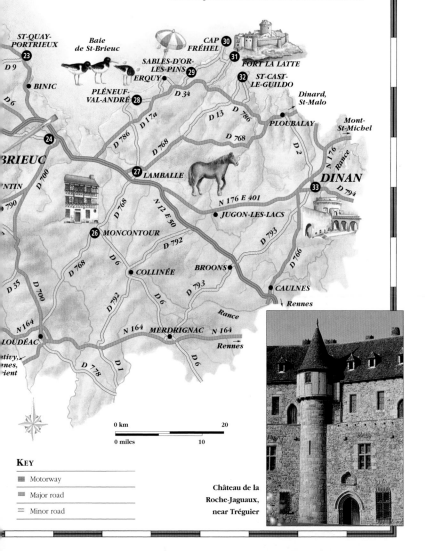

KEY

▬ Motorway

▬ Major road

= Minor road

**Château de la
Roche-Jaguaux,
near Tréguier**

Mûr-de-Bretagne ❶

Road map D2. 17 km (11 miles) west of Loudéac via the N164. 🏠 *2,140.* 🚉 *Place de l'Église; (02) 96 28 51 41.* 🚌 *Jul–Aug: Fri.* 🎭 *Festival des Arts Traditionnels (Jul).*

T HE TOWN OF Mûr marks the linguistic boundary between the Celtic, western part of Brittany and the eastern part.

The menhirs in the vicinity, especially the Neolithic **Menhir de Botrain** and **Menhir de Boconnaire**, as well as the numerous burial mounds, show that the region was quite densely populated in prehistoric times.

The **Chapelle Ste-Suzanne**, north of Mûr, in a stand of oak trees, was painted by Corot (1796–1875). It was built in 1496, although the choir (1694) and belfry (1752–64) are later.

Lac de Guerlédan and Forêt de Quénécan ❷

Road map D2. 22 km (14 miles) west of Loudéac via the N164. **Watersports centre** 🚉 *(02) 96 67 12 22.* **Holiday village** 🚉 *(02) 96 28 50 01.* 🚉 *(02) 96 28 51 41.* 🎭 *Fête du Lac (15 Aug).*

F ILLING A VALLEY that was flooded when a hydroelectric dam was built in 1930, the Lac de Guerlédan, just west of Mûr-de-Bretagne, stretches for 12 km (8 miles). A watersports centre, a camp site and a holiday village, it attracts lovers of the great outdoors.

From the banks of the Blavet, there is a stunning view of the **Barrage de Guerlédan**. Both the dam and the power station are open to visitors. The **Musée de l'Électricité** nearby illustrates the history of electricity production, and the ways in which electricity is used.

Southwest of the lake is the 3,000-ha (7,400-acre) Forêt de Quénécan, with beech, spruce and pine. Like the Forêt de Paimpont, it is a vestige of the Forêt de Brocéliande (*see p62*).

🏕 **Barrage de Guerlédan** ◻ *Summer.* 🚉 *(02) 96 28 51 41.* 🏛 **Musée de l'Électricité** St-Aignan. 🚉 *(02) 96 28 51 41.* ◻ *All year.* ● *Tue.* 📷

Gorges de Daoulas ❸

Road map C2. 30 km (18.5 miles) west of Loudéac via the N164.

T HE HIGH escarpments and the plant life of the Gorges de Daoulas give this gorge the appearance of an Alpine defile. The river here has eroded the schist, and the water flows swiftly between high cliffs that have a wild beauty.

The partially ruined **Abbaye de Bon-Repos**, just off the N164, was built in the 13th century. The monastic buildings and cloister both date from the 18th century. An exhibition of mineral stones is laid out in the mill at the abbey.

Abbaye de Bon-Repos, founded in the 12th century and now partly in ruins

🏰 **Abbaye de Bon-Repos** St-Gelven. Via the N164. 🚉 *(02) 96 24 80 41.* ◻ *Mid-Jun–mid-Sep: daily; mid-Sep–mid-Jun: Wed–Fri & Sat–Sun, pm.* **Son et Lumière** *(second weekend in Aug).*

Guingamp ❹

Road map C2. 🏠 *8,830.* 🚉 *2 Place du Champ-au-Roy; (02) 96 43 73 89.* 🚇 🚌 *St-Brieuc.* 🚌 *Fri.* 🎭 *Bugale Vreizh (Breton dancing and Pardon de Notre-Dame, early Jul); Fête de la St-Loup (15 Aug).*

S TANDING AT a crossroads and once fortified, Guingamp is an attractive town with fine timber-framed houses, particularly on Place du Centre.

The **Basilique Notre-Dame**, in Rue Notre-Dame, was built in several stages between the 13th and 16th centuries, and therefore exhibits several different styles. While the columns at the crossing, which are decorated with grotesque figures, are typically Romanesque, both the west door and the triforium are in an accomplished Renaissance style. The apse, by contrast, is Gothic.

The **Hôtel de Ville**, on Place Verdun, occupies the former Monastère des Hospitalières, dating from the early 17th century. The Baroque chapel here contains paintings by the Pont-Aven group (*see p169*). Ramparts on Place du Petit-Vally are all that remains of the 15th-century castle, which was demolished in 1626.

ENVIRONS: 10 km (6 miles) west of Guingamp is the holy mountain of **Menez-Bré**. From the summit, there are spectacular views of the Trégor. The 17th-century

The Lac de Guerlédan, offering many watersports activities

chapel here is dedicated to St Hervé, healer, exorcist and patron of bards. The fountain 300 m (330 yds) from the chapel is said to have sprung at his command. Sick children were dipped in its miraculous waters in the hope of curing them.

Châtelaudren, 13 km (8 miles) east of Guingamp via the N12-E50 then the D7, is well worth the detour for the Chapelle Notre-Dame-du-Tertre, which contains 132 remarkable 15th-century frescoes on biblical themes.

The nave of the Basilique Notre-Dame in Guingamp

Bulat-Pestivien ❺

Road map C2. 18 km (11 miles) southwest of Guingamp via the D787 then the D31. 🏠 *440.* 🎭 *Pardon (early Sep).*

THIS SMALL VIILLAGE (famous, rather quirkily, as a centre for the breeding of the Breton spaniel) boasts a magnificent 14th-century **church**. Its tower is the earliest example of Renaissance architecture in Brittany. Like those of the church at Loc-Envel *(see below)*, the exterior walls are covered in gargoyles, monsters and grimacing *ankous* (skeletons). Both the porch and the main entrance dazzle with their elaborate decoration. According to legend, this church was built by a lord in thanks to the Virgin Mary, who restored his son to him when the child was snatched by a monkey.

This strange scene is depicted in the sacristy.

ENVIRONS: One km (0.5 mile) to the north is a charming **parish close** with a calvary dating from 1550. The **Gorges du Corong**, 10 km (6 miles) south of Bulat-Pestivien, are wreathed in ferns and have a wild and dramatic beauty. According to legend, the great rocks beneath which the river flows are the stones that a giant shook out of his clogs.

Belle-Isle-en-Terre ❻

Road map C2. 18 km (11 miles) west of Guingamp via the N12. 🏠 *1,110.* 🛈 *15 Rue du Chrec'h-Ugen; (02) 96 43 01 71.* 🚉 *Guingamp.* 🚌 *Wed.* 🎭 *Pardon (mid-Jul).*

THIS TOWN LIES between the rivers Guer and Guic, which join to form the Léguer, the river that flows into the Baie de Lannion. The meadows and woods round about are ideal walking country.

The castle here houses the **Centre Régional d'Initiation à la Rivière**, dedicated to environmental protection. Its aquarium is open to visitors. It is owned by a local woman, who, having married Robert Mond, chief executive of Nickel Mond Co., became Lady Mond (nicknamed "the Queen of Nickel") in 1922.

🏛 **Centre Régional d'Initiation à la Rivière**
Belle-Isle-en-Terre.
🕿 *(02) 96 43 08 39.* ◻ *Tue–Sun.*

The church at Bulat-Pestivien, in the Renaissance style

ENVIRONS: The village of **Loc-Envel**, 4 km (3 miles) southwest of Belle-Isle via the D33, stands on the edge of the **Forêt de Coat-an-Noz**.

Loc-Envel is well worth a visit for its 16th-century church. The belfry, with gargoyles, is in the Gothic style, but it is the interior that is particularly fascinating. The rood screen, richly decorated in the Flamboyant Gothic style, and the vaulting of the nave, from which hosts of carved monsters stare down, are remarkable.

The forest, with age-old trees whose branches are covered with moss, lichen and ferns, is a magical place in which to stroll. The forest's undulating terrain, and the paths that wind between clumps of box-tree dating from Roman times, make it interesting walking country.

The Flamboyant Gothic rood screen in the church at Loc-Envel

The Château de Rosanbo, owned by the same family for 600 years

Plestin-les-Grèves ❼

Road map C1. 15 km (9 miles) southwest of Lannion via the D786. 🏠 3,237. 🚉 Morlaix, Lannion and Plouaret. 🛈 Place de la Mairie; (02) 96 35 61 93. 🛒 Sun.

THE JEWEL IN the area around Plestin (*Plistin* in Breton) is a wide, soft sandy beach known as **Lieue de Grève**. This beach, which stretches for miles when the tide is out, has held a strong appeal for holiday-makers since the 1930s. Several holiday residences, including the Villa Trenkler (House of the Eagle) and Villa Lady Mond *(see p91)* at the coastal village of St-Efflam, date from this period.

Unfortunately, since 1970, the water on this small stretch of coastline has been regularly infested with prolific, foul-smelling green algae. However, if taking the sea air is out of the question, it is possible to climb up to the Grand Rocher, which, 80 m (262 ft) high, overlooks the beach, or to follow the coast road, the Corniche de l'Armorique (D42), for a view of the Baie de Locquirec *(see p119)*. Several species of birds, including sheldrake and sandpiper, can also be seen here.

ENVIRONS: The **Château de Rosanbo**, which has been in the same family for 600 years, is located just 6 km (4 miles) from Plestin-les-Grèves. This fine residence was restored in the Neo-Gothic style in 1895. The chateau's formal garden, with hedgerows and bowers, was designed by Duchêne, the landscape gardener who laid out the gardens at Vaux-le-Vicomte. The architect Lafargue designed the library for the 8,000-book collection of Claude Le Pelletier, who was to succeed Colbert as Louis XIV's finance minister. The dining room was reconstructed on the basis of 18th-century inventories.

The church in the village of **Lanvellec** is also worth a visit. It contains a fine organ built by Robert Dallam in 1653.

Château de Rosanbo
Lanvellec (D22). 【 (02) 96 35 18 77. ◯ Apr–Aug: daily; Sep–Oct: Sun. 🌐

Ploubezre ❽

Road map C1. 3 km (2 miles) south of Lannion via the D11. 🏠 2,700. 🛈 Mairie; (02) 96 47 15 51.

TO DISCOVER so fine a chapel in a remote location such as this is always a pleasant surprise. **Notre-Dame de Kerfons**, in Ploubezre, is one of the finest examples of religious architecture in Brittany.

The chapel was built in the Flamboyant Gothic style, probably under the aegis of a powerful local lord. When it was remodelled in the Renaissance style, its builders took the trouble to use stones from the same quarry, the better to blend the new style with the old.

The detailed and elaborate decoration of the interior culminates in the rood screen, a tracery of painted and gilt wood, with reliefs depicting Christ, the 12 Apostles, St Barbara and St Mary Magdalen.

Altarpiece in the Chapelle de Notre-Dame de Kerfons

The **Château de Kergrist**, built in 1537 by Jean de Kergrist and remodelled in the 17th and 18th centuries, is characteristic of the great Renaissance residences built by the Breton aristocracy. The Huon de Penanster family, which has owned the castle since 1860, has opened to visitors the gardens and one of the three blocks that frame the main courtyard. The interior is filled with interesting examples of traditional Breton furniture, including a *malouine* (wardrobe from St-Malo) decorated with chequered patterns, and tapestry door screens.

♠ Notre-Dame de Kerfons
Kerfons (D31b). ◯ Mid-Jun–mid-Sep: daily. 🌐
♣ Château de Kergrist
Ploubezre (D11). 【 (02) 96 38 91 44. ◯ Jan–Mar: Sat–Sun, pm; Apr–May: daily pm; Jun–Sep: daily; Oct–Dec: Sat–Sun, pm. 🌐
🔾 Garden & ground floor only.

Lieue de Grève, a wide sandy beach north of Plestin-les-Grèves

The ruined 13th-century Château de Tonquédec

ENVIRONS: About 2 km (1 mile) from the Château de Kergist stands the impressive ruins of the **Château de Tonquédec,** built in the 13th century by the lords of Tonquédec. During the Wars of the Holy League, the castle had become a Huguenot stronghold. Because of this, it was partly demolished in 1626 on the orders of Cardinal Richelieu, principal minister to Louis XIII. The fortificiations consist of 11 towers and a courtyard in which attackers could easily be trapped. From the rampart walk there is a panoramic view of the wooded valley of the Léguer.

♣ **Château de Tonquédec**
Tonquédec (D31b). 🄲 (02) 96 47 18 63/47. ⬜ Apr–Sep: daily. 🖼

Lannion ⑨

Road map C1. 👥 19,350.
🚶 🚉 🄷 Quai d'Aiguillon; (02) 96 46 41 00. 🎵 Festival d'Orgue et de Musique en Trégor (Jul–Aug); Festivales de la Photographie (Jul–Sep). 🛒 Thu.

T HIS BUSTLING TOWN has profited handsomely from the installation of the Centre National d'Études des Télécommunications here in 1960, and from the new TGV (high-speed-train) link. The nexus between the telecommunications centre at Pleumeur-Bodou (*see p94*) and newly installed optical industries, Lannion (*Lannuon* in Breton) has attracted thousands of researchers and students of

engineering specializing in state-of-the-art technology.

Such dynamism might have altered the town's identity and picturesque character. Far from it: Breton is still spoken in the busy market square. The heart of the old town has ancient paved alleyways and some charming timber-framed, granite and cob houses, such as those at Nos. 1–3 Rue des Chapeliers, which escaped destruction during the Wars of Religion (1591), and Nos. 29–31 Place du Général-Leclerc, which were rebuilt after 1630. These houses are clad in slate and decorated with human figures, animals, crosses and lozenges. Some have overhanging windows.

Of all the religious buildings in Lannion, the most appealing is the **Église de Brélévenez**. It is reached via a flight of steps lined with small, attractive houses decorated with statues of patron saints or ceramic friezes. The church was founded in the 12th century by a branch of the order of the Knights Templar, the

Half-timbered houses in the historic centre of Lannion

Trinitarians of St John. The choice of materials used in its construction reflects the importance of this church: pink and yellow granite for the south porch, large ashlars for the apse, black marble and tufa for the high altar, and painted wood for the altarpiece (1630) in the north transept – a slightly macabre reminder of the Day of Judgment. Concerts take place in the church in summer, especially during the popular Trégor festival of organ music.

🔒 **Église de Brélévenez**
⬜ Jul–Aug: Mon–Sat. 🖼

Le Yaudet, in a beautiful setting on the Léguer estuary

ENVIRONS: About 3 km (2 miles) west of Lannion, on the left bank of the Léguer, is **Loguivy-lès-Lannion** (*Logivi* in Breton), whose parish close has a notable portal and a Renaissance fountain. The oak altarpiece inside features a wealth of carvings.

The coast road leads on to the scenic hamlet of **Le Yaudet** (*Ar Yeoded* in Breton), whose granite houses cling to the hillside. Uniquely in Brittany, the village chapel contains a depiction of a recumbent Virgin next to the figure of Christ.

Set on a promontory, with a stunning view of the Léguer estuary, Le Yaudet has one of the most beautiful natural settings in the Trégor. Excavations led by archaeologists from Brest and Oxford have uncovered a Gallo-Roman fishing village on the promontory.

🌿 **Le Yaudet**
Le Yaudet (D88). 🄲 (02) 96 48 35 98. 🖼 Mon & Fri. 🖼

A beach at the popular coastal resort of Trébeurden

Trébeurden ❿

Road map C1. 7 km (4 miles) northwest of Lannion via the D65. 🚉 *Lannion.* 👥 *3,540.* ℹ️ *Place de Crec'h-Héry; (02) 96 23 51 64.* 🚌 *Tue.* 🎪 *Fête des Battages during Fest-noz (Aug); concerts (Wed in summer).*

A POPULAR coastal resort, Trébeurden has several beautiful beaches either side of Le Castel, a rugged peninsula with pink granite rocks. The **Île Milliau**, opposite the peninsula, is accessible at low tide. More than 270 species of plants grow there. The island was inhabited 7,000 years ago; evidence of human habitation is a Neolithic passage grave, the **Allée Couverte de Prajou-Menhir**, 14 m (46ft) long and with carvings on its stones. The **Marais du Kellen**, behind Plage de Goas-Trez, attracts snipe, teal grebe and other birds.

Pleumeur-Bodou ⓫

Road map C1. 6 km (4 miles) northwest of Lannion via the D65 then the D21. 🚉 *Lannion.* 👥 *3,820.* ℹ️ *11 Rue des Chardons; (02) 96 23 91 47.* 🚌 *Sat.*

B RISTLING WITH giant antennae that provide worldwide communication, Pleumeur-Bodou is well known as the site of the telecommunications centre where the first satellite link between the United States and Europe was made, in 1962. The radar dome, a gigantic sphere 50 m (160 ft) high, is open to visitors.

There is also a **Museum**, tracing the 150-year history of telecommunications from their earliest days to the age of the Internet, and a **Planetarium**, with a screen measuring 600 sq m (6,460 sq ft).

Opposite the planetarium is the reconstruction of a Gaulish settlement, the **Village de Meem le Gaulois**. This whole complex goes under the name **Cosmopolis**.

🏛 Musée des Télécommunications
📞 *(02) 96 46 63 80.* ⏰ *May–Aug: daily; Apr & Sep: Sun–Fri; Oct–Mar: Mon-Fri.*

🏛 Planetarium
📞 *(02) 96 15 80 30.* ⏰ *Apr–Sep & school holidays: daily.* ⏰ *Oct–Mar: Wed & Sat; may be closed in Jan: phone for details.*

🏛 Village de Meem le Gaulois
📞 *(02) 96 91 83 95.* 🌐 *www.levillagegaulois.asso.fr* ⏰ *Jul–Aug: daily; Easter–Jun & Sep: Sun–Fri.*

ENVIRONS: The **Île Grande**, north of Trébeurden, is accessible via a bridge on the D788. As well as beaches and footpaths, the island has an ornithological centre. The **Maison LPO**, a centre set up by an organization for the protection of birds, highlights the rich flora and fauna of the Sept-Îles archipelago. Tours are also organized from here. The **Menhir de St-Uzec**, 2 km (1 mile) from

Board for Aquarium Marin, Trégastel

Penvern, is a standing stone 8 m (26 ft) high, one of the finest in Brittany. In the 17th century, a cross and a depiction of the Passion of Christ were carved on it to convert it into a Christian monument.

🦅 Maison LPO
Île Grande. 📞 *(02) 96 91 91 40.* ⏰ *Jun–Aug: daily; school holidays: daily pm; other times: Sat–Sun pm.*

Trégastel-Plage ⓬

Road map C1. 6 km (4 miles) west of Perros-Guirec via the D788. 🚉 *Lannion.* 👥 *2,290.* ℹ️ *Place Ste-Anne; (02) 96 15 38 38.* 🚌 *Mon.* 🎪 *Fest-noz (Jun); 24 Heures de la Voile (mid-Aug).*

T HIS RESORT is famous for the blocks of pink granite that rise up behind its beaches, Plage du Coz-Pors and Plage de Grève-Blanche. The orientation table between these two beaches offers a splendid panorama of the coast and of the countryside inland. At the **Aquarium Marin**, housed in a cave, visitors can see fish and other marine life of the waters around Brittany. **Kerguntuil**, 2 km (1 mile) south, on the D788 towards Trebeurden, is of interest for its Neolithic passage grave and dolmen.

🐟 Aquarium Marin
Boulevard de Coz-Pors. 📞 *(02) 96 23 48 58.* ⏰ *Apr–Nov: daily; school holidays: daily pm.*

Meem le Gaulois, the reconstruction of Gaulish village, Pleumeur-Bodou

Ploumanac'h ⑬

ON ACCOUNT OF its spectacular rocks, this former fishing village, now a district of Perros-Guirec, is one of the greatest tourist attractions in Brittany. **Pointe de Squewel**, one hour's walk along the coast path from Plage St-Guirec, north of Ploumanac'h, is a promontory with gigantic piles of rocks that suggest such incongruous shapes as tortoises, rabbits and tricorn hats. The **Maison du Littoral**, level with the lighthouse, contains displays explaining how the rocks were formed, and describing local flora and fauna.

The **Chapelle Notre-Dame-de-la-Clarté** (1445), midway between Ploumanac'h and Perros-Guirec, is the focus of a very lively annual pardon. The chapel has an interesting porch with relief decoration, and, inside, a stoup (1931) decorated with heads of Moors and the Stations of the Cross. It was made by Maurice Denis, a founder of the group of

Granite rocks at Pointe de Squewel, a major tourist attraction

painters known as the Nabis. The **Vallée des Traouïéros**, between Ploumanac'h and Trégastel, runs between blocks of granite and lush vegetation. The restored tidal mill here dates from the 14th century.

🗡 Maison du Littoral
Opposite the lighthouse. 【 (02) 96 91 62 77. ◯ Mid-Jun–mid-Sep: daily; school holidays: Tue–Sun pm.

Plage de Trestraou, one of several beaches at Perros-Guirec

Perros-Guirec ⑭

Road map C1. 🚉 Lannion.
🏘 7,890. 🛈 21 Place de l'Hôtel-de-Ville; (02) 96 23 21 15; in season: Fri & Sun. 📅 Festival de la Bande Dessinée (Apr); Fête des Hortensias (Aug); Ploumanac'h Regatta (Aug); Pardon de Notre-Dame-de-la-Clarté (15 Aug).

WITH ABOUT a dozen beaches and many hotels, this coastal resort attracts large numbers of visitors in summer. As at Ploumanac'h, the coast here has extraordinary rock formations shaped by the erosion of wind and rain.

The coast path, running the 6 km (4 miles) between Plage de Trestraou and the famous rocks at Ploumanac'h, offers stunning views.

ENVIRONS: From Perros-Guirec there is a boat service to the **Sept-Îles Archipelago**, one of the best places to see sea birds. One of the islands, the **Île aux Moines**, is named after the Franciscan friars who settled there in the Middle Ages. Also on the island is a lighthouse and a small fort built by Garangeau, the architect responsible for St-Malo's fortifications (see pp78–83).

⚓ Embarcadère des Sept-Îles
(boarding point for boat service), Plage de Trestraou. 【 (02) 96 91 10 00. ◯ Apr–Sep & school holidays: daily; rest of the year: by arrangement.

SEPT-ÎLES BIRD SANCTUARY

Although the islands' best-known inhabitant is the puffin, the Sept-Îles archipelago, a protected area, is also home to fulmars, kittiwakes, pied oystercatchers, gulls, crested cormorants and other sea birds. Twenty thousand pairs breed in this protected area. Only one island, the Île aux Moines, is accessible to the public, although the birds on the other islands can be observed from motorboats. On the Île de Roizic, 15,130 pairs of gannets and 248 pairs of puffins nest in the craggy rocks. Grey seals can sometimes be seen at the foot of the cliffs in the islands' secluded creeks.

The puffin, emblematic inhabitant of the Sept-Îles

Stained-glass window in the Église Ste-Catherine in La Roche-Derrien

La Roche-Derrien ⑮

Road map C1. 15 km (9 miles) northeast of Lannion via the D786 then the D6. 🚆 *Guingamp or Lannion.* 👥 *1,012.* ℹ️ *Pays du Trégor-Goëlo, 9 Place de l'Église; (02) 96 91 50 22.* 📅 *Fri.*

IN THE MIDDLE AGES, La Roche Derrien (*Ker Roc'h* in Breton, meaning Town of the Rock), was a fortified town over which many battles were fought. The castle, overlooking the Jaudy valley, was besieged during the War of the Breton Succession, a conflict between the English, the French and the Bretons (*see p40*). In the 14th century, the castle passed into the hands of Bertrand du Guesclin (*see p41*). He is said to have planted the yew tree still standing in the close of the 18th-century Chapelle de Notre-Dame-de-la-Pitié, on the road to Kermezen.

Today, La Roche-Derrien offers pleasant walks on the banks of the Jaudy. In the town, several timber-framed houses line Place du Martray. The Église Ste-Catherine, built in the 12th and 15th centuries, contains an elaborate 17th-century altarpiece. The modern stained-glass window in the transept depicts the battle between supporters of Charles of Blois and the English.

Altarpiece in the chapel at Confort

ENVIRONS: The 16th-century chapel at **Confort**, 13 km (8 miles) southwest of La Roche-Derrien on the D33, is built in a combination of the Flamboyant Gothic and Renaissance styles. The belltower, in the style of Lannion belfries, incorporates a stair turret. The chapel contains an altarpiece in which the Virgin is depicted in the likeness of Anne of Brittany and the Angel Gabriel in that of Louis XII, king of France (*see pp42–3*).

About 6 km (4 miles) southeast of La Roche-Derrien on the D8, the church at **Runan**, dating from the 14th–16th centuries, was once owned by the Knights Templar, then by the Knights of St John of Jerusalem. It has a richly decorated façade and the south porch, with a pointed arch, has some notable reliefs. While the lintel is carved with a scene of the Annunciation and with a Pietà, the side panels feature a host of carved figures, four of whom stick out their tongues at the viewer. In front of the church is a rare 15th-century outdoor pulpit.

Port-Blanc ⑯

Road map C1. 8 km (5 miles) northwest of Tréguier via the D70a, the D70 then the D74. 🚆 *Lannion.* 👥 *2,700.* ℹ️ *12 Place. de l'Église, Penvenan; (02) 96 92 81 09.* 📅 *Sat.* 🎉 *Pardons (Whitsun & 15 Aug).*

LYING WEST of Plougrescant and sheltered by a barrier of dunes, the coastal village of Port-Blanc is a pleasant holiday resort. The highly picturesque 16th-century **chapel**, which nestles among rocks, is the focal point of the village. The chapel's roof is unusual in that it reaches almost to the ground. The 17th-century calvary in the close depicts St Yves, St Joachim, St Peter and St Francis. The chapel contains several old statues, including the traditional group depicting St Yves between a rich and a poor man.

From the harbour, trips out to sea are offered in an old sardine boat, the *Ausquémé*. The coast path from Port-Blanc to Buguélès commands some magnificent views.

🚤 *Ausquémé*
📞 *(02) 96 92 00 65.* ⏰ *Jul–Aug: daily; Sep–Jun: by arrangement.*

The 16th-century chapel at Port-Blanc

The Sillon de Talbert, a natural spit of land with the Héaux lighthouse in the distance

Plougrescant ⑰

Road map C1. 6 km (4 miles) north of Tréguier on the D8. 🚂 *Guingamp or Lannion.* 🚶 *1,430.* ℹ️ *Pays du Trégor-Goëlo, 9 Place de l'Église, La Roche-Derrien; (02) 96 91 50 22.*

THE MOST PROMINENT feature of Plougrescant is its chapel, the **Chapelle St-Gonery**, which has an eye-catchingly crooked belfry. The church consists of two sections, the first of which is Romanesque, dating from the 10th century. From this section rises the belfry, built in 1612. The other part is the nave, which was built in the 15th century.

The chapel is of interest chiefly for its remarkable 15th-century frescoes. Covering the barrel-vaulted ceiling, they loosely depict scenes from the Old and New Testaments. These scenes, which are depicted on an ochre background dotted with stars, are in a naive style. The contrasting colours, and areas of black and white, emphasize outlines and accentuate perspective.

The strikingly fine monuments inside the chapel include the tomb of Guillaume du Halgouët, bishop of Tréguier, and an alabaster statue of the Virgin, both dating from the 16th century, and a reliquary with finely carved panels.

During the summer, trips out to sea in an old sailing boat, the ***Marie-Georgette***, depart from the harbour.

🚤 ***Marie-Georgette***
☎ *(02) 96 92 51 03/ 58 83.*
🕐 *July–Aug: daily; Sep–Jun: by arrangement.*

Sillon de Talbert ⑱

THIS NATURAL spit of land extends for 3 km (2 miles) from the tip of the Presqu'île Sauvage, the peninsula between Tréguier and Paimpol. Made up of sand and pebbles, the spit was created by the opposing currents of two rivers, the Trieux and the Jaudy. It is now a protected site, as, were it to disappear, the two inlets on each side of the peninsula would be at the mercy of tidal currents. A kite festival takes place on the spit in July each year. The Héaux lighthouse can also be seen from here.

FAMOUS NAMES IN PORT-BLANC

Théodore Botrel

Port-Blanc has appealed to a variety of different people, from authors and songwriters to scientists and pioneers of aviation. In 1898, the writer Anatole Le Braz bought the property known as Kerstellic. He recorded Breton stories and legends that he heard told by the inhabitants of the Trégor. *La Légende de la Mort* (1893), is considered by Armorican Bretons to be his best work. Le Braz's friend and neighbour was the writer Ernest Renan *(see p101)*, who lived at Rosmapamon. The songwriter Théodore Botrel, who wrote *La Paimpolaise*, bought land at Port-Blanc on which he built a house that he named *Ty Chansonniou* (House of Songs). He later left to live in Pont-Aven. In 1922, Alexis Carrel, winner of the Nobel Prize for Medicine, purchased the Île St-Gildas, where he was buried in 1944. His friend Charles Lindbergh was a frequent visitor. In 1938, after his pioneering flight across the Atlantic, Lindbergh acquired the Île d'Illiec, where he briefly lived before returning to the United States.

Île de Bréhat ⓳

BECAUSE OF THE luxuriant vegetation that thrives in its gentle climate, the Île de Bréhat is also known as the Island of Flowers. Bréhat, a paradise for walkers and a haven for artists, actually consists of two large islands linked by a bridge. In the north, heathland predominates and the indented coastline is reminiscent of Ireland. In the south, the landscape is softer, with pine trees, pink pebble beaches and Mediterranean plants. There is no motorized transport, but it is easy to walk or cycle along the island's sunken paths.

Phare du Paon ④
Destroyed by German forces during World War II, the lighthouse was rebuilt in red porphyry in 1947. Stairs lead up to the platform, from which there is a view of the open sea.

Chapelle St-Michel ⑥
Perched on a rise 26 m (85 ft) high, the Chapelle St-Michel overlooks the whole island. It was rebuilt in 1852, and has long served as a landmark for shipping. The path leads straight down to an old tidal mill.

Phare du Rosedo ⑤
The 19th-century lighthouse overlooks the heathland of the northwest of the island. Ernest Renan *(see p101)* came here to enjoy the beauty of the surroundings.

Le Goareva ⑦
This fort is a fine example of 18th-century military architecture.

Port-Clos ①
In 1770, Charles Cornic built this harbour, a port of call for ships from the mainland.

Chaîse de Renan
Pointe du Rosedo
Signal station
ÎLE NORD
Chapelle St-Rion
Île ar-Morbic
Anse de la Corderie
Île Séhérès
la Croix de Maudez
Étang de Birlot
Moulin de Crec'h Tarek
Île Lavrec
Raguénès Meur
ÎLE SUD
Île Logodec
Plage du Guerzido

KEY

▬ Suggested route

▪▪ Footpaths

⁝ Other routes

☀ Viewpoint

POINTE DE L'ARCOUEST

0 m	1000
0 yards	1000

Chaussée Vauban ③
A bridge built by Vauban links the south and north islands. The harbour in the Anse de la Corderie, west of the bridge, was once Bréhat's port.

Bréhat, the island's flower-filled town

The town ②
Bréhat consists of houses clustered around a 12th-century church with 17th–19th-century alterations.

TIPS FOR VISITORS

Tour: about 9 km (5.5 miles).
Access: 10 minutes from Pointe de l'Arcouest; information ℂ (02) 96 55 79 50. Bicycles can be hired in Port-Clos.
Stopping-off places: La Potinière, on Plage du Guerzido offers oysters and mussels; Le Paradis Rose, in the north, serves crêpes.

Paimpol ⑳

Road map D1. 🚉 8,420.
🚌 Avenue Général-de-Gaulle. 🚌
ℹ️ Place de la République; (02) 96 20
83 16. 🚢 Tue. 🎪 Fête des Terre-
Neuvas et des Islandais (third Sun in
Jul) ; songs of the sea (Aug); concerts
of Celtic music (14 Aug); Fest-noz
(Whitsun).

ALTHOUGH PLEASURE boats have now replaced the schooners that once filled the harbour, this is still the heart of Paimpol, with coasters and trawlers tied up alongside the quais. As Pierre Loti, in his novel *Pêcheurs d'Islande (An Iceland Fisherman)*, so eloquently described, the sea has exacted a heavy price from Paimpol: 100 schooners and 2,000 men were lost in the fishing expeditions that left Paimpol for Iceland.

The first left in 1852 and, in 1895, 82 schooners of 400 tonnes burden set sail for the North Sea. Each was crewed by about 20 seamen, who for six months endured not only cold and great physical strain, but also separation from their families. Their wives, the famous *Paimpolaises* immortalized by Théodore Botrel, would scour the horizon for their return at the Croix des Veuves-en-Ploubazlanec, north of the town. When the ships came in, there were either joyful reunions or scenes of mourning. The last expedition to Iceland left Paimpol in 1935.

The Place du Martray, in the town centre, is lined with 16th-century houses. On the corner of Rue de l'Église is a shipowner's house in the Renaissance style, with a turret. The house was used as

The 13th-century Abbaye de Beauport, in Paimpol, now in ruins

a hunting lodge by the Rohans, a powerful Breton dynasty. The **Musée du Costume**, in Rue Pellier, contains displays of *coiffes* and costumes from the Trégor and Goëlo. Through photographs, models, ships' logs, nautical equipment and votive offerings, the **Musée de la Mer**, in a building once used for drying cod, describes the fishing expeditions to Newfoundland and Iceland.

From Paimpol, visitors may take a **boat trip** out to sea in an old sailing boat, or a ride on a **steam train** up the Trieux valley to Pontrieux.

🏛 **Musée du Costume**
Rue Raymond-Pellier. 🕐 Jul–Aug: daily.
🏛 **Musée de la Mer**
Rue Labenne. 📞 (02) 96 22 02 19.
🕐 Jun–mid-Sep: daily; May: Sat–Sun.

🚢 **Boat Trips**
📞 (02) 96 20 59 30.
🕐 Jul–Aug: daily; Sep–Jun: Sat–Sun. Booking obligatory.
Steam Train 📞 (02) 96 20 52 06. 🕐 Mid-Jun–Sep: daily.

ENVIRONS: The ruined Romanesque **Abbaye de Beauport**, 2 km (1 mile) south of Paimpol via the D786, is one of the most beautiful abbeys in Brittany. Built in the Anglo-Norman style in the early 13th century, it was an important centre of religion. Visitors can see the chapterhouse, cloisters, refectory and storerooms. From the abbey, a road leads to the **Chapelle Ste-Barbe**, the starting point of a coastal path.

The **Pointe de l'Arcouest**, reached via the D789 from Paimpol, is the main boarding point for the Île de Bréhat. **Loguivy-de-la-Mer**, 4 km (2.5 miles) north of Paimpol, is one of the oldest harbours in Brittany, and it is renowned for the sea crayfish, lobsters and crabs that are landed here. Trawlers and other fishing boats continue Loguivy's ancient fishing tradition.

🔒 **Abbaye de Beauport**
On the D786. 📞 (02) 96 55 18 58.
🕐 Mid-Jun–mid-Sep: daily.
🚢 **Pointe de l'Arcouest**
Jul–Aug: hourly departures.
📞 (02) 96 55 79 50.

ARTISTS ON BRÉHAT

Between the late 19th and early 20th centuries, many writers and artists came to Bréhat. Writers included Ernest Renan, the Goncourt brothers, Pierre Loti and Théodore Botrel, and the artists Henri Rivière, Paul Gauguin, Henry Matisse, Tsugouharu Foujita, Henri Dabadie and many others. All found inspiration in the island's landscapes, but they also frequented the town's cafés. Mme Guéré, the fearsome landlady of a certain café, once threatened to behead a customer if he failed to settle his slate. Taking her at her word, the miscreant painted his face on the side of his glass. Ever since, artists have customarily painted their portraits on glasses at the Café des Pêcheurs, which now has a collection of 200 such glasses.

Une Rue à Bréhat, a painting by Henri Dabadie

Steam train in the station at Pontrieux

Tréguier **㉑**

Creatures from Tréguier cathedral

THE CAPITAL OF the Trégor and an ancient bishopric, Tréguier is today a quiet city. The narrow streets around the splendid cathedral are lined with timber-framed houses and grander granite residences. The 16th-century timber-framed house in Rue Renan that is the birthplace of the writer Ernest Renan is now a museum, and visitors can see the nursery, Renan's studio and various other exhibits relating to his life and work. The Flamboyant Gothic Cathédrale St-Tugdual, one of the finest examples of Breton religious architecture, dominates Tréguier. The Pardon de St-Yves, in May, honours the cathedral's patron saint, who is also that of lawyers.

VISITORS' CHECKLIST

Road map C1. ▣ Paimpol or Lannion. ▨ 2,950. ▯ 1 Place du Général-Leclerc; (02) 96 92 22 33. ▣ Wed. ▧ Pardon de St-Yves (third Sun in May); Festival en Trégor (concerts; Jul–Aug).

⛪ **Cathédrale St-Tugdual**
Place du Martray. ◯ Jul–Aug: 9:30am–7pm daily; Sep–Jun: 9:30am–noon & 2:30–6:30pm. ⬤ to visitors during services.
The cathedral was built on the site of a 12th-century Romanesque church, the only vestige of which is the Tour Hastings. The Porche des Cloches, in the south side, features a Flamboyant Gothic stained-glass window, and from the tower rises an 18th-century spire. The outer wall on the south side is covered in Gothic tracery.

CATHÉDRALE ST-TUGDUAL
A masterpiece of Breton Gothic religious architecture, the cathedral was built in the 14th–15th centuries.

The Tour Hastings, with Romanesque arches, is the cathedral's oldest tower.

The courtyard was hired out to traders during the city's fair.

The spire, 72 m (236 ft) high, is covered with playing-card symbols, as the Loteries de Paris contributed to the cost of its rebuilding.

The Gothic tower over the crossing once contained a bell.

The Chapelle au Duc contains the body of John V, Duke of Brittany.

Nave

Buttresses

The west door is framed by an arch with a terrace above.

The south door is a pointed archway divided by a column. Above is a rose window.

The Porche des Cloches is crowned by a Flamboyant Gothic stained-glass window.

The arches inside rise in three tiers to a height of 18 m (59 ft) above the nave, and grotesques stare down from the base of some of the arches. The choir, in the Anglo-Norman style, has 46 Renaissance stalls with strikingly realistic decoration. The cathedral also contains the tomb of John V, Duke of Brittany, the tomb of St Yves (1890), and the saint's reliquary. The 15th-century cloisters north of the choir are the best-preserved in Brittany. The ambulatory is filled with sculptures of recumbent figures.

🏛 **Maison Ernest-Renan**
20 Rue Ernest-Renan. 📞 *(02) 96 92 45 63.* 🕐 *Apr–Jun: Wed–Sun; Jul–Aug: daily; Sep: Wed–Sun.* ⬤ *Oct–Mar.*

ENVIRONS: The village of **Minihy-Tréguier**, 1 km (0.5 mile) south of Tréguier, is famously associated with

---

ERNEST RENAN

Ernest Renan, a native of Tréguier

Born in Tréguier, Ernest Renan (1823–92) intended to join the priesthood, but his reading of the philosopher Hegel turned him against this vocation. A philologist who specialized in Semitic languages, he published writings that were thought to be scandalous because they proposed a rational, analytical approach to Christianity. Renan's *Vie de Jésus* (Life of Jesus) had particularly dramatic repercussions. When his statue was unveiled in 1903, the police were forced to act to prevent its desecration.

Yves Helory de Kermartin, who was canonized in 1347. A member of the local nobility, he became a protector of the poor, and turned the village into a refuge *(minihy)*. An annual pardon *(third Sun in May)* is held in his honour. The 15th-century church contains painted wooden statues of St Yves, shown, as usual, between a rich and a poor man.

The **Château de La Roche-Jagu**, 14 km (9 miles) southeast of Tréguier, was built in the 15th century, on the site of one of the ten forts that, from the 11th century, defended the Trieux valley.

⛪ **Château de La Roche-Jagu** 📞 *(02) 96 95 62 35.* 🕐 *Feb–Nov: daily; Dec–Jan: by arrangement.* 🈲

Fresco of the Dance of Death in the Chapelle de Kermaria-an-Iskuit

Chapelle Kermaria-an-Iskuit ㉒

Road map D1. 11 km (7 miles) northwest of St-Quay-Portrieux via the D786 then the D21.
🎏 *Pardon (third Sun in Sep).*

ABOUT 3 KM (2 miles) from Plouha, via the D21, stands the Chapelle Kermaria-an-Iskuit, "Chapel of Mary Restorer of Health". Founded in the 13th century by a former Crusader, it contains some extremely rare frescoes. One of them (1501) depicts the Dance of Death, which expresses the

fear of death that was widespread in late medieval Europe. Regardless of their rank, the *Ankou* (skeletal figure) leads men, from pope and king to knight and peasant, in a macabre dance.

St-Quay-Portrieux ㉓

Road map D1. 🚉 *St-Brieuc.*
🏘 *3,430.* 🚢 *Motorboat service to Île de Bréhat mid-Jun–mid-Sep.*
ℹ *17 bis Rue Jeanne-d'Arc; (02) 96 70 40 64.* 🦞 *Mon & Fri.*

THE PLEASANT COASTAL resort of St-Quay-Portrieux, north of St-Brieuc, once relied for its livelihood on fishing

off Newfoundland. Uniquely for a town of this size, the deep-water harbour here can berth 1,000 boats. A coast path leads to a signal station.

ENVIRONS: The popular resort of **Binic**, 7 km (4 miles) south of St-Quay-Portrieux, was a large port in the 19th century. The **Musée d'Arts et Traditions Populaires** is devoted to local history, especially the Newfoundland fishing industry. A collection of Breton headdresses is also on display.

🏛 **Musée d'Arts et Traditions Populaires**
Avenue du Général-de-Gaulle, Binic. 📞 *(02) 96 73 37 95.* 🕐 *Jul–Aug: daily pm; mid-Apr–Sep: Wed–Mon.*

The bay at St-Quay-Portrieux, a coastal resort with beautiful beaches

St-Brieuc 24

Carved figures in a panel in Rue Fardel

THE HISTORY OF St-Brieuc is closely linked to its evolution as a centre of religion. In the 5th century, Brieuc, a Gaulish monk, founded an oratory on the site of the present Fontaine St-Brieuc, in Rue Notre-Dame. The city was sacked in the late 16th century, during the Wars of the Holy League *(see p44)*, although stability returned in the 17th and 18th centuries. Lying between the valleys of the Gouédic and the Gouët, St-Brieuc, capital of the Côtes d'Armor, is a pleasant city. Also a dynamic centre of culture, it has spawned cultural organizations and hosts events such as Art Rock *(see p28)*. It also has associations with several great French writers.

One of the towers on the fortified Cathédrale St-Étienne

⛪ Old Town

Built in the 14th and 15th centuries, the **Cathédrale St-Étienne**, on Place du Martray, has the appearance of a fortress. Its central porch is flanked by two sturdy towers: the 14th-century Tour Brieuc, 28 m (92 ft) high, and the 15th-century Tour Marie, 33 m (108 ft) high. Both are pierced with openings that allowed defensive weapons of many kinds to be used.

The large Chapelle de l'Annonciation, dating from the 15th century, has a notable altarpiece made by Yves Corlaix in 1745. With rocaille decoration, gilt polychrome and curves and counter-curves, it is a masterpiece of Baroque art. In the choir, some of the capitals are carved with grotesques or foliage. The organ was built by Cavaillé-Coll, who also built the organ in St-Sulpice in Paris.

Rue Pohel, Rue Fardel and Rue Quinquaine, in the vicinity of the cathedral, are lined with many timber-

Timber-framed house in Rue Fardel, in the old town of St-Brieuc

framed houses dating from the 15th and 16th centuries.

The 15th-century house in Rue Fardel known as **Maison Ribault** is the oldest house in St-Brieuc. In Rue Quinquaine, the Hôtel des Ducs de Bretagne, the ducal residence built in 1572, is also of interest for its elegant Renaissance façade with grotesque masks and figures carved in relief. On Place du Chai, modern buildings stand alongside restored wine warehouses. A covered passageway links the square with Rue Houvenagle, which is lined with ancient timber-framed houses faced with pilasters and featuring overhanging upper storeys. Three pedestrianized streets, Rue St-Guéno, Rue Charbonnerie and Rue-Guillaume, the city's main shopping area, are also worth seeing.

🏛 Musée d'Art et d'Histoire
Rue des Lycéens-Martyrs.
📞 *(02) 96 62 55 20.* ⏰ *Tue–Sat; Sun pm.*
Through models, paintings, objects from everyday domestic life, films and dioramas, this museum presents the history of the the *département* of the Côtes d'Armor from its origins in the 18th century up until the 20th century. The displays illustrate several themes, including fishing, ship-building, the cloth and linen trade, agriculture and land reclamation, as well as popular traditions.

LITERARY LIFE IN ST-BRIEUC

Jean Grenier

Growing up in St-Brieuc in the early 20th century, Jean Grenier and Louis Guilloux formed a strong friendship. While the latter spent his life in St-Brieux, Grenier left in 1930 to teach at the *lycée* in Algiers, where one of his pupils was the young Albert Camus. As a teacher, Grenier influenced Camus' later work. Camus, the author of *L'Homme Révolté* and winner of the Nobel Prize for Literature in 1957, was steeped in the writings of both Grenier and Guilloux, and of Georges Palante, another philosopher who was a native of St-Brieuc. Guilloux came to the attention of the publisher Gaston Gallimard, winning the Prix Renaudot with *Le Jeu de Patience* (1949). Gide and Malraux judged his novel *Le Sang Noir* (1935) to be a work of major importance.

Anse d'Yffiniac, seen from the Maison de la Baie

🌿 **Les Grandes Promenades**

These walks circle the law courts. East of Rue St-Guillaume, the municipal garden, decorated with sculptures, follows the outline of the old city walls. On the right of the law courts stands a bust of the writer Villiers de l'Isle-Adam, who was born in St-Brieuc, by Elie Le Goff, and a sculpture entitled *La Forme se Dégageant de la Matière* (Form Emerging from Matter) by Paul Le Goff. There is a monument to Paul Le Goff on Boulevard de La Chalotais.

ENVIRONS:
Lying some 3 km (2 miles) inland, St-Brieuc is linked to the sea by the port of **Légué**, on the Gouët estuary. Here, shipowners' houses evoke the great age of the 19th-century Newfoundland cod-fishing industry, which has been replaced by the scallop industry. A footpath runs around the Pointe du Roselier. From the point, there is a view of the whole bay, from Cap d'Erquy in the east to the Île de Bréhat in the northwest. After passing an 18th-century cannon-ball foundry, the long-distance footpath GR34 leads to Martin-Plage. The Anse d'Yffiniac, an inlet behind the bay, is a sea-bird sanctuary: 50,000 birds of various species nest in this protected site. They arrive from northern Europe at the end of summer. Most spend the winter here. The **Maison de la Baie**, north of Hillion, contains displays documenting the bay's flora and fauna and describing its seafaring economy.

Near Hillion, long paths leading far into the Dunes de Bon-Abri allow walkers to have a closer look at the plant life of the protected site.

🏛 **Maison de la Baie**
📞 (02) 96 33 32 50. ⬜ Apr–Jun & Sep–Nov: 10am–12.30 & 2–6pm Mon–Fri; Jul–Aug: 10am–7pm Mon-Fri; 2–7pm Sat–Sun. ⬤ Dec–Mar, except school holidays: 10am–6pm.

VISITORS' CHECKLIST

Road map D2. 🚌 *Boulevard Charner.* 🚆 *6 Rue du Combat-des-Trente.* 👥 *48,900.* ℹ️ *7 Rue St-Gouénon; (02) 96 33 32 50; Comité Départemental, 29 Rue des Promenades; (02) 96 62 72 00.* 🛒 *Wed & Sat.* 🎭 *Art Rock (Whitsun); L'Été en Fête (theatre, dance & concerts, mid-Jul–mid-Sep).* 🌐 *www.mairie-saint-brieuc.fr*

ST-BRIEUC CITY CENTRE

Cathédrale St-Étienne ①
Grandes Promenades ④
Maison Ribault ②
Musée d'Art et d'Histoire ③

Brest

PLACE SAINT-MICHEL

RUE QUINQUAINE
R. HOUVENAGLE
RUE CHARBONNERIE
RUE MARECHAL FOCH
RUE CHATEAUBRIAND
R. LAMENNAIS

②

PL. DU GÉNÉRAL DE GAULLE
①

RUE SAINT BENOÎT

PL. G. BIZOIN

SÉVIGNÉ

④ GRANDES PROMENADES

PL. DE LA RÉSISTANCE

RUE SAINT PIERRE
R. P. CORBION
DE ROHAN
RUE DES

RUE VICAIRE

③

ALLÉE DES PROMENADES
BD LA CHALOTAIS
BD BOULEVARD

VALLÉE DU GOUÉDIC

Guingamp, Brest

RUE CH. LE MAOUT

RUE DES LYCÉENS MARTYRS

PL. SAINT-GUILLAUME

PL. DU 8 MAI 1945
BD SÉVIGNÉ

Lamballe, Rennes

RUE DU 71E RÉGIMENT D'INFANTERIE

PL. S. ALLENDE

CHAMP DE MARS

PL. DU GUESCLIN

AV. DE LA LIBERATION
RUE DE WALDECK ROUSSEAU

Railway station

Loudéac, Pontivy

R. DU COMBAT DES TRENTE

BD GOUÉDIC

KEY

🚌 Bus station

🅿️ Parking

ℹ️ Tourist information

✉️ Post office

✝️ Church

0 m   200
0 yards   200

The elegant Château de Quintin, built in the 17th century

Quintin ㉕

Road map C2. 18 km (11 miles) southwest of St-Brieuc via the D700, the D790 and the D7. ▦ *St-Brieuc.* ▨ *2,930.* ▮ *6 Place 1830; (02) 96 74 01 51.* ▨ *Jul–Aug: Thu pm.* ▧ *Tue.* ▨ *Pardon de Notre-Dame (second Sun in May); St-Jean (son et lumière, Jun); Fête des Tisserands (early Aug).*

D URING THE 17th and 18th centuries, Quintin was an important centre of the linen cloth industry. This age of prosperity gave the town its chateau as well as the timber-framed houses and fine granite-built residences that line Place 1830, Place du Martray and Grande Rue. The **Musée-Atelier des Toiles**, in Rue des Degrés, documents this period of the town's history.

The 19th-century Neo-Gothic Basilique Notre-Dame, in Rue de la Basilique, is dedicated to the patroness of spinners. A relic reputed to be a piece of the Virgin's girdle is kept in the basilica. It is particularly venerated by pregnant women.

Opposite the tourist office, the chateau, built in the 17th–18th centuries, houses a Musée de la Porcelaine (porcelain museum).

♦ Château de Quintin
Entrance on Place 1830. ▮ *(02) 96 74 94 79.* ◯ *Mid-Jun–mid-Sep: daily; Whitsun & Easter: daily pm; other times: Sat–Sun pm.*

🏛 Musée-Atelier des Toiles de Quintin
Rue des Degrés. ▮ *(02) 96 74 01 51.* ◯ *Jun–Sep: Tue–Sun.*

Moncontour ㉖

Road map D2. 15 km (9 miles) southwest of Lamballe via the D768. ▦ *Lamballe.* ▨ *1,000.* ▮ *4 Place de la Carrière; (02) 96 73 49 57 in summer; (02) 96 73 44 92 out of season.* ▨ *Pardon de St-Mathurin (Whitsun); Fête Médiévale (second 2 weeks Aug); Festival de Musique (Sep).*

T HIS MEDIEVAL WALLED town stands on a promontory at the point where two valleys meet. Fine 16th- and 18th-century residences and half-timbered houses line **Rue des Dames** and **Place de Penthièvre**, where a linen market was once held. The **Église St-Mathurin**, dating from the 16th–18th centuries, is well worth a visit for its 16th-century stained-glass windows. Those showing scenes from the life of St Yves, on the left of the nave, show Flemish influence.

Pietà in the Église St-Mathurin

Lamballe ㉗

Road map D2. ▦ *Boulevard Jobert.* ▨ ▨ *11,200.* ▮ *Maison du Bourreau, Place du Martray; (02) 96 31 05 38.* ▧ *Thu.* ▨ *Foire des Potiers (Jun); Festival des Ajoncs d'Or (early Aug); traditional threshing (mid-Aug); Pardon de Notre-Dame (6 Sep).*

F OUNDED IN THE sixth century, Lamballe began to develop in the 11th century, when it became the capital of the duchy of Penthièvre. Until the 18th century, the latter was in repeated conflict with its rival, the house of Brittany.

The **Musée d'Art Populaire du Pays de Lamballe**, on Place du Martray, is laid out in a charming half-timbered house that also contains the tourist office. With exhibits dating from prehistory, as well as local costumes, headdresses and tools, the collections illustrate the daily life in Lamballe and its environs in historical times.

The **Musée Mathurin-Méheut**, on the first floor, has a large collection relating to this local painter, who was also a leading exponent of Art Nouveau. About 4,000 of his works are exhibited in rotation, illustrating a different theme each year.

The **Collégiale Notre-Dame-de-Grande-Puissance** in Rue Notre-Dame, has the appearance of a fortified church. It is built in a combination of Romanesque

LINEN CLOTH

The linen cloth industry brought prosperity to Brittany in the 17th and 18th centuries. St-Brieuc, Quintin, Uzel, Loudéac and Moncontour – which, between them, had more than 8,000 weavers – were the main centres of production. In 1676, a statute was passed regulating the standards of quality of the linen cloth woven in western Europe. That produced in Brittany was then acknowledged to be the best in France. Loaded onto ships in St-Malo and Nantes, it was exported worldwide.

A loom on which linen cloth was once woven

MATHURIN MÉHEUT

Painter, interior decorator, illustrator, designer of jewellery and wallpaper, Mathurin Méheut (1888–1958) was a multi-talented artist. One of the earliest exponents of Art Nouveau, Méhuet was commissioned to design the interior decoration of 27 liners. This included producing four oil paintings for the *Normandie*. After World War II, he was appointed painter to the French Navy and produced many fishing scenes. In 1923, a retrospecive exhibition of his work was held in San Francisco.

Mathurin Méheut, a pioneering exponent of Art Nouveau

Louis XIII organ loft of 1741. Near the church, a walk has been made on the site of a castle that was destroyed in 1626.

The **Haras National**, in Place du Champ-de-Foire, in the west of Lamballe, is the second-largest national stud in France. Set up in 1825, it was well regarded in the early 20th century, and is still important today. It has capacity for 400 animals, and the horses bred here include Breton post-horses, thoroughbreds and Connemaras, thus helping to preserve these breeds.

The Maison du Bourrreau, in Lamballe, housing two museums and the tourist office

⏻ Haras National
Place du Champ-de-Foire.
[(02) 96 50 06 98.
Mid-Jun–mid-Sep: daily; school holidays: daily pm; other times: Wed, Sat & Sun pm.

ENVIRONS: Northeast of Lamballe, not far from Pléven, are the ruins of the **Château de La Hunaudaye**. In summer, for the benefit of visitors, actors in costume populate the castle. Of particular interest is the 15th-century keep, pierced by loopholes, the seigneurial quarters, with a fine Renaissance staircase, and two 13th-century towers.

♟ Château de La Hunaudaye
On the D28. [(02) 96 34 82 10.
Apr–Jun & Sep: Sun & public holidays, pm; Jul–Aug: Mon–Sat; Sun pm.

🏛 Musée d'Art Populaire du Pays de Lamballe
Maison du Bourreau. [(02) 96 31 05 38. Jul–Aug: Mon–Sat; Sun am; Sep–Dec & Feb–Jun: Sun. Jan.

🏛 Musée Mathurin-Méheut
Maison du Bourreau.
[(02) 96 31 19 99. Jun–Sep & spring school holidays: Mon–Sat; other times: Tue, Fri & Sat, pm. Jan.

⛪ Collégiale Notre-Dame-de-Grande-Puissance
Rue Notre-Dame. Mid-Jun–mid-Sep: Mon–Sat.

and Gothic styles. The north door, dating from the 12th century, has capitals carved with foliage. The thick columns and floral motifs in the nave show Norman influence, while the Flamboyant Gothic rood screen (1415) is perfectly counterbalanced by the

The charming medieval village of Moncontour, perched on a promontory

The Château de Bien-Assis, near Pléneuf-Val-André

Pléneuf-Val-André ㉘

Road map D2. 🚉 🚌 *Lamballe.*
🏠 *3,770.* ℹ️ *Cours Winston-Churchill;
(02) 96 72 20 55.* 🗓 *Tue
in Pléneuf; Fri in Val-André.* 🎉 *Fête
du Nautisme & regatta (May); jazz
(Jul–Aug: every Tue); Pardon
de Notre-Dame-de-la-Garde (Aug);
Fête de la Mer (mid-Aug).*

ORIGINALLY NO MORE than a
quiet fishing harbour,
Pléneuf Val-André was
transformed in the late 19th
century, when developers
turned it into one of Brittany's
most sophisticated holiday
resorts. With a beautiful sandy
beach 2 km (1 mile) long, it
soon became very popular.

From the 16th century,
fishermen from the neigh-
bouring village of Dahouët
came to Pléneuf Val-André to
prepare for cod-fishing expeditions off Newfoundland. In
those days, ships' captains
would call at local inns to
enlist sailors, whose drunkenness would guarantee that they
signed up without protest.

From Pléneuf Val-André, two
walks, to Pointe de la Guette
and to Pointe de Pléneuf, offer
spectacular views. The **Îlot
du Verdelet**, opposite Pointe
de Pléneuf, is a bird sanctuary,
and it is accessible at low tide.
Trips out to sea on the sailing
boat ***Pauline*** are organized
during the holiday season.

🚢 *Pauline*
Port de Dahouët. 📞 *(02) 96 63 10 99.*
🕐 *Jun–Sep: daily; Oct–May:
by arrangement.*

ENVIRONS: The **Château de
Bien-Assis**, 4 km (3 miles)
east of Pléneuf-Val-André, was
built in 1400 and has been
remodelled several times since.
The only surviving part of the
original building is a tower
behind the present chateau.
Destroyed during the Wars of
the Holy League *(see p44),*
the chateau was rebuilt in the
17th century: the part framed
by towers dates from this
phase. The interior contains
Breton Renaissance furniture
and a monumental stairway.
There is also a formal garden.

⛪ Château de Bien-Assis
Sur la D786. 📞 *(02) 96 72 22 03.*
🗓 *Mid-Jun–mid-Sep: Mon-Sat,
Sun pm: mid-Sep–mid-Jun:
by arrangement.* 🏞

The fishing port of Erquy, base of many
deep-sea trawlers

Sables-d'Or-les-Pins ㉙

Road map E1. 8 km (5 miles)
southwest of Cap Fréhel via the D34a.
🏠 *2,100.* 🚉 🚌 *Lamballe.*
ℹ️ *La Grande Abbaye, Fréhel;
(02) 96 41 53 81 all year; (02) 96 41
51 97 summer only.* 🗓 *Tue.*

THIS COASTAL RESORT with
smart villas in the neo-
Norman style was created in
the early 1920s as a rival to
Deauville. With a 3-km (2-
mile) long sandy beach and
pine trees, it is very popular
with holidaymakers.

ENVIRONS: Erquy, on the
D786 west of Sables-d'Or, is
renowned for its clams and
scallops. It is also the base for
a large fleet of deep-sea
trawlers. Of all the beaches
nearby, the Plage de Caroual
is the best. In summer, the
tourist office organizes boat
trips to the Île de Bréhat *(see
p98)* and the Baie de St-
Brieuc *(see p103).*

Cap d'Erquy is less well
known than Cap Fréhel, yet it
is one of the most beautiful
headlands in Brittany. Many
marked footpaths cross the
flower-covered heath here
and run along the indented
cliffs, beneath which are
shingle beaches. The views
from the headland are
stunning; to the west,
there is a panorama
across the Baie de
St-Brieuc and to Pointe
de Pléneuf beyond.

One of the paths on
the promontory passes
an *oppidum* popularly
known as Caesar's
Camp; it was, in fact,
a fortified Gaulish
settlement and its
Iron Age earthworks
are still visible.
Classified in 1978, the
site was bought by the
local authority in 1982
so as to protect it from
erosion caused by
motorcyclists using it
as a rough circuit. In
summer, daily walks
on Cap d'Erquy are
organized by the
Syndicat des Caps
(02 96 41 50 83).

Fort La Latte, built in the 13th century, with a commanding view of the sea

Cap Fréhel ③⓪

Road map E1. ❶ *Syndicat des Caps, Rue Notre-Dame, Plévenon; (02) 96 41 50 83.* ⍟ *Mid-Jun–mid-Sep & school holidays out of season: daily.* ⛴ *Emeraude Line Dinard; (02) 99 46 10 45.* ⛴ *Emeraude Line St-Malo; (02) 23 18 11 81.*

T HE SPECTACULAR headland of Cap Fréhel is one of the most beautiful landscapes in Brittany. Heathland covered with heather and gorse stretches to infinity, and sheer pink limestone cliffs rise vertically from the sea to heights of 70 m (230 ft).

The view from here stretches from Pointe du Groin in the east to the Île de Bréhat in the west. In clear weather, it is even possible to see the Channel Islands. Sea birds, such as fulmars, kittiwakes, cormorants, guillemots and pied oystercatchers, nest in nooks in the cliffs and on the neighbouring small islands.

There are two lighthouses on the promontory: one built by Vauban in the 17th century and the other dating from 1950. The latter is open to visitors; the effort of climbing to the top is rewarded by the view. In summer, the Syndicat des Caps organizes walks on the promontory every day. Trips by motorboat from Dinard and St-Malo allow visitors to admire the cliffs from the sea.

⚲ Lighthouse
❶ *(02) 96 41 40 03.* ⍟ *Jul–Aug: daily; Sep–Jun: by arrangement.*

Fort La Latte ③①

Road map E1. 4 km (3 miles) southwest of Cap Fréhel via the D16. ❶ *(02) 96 41 40 31.* ◐ *Apr–Sep: daily; Oct–Feb: Sat–Sun; winter school holidays: daily pm.* ⛴ *Emeraude Line Dinard; (02) 99 46 10 45.* ⛴ *Emeraude Line St-Malo; (02) 23 18 11 81.*

T HIS IMPRESSIVE FORTRESS overlooking the sea was built in the 13th century by the powerful Goyon-Matignon family. It was captured by Bertrand du Guesclin *(see p41)* in 1379 and was besieged by the English in 1490, then by the Holy League in 1597. On Vauban's orders, Garangeau *(see p80)* restored it in the 17th century. The keep and the cannon-ball foundry are of particular interest to visitors.

From the rampart walk, there is a sublime view of the Côte d'Émeraude. Abandoned in the 19th century, the fort passed into private ownership in 1892, and was classified as a historic monument in 1931.

The spectacular headland at Cap Fréhel, with sheer limestone cliffs

St-Cast-Le Guildo ③②

Road map E1. ⊟ ⊟ *Lamballe.* ⍟ *3,290.* ❶ *Place Charles-de-Gaulle; (02) 96 41 81 52.* ⊜ *Fri: in season: Mon & Fri.* ⌖ *Concerts (Jul–Aug).*

N OW A POPULAR coastal resort, St-Cast-Le Guildo has no less than seven beaches, and in summer its population increases ten-fold. Its expansion began at the end of the 19th century, when the painter Marinier purchased the headland and set about developing it.

The ruins of the **Château du Guildo**, in the parish of Créhen, recall the fratricidal conflict between Giles of Brittany, son of John V, Duke of Brittany, whose allegiance was to the English crown, and his brother Francis I of Brittany, a supporter of the king of France. Francis murdered Giles, but the latter had prayed to God that his brother might outlive him by just 40 days; Francis indeed died exactly 40 days later. It was not until 1758 that the English, who suffered defeat at St-Cast, finally relinquished their intentions of invading the coast of Brittany.

From here, visitors may enjoy two walks along part of the GR34 long-distance footpath. One goes south to Pointe de la Garde, which offers a beautiful panorama of the Ebihens archipelago and Presqu'île St-Jacut; the other goes north, to the Pointe de St-Cast, which commands a fine view of Fort La Latte and Cap Fréhel.

The fort and Cap Fréhel can also be admired from the sea by taking a trip in the *Dragous*, an old sailing boat, which leaves from St-Cast-Le-Guildo.

The town's **church** contains a 12th-century Romanesque stoup decorated with grotesques and a statue of St Cast, the monk who established a hermitage here in the 6th century.

⛴ Dragous
Port de St-Cast. ❶ *(02) 96 41 86 42.* ◐ *Jul–Aug: daily; Easter–Nov: by arrangement.*

Street-by-Street: Dinan 🟤

IN THE WORDS OF Victor Hugo, Dinan perches "on an overhanging precipice…like a swallow's nest". From the 14th to the 18th centuries, a flourishing trade in linen cloth, leather, wood and cereals – cargoes that left Dinan from its harbour on the Rance – led to the creation of an exceptionally rich architectural heritage: the old town has some extremely fine half-timbered houses. The town is enclosed by 3 km (2 miles) of walls that are both the most massive and the oldest in Brittany. The 14th-century machicolated keep known as the Donjon de la Duchesse Anne, as well as the Basilique St-Sauveur, with a magnificent Romanesque porch, are some of the other attractions of this medieval town.

★ Basilique St-Sauveur
This is built in a style combining Byzantine, Persian and Romanesque influences.

Tour Ste-Catherine
The oldest tower in the town's 13th-century walls commands a splendid panorama of the harbour and the Rance valley.

Tour du Gouverneur

Porte de St-Malo

Franciscan Monastery
Built in the 13th century, this former Franciscan monastery now houses a private school.

★ Rue de Jerzual
Until 1783, when the viaduct was built, travellers entering Dinan would follow this street, which was once a steep track.

★ Castle and Town Walls

The castle consists of a keep, the Tour de Coëtquen and the Porte du Guichet. The 14th-century keep houses a museum of local history.

Benedictine monastery

KEY

– – – Suggested route

```
0 m          100
0 yards      100
```

Porch of the Hôtel Beaumanoir
The street entrance of this residence is framed by a stone archway decorated with carved dolphins.

Tour de l'Horloge

★ Place des Merciers

In the heart of the old town, the Place des Merciers (Haberdashers' Square) is lined with medieval timber-framed houses. The Restaurant de la Mère Pourcel, a 15th-century timber-framed building with overhanging upper storey, also lines the square.

Exploring Dinan

THE HISTORY OF DINAN is closely linked to events in Breton political history. In about 1000, noblemen from a family called Dinan took possession of the town and, in 1238, it came under the control of the duchy of Brittany. Dinan enjoyed an initial period of prosperity thanks to its maritime trading links with Flanders and England, and to the trade in linen sheets and cloth. In the 14th century, the Wars of the Breton Succession, during which Dinan supported the king of France, curtailed the town's development. However, from the 16th century, Dinan was again prosperous and it enjoyed a second golden age in the 17th and 18th centuries. This can be seen from the fine timber-framed houses that line the town's streets. At this time, religious orders also established several large convents and founded new churches in Dinan.

The old town of Dinan, on the banks of the Rance

🏛 Old Town and Harbour

In the harbour, the commercial activity that once brought Dinan such riches has been replaced by a flotilla of pleasure boats. The leafy banks of the Rance offer the opportunity for scenic walks.

Rue du Quai leads to **Rue du Petit-Fort**. At No. 24 is the **Maison du Gouverneur**, a fine 15th-century residence. Before the viaduct was built in 1783, travellers would enter Dinan via **Porte du Jerzual**, a 14th-century gate with Gothic arcades. They would then follow **Rue du Jerzual**, which is lined with timber-framed houses dating from the 15th and 16th centuries. Once filled with traders, the street has been taken over by glass-blowers, cabinet-makers and gilders.

Rue de l'Apport has several well-restored houses. This street leads to **Place des Merciers**, which also contains attractive houses with wooden porches

and overhanging upper storeys. In **Rue de l'Horloge**, the tourist office, at No. 6, is housed in the **Hôtel de Keratry**, a 16th-century mansion with granite columns.

🏛 Town Walls

These were built in the 13th century and strengthened in the 15th century by Francis I, Duke of Brittany. They were renovated in the 17th century by Garangeau (*see p80*) on the orders of Vauban. The walls are set with six towers, the most impressive of which is the Tour Beaumanoir.

Two walks along the walls, the Promenade de la Duchesse Anne and the Promenade des Grands Fossés, offer views of the town and of the Rance.

🏛 Franciscan Monastery

Place des Cordeliers. ⬤ *Mon–Fri.*
This former monastery was established in the 13th century by a Crusader who

became a Franciscan friar. Several 15th-century buildings survive. Among them are the Gothic cloisters, the main courtyard and the chapter-house, which is used as a refectory by the school that now occupies the monastery.

🔒 Église St-Malo

Grande-Rue. ⬤ *daily, 9am–4pm.*
⬤ *to visitors during services.*
The church, with a slate-covered bell-turret, was begun in the 15th century and completed 400 years later. The exterior has a remarkable Renaissance doorway. Pillaged during the Revolution, the interior is somewhat bare, apart from more recent additions such as the high altar (1955) in granite carved by Gallé and a series of stained-glass windows (1927) by Merklen, depicting various quarters of Dinan, such as the Jerzual and Place des Cordeliers.

🔒 Basilique St-Sauveur

Place St-Sauveur. ⬤ *daily, 9am–4pm.*
⬤ *to visitors during services.*
Built in a combination of Romanesque and Byzantine styles, the basilica is unique in Brittany. It was founded by a knight who had safely returned from a crusade against the Saracens. Begun in the 12th century, it was not completed until the 16th century.

The façade has a remarkable Romanesque doorway carved with depictions of the vices and with such monstrosities

Rue du Petit-Fort, lined with fine 15th-century houses

BIRTH OF A LEGEND

In 850, some monks dressed in rags met King Nominoë (*see p37*) and asked him to help them. The king agreed on condition that he be given some relics in return. To fulfil this obligation, the monks set sail for Sark, in the Channel Islands, where they found the body of St Magloire (525-605), Bishop of Dol. On their return, the king fell to his knees before the relic and founded the Prieuré de St-Magloire-de-Lehon.

Relic of St Magloire

VISITORS' CHECKLIST

Road map E2. 15,000. 6 Rue de l'Horloge; (02) 96 87 69 76. Apr–Jun & Sep: Sat; Jul–Aug: daily. Place du 11-Novembre-1918. Thu. Festival de Harpe Celtique (first week in Jul); Fête des Remparts (third weekend in Jul) ; Fête de la Pomme (first weekend in Nov).

as sirens, human-headed serpents and a toad at a woman's breast. The interior combines the Romanesque and Flamboyant Gothic styles. The heart of Bertrand du Guesclin (*see p41*) is entombed in one of the chapels. There are also some fine stained-glass windows, both ancient and modern.

The former cemetery is now a terraced garden with a view of the Rance valley. In the garden are busts of the explorer Auguste Pavie and of Néel de la Vigne, mayor of Dinan during the Revolution.

⊞ Tour de l'Horloge
Rue de l'Horloge.
☐ Apr–Sep: daily.
The top of the tower commands an extensive view over Dinan. The bell was a gift to the town made in 1507 by Anne of Brittany.

⊞ Benedictine Monastery
Rue de Léhon. ☐ Mon–Fri.
Built in the 17th and 18th centuries, the monastery now houses a private school where Chateaubriand (*see p69*) was once a pupil.

♣ Castle & Museum
Rue du Château. 📞 (02) 96 39 45 20
☐ Wed–Mon. ● Jan.
The castle consists of a 14th-century keep – the Donjon de la Duchesse Anne – the 13th-century Porte du Guichet and the Tour de Coëtquen. Strengthened by Mercœur, leader of the Holy League (*see p44*), the castle withstood attack by Protestant soldiers but, with the help of the

Statue from the castle

people of Dinan, Henry IV managed to break through the Porte de St-Malo.

The keep, built in 1380, must have served both as a fortress and as living quarters, as it features spy-holes and look-outs as well as mullioned windows and monumental chimneys. A platform at the top of the keep offers a magnificent view of Dinan and its environs.

Tour Coëtquen, with tomb effigies, was built by Estienne Le Fur, who also built the keep here and Tour Solidor in St-Servan, south of St-Malo (*see pp82–3*).

The **museum** of local history, in the keep, contains archaeological artifacts, Breton headdresses, paintings and sculpture.

🏛 Maison d'Artiste de la Grande-Vigne
103 Rue du Quai. 📞 (02) 96 87 90 80.
☐ Jun–Sep: daily.
This house was the home of Yvonne Jean-Haffen (1895–1993), an artist who

The Tour de l'Horloge, offering a wide view over Dinan

was a pupil and friend of Mathurin Méheut (*see p105*). Among the 4,000 works that Jean-Haffen bequeathed to the town are engravings, ceramics and watercolours depicting scenes of Brittany in a bygone age.

Exhibited in rotation, these works illustrate a variety of themes.

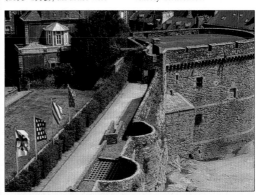

Tour de Coëtquen, built by the architect Estienne Le Fur

NORTHERN FINISTÈRE

TWO VERY DISTINCT *geographical and historical entities make up northern Finistère. West of the Morlaix river lies the territory of the former diocese of the Léon, whose religious and economical capital was St-Pol. East of Morlaix is a small section of the Trégor, the neighbouring diocese that became part of Finistère after the Revolution.*

The Trégor Finistérien, that part of the Trégor annexed to Finistère, is a charming part of Brittany, a patchwork of valleys and sunken lanes. The Léon, by contrast, is a large plateau that in the 1960s was stripped of its trees to maximize intensive agriculture. This is especially true of the Haut-Léon, a prime producer of artichokes and cauliflowers. Its commercial dynamism even led to the creation of Brittany Ferries, founded to export the Léon's prized local produce.

Commercially successful, the Haut-Léon is also deeply religious. Not for nothing is it known as "the land of priests", and it boasts some of Brittany's architectural jewels: the parish closes, built with funds provided by local rural inhabitants who, from the 13th century, had grown rich through the thriving linen cloth trade.

The Bas-Léon, surrounded on three sides by the sea (the Abers, the Mer d'Iroise and the Rade de Brest), has a quite different landscape. Here are wide deserted beaches and narrow secret creeks, wooded estuaries and cliffs topped by lighthouses, banks of dunes and windswept promontories. In the extreme west, battered by the Atlantic Ocean, lies Ouessant, the end of the known world in ancient times, and the low-lying islands of the Molène archipelago, which, like the Monts d'Arrée and the magical forest of Huelgoat, form part of the Parc Régional d'Armorique.

Each of these different environments offers wonderful walking country, providing unlimited peace, fresh air and unspoiled landscapes.

Halyards and stays coiled and hung to dry on belaying pins after fishing

◁ The Parc du Menez Meur in the Monts d'Arrée

Exploring Northern Finistère

The northern part of Finistère, meaning "Land's End", consists of several protected environments. Among these are the Baie de Morlaix, the heathland of the Monts d'Arrée *(see pp140–41)*, the dunes of Keremma, the deeply indented Côte des Abers *(see pp126–7)* and the Ouessant archipelago, battered by wind and spray. As the distances between these areas are small, it is easy to explore them while also stopping off to visit the chateaux, manor houses and parish closes that make up the rich architectural heritage of the area, once the diocese of Léon. Alternating between coastal and inland areas, particularly around Landerneau and Landivisiau, visitors will appreciate the many facets of this rugged region, which is bathed in a pearly light.

The church at Lannédern, north of Pleyben

CÔTE DES ABERS

OUESSANT

OUESSANT ARCHIPELAGO
ÎLE MOLÈNE

POINTE ST-MATHIEU

Rade de Brest

SEE ALSO

- *Where to Stay* pp221–3
- *Where to Eat* pp236–7

0 km   20

0 miles   10

NORTHERN FINISTÈRE AT A GLANCE

KEY

▬ Motorway

▬ Major road

═ Minor road

The small town on the Île de Batz

ÎLE DE BATZ **5**

Baie de Morlaix

ROSCOFF **4**

ST-POL-DE-LÉON **3**

PLOUGASNOU

LOCQUIREC

6 PLOUESCAT

D 10

CARANTEC **2**

D 73

D 46

D 786

D 64

Lannion

CHÂTEAU DE KERJEAN

D 69

7

D 58

D 30

D 19

N 12 E 50

1 MORLAIX

N 12 E 50

Guingamp, St-Brieuc

DILIS **22**

N 12 E 50

ST-THÉGONNEC **25**

27

NDIVISIAU

LAMPAUL-GUIMILIAU **23**

À ROCHE-MAURICE

GUIMILIAU **24**

D 769

D 42

LANNÉANOU

MONTS D'ARRÉE

21

D 30

D 11

D 111

D 785

D 111

D 9

MARTYRE

D 764

D 18

D 11

D 42

SIZUN *D 764*

D 18

D 14

HUELGOAT **26**

D 785

D 14

D 764

D 769

'hâteaulin, Quimper

Pleyben

Carhaix-Plouguer, Lorient

GETTING AROUND

Morlaix and Brest, the two major towns in northern Finistère, are linked by a motorway, the N12, and by the TGV (high-speed train) service. The TGV journey time between these two towns is 45 minutes. The port of Roscoff, a ferry terminal for services to and from Britain and Ireland, is served by buses and TER trains run by the French state railway company, SNCF. Several coach companies (such as Bihan, CAT, St-Mathieu, Douguet, Kreisker and Leroux) provide regular links between the towns of the Léon. Particularly scenic routes are the coast roads D73 (Morlaix to Carantec), D76 (Plouézoc'h to Térénez) and D127 (Portsall to Argenton), as well as those that follow the estuaries of the Côte des Abers and along the banks of the Élorn (D712 and D30) and Queffleuth rivers (D769).

Wooded countryside around St-Rivoal, southeast of Sizun

Street-by-Street: Morlaix 1

The Morlaix viaduct, with a pedestrian bridge on the lower of its two levels

O N THE BORDER of the Léon to the west and the Trégor to the east, and with the sea to the north and the Monts d'Arrée to the south, Morlaix *(Montroulez* in Breton) was once one of the largest ports on the English Channel. From early times, shipowners, privateers and merchants exploited to the full the town's favourable geographical location. Its focal point were the docks, from which ships bound for Spain were laden with delicate linen cloth woven inland, and those bound for Holland with salt from Guérande, lead from the mines of Huelgoat, leather and wine from the vineyards of Bordeaux. In the 19th century, ships could still sail up the estuary to a point level with Morlaix's town hall. Lined with arcades and warehouses, the quays were as busy as any modern stock exchange.

★ **Place des Otages**
The square is lined with 17th-century mansions, such as that at No. 15, built for a member of the Breton parliament, and with charming timber-framed houses, like that at No. 35, shown here. It contains the bookshop La Nuit Bleu Marine.

RUE ANGE-DE-GUER...

PLACE DES OTAGES

PLACE ÉMILE SOUVESTRE

RUE

Église St-Melaine and Viaduct
The impressive viaduct that bestrides Morlaix's old town was built by the engineer Victor Fenoux in 1861 to carry a stretch of the Paris–Brest railway. The church is dedicated to Melaine (462–530), a priest who was chancellor to Hoel II, a Breton king, and counsellor to Clovis, king of France.

The town hall was built in 1841.

STAR SIGHTS

★ **No. 9 Grand'Rue**

★ **Place des Otages**

0 m   100

0 yards   100

The old town walls are vestiges of medieval Morlaix.

Rue Ange-de-Guernisac is lined by houses with slate-clad façades.

★ No. 9 Grand'Rue

This was the street where the linen cloth market was once held. The house at No. 9 has a pondalez, a staircase that is typical of residences in Morlaix. The building also features windows with sliding shutters and 17th-century painted beams.

Maison de la Duchesse Anne

This is one of the fine town houses built in the 15th and 16th centuries for the nobility of Morlaix and for rich merchants in the linen cloth trade.

Musée des Jacobins

One room in this museum contains several gwele kloz (traditional Breton box beds), made in oak or cherrywood in the 18th and 19th centuries. Some beautiful stained-glass is also on display.

Église St-Mathieu

The tower (1548) was once crowned by a dome. Inside the church is a rare "vierge ouvrante", a statue of the Virgin and Child that opens to reveal the Holy Trinity.

PLACE VIARMES

RUE AU FIL

D'AIGUILLON

PLACE DES JACOBINS

GRAND'RUE

RUE DE PARIS

PLACE SALVADOR ALLENDE

PLACE DU DOSSEN

DU

MUR

VENELLE DES ARCHERS

RUE BASSE

RUE HAUTE

Place Allende
was once the market square.

New market

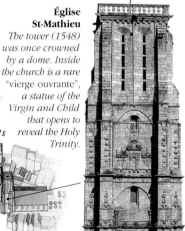

KEY

– – – Suggested route

Exploring Morlaix

MORLAIX SADLY LOST much of its character when, in 1897, its docks were filled in and covered by two squares, the Place des Otages and Place Cornic. Efforts are now being made to make the town more vibrant and to renovate the historic quayside buildings – mansions with dormer windows and houses with *pondalez* (spiral staircases) – that merchants built in a more prosperous age. Pleasure boats are the only vessels that now tie up in the harbour, as, with the closure of the tobacco-processing plant, it is now devoid of the ships that once serviced that industry. The resulting loss of 2,000 jobs has forced Morlaix, the third-largest town in the Finistère, to seek prosperity in other industries.

Stained-glass window in the Église St-Mathieu

Timber-framed and slate-clad houses in Morlaix

🔒 Église St-Melaine
Rue Ange-de-Guernisac.
📞 *(02) 98 88 45 19.*
Built in the Flamboyant Gothic style by the Beaumanoirs and completed in 1489, St-Melaine is the oldest church in Morlaix. As well as an organ built by Thomas Dallam in 1682, it contains painted wooden statues of saints and has fine 16th-century beams carved with plant motifs, angels, animals, including ermines (emblem of Anne of Brittany) and, amusingly, caricatures of prominent people of the time.

🏛 Musée des Jacobins
Place des Jacobins. 📞 *(02) 98 88 68 88.* ⬤ *Jun–Sep.* ⬤ *Tue & Sat am.*
Housed in a former convent founded in the 13th century, the museum focuses on several themes: local history, painting inspired by Brittany and contemporary art.

Of particular interest are the 15th- to 17th-century religious statuary, including an *Ankou* (skeletal figure in the Dance of Death), and the Breton antique furniture, which includes grain chests, linen presses and box beds.

🔒 Église St-Mathieu
East of the Rue de Paris.
📞 *(02) 98 88 45 19.*
This church, rebuilt in 1824, is notable for its tower, one of the earliest examples of the Renaissance style in Brittany, and for the curious statue that it contains. Made in about 1390 in a workshop in Westphalia, it depicts the Virgin and Child but opens to reveal the Holy Trinity. It is especially precious since most such statues were destroyed after the Council of Trent (1563): theologians feared that they might give rise to the idea that the Virgin could have engendered the Holy Trinity.

Furniture detail, Musée des Jacobins

🏠 Maison de la Duchesse Anne
33 Rue du Mur. 📞 *(02) 98 88 23 26.* ⬤ *Jul–Aug: daily.* ⬤ *Sun & public holidays, am.* 🈺
This house, one of several in the region where Anne of Brittany is reputed to have stayed, consists of three sections, the central part with a monumental chimneypiece rising the full height of the building.
    The house also has a staircase known as a *pondalez.* This is a spiral staircase that, by means of a walkway, allows access to the rooms in the different parts of the house.

Windows of the Maison de la Duchesse Anne

🏠 No. 9 Grand'Rue
📞 *(02) 98 88 03 57.* ⬤ *winter: Wed, Fri–Sat; summer: Tue–Sat.* 🈺
Restored in 1997, the house at No. 9 Grand'Rue is another 16th-century residence with a *pondalez* staircase. The latter is supported by a single oak beam, which is decorated with profuse carvings. The windows of the house were designed to allow merchants to display their wares.
    The timber-framed façades of houses like these were often decorated with depictions of patron saints or with amusing representations of people.

Caplan & Co

This café and bookshop, which opened in 1933, is one of the most atmospheric places in Finistère Nord. It is housed in a former grocer's shop overlooking the beach at Poul-Rodou, on the coast road between Locquirec and Guimaëc. Outside, there is a terrace with tables. Inside, where the décor replicates a school classroom, is an excellent selection of books by an international range of authors.

Caplan & Co, one of the region's most famous cafés

ENVIRONS: The **Trégor Finistérien**, the small region of heath and woodland between Morlaix and Locquirec, is worth exploring, not least for its archaeological sites and beautiful coastal landscapes. From Morlaix, take the D76 that runs along the estuary to Dourduff-en-Mer.

Cairn de Barnenez
Presqu'île de Barnenez, Plouézoc'h. ((02) 98 67 24 73. ◯ Apr–Sep: daily. ● winter: Mon.
This megalithic monument crowns the Presqu'île de Barnenez. Built in about 4,500 BC, it is the largest and oldest cairn in Europe. It contains 11 dolmens, and excavations have uncovered pottery, bones and engraved motifs. From the tip of the peninsula, there is a superb view of the Château du Taureau *(see p120)*, the Île Stérec and the small fishing harbour of Térénez.

Plages de Plougasnou
The beaches tucked away along the coast between Térénez and St-Jean-du-Doigt are the most beautiful in the Trégor

Finistérien. They are at Samson, Guerzit and Port-Blanc (reached via the D46A2) and Primel-Trégastel (via the D46).
Walkers will enjoy the coast path that runs round the Pointe du Diben. The headland bristles with rocks in strange zoomorphic shapes, such as those of a dromedary and a sphinx. The Pointe de Trégastel offers a wide panorama of the English Channel, the Île de Batz and the Île Grande.

St-Jean-du-Doigt
6 km (4 miles) northeast of Morlaix via the D46. ◻ from Morlaix.
In the late 19th century, the pardon held in this small town (*Sant Yann ar Biz* in Breton) would attract up to 12,000 faithful. It is named after a famous relic, the finger of St John the Baptist, that is kept in the church here.
The relic reputedly has the power to restore sight, and, in the 16th century, Anne of Brittany came to seek a cure for a troublesome left eye. Duly healed, she funded the building of the church, whose spire and three bell-turrets

were struck by lightning in 1925. The town also has an elegant fountain decorated with lead statues.

Musée des Vieux Outils
Le Prajou, Guimaec, 13 km (8 miles) northeast of Morlaix. ((02) 98 67 54 77. ◯ summer: daily pm.
The museum is housed in a barn on the road running between the small town of Guimaec and the wild coast around Beg an Fry. It contains almost 2,500 traditional tools and implements of the Trégor, including flails, gorse-crushing hammers, combs for carding linen, cream separators and old stills.

Fountain in St-Jean-du-Doigt, decorated with lead statues

Locquirec
Road map C1. 19 km (12 miles) northwest of Morlaix on the D786 then the D64. ⚐ 1,242. ◻ & ◻ from Morlaix. ℹ Place du Port; (02) 98 67 40 83. ◻ Wed am.
It was in this small fishing village on the border between the Trégor and the Côtes d'Armor that the thick, heavy Locquirec slate – with which almost all local buildings are roofed – was once mined. Locquirec (*Lokireg* in Breton) is now a coastal resort, with nine beaches, a large hotel and a coast path that offers a fine view of the bay. The church, with a belfry built by Beaumanoir in 1634, is as dainty and intimate as the village itself. It has a painted wooden ceiling and a charming statue of Our Lady of Succour. The **Chapelle Notre-Dame-des-Joies**, 5 km (3 miles) further south, has a 16th-century oak chancel decorated with fruits, flowers and chimeras, and a *Virgin and Child*.

Cairn de Barnenez, one of the most remarkable burial mounds in Europe

The beach at the elegant coastal resort of Carantec

Carantec ❷

Road map B1. 🚶 2,650.
🚌 from Morlaix. 🛈 4 Rue Pasteur;
(02) 98 67 00 43. 🕑 Thu am.
🎭 Pardon de Notre-Dame-de-Callot
(Sun after 15 Aug).

WITH THE ARRIVAL of the
first foreign visitors,
between the 1870s and the
1900s, the history of Carantec
(*Karanteg* in Breton) took a
decisive turn. One of these
visitors found the location
enchanting, and largely
thanks to him, this farming
village was transformed into a
fashionable coastal resort. The
smart hotels and elegant villas
that were built no longer
exist, however.

The magical views here can
be enjoyed by following a
marked footpath running
from Grève Blanche to the
pine wood at Penn al Lann.
The two-hour walk takes in
Porspol beach, a rocky
platform known as the
Chaise du Curé (Parson's
Chair) and another beach,
Le Cosmeur. There are also
views of the **Île Callot**, with
sandy inlets, and the Île Louët,
a small island with a lighthouse
and a keeper's cottage, as well
as the **Château du Taureau**.
The castle was built by the
inhabitants of Morlaix as a
defence against the incursions
of English pirates. Strengthened
by Vauban, it became a
prison. It is scheduled to
open to visitors in 2004.

In Carantec itself, the small
Musée Maritime contains
some vintage sailing boats,
including a boat in which 193
British pilots and members of
the Résistance crossed the
Channel during World War II.

⚓ **Château du Taureau**
🔵 closed for renovation. Reopening
scheduled for 2004. Information from
the Chambre de Commerce et Industrie
in Morlaix. 📞 (02) 98 62 39 39.
⛵ **Île Callot**
Accessible from Grève Blanche at low
tide. Check with the tourist office.
🏛 **Musée Maritime**
8 Rue Albert-Louppe. 📞 (02) 98 67
00 43. 🔵 Jul–Aug. 🔴 Thu.

St-Pol-de-Léon ❸

Road map B1. 🚶 7,256. 🚉
🛈 Place de l'Évêché; (02) 98 69 05 69.
🕑 Tue.

THIS CITY IS THE capital of
Brittany's artichoke- and
cauliflower-growing region.
St-Pol (*Kastell Paol* in Breton)
is named after Pol-Aurélien, a
Welsh evangelizer who founded
a monastery here in the 6th
century. Soon after, it became
the see of the diocese of Léon.
The clergy's powerful influence
here is evident both from the
number of religious institutions
– monastic communities and
seminaries – and from its
religious buildings.

The 12th-century **cathedral**,
which towers over the market
square, is one of the very few
churches in Brittany still to have
its original ciborium (canopy).
This one takes the form of a
palm tree, its spreading
branches covered in putti,
vine leaves and ears of corn.
According to an ancient tradition, the ciborium is suspended
over the altar, which here is
made of black marble. Other
notable features are a 16-petal
rose window (1431), trompe-
l'œil decoration on the organ,
built by Robert Dallam, 16th-
century choir stalls with carvings
of fabulous animals, and
reliquaries containing skulls.

The most remarkable building in St-Pol is, however, the
**Chapelle Notre-Dame-du-
Kreisker**, whose belfry is the
tallest in Brittany; the climb
up its 170-step spiral staircase
is rewarded by a breathtaking
view of the bay, the fields
forming the Ceinture Dorée
(the "golden belt" that is a
prime producer of early
vegetables), and, below, the
old town of St-Pol. From this
vantage point there is a
bird's-eye view of other
jewels of St-Pol's Renaissance
architecture, such as the
Maison Prébendale (canons'
house) on Place du 4-Août-
1944, the Hôtel de Keroulas
in Rue du Collège, and the
Manoir de Kersaliou, on the
road to Roscoff, a charming
16th-century manor house.

🔒 **Chapelle
Notre-Dame-du-Kreisker**
Town centre. 📞 (02) 98 69 01 15.
🔵 mid-Jun–mid-Sep: daily. 🚩 Belfry
& chapel, Jul–Aug.

View of St-Pol-de-Léon from the belfry of Notre-Dame-du-Kreisker

THE STORY OF THE JOHNNIES

When Henri Olivier, an inhabitant of Roscoff, sailed for Plymouth in a ship loaded with onions, he was unwittingly establishing a tradition. Hundreds of agricultural workers, many of whom were very young, followed Olivier's example, going from from port to port in Wales, Scotland and England selling strings of onions to housewives, who nicknamed them Johnnies. Until the 1930s, this seasonal migration was an essential opportunity for trade, and many families who lived on the coast of Brittany began to adopt such British habits as drinking tea and playing darts. They also began to speak Breton interspersed with various English words and expressions.

Johnnies with their strings of onions

Roscoff ●

Road map B1. 🏠 *3,709*. 🚉
🚌 *from Morlaix.* 🚢 ℹ️ *46 Rue Gambetta; (02) 98 61 12 13.* 🕐 *Wed am.* 🎭 *Pardon de Ste-Barbe (mid-Jul).*

FROM THE FISH FARMS at Ste-Barbe to the seaweed boats in the old harbour, everything in Roscoff is focused on the sea. The **Église Notre-Dame-de-Kroaz-Baz** (1515), built with funds provided by merchants and privateers, has caravels carved on the exterior of its walls. The church also contains alabaster reliefs from a workshop in Nottingham, England.

Roscoff *(Rosk o Gozen* in Breton), whose port handles ferry links with Plymouth, has longstanding, if sometimes stormy, connections with Britain. Not only did Roscovites fight naval battles with the British and suffer their raids, they were also accomplices in smuggling. In the 18th century, enormous quantities of contraband tea, brandy and other liquor left Roscoff to be landed in Britain. Shipowners grew prosperous, as the fine houses that they built in Rue Armand-Rousseau, Rue Amiral-Réveillère and Place Lacaze-Duthiers clearly show.

Roscoff also has a centre of thalassotherapy (medical treatment using sea water), at Roc'h Kroum, and an **Aquarium**, where visitors can see the flora and fauna of the Breton coast.

➤ Aquarium
Place Georges-Teissier.
📞 *(02) 98 29 23 25.* 🕐 *Apr–Oct.*

Île de Batz ●

Road map B1. 🏠 *740*.
🚢 *4 motorboats run by CFTM (02 98 61 78 87) & ARMEIN (02 98 61 77 75) from Roscoff.* ℹ️ *(02) 98 61 75 70.*
🎭 *Pardon de Ste-Anne (late Jul).*

SEPARATED FROM Roscoff by a narrow channel, the Île de Batz *(Enez Vaz* in Breton) is a small island just 4 km (3 miles) long and 2 km (1 mile) wide. It has about 20 sandy beaches and creeks.

As the crossing from Roscoff's old harbour or from the groyne takes only 20 minutes, the island attracts crowds of visitors, up to 4,000 a day over certain summer weekends. Outside the high season, however, Batz is a haven of tranquility, with far fewer visitors than continue to flock to the Île de Bréhat *(see p98)*.

Most of the islanders are market gardeners. The seaweed that they spread on their small plots of land helps produce the best fruit and vegetables in the region.

From the landing stage, an alley to the right leads to the

Jardin Georges-Delaselle, the colonial garden on the Île de Batz

ruined Romanesque Chapelle de Ste-Anne and the a **Jardin George-Delaselle**, in the southeast of the island, created in 1897. Some 1,500 plants from southern Africa, California and New Zealand thrive in the island's gentle microclimate.

🌺 Jardin Georges-Delaselle
Porz an Iliz. 📞 *(02) 98 61 75 65.*
🕐 *Apr–Oct: daily pm; Oct: Sat–Sun pm.*
⬤ *Tue.* 🎨 🚫

Île de Batz, a small treeless island with sandy beaches, off Roscoff

The 16th-century covered market in Plouescat, a rare sight in Brittany

Plouescat **❻**

Road map B1. 14 km (9 miles) west
of St-Pol-de-Léon via the D10.
🏠 *3,689.* 🚆 *Brest then change at
Lesneven.* 🛈 *8 Rue de la Mairie; (02)
98 69 62 18.* 🅿 *Sat am.* 🐎 *Horse
racing in the Baie du Kernic (Aug).*

T HE TWO MOST memorable
features of Plouescat
(*Ploueskad* in Breton), a major
coastal resort and centre of
vegetable production, are its
beach, the Plage du Pors
Meur, and the 16th-century
covered market, one the few
remaining in Brittany.

ENVIRONS: Further inland are
several interesting chateaux.
Among them is the **Château
de Traonjoly**, an attractive
Renaissance manor 4 km
(3 miles) northeast of Plouescat.
The main building is flanked
by wings set at right angles to
it. A balustraded terrace
closes the fourth side, thus

The Château de Traonjoly, a
charming Renaissance manor

forming the main courtyard.
The more austere **Château
de Kerouzéré**, 9 km (5 miles)
east of Plouescat, is a fortified
castle with a machicolated
rampart walk and thick
granite walls. Built between
1425 and 1458 by Jehan de
Kerouzéré, it was twice
besieged during the Wars of
the Holy League *(see p44).*

The **Château de Maillé**,
3 km (2 miles) south of
Plouescat, is different again.
Remodelled in about 1560 in
the late Renaissance style by
the Carman-Goulaine family,
it has an elegant pavilion.

The most romantic of all
these castles is the **Château
de Kergournadeac'h**, 6 km
(4 miles) south of Plouescat,
although it is gutted. Built in
the 17th century by the
Kerc'hoënt and Rosmadec-
Molac families, it was
destroyed a century later on
the orders of its owner, the
Marchioness of Granville; it
is said that she feared that
so beautiful a residence
would keep her son away
from the royal court.

⚜ **Château de Traonjoly**
Cléder. 🎟 *(02) 98 69 40 01.*
🕑 *by arrangement.*
⚜ **Château de Kerouzéré**
Sibiril. 🎟 *(02) 98 29 96 05.*
🕑 *Jul–Aug: 2:30–5pm daily.*
⚜ **Château de Maillé**
Plounévez-Lochrist. 🎟 *(02) 98 61
44 68.* 🕑 *by arrangement.*
⚜ **Château de
Kergounadeac'h**
5 km (3 miles) south of Plouescat on
the D30. 🕑 *Jul–Aug: by arrangement;
contact the tourist office in Cléder
(02) 98 69 43 01.*

ENVIRONS: In the countryside
around Plouescat are two
jewels of religious architecture:
the parish close of Notre-Dame
de Berven, 5 km (3 miles)
northeast of Plouescat, and
the Chapelle Notre-Dame-de-
Lambader, 9 km (5 miles) to the
east of the town.

In the **Église Notre-Dame-
de-Berven**, the Virgin is
traditionally invoked to help
young children learn to walk
at an early age. The church
has a stone chancel and a
wooden rood screen with
reliefs showing the four scenes
from the Passion of Christ. A
superb late 16th-century
Virgin of Jesse of Flemish or
Rhenish inspiration stands in
a shuttered niche.

Notre-Dame-de-Lambader,
in a more bucolic setting, has
an attractive balustraded belfry
with four corner-towers like
that of Notre-Dame-du-Kreisker
in St-Pol-de-Léon *(see p120).*
The Flamboyant Gothic rood
screen (1481) is flanked by a
spiral staircase and a 16th-
century statue of the Virgin
that is carried in procession
at the Whitsun pardon.

Château
de Kerjean **❼**

See pp124–5.

Goulven **❽**

Road map B1. 23 km (14 miles) west
of St-Pol-de-Léon via the D10. 🏠 *482.*
🛈 *Pounéour-Trez; (02) 98 83 45 03.*

T HE 16TH-CENTURY church in
Goulven has an interesting
interior. It contains a small altar
with reliefs of the six miracles
performed by St Goulven,
and painted wooden panels
depicting the saint with
Count Even de Charruel, who
fought at the Battle of Thirty
(see p40). The belfry, built on
the model of that of Notre-
Dame-du Kreisker in St-Pol-
de-Léon *(see p120),* overlooks
a wide bay. At low tide the
sea retreats 5 km (3 miles),
making the bay a favourite
spot for sand yachting. It also
attracts many different species
of birds, including curlew,
teal and sandpiper.

**The Pontusval lighthouse,
near Brignogan**

ENVIRONS: Keremma, 3 km (2 miles) east of Goulven, is one of the most scenic places on the coast of the Léon. It has a long string of dunes created in 1823 by one Louis Rousseau (1787–1856). With his wife Emma, Rousseau purchased the marshy Plaine de Tréflez. Having installed a dyke and drained the land, he built over 80 farms and villas. This newly created polder (see p71) increased the agricultural land of the parish by a quarter.

Louis Rousseau's descendants, who still come to spend the summer here, have entrusted the dunes to the Conservatoire du Littoral, a conservation body.

The coastal resort of **Brignogan**, 5 km (3 miles) further north, has a beautiful white sandy beach (below the Pontusval lighthouse) and a *men marz*, 8.50 m (28 ft) high, one of a small number of Christianized menhirs.

Lesneven ❾

Road map B2. 22 km (13.5 miles) north of Brest on the D788. 🚶 6,250. 🚌 *Brest or Landerneau.* 🛈 *14 Place du Général-Le-Flô; (02) 98 83 01 47.* 🅰 *Mon.*

APART FROM some old houses – at No. 21 Place du Général-Le-Flô and No. 1 Rue du Comte-Even – the main focus of interest in Lesneven is the **Musée du Léon**, which is housed in a wing of a former Ursuline convent.

The exhibits trace the history of the parish, which, until the Revolution, was the seat of the seneschalsy (stewardship) of the Léon. The museum documents the frightful scenes of terror that occurred in the town in 1793, when many local peasants resisted conscription to the revolutionary cause and were massacred by Republican soldiers.

The museum also has an attractive display of costumes of the 1830s. They include a red silk skirt, an embroidered apron and a gold-embroidered bodice (see pp26–7), a feast-day outfit that would be worn, with a square *coiffe*, by the women of Kerlouan.

🏛 Musée du Léon
12 Rue de la Marne. ⬛ (02) 98 21 17 18. ⬛ May–Sep: Wed–Mon; Oct–Apr: Fri. ⬛

Le Folgoët ❿

Road map B2. 20 km (13 miles) north of Brest via the D788. 🚶 3,094. 🚌 *Brest.* 🎪 *Grand Pardon (8 Sep).*

THE NAME OF THIS small town means "Fool's Wood", and its origins lie in a strange story. There was once a simpleton named Salaün who lived near a spring on the edge of the wood near Lesneven, and who tirelessly repeated the words "Ave Maria". The villagers nicknamed him *fol goad* (madman of the woods). One day, in 1358, Salaün was found dead near the fountain. Some time afterwards, a lily sprouted on his neglected grave; it bore two words in golden letters: Ave Maria.

The story of this miracle was broadcast throughout the duchy. John V, Duke of Brittany, and the duchy's noble families then offered to finance the building of a collegiate chapel in Le Folgoët. This is the imposing **Basilique Notre-Dame** (1422–60). One of the most illustrious places of pilgrimage in Brittany, it has a delicate *kersanton* (granite) rood screen.

🔒 Basilique Notre-Dame
⬛ (02) 98 83 09 78. ⬛ Jul–Aug.

Basilique Notre-Dame, in Folgoët, built as the result of a miracle

Château de Kerjean ❼

Christ, in the chapel

IN 1618, LOUIS XIII described this stately residence as "one of the most beautiful in the kingdom". It was built between 1566 and 1595 by Louis Barbier, with the fortune that his uncle Hamon, a rich canon of St-Pol-de-Léon, had amassed. It has the characteristics both of a traditional Breton manor and of a French chateau. The architect in charge of the project was clearly familiar with the architectural treatises of the period and also with Renaissance decorative motifs.

He remains anonymous, but his style was to influence future buildings in the Léon, including the churches at Berven and Bodilis and the parish close at St-Thégonnec. Ransacked in 1793, Kerjean was sold to the state in 1911. It now contains a fine collection of 17th- and 18th-century furniture of the Léon.

Dormer Windows
The richly decorated dormer windows relieve the plainness of the façades.

The Kitchen
This large, 6-m (20-ft) high room has two hearths and a bread oven.

Pediment over the Central Doorways
The doorways of the stable wing are topped by pediments set with urns.

Main entrance

The wooden beams of the chapel ceiling are decorated with representations of the Four Evangelists and Mary Magdalen.

A museum of stonework is housed in one of the guardrooms.

★ Main Entrance
Elaborate ornamentation, with caryatids and volutes, crowns the main entrance.

STAR FEATURES

★ Chapel

★ Main Entrance

General view of the chateau from the grounds

VISITORS' CHECKLIST

Road map B1. St-Vougay. 32 km (20 miles) west of Morlaix via the N12 then the D30. (02) 98 69 93 69. ○ *Apr–May: Wed–Mon pm; Jun–Sep: Wed–Mon; Oct–Mar: Wed & Sun, pm; groups by arrangement.* *Exhibitions of contemporary art & workshops.*

Surviving walls of the part of the chateau destroyed by fire in 1755. It contained the armoury.

Well
The elegant canopy is based on a design provided by the architect Androuet du Cerceau in 1561.

In the projection room, a film traces the chateau's history.

★ **Chapel**
The chapel has interesting vaulting and contains some fine carved reclining figures. It is located above a room that was used as a guardroom.

BRETON FURNITURE AT KERJEAN

As well as grain bins and chests that double as seats, Kerjean contains a few pieces of furniture that are typical of the Léon. These are *gwele kloz* (box beds), some of which are decorated with the monograms of Christ and of the Virgin, and *pres lin* (linen presses), in which cloth was kept before it was taken for sale. These presses are valuable items associated with the weaving industry that brought prosperity to the region.

Linen press

Box bed

Côte des Abers ⓫

Aber Wrac'h, a popular sailing and diving centre

THREE LONG, FJORD-LIKE indentations scar the coastline between Brignogan and Le Conquet. These are known as *abers* – a Celtic word meaning "estuary". They were formed as glaciers began to melt at the end of the Ice Age, 10,000 years ago. As sea level rose, sea water flowed up the valleys far inland, where it met the fresh water of the streams. These estuaries are very characteristic of this part of Brittany, and they are strikingly different from the coastline itself. There are no gleaming mud flats along the *abers* but piles of rocks and white, sandy dunes where the local inhabitants once spread seaweed out to dry.

KEY

▬ Suggested route

═ Other roads

☆ Viewpoint

0 km   5

0 miles   3

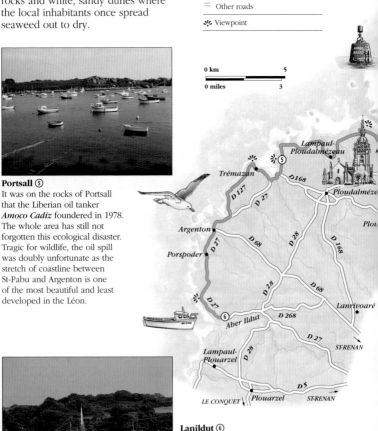

Portsall ⑤

It was on the rocks of Portsall that the Liberian oil tanker *Amoco Cadiz* foundered in 1978. The whole area has still not forgotten this ecological disaster. Tragic for wildlife, the oil spill was doubly unfortunate as the stretch of coastline between St-Pabu and Argenton is one of the most beautiful and least developed in the Léon.

Lanildut ⑥

The village (*Lannildud* in Breton) is the largest seaweed-processing port in France, handling almost 50 per cent of the national harvest. The coastline is riddled with the ovens in which laminaria, a green seaweed, was once burned to produce soda, from which iodine was in turn extracted.

MISSION PICTURES

In 1613, Michel Le Nobletz, a native of Plouguerneau and a zealous missionary, developed an ingenious method of teaching Christian doctrine and backing up the teachings of the Church. On his evangelizing missions, he showed the inhabitants of local coastal parishes pictures of biblical scenes and parables annotated in Breton. These moralizing paintings (*taolennou*) were highly successful. Used until 1950 by missionaries in other countries, they have been translated into 256 languages.

Le Miroir du Monde, by Michel Le Nobletz

TIPS FOR DRIVERS

Tour length: 56 km (35 miles).
Stopping-off places: The coast has many crêperies where you can enjoy a pancake washed down with local cider. There is also the Auberge des Abers in Lannilis (see p236). Alternatively, the oyster farms and bakeries in Lannilis will provide all you need for a picnic to enjoy on one of the small islands along the abers (but take care not to become marooned by rising tides). For a night stop, there is the Hôtel de la Baie des Anges, 350 Route des Anges, Aber Wrac'h village.

Lilia ①
At 82.5 m (270 ft) high, the Île Vierge lighthouse, opposite Lilia, is the tallest manned lighthouse in Europe. It was built in 1902 to protect shipping from treacherous rocks along a stretch of the coast known as Bro Bagan, "pagan country".

Plouguerneau ②
The Écomusée des Goémoniers de Plouguerneau is an open-air museum devoted to the local seaweed-gathering industry. Also of interest is Iliz Koz, where ruins of a church engulfed by sand in the 18th century have been uncovered.

Seaweed being carried from the coast on an *ar gravazh*, a wooden stretcher

Aber Benoît ④
A footpath runs along the south bank of the *aber*. The walk from the coast to the end of the *aber* takes three to four hours, and reveals every aspect of the estuary.

Aber Wrac'h Harbour ③
This small fishing harbour is now a very popular stopping-place for pleasure boats, and has a diving centre. It is also an ideal base for exploring Aber Wrac'h, the longest and least developed of the three *abers* that indent this stretch of the coast of Brittany.

St-Renan ⑫

Road map B2. 9 km (6 miles)
northwest of Brest via the D5.
🚶 6,749. 🚌 from Brest or
Landerneau. 🛈 22 Rue St-Yves; (02)
98 84 23 78. 🛒 Sat. 🎭 Medieval
festival, in costume (mid-Jul).

Until the early 17th century, St-Renan (*Lokournan* in Breton) was an important town with a court of justice that served no fewer than 37 parishes, including Brest. The town's few surviving granite or timber-framed houses, the finest of which are around the Église Notre-Dame-de-Liesse and on Place de la Mairie, date from this period. The weekly market held on this square is widely renowned for the local produce that is sold there.

The history of these markets and of the horse fairs for which St-Renan was also famous is illustrated in a small museum, the **Musée du Patrimoine**. Breton head-dresses, furniture, domestic objects and exhibits relating to the rich tin mines of the parish are also displayed.

The **Menhir de Kerloas** stands 4 km (2.5 miles) west of St-Renan. Erected on a crest, it is one of the tallest megaliths in Brittany. Newly married couples who wanted children would come to rub their abdomens against the stone.

🏛 Musée du Patrimoine
16 Rue St-Mathieu. 🟦 (02) 98 32
44 94. 🕐 Sep–Jun: Sat am; Jul–Aug:
daily pm; groups by arrangement.

**Timber-framed houses on
Place du Marché in St-Renan**

The fishing harbour at Le Conquet, seen from Pointe de Kermorvan

Le Conquet ⑬

Road map A2. 20 km (12 miles)
southwest of Brest via the D789.
🚶 2,159. 🚌 from Brest or
Plougonvelin. 🚢 Île Molène & Île
d'Ouessant. 🛈 Parc de Beauséjour;
(02) 98 89 11 31. 🛒 Tue am.
🎭 Blessing the sea (mid-Aug).

For many Bretons, the name of this small, busy fishing port is associated with the radio station on Pointe des Renards that, from 1948 to 2000, broadcast shipping forecasts.

Le Conquet (*Konk Leon* in Breton) has few old buildings besides those known as the *maisons anglaises* (English houses), which the English spared when they attacked the port in 1558, and the Chapelle Notre-Dame-de-Bon-Secours, which contains mission pictures invented by Michel Le Nobletz (*see p127*).

By contrast, the coast between Le Conquet and Lampaul-Plouarzel has some splendid and varied landscapes for walkers. Beyond the Presqu'île de Kermorvan, a peninsula that offers a fine view of the Île Molène and Île d'Ouessant, the long-distance footpath GR34 runs along the dunes of Blancs-Sablons, the beach at Porsmoguer and the cliffs of Le Corsen, 12 km (7.5 miles) to the north. On this rocky headland, the most westerly point in France, stands CROSS, the centre that coordinates rescue operations and monitors maritime traffic in the approaches to Ouessant.

The **Trézien lighthouse**, 2 km (1 mile) northeast, is open to visitors. It is part of the navigation aids (17 light-houses on land and 13 at sea, 85 lightships and 204 buoys) installed in the 19th century to alert seamen to the hidden dangers of the Mer d'Iroise.

🗼 Phare de Trézien
Trézien en Plouarzel. 🟦 (02) 98 89
69 46. 🎫 Jul–Aug: daily pm.

**Lobster pots stacked on the quay
at Le Conquet**

Pointe St-Mathieu ⑭

Road map A2. 22 km (14 miles)
southwest of Brest via the D789 then
the D85. 🚌 from Brest, changing at
Plougonvelin. 🛈 Trez Hir in
Plougonvelin, Boulevard de la Mer.
🟦 (02) 98 48 30 18.

The lighthouse on Pointe St-Mathieu, built in 1835, is open to visitors. Its beams project 60 km (37 miles) across the Mer d'Iroise and its many reefs, including those known as Les Vieux-Moines and La Chaussée des Pierres-Noires.

At the foot of the lighthouse are the ruins of a monastery that was probably founded in the 6th century. At nightfall, the Benedictine monks who settled in this windswept abbey in 1656 would light a fire at the top of the church tower in order to guide ships.

Ouessant Archipelago 🕒

Road map A1. 🏠 1,207.
🚢 *Motorboats run by Penn Ar Bed (02 98 80 80) & Finist'Mer (02 98 89 16 61) from Brest or Le Conquet.*
🛈 *Place de l'Église, in Lampaul; (02) 98 48 85 83.*

Pointe St-Mathieu, where Benedictine monks once settled

BATTERED BY strong westerly winds and lashed by the sea, the seven islands and dozen islets that make up the Ouessant archipelago lie some 20 km (13 miles) off the mainland. Only two of the islands – Ouessant (*Eussa* in Breton) and Molène (*Molenez*) are inhabited. Each of these islands preserves its identity and rich natural environment and wildlife.

With heathland lapped by the waves, piles of lichen-covered rocks and an exceptionally varied plant life that thrives in the moist salt air, the fascinating Ouessant archi-pelago is a world like no other. In 1989 UNESCO declared it a World Biosphere Reserve.

Shelduck on the Ile d'Ouessant

Just 1.2 km (0.75 mile) long and 800 m (875 yds) wide, the **Île Molène** can be walked around in half an hour. At first sight, the tiny bare, low-lying island's only interesting feature is a small town of 277 inhabitants huddled behind a breakwater.

But Molène deserves a closer look: it is a welcoming place in which to linger. Quirkily, it keeps English time. It offers one great advantage – no cars – and

three specialities: lobster, seaweed-smoked sausage and sea rescue. A small museum pays tribute to the courage of the islanders who, in 1896, came to the rescue of passengers on the wrecked *Drummond Castle*.

From the top of the former signal station there is a view of the islands of the archipelago: Beniget, with a population of wild rabbits, and Banneg, Balaneg and Trielen, which were inhabited until the 1950s and which are today classified nature reserves. They are home to a small colony of otters, shelducks and gulls, and 120 species of plants, including the curiously named Sabot du Petit Jésus (Baby Jesus's Slipper) and Cierge de Marie (Mary's Candle).

The largest and highest island in the archipelago, the **Île d'Ouessant** is a wild granite plateau. With its rugged landscapes, the island has been the subject of the

most fanciful legends. In ancient times, the Celts considered it to be the final gateway to the Otherworld.

A striking feature of Ouessant is that it is divided into extremely small parcels of land, of which there are about 55,000. The population is widely spread over 92 hamlets and a small town, Lampaul.

The parish church of St-Pol-Aurélien, in Lampaul, has a spire that was built with funds provided by the British crown. Queen Victoria wished to thank the islanders for their valiant actions after the *Drummond Castle* was wrecked.

Walkers who do not have time to explore the whole island should make for the northwestern part, starting with a visit to the houses in Le Niou Huella and the Musée des Phares et Balises (*see pp130–1*).

🏛 Musée Drummond Castle
Mairie, Île Molène. 📞 (02) 98 07 38 41. ⏰ *Apr–Sep: daily pm.*

The Ile d'Ouessant, the largest and highest island in the Ouessant archipelago, seen from Corz

Exploring Ouessant

W ITH ITS 45 KM (28 miles) of coastal paths and its breathtakingly beautiful landscape, Ouessant attracts some 120,000 visitors – walkers and city-dwellers in search of fresh air – every year. The island's wildness is accentuated by its location. At the point where the Atlantic Ocean and English Channel meet, Ouessant is ceaselessly washed by waves and salt spray.

The Phare du Stiff, and to the right, a radar station, on Ouessant

Lampaul, 4 km (2.5 miles) from the landing stage, is Ouessant's main town. A good place to start out from on an exploration of the island is the hamlet of Niou Huella, where the **Écomusée d'Ouessant** opened in 1968.

This open-air museum has two traditional houses which themselves make a perfect introduction to the island's history and traditions. One of the houses contains pieces of furniture made with *pense an aod* (wood from wrecks washed up on the shore) and painted in blue, white and other bright colours, the remains of the paint used to decorate the hulls of ships. The other house contains a display of tools, costumes, souvenirs of shipwrecks and objects relating to the ritual of the *proëlla*, a small wax candle symbolizing the body of a sailor lost at sea.

The **Phare de Créac'h**, which towers over the surrounding heathland, is one of the most powerful lighthouses in the world, with a beam that carries for 80 nautical miles (150 km/93 miles). Since it was inaugurated in 1863, its xenon lamps (which emit two white flashes every 10 seconds) have guided more than 100,000 vessels through one of the busiest and most hazardous shipping lanes – the infamous Ouessant strait linking the Atlantic Ocean and the English Channel.

The **Musée des Phares et Balises**, on the subject of lighthouses and buoys, has opened in the lighthouse's former generator room.

Exhibits in the Musée des Phares et Balises, in the Phare de Créac'h

KEY

▬	Main road
▬	Minor road
=	Track
--	Footpath
...	Ferry route

Île Cadoran

Île de Keller

Baie de Béninou

Phare du Stiff

Porz Yusin

Frugullou

Baie du Stiff — MOLÈNE, LAN, LE CONQUET,

Phare de Créac'h

Niou Huella

Pen ar Lan

Pha Men

Pointe de Créac'h

Loqueltas

D 81

Lampaul

D 181

Porz ar Lan

Pointe de Pern

Corz

Porsguen

Phare de Nividic

Baie de Lampaul

Feunteun Vélen

Baie de Penn ar Roc'h

MOLÈNE, LE CONQUET, BREST

Phare de Kéréon

0 km 2

0 mile 1

Phare de la Jument

OUESSANT'S SHEEP

Out of the high season, Ouessant's sheep graze freely on the island's salty pastures. Then, on the first Wednesday in February, the day of Porzgwenn's traditional fair, they are collected by their owners. Although sheep-rearing has always been an important activity on Ouessant, the local breed, which is related to the ancient wild sheep of Asia Minor, has almost disappeared from the island. This small, hardy black sheep is being rivalled by the white-fleeced merino.

One of Ouessant's black sheep

The Phare du Stiff, built by Vauban in 1695

From the Musée des Phares et Balises, a coast path runs between pebble ridges and low dry-stone walls, leading to the **Pointe de Pern**, the island's most westerly point. Beyond the tip of this spectacular promontory, with rocks eroded into strange and fantastic shapes, rises the Phare de Nividic, bathed in spray.

The island's northern coast has been colonized by sea birds, including herring gulls, common gulls, puffins, pied oystercatchers and kittiwakes. Further east, grey seals can be seen in the narrow inlets of the Presqu'île de Cadoran. They can also sometimes be seen basking in the sun on rocks at Toull Auroz and Beninou.

The path continues towards the **Phare du Stiff**, which stands on the island's highest point (65m/213 ft). Built by Vauban in 1695, it is one of the oldest lighthouses in France. From here, in clear conditions, it is possible to see the whole archipelago, the west coast of the Léon and the Île de Sein. Below nestles Stiff harbour, where the *Enez Eussa*, the *Fromveur* and other vessels from the mainland tie up each day.

The **Presqu'île de Pen ar Lan**, southeast of Stiff, is worth a visit primarily for its small sandy inlet, which attracts fewer visitors than Corz, the beach at Lampaul, and for its cromlech, dating from 2,000 BC. This is an elliptical arrangement of menhirs that probably served astronomical purposes.

These are not the only signs of prehistoric habitation on Ouessant. At the foot of the Colline St-Michel, in Mez Notariou, archaeologists have discovered fragments of pottery and pieces of amphora that show that Ouessant was an early and important centre of trade.

Out at sea opposite Porz ar Lan is the Phare de Kéréon, built in 1907 in extremely difficult conditions. Another lighthouse, the Phare de la Jument, dating from 1904, protects shipping from the dangerous rocks that extend the **Presqu'île de Feunteun Velen**, to the southwest.

Écomusée d'Ouessant
Niou Huella. **C** *(02) 98 48 86 37.*
☐ *Jun–Sep: daily.* ✍

🏛 Musée des Phares et Balises
Créac'h. **C** *(02) 98 48 80 70.*
☐ *May–Sep: daily.* ✍

The rocky Pointe du Créac'h, on the southwest side of Ouessant

Brest ⓰

THE SECOND-LARGEST TOWN in Brittany after Rennes, Brest has always played a leading military role. From the early days of the Roman Empire, legionnaires had seen the advantage of establishing a secure base on the rocky spur here, overlooking a river, the Penfeld, and perfectly protected by a peninsula, the Presqu'île de Crozon. At the instigation of Richelieu, Colbert and Vauban, who throughout the 17th century worked to transform this natural harbour into the kingdom's foremost naval base, life in the city revolved around the naval dockyard. Brest remained a major shipyard until World War II. After 165 bombing raids and 43 days of siege, the conflict reduced Brest to rubble.

Navy vessel and pleasure craft in the roadstead at Brest

Exploring Brest

A city of rigidly straight streets, regimented residential blocks and lifeless districts, Brest, which was entirely rebuilt after World War II, cannot be described as a prime tourist destination. Yet, visitors who take the trouble to explore it will be rewarded.

Although there are no old buildings here, the town has a pervading and stimulating naval atmosphere. There are dry docks, warships in the naval dockyard, vessels in the roadstead (sheltered anchorage), where there is a viewing platform, and everywhere the cry of seagulls. Of special interest are the opportunity to experience the undersea world at Océanopolis (*see p135*) and, every four years, the great international gathering of tall ships in the harbour.

Rue de Siam, Brest's lively commercial thoroughfare

🚇 Rue de Siam

The name of this lively commercial thoroughfare commemorates the arrival in Brest of ambassadors sent by the king of Siam to the court of Louis XIV in 1686.

More prosaically, Rue de Siam is a perfect example of 1950s town planning. It has a very uniform appearance. Here, as in the entire district between the Pont de Recouvrance and the town hall, large four-storey residential buildings are arranged symmetrically on a strictly rectilinear axis. However, the recent installation of seven black fountains by the Hungarian sculptor Marta Pan has given the Rue de Siam a noticeable lift.

🔒 Église St-Louis

Place St-Louis, Rue de Lyon.
🕐 *8 Jul–5 Aug: daily.* 📷 ♿

Built between 1953 and 1958 on the site of the original church of St-Louis, which was destroyed in 1944, this place of worship is the largest of all those built in France in the post-war period.

The materials used – yellow stone from Logonna-Daoulas and reinforced concrete – are a clear departure from Breton architectural traditions, and they produce an admirable effect. The bold lines and restrained decoration of the interior are no less impressive.

The church has two notable features: stained-glass windows on the west front, by Paul Bony, and a lectern in the shape of an eagle, one of the very few pieces that were salvaged from the original church.

🚇 Quartier St-Martin

The former outlying district of St-Martin, which became part of Brest in 1861, is one of the few surviving quarters of the old town. It is also one of the most convivial, judging by the cafés and Irish pubs here, which attract many students from the Université de Bretagne Occidentale.

Retired people and idle onlookers also gather here, to stroll in the market or play boules on Place Guérin, between the school and the Église St-Martin (1875), two buildings that survived the wartime bombings.

The Neo-Romanesque-Gothic church in the Quartier St-Martin

La Mer Jaune, by Georges Lacombe, Musée des Beaux-Arts

VISITORS' CHECKLIST

Road map B2. ⚑ *153,099.*
✈ *Brest-Guipavas, 9 km (5.5
miles) from the town centre.*
🚇 *Place du 19ᵉ-R-I.* 🚌 *Place du
19ᵉ-R-I.* 🛈 *Place de la Liberté;
(02) 98 44 24 96.* 🛒 *Mon–Sat in
Halles St-Martin.* 🎭 *Fête
Internationale de la Mer et des
Marins (mid-Jul; every four
years); Jeudis du Port Jul–Aug;
Festival International du Film
Court (Nov); Festival du Conte
(late Nov).*
🌐 *www.mairie-brest.fr*

🏛 Musée des Beaux-Arts

24 Rue Traverse. 📞 *(02) 98 00 87 96.*
⏱ *Wed–Mon.* 🔴 *Public holidays.*
🎫 *Oct–May.* 📷

The original collection held by this museum was quite literally annihilated by bombing in 1941. However, thanks to the efforts of the curator, the collection has been rebuilt, now consisting of around 300 works of art.

There is a fine collection of Baroque paintings on the first floor, where Guerchin's *Judith and Holophernes* is the centrepiece, and an interesting assemblage of paintings by members of the Pont-Aven School *(see p169)* on the ground floor. Among the most notable works in the collection are *Vue du Port de Brest* by Louis-Nicolas Van Blarenberghe, a Dutch artist who painted siege and battle scenes for Louis XV. Although the artist took liberties with his depiction of the course of the Penfeld river, this painting is of great documentary value as it shows in minute detail the work carried out by convicts and carpenters in the naval dockyards of Brest in 1774.

BREST CITY CENTRE

Cours Dajot ④
Église St-Louis ②
Musée de la Marine ⑥
Musée des Beaux-Arts ③
Musée de la Tour Tanguy ⑨
Naval Dockyard ⑦
Quartier de Recouvrance ⑧
Quartier St-Martin ⑤
Rue de Siam ①

0 m   200
0 yards   200

KEY

🚊 Railway station
⛴ Ferry port
🚌 Bus station
🛈 Tourist information
⊠ Post office

🏛 Cours Dajot

This promenade on the southern part of the town walls was built by convicts in 1769, to a plan by Dajot, a pupil of Vauban. It offers a panoramic view of the commercial port, built in 1860, and of Brest's famous roadstead, which has long given it a strategic and military advantage. Like a huge marine amphitheatre, the roadstead covers 150 sq km (60 sq miles) between the Elorn estuary and the Pointe des Espagnols, with the Île Longue, where there is a nuclear submarine base, in the background.

Of passing interest is the 1900s-style Maison Crosnier, on the corner of Rue Traverse. This is the only house on Cours Dajot that was not destroyed during the war.

Forteresse de Brest, built in the 15th and 16th centuries

🏛 Musée de la Marine

Château de Brest. 📞 *(02) 98 22 12 39.* ⭘ *daily.* ⬤ *15 Nov–15 Dec.* 📷 *Apr–Sep.* 🕿

This great fortress on the Penfeld estuary was built in the 15th and 16th centuries. It was a lynchpin in the duchy of Brittany's defences and, for many years, the English had designs on it. It withstood many attacks, including assaults by the Holy League in 1592 and the Bonnets Rouges in 1675, and was later used as barracks and as a prison.

The castle now houses the naval prefecture as

well as a small naval museum. The keep, built by Vauban in 1683, contains the oldest exhibits, which include ship models, lanterns, pieces salvaged from wrecks and wooden figureheads carved in the workshops of the naval dockyard. The modern collections, with navigational instruments, a German mini-submarine, and other exhibits, are displayed in the gatehouse towers.

From the top of the keep there is a fine view of the Quartier de Recouvrance and the Penfeld river.

🏛 Quartier de Recouvrance

The Penfeld river, like a fjord, separates the town centre from the Quartier de Recouvrance. The river is spanned by the Pont de Recouvrance, a vertical-lift bridge built in 1954. Its 525-tonne roadway can be raised 26 m (85 ft) in less than three minutes.

The Quartier de Recouvrance used to be a run-down district, as can be seen from the derelict houses in Rue de St-Malo. Before World War II, it was populated by the families of fishermen and of naval dock-yard workers. Though slightly insalubrious, with illegal bars and inebriated sailors, the quarter inspired the writers Mac Orlan and Jean Genet (in *Querelle de Brest*).

The 18th-century Maison de la Fontaine, at No. 18 Rue de l'Église, is one of the oldest houses in Brest. It has a fountain dating from 1761 and a 15th-century medieval granite cross.

Crew hoisting sails in the rigging of a tallship

🏛 Musée du Vieux Brest

Tour Tanguy. 📞 *(02) 98 00 88 60.* ⭘ *Summer: daily; winter: Wed–Thu & Sat–Sun pm.* 📷 *Groups only, by arrangement.*

A fuller picture of the Quartier de Recouvrance as it was in the past, with its dives and its shady streets, can be gained through a visit to the Musée du Vieux Brest, in the Tour Tanguy.

Built in the 14th century, the Tour de la Motte-Tanguy was once owned by the powerful Chastel family. In 1964, the tower was converted into a museum devoted to historic Brest.

By means of dioramas, documents and other exhibits, the museum illustrates such major events in the town's history as the naval battle fought by Hervé de Portzmoguer in 1512, the arrival of ambassadors from Siam in 1686, and a visit by Napoleon III in 1858.

The Pont de Recouvrance, a vertical-lift bridge across the Penfeld river

LE TOUR DU MONDE

The bar Le Tour du Monde

The regular haunt of the famous yachtsman Olivier de Kersauson *(see p25)*, this bar is located above the port authority building. Le Tour du Monde (Round the World) was opened in 1997, the year that Kersauson won the Jules Verne round-the-world yachting trophy in his trimaran *Port-Elec*. The yacht is moored near the bar. When he is not at sea, the Admiral, as Kersauson is affectionately known, can often be seen in this wood-panelled bar, which is filled with all manner of souvenirs of his yachting exploits.

⚓ Naval Dockyard

Route de la Corniche. [(02) 98 22 11 78. ◯ Easter, 15 Jun–15 Sep: daily. ✗ Admission restricted to nationals of countries that are accessors to the Schengen Convention (the UK is not). Identification compulsory.

Brest's naval dockyard (Arsenal) was established at the instigation of Cardinal Richelieu. Work began in 1631, and workshops, dry docks and rope-works appeared on the banks of the Penfeld. It was here also that

Rope-works on the banks of the Penfeld

workmen and convicts fitted out ocean-going vessels and provided the labour for further installations. Between 1749 and 1858, 70,000 convicts worked here. Replaced by the penal settlement in Cayenne, French Guiana, the convict centre in Brest closed in 1858.

The guided tour of the naval dockyard takes in the installations that were built at the mouth of the estuary after 1889. They include the naval college, which opened in 1935, the former submarine

base and the quays, where the most advanced vessels of the French navy are tied up. The reorganization of the French navy and of its dockyards threatens the future of Brest, which is focused on naval defence.

🌿 Conservatoire Botanique

52 Allée du Bot. [(02) 98 41 88 95. **Park:** ◯ daily. **Greenhouses**: ◯ Jul–Sep: Sun–Thu, pm; out of season: admittance at 4:30pm Sun. ♿ ⬛ for groups, by arrangement.

This, one of eight similar institutes established in France, is the first to have seriously addressed the issue of saving endangered species of plants from extinction.

Specializing in the plants of the Armorican massif and of the former French colonies (including Madagascar, Martinique and Mauritius), the institute has four greenhouses, in each of which different climatactic zones have been re-created.

A Noah's Ark of the plant kingdom, the institute has been able to reintroduce certain species into their original environment. One such is loosestrife, which became extinct in Spain's Balearic Islands in about 1925.

The park, covering 22 ha (54 acres), is laid out in the little valley of the Stangalar, just north of the greenhouses. It is a paradise for both nature-lovers and joggers.

Part of the tropical pavilion at Océanopolis

🐟 Océanopolis

Moulin-Blanc Marina. [(02) 98 34 40 40. ◯ Summer: daily. ◯ Oct–Apr: Mon & two weeks in Jan. ♿ ⬛ ⬛

A day is hardly long enough to explore Océanopolis. Three pavilions re-create polar, temperate and tropical marine conditions. With a spectacular presentation and state-of-the-art technology, the centre is simultaneously educational, fascinating and entertaining.

Visitors can ride in a glass-sided lift that descends through a pod of sharks, or step into a bathyscaph (submersible vessel) to float through leathery fronds of seaweed. In environments ranging from from ice floes to coral reefs, 1,000 species of sea creatures can be observed in elaborate aquariums with viewing tunnels running through them. There is also a colony of penguins.

The Tour Tanguy, home to the Musée du Vieux Brest

Plougastel-Daoulas ⑰

Road map B2. 👥 *11,200.* 🚌 *from Brest.* ℹ️ *Place du Calvaire; (02) 98 40 34 98.* 🍴 *Thu am.* 🎭 *Fête des Fraises (second Sun in Jun); Pardon de la Fontaine-Blanche (15 Aug).*

L YING BETWEEN the Elorn and Daoulas rivers, the Plougastel peninsula is a world apart. Plougastel-Daoulas (*Plougastell-Daoulaz* in Breton) itself only came under the administration of Brest in 1930.

The special character of this part of Brittany is well illustrated by the collections in the **Musée de la Fraise et du Patrimoine Local**. These focus on local culture (furniture, ceremonial dress and the tradition of *pain des âmes*, special loaves eaten on All Soul's Day) and on the history of strawberry-growing in the area, from the time that the first plants were brought back from Chile by Amédée-François Frézier in 1712 to the conquest of the British market in the early 20th century.

In 1602, the inhabitants built an elaborate calvary to thank God for the passing of an epidemic of the plague. Similar to that at Guimiliau *(see p138)*, it has 180 figures depicting scenes from the life of Christ.

Poster, Musée de la Fraise

🏛 **Musée de la Fraise et du Patrimoine Local**
Rue Louis-Nicolle. 📞 *(02) 98 40 21 18.* 🕐 *Mon–Fri; Sat–Sun pm.* ⚫ *Winter: public hols, Sat & Sun.* 🅿️ *All year, by arrangement.* 📷 ♿

The Abbaye de Daoulas, founded in 1167 by Augustinians

Daoulas ⑱

Road map B2. 👥 *1,866.* 🚌 *From Brest.* ℹ️ *Place du Valy; (02) 98 25 84 44.* 🍴 *Sun am.*

T HE TOWN OF Daoulas (*Daoulaz* in Breton) developed thanks to the linen-weaving and kaolin-extraction industries.

The **abbey** here was founded in 1167 by Augustinian canons. When they left, in 1984, the *département* of the Finistère purchased the buildings, which had been abandoned in the 19th century. They have been converted into a cultural centre and exhibition space devoted to the world's great civilizations.

Of particular interest are the remains of the cloisters, with 32 arcades and a monolithic fountain, decorated with masks and geometric motifs such as stars, guilloche patterns, wheels and crosses.

The monastic tradition of growing medicinal herbs continues in a garden near the cloisters that contains 300 species native to Brittany, Asia, Africa and Oceania. At the far end of the abbey grounds is Notre-Dame-des-Fontaines, a charming oratory of 1550.

⛪ **Abbaye de Daoulas**
21 Rue de l'Église. 📞 *(02) 98 25 84 39.* 🕐 *May–Nov: daily.* 📷

Landerneau ⑲

Road map B2. 👥 *15,035.* ℹ️ *Pont de Rohan; (02) 98 85 13 09.* 🚉 *Place François-Mitterrand.* 🚌 *Quai Barthélemy-Kerros.* 🍴 *Tue & Fri, am, Sat.* 🎭 *Festival Kann al Loar (Jul); Festival Lunatic (mid-Aug).*

O NE OF THE MOST striking features of Landerneau (*Landerne* in Breton) is the **Pont de Rohan**, built in 1510 and one of the few surviving habitable bridges in Europe.

The historic Pont de Rohan in Landerneau, a bridge all but hidden by the buildings on it

The houses and shops of metalworkers, millers and cloth merchants were built on piles or, like the superb house of the magistrate Gillart (1639), built directly on the riverbed.

Although the Elorn, which flows through the town, now carries hardly any river traffic, Landerneau was for centuries a busy port. All kinds of goods bound for the naval dockyard in Brest, as well as linen cloth, passed through Landerneau.

Most of the old houses beside the river date from this age of prosperity (1660–1720). Built in yellow stone from Logonna, they have dormer windows, pepperpot roofs and ornate cornices. Every Wednesday throughout the summer, the tourist office here organizes an architectural walk through the town.

Of particular interest on the south bank are the old Auberge de Notre-Dame-de-Rumengol, at No. 5 Rue St-Thomas, and the houses at Nos. 11, 13 and 15 Rue Rolland. On the north bank is the Maison de la Sénéchaussée at No. 9 Place du Général-de-Gaulle, with one façade of dressed stone and another clad in slates; the residence of the ship-owner Mazurié de Keroualin at No. 26 Quai de Léon; the Ostaleri an Dihuner (Inn of the Alarm Clock) at No. 18 Rue du Chanoine-Kerbrat; and the house of the merchant Arnaud Duthoya, at Nos. 3–5 Rue du Commerce.

La Roche-Maurice ⑳

Road map B2. 4 km (3 miles) northeast of Landerneau via the D712. 🏠 *1,740.* 🚉 *Landerneau.* 🛈 *Ossuary; (02) 98 20 43 57.* 🎭 *Pardon de Pont-Christ (Aug).*

AS IN MANY other small towns and villages in the Léon, the **church** here is an architectural gem. The belfry, which has two superimposed bell chambers, is decorated with Gothic spires, gargoyles and Renaissance lanterns.

Rood screen figure, La Roche-Maurice

Inside, the wooden ceiling features angels on a blue background, while the rood screen is striking for its skilled craftsmanship and decoration of fauns and gorgons, apostles and saints. Other notable features are the stained-glass window of the Passion of Christ (1539) by Laurent Sodec, of Quimper, and, above the stoup at the ossuary (1639), an *Ankou* (skeletal figure) with his spear and his motto "Je vous tue tous" ("I kill you all").

The **castle** above the town was one of the main residences of the viscounts of Léon. It passed into the ownership of the dukes of Rohan, who bequeathed it to the parish in 1985. The view from the keep stretches as far as the Elorn estuary.

La Martyre ㉑

Road map B2. 7 km (4 miles) east of Landerneau via the D35. 🏠 *608.* 🛈 *Town centre; (02) 98 25 13 19.* 🚉 *Landerneau.* 🎭 *Pardon de St-Salomon (Jul).*

THIS FORTIFIED CLOSE was begun in the 9th century. The house on the left of the entrance was once the look-out post from which the borders of the medieval kingdom, then duchy, of Cornouaille were watched.

The annual fair that was held here would draw crowds of merchants from England, Holland and Touraine, who came to deal in linen cloth, livestock and horses. As it levied taxes on every trans-action that took place, the parish grew rich and could thus afford to commission the best workshops to decorate the close and the church.

Everything about the church, dedicated to St Salomon, is, indeed, remarkable: from the 16th-century door and rampart walk, to the tympanum over the south porch, the beams over the north aisle and the stained-glass window of the Crucifixion. Over the ossuary, two angels hold banners that are inscribed in Breton with words that, loosely translated, read: "Death, judgment, freezing hell. Think on that and fear it. Foolish is he who does not know that he must die."

Bodilis ㉒

Road map B2. 21 km (13 miles) northeast of Landerneau via the D770, the N12 and the D30. 🏠 *1,222.* 🛈 *Jul–Aug; (02) 98 68 07 01.*

THE 16TH-CENTURY church in Bodilis (*Bodiliz* in Breton) is another jewel of religious architecture in Haut-Léon. It has a superb Renaissance porch (1585–1601), which the stoneworkers of Kerjean decorated with statues of the 12 apostles. The interior has a painted wooden ceiling, a Baroque high altar and beams richly decorated with scenes of labour and, somewhat unexpectedly, of drunkenness: a man is shown drinking from a barrel while worms infest a skull.

The fortified close of La Martyre, built by Hervé VII of Léon

The church in St-Thégonnec, once one of the richest in Léon

Lampaul-Guimiliau 23

Road map B2. 3 km (2 miles) west of Guimiliau. 🏘 2,037. 🚇 Landivisiau. 🛈 14 Avenue Foch, Landivisiau; (02) 98 68 33 33.

THE PARISH CLOSE at Lampaul (*Lambaol* in Breton) was built in stages, starting with the porch in 1533 and ending with the sacristy in 1679. Masterpieces here are six stunning altarpieces and an *Entombment of Christ* by Antoine Chavagnac, a sculptor to the French Navy in Brest.

Guimiliau 24

Road map B2. 🏘 791. 🚇 Landivisiau. 🛈 14 Avenue Foch, Landivisiau; (02) 98 68 33 33.

THE CALVARY IN the parish close at Guimiliau (*Gwimilio* in Breton) dates from 1588. Almost

200 figures in amusing or pathetic attitudes make up an earthy and unusual depiction of the life of Christ.

Inside the church is an organ built by Thomas Dallam, and an altarpiece of St Joseph in the Laval style. The baptismal fonts, dating from 1675, are graced by elegant spiral columns.

St-Thégonnec 25

Road map C2. 13 km (8 miles) south of Morlaix via the D769. 🏘 2,139. 🚇 Morlaix. 🛈 Park ar Iliz; (02) 98 79 69 26/80 (Jul–Aug).

THE PORCH OF the **parish close** here is in a triumphal and ostentatious style that perfectly reflects the opulence that St-Thégonnec (*Sant Tegoneg* in Breton) enjoyed during the Renaissance, when it was one of the richest parishes in the Léon.

Although the church was severely damaged by fire in 1988, some 16th- and 17th-century masterpieces survive. Among them is a priest's chair decorated with medallions and putti, and with armrests in the shape of dolphins' heads. There is also a Rosary altarpiece; a shuttered niche with the Tree of Jesse; a pulpit, which was originally gilded; and an organ built by Thomas Dallam.

The ossuary contains a beautiful painted wood *Emtombment of Christ* dating from 1702. Like the triumphal porch, the architecture of the ossuary is exuberant, with bell-turrets, windows and slender columns.

The altarpiece, set at the back of the altar, provides a focal point for prayer. This one depicts St Joseph.

GUIMILIAU PARISH CLOSE

This is a typical parish close, with three essential features: an entrance framed by an arch or a monumental gateway, a calvary with figures depicting biblical scenes, and an ossuary attached to the church.

The cemetery, where members of the small parish community were buried.

Calvaries were built for the elevation of the souls of believers towards God, but they also provide an insight into daily life in the past.

The Emtombment of Christ, part of the calvary at Lampaul-Guimiliau

Parish Closes

THE PHENOMENON OF Brittany's parish closes *(enclos paroissiaux)*, of which there are almost 70 in Lower Brittany, is closely connected to the rise of the linen industry in the 16th and 17th centuries. The most numerous and elaborate parish closes are those in the Élorn valley. Here, encouraged by evangelizing missions, the religious fervour of the faithful and the generosity of the rich *juloded* (local linen merchants), parishes would virtually rival one another in their efforts to build the finest close. Centred around cemeteries, these remarkable religious complexes consist of a church, an ossuary, a calvary and a triumphal entrance, with Baroque altarpieces and sculptures carved in lacelike detail.

In the ossuary, the bones of the deceased exhumed from the cemetery would be stored. The ossuary was considered a bridge between the living and the dead.

The triumphal entrance was the gateway through which the faithful entered the close. It was intended to prefigure the entry of the righteous into the kingdom of heaven.

Church

Calvary

Funeral chapel

Field of the Dead

South porch

Triumphal arch

The funeral chapel (that at Sizun is shown here) was used as a repository for bones when there was no more room in the church. The dead were originally buried beneath the floor of the church.

The Blindfolded Christ, *with two guards in 17th-century clothes, was carved by Roland Doré. The sculpture is from the calvary at St-Thégonnec.*

The Moulin du Chaos, at the start of Huelgoat's impressive rocks

Huelgoat ㉖

Road map C2. ☐ *Morlaix*. ᚛ *1,748.* ᚛ *Moulin du Chaos; (02) 98 99 72 32.* ᚛ *Thu.*

A SHINING RIVER, a mass of strangely shaped fallen rocks, great moss-covered trees and menhirs make Huelgoat (High Wood) a mysterious and atmospheric place around which popular imagination has woven many legends.

From the Moulin du Chaos, marked footpaths link various places of interest in the area around Huelgoat, which is now part of the Parc Naturel Régional d'Armorique *(see right)*. The river, which from 1750 to 1867 worked the wheels of a lead mine, winds between the Grotte du Diable (Devil's Cave), the first stop on the Chemin de l'Enfer (Path to Hell) of legend, and the famous Roche Tremblante (Shaking Rock), a 100-tonne stone that can be made to rock back and forth simply by applying pressure to it in the right place.

Keen walkers will want to continue to the Mare aux Sangliers (Wild Boars' Pond) and the Camp d'Artus, a Gaulish *oppidum* (fortified settlement), where the fabulous treasure of King Arthur *(see p63)*, is said to lie.

The **Jardin de l'Argoat** and the **Arboretum du Poërop** contain various plants and trees in danger of extinction, including 66 species of hydrangea and 128 of magnolia and orchards with ancient varieties of fruit trees.

♣ **Arboretum du Poërop and Jardin de l'Argoat**
55 Rue des Cieux. ☐ *(02) 98 99 95 90.* ☐ *May–Sep: daily.*

Tour of the Monts d'Arrée ㉗

THE HILLY AREA between Léon and Cornouaille can hardly be described as mountainous, as nowhere does it exceed an altitude of 384 m (1,260 ft). Nevertheless, the Monts d'Arrée, covering 60,000 ha (148, 000 acres), are the spine of Finistère. With fewer than 40 inhabitants per square kilometre (103 per square mile), it is sparsely populated. It contains spectacular landscapes, with huge areas of heath, hilly crests and peat bogs, level expanses of granite, ubiquitous lichens and rare species of ferns. Rich in legends and tales of sorcery, this arid region becomes even more extraordinary when the marshy Yeun Elez depression is shrouded in mist. Threatened by forest fires, encroaching wasteland and desertification, it is a fragile environment. The Parc Naturel Régional d'Armorique is working to protect its plant life and to ensure that the local economy remains viable.

KEY

▭ Suggested route

＝ Other roads

❄ Viewpoint

LANDIVISIAU, LANDERNEAU

LE FAOU

④

⑤

D 18

D 764

D 18

Élorn

D 30

Barrage du Drenr

St-Cadou

D 342

D 42

D 21

D 121

LE FAOU

PONT-DE-BUIS-LÈS-QUIMERC'H

Sizun ④
Renowned for its salmon-rich rivers, Sizun is also worth a visit for its church, with a fine organ case by Thomas Dallam and a 17th-century high altar with dramatic décor. The triumphal entrance leads to the ossuary, which is decorated with apostles and which contains a small museum of religious art.

Maison Cornec ③
This historic farm just outside the small town of St-Rivoal is a prime example of rural architecture. It also offers an excellent insight into country life in Brittany in the 18th century.

Moulin de Kerhouat ⑤
Built in 1610 and in use until 1942, the Moulin de Kerhouat (High Mill) has been converted into an open-air museum of the daily life and work of local millers.

TIPS FOR VISITORS

Tour length: 77 km (48 miles).
Stopping-off places: There are good crêperies in Huelgoat and Sizun. Gîtes and chambres d'hôte (rooms in private houses) can be rented in Botmeur, Brasparts, Brennilis and Commana. In St-Rival, visitors may sample and purchase local delicacies.

Commana ⑥
The parish church here contains two painted wooden altarpieces, one depicting St Anne and the other, of 1682, Christ displaying his wounds.

Brennilis ⑦
A village strongly associated with legends, Brennilis is located near a strange peat bog – the Yeun Elez – which reputedly marks the entrance to Hell. The church has two 16th-century altars.

St-Herbot ①
The chapel, dedicated to St Herbot, patron saint of livestock, has a chancel and two stone tables on which people placed offerings when requesting his aid.

Montagne St-Michel ②
A stony track leads to the summit of this bare mountain, 380 m (1,247 ft) high, from which there is a panoramic view of one of the wildest areas of Brittany.

SOUTHERN FINISTÈRE

THIS PART OF BRITTANY *has wild and rugged coastline but also some very sheltered beaches, and is swept by strong winds while also enjoying a temperate climate. The outstanding cultural heritage of southern Finistère is amply evident in Quimper, the capital city, and during the Festival de Cornouaille that is held here.*

Corresponding to the historic kingdom of Cornouaille, southern Finistère is bordered to the north by the Monts d'Arrée and the Presqu'île de Crozon, and to the east by the Montagnes Noires. Like northern Finistère, to the north, and the Morbihan, to the southeast, the region has an indented coastline with impressive promontories, wide bays and sheltered coves.

The Pointe du Van and Pointe du Raz, two promontories at the western extremity of southern Finistère, are among the region's wildest and most beautiful places. It is here, on the edge of the Atlantic, that the four of the largest inshore and deep-sea fishing ports in Brittany – Concarneau, Douarnenez, Le Guilvinec and Camaret – have developed.

Inland, southern Finistère is an area of unspoiled countryside, with lush woods and narrow rivers running through deep valleys where unexpectedly splendid chapels, many with splendid altarpieces and calvaries, can be discovered.

It is also in southern Finistère, together with the Morbihan, that the spirit of ancient, mythical, pre-Christian Brittany most tangibly lives on. The Breton spirit is suffused with the otherworldly, with ancient pagan ideas and rituals that have given birth to legends surrounding countless saints. Armorica is also the land of the Knights of the Round Table and the companions of King Arthur, whose legends enliven a part of this region's enthralling and romantic history.

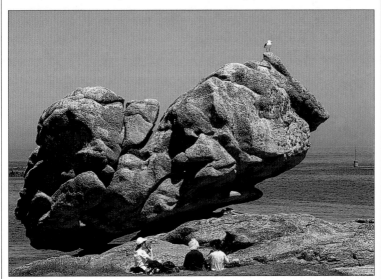

Picnicking at the foot of a rock on the Île de Sein

◁ **The triumphal entrance to the parish close at Argol, built in 1659**

Exploring Southern Finistère

THE NORTHWESTERN PART of this region is made up of the Parc Naturel Régional d'Armorique, which consists of a small section of the Montagnes Noires and the whole Presqu'île de Crozon. The Châteaulin basin, in the centre of Finistère Sud, is drained by the Aulne river. Further south, at the confluence of the Steir and the Odet, is Quimper, Cornouaille's administrative and cultural capital.

The region has two major towns: Douarnenez, in the west, a seafaring town built around an extensive bay, and the fortified town of Concarneau in the south.

With a mainly southern orientation, southern Finistère encourages a relaxed way of life. Sheltered coastal resorts, like Morgat, contrast strongly with the rugged Ménez-Hom and Pointe du Raz.

The Glénan archipelago, the Île Tristan and Île de Sein each offer superb ports of call for yachtsmen and much that will interest divers.

POINTE
DES ESPAGNOLS
③

CAMARET
POINTE   ④
DE PEN-HIR ⑤   D 355   CROZON   D 791   D 60
D 8   ②
D 255   ⑥ MORGAT   D 887

LANDÉVENNEC ①

ARGOL
MÉNEZ-

POINTE
DU VAN
BAIE ⑬
DES
TRÉPASSÉS
⑮
ÎLE DE SEIN   ⑭
POINTE
DU RAZ   CHAPELLE
ST-TUGEN

RÉSERVE
DU CAP SIZUN
⑫
D 7

DOUARNENEZ
⑪

LOCRON

D 765

D 143

D 784

⑯ AUDIERNE

D 2

D 784

KEY

▰▰	Motorway
▰▰	Main road
▰▰	Minor road

0 km   10
0 miles   10

PONT-
L'ABBÉ
NOTRE-DAME- ⑰
DE-TRONOËN   D 57   ㉒
POINTE DE LA TORCHE ●   MANOIR
DE KÉRAZAN
PENMARC'H ⑱   D 53 LOC
⑲
PHARE D'ECKMÜHL   LE GUILVINEC

The wide Plage de Veryach at Camaret

GETTING AROUND

From Paris, Quimper can be reached in four hours by TGV (high-speed train). The principal roads linking Quimper and Nantes and Quimper and Rennes are, respectively, the N165 motorway in the north, and the N164, which follows the course of the Aulne river, then leads to Châteaulin and the Presqu'île de Crozon via the D791. Quimper-Cornouaille, the regional airport, is located at Pluguffan, 10 km (6 miles) from Quimper via the D785.

SIGHTS AT A GLANCE

The picturesque mill at Pont Aven

The Pointe du Van, where the cliffs are 65 m (210 ft) high

SEE ALSO

Ruins of the Abbaye de Landévennec, founded in the 5th century

Landévennec ❶

Road map B2. 18 km (11 miles) south of Crozon via the D791 and the D60. 🏠 370. 🚌 Brest or Quimper, then taxi or bus. 🚌 ℹ️ (02) 98 27 78 46 (summer); (02) 98 27 72 65 (winter).

IN THE FIFTH CENTURY, where Landévennec (*Landevenneg* in Breton) now stands, St Guénolé founded an abbey . Destroyed by the Normans in 913, rebuilt in the 13th century, pillaged by the English in the 16th and dissolved during the Revolution, the abbey remained an important centre of Christianity despite these vissicitudes.

Among the ruins of this fine example of Romanesque architecture are a 16th-century statue of St Guénolé and a tomb that is said to be that of Gradlon, legendary king of Cornouaille. The capitals and the bases of the abbey's columns are well preserved, and they bear Celtic patterns and animal motifs.

The **Musée de l'Ancienne Abbaye** presents the history of this religious centre in the context of Christianity in Brittany. Artifacts, such as manuscripts and statues, that were discovered during archaeological excavations here, are also on display.

The **Corniche de Térénez**, leading towards Le Faou, follows the Aulne estuary and leads to a viewpoint offering a splendid panorama of the meandering river and a view of the French navy's scrapyard.

🏛 **Musée de l'Ancienne Abbaye**
🎫 (02) 98 27 35 90. ◯ all year (groups by arrangement). 🏷

Crozon ❷

Road map B2. 🏠 7,535. 🚌 Brest or Quimper. 🚌 🚆 to Brest (summer only). ℹ️ Boulevard de Pralognan-la-Vanoise; (02) 98 27 07 9. 🛒 second & fourth Wed in the month.

IN SUMMER the coast here becomes a paradise of beautiful turquoise lagoons and white sandy creeks.

According to the Cartulaire de Landévennec, King Gradlon gave a third of the land around Crauthon (the old name of Crozon) and its church to St Guénolé. Because of its strategic location, Crozon (*Kraozon* in Breton) was invaded by Normans in the 10th century, by English allies of the Montforts in the 14th century, by the English again in the 15th and 16th centuries and later by the Spanish. It also suffered bombing during World War II.

Although the Église St-Pierre has been damaged by vandals and the ravages of time, it still has its 16th-century porch and a magnificent painted

wooden altarpiece of the Ten Thousand Martyrs (*see pp148–9*), also dating from the 16th century.

Pointe des Espagnols ❸

THIS PROMONTORY on the north side of the Presqu'île de Crozon encloses Brest's roadstead (*see p134*) and also offers a view of Île Longue, where there is a nuclear submarine base.

The promontory (Spaniards' Point) is named after a fort that the Spaniards, allies of the Holy League, built in 1594 during their war with Henry IV. It was, however, captured and destroyed by the king's soldiers.

Camaret ❹

Road map A2. 9 km (6 miles) west of Crozon via the D8. 🏠 2,735. 🚌 🚌 ✈️ Brest-Guipavas or Quimper-Cornouaille. ℹ️ Quai Kléber; (02) 98 27 93 60. 🏷 Pardon de Notre-Dame de Rocamadour (first Sun in Sep). 🛒 third Tue in the month (daily in summer).

ONCE A SARDINE port, Camaret (*Kameled* in Breton) turned to the crayfish industry at the beginning of the 20th century. Ships take on cargoes of crayfish from the farms located all along the coast of Brittany. Foreign competition has, however, somewhat curtailed this industry.

The **Tour Vauban**, begun in 1689 and rendered in orange, is the focal point of the fortifications that Vauban (*see p167*) built around

Pointe du Tourlinguet, between Pointe de Pen-Hir and Camaret

One of the beaches at the small coastal resort of Morgat

Camaret. It was these fortifications that made possible the destruction of the Anglo-Dutch fleet when it made an attempted landing here in 1694.

The **Chapelle de Notre-Dame-de-Rocamadour** was built on a shingly spit, the Sillon de Camaret, in the 16th century. It is named for the pilgrims who stopped there on their way to the Église de Notre-Dame in Rocamadour, southwestern France. The top of the belfry was destroyed by a cannon ball fired by the English in 1694. In stormy weather, the church bells are rung to guide seamen.

ENVIRONS: Just off the road from Camaret to Pointe du Tourlinguet are the **Alignements de Lagatjar**, 142 menhirs that stand facing the sea. Opposite are the ruins of the Manoir de Coecilian, where St-Pol Roux, a poet and pioneer of Surrealism, lived from 1905.

🏛 **Tour Vauban**
[(02) 98 27 91 12/93 60. ⬤ details from the tourist office. Temporary exhibitions.
🏛 **Alignements de Lagatjar**
D8, towards the Pointe du Tourlinguet.

Pointe de Pen-Hir ❺

Road map A2. 5 km (3 miles) west of Crozon via the D8, or 6 km (4 miles) via the D355.

RISING TO A HEIGHT of 63 m (207 ft), Pointe de Pen-Hir offers one of the most breath-taking panoramas in Brittany. Breaking the waves just below the point is a cluster of rocks, the Tas de Pois (Pile of Peas). On the left is Pointe de Dinan, and on the right Pointe du Tourlinguet and Pointe de St-Mathieu.

The **Musée du Mur de l'Atlantique**, on the road running round Pointe de Pen-Hir, describes the German occupation of the coast here. The **Musée Ornithologique de Pen-Hir** is a good source of information on the sea birds of Brittany.

🏛 **Musée du Mur de l'Atlantique**
Kerbonn, *commune* of Camaret. **on Pen-Hir**
[(02) 98 27 92 58. ⬤ irregular hours. 🎟
🦅 **Musée Ornithologique de Pen-Hir**
Kerbonn, *commune* of Camaret. [(02) 98 27 92 58. ⬤ Jul–Aug. 🎟

Cormorant

Morgat ❻

Road map A2. 4 km (3 miles) south of Crozon via the D887. 🚉 🏨 *Place d'Ys;* (02) 98 27 29 49 (summer only). ⬤ Jul–Aug: first & third Wed in the month. 🎣 Fête du Thon (15 Aug).

THE SMALL COASTAL resort of Morgat (*Morgad* in Breton) developed at the beginning of the 20th century, thanks to the publicity that it gained from its association with the Peugeot family, who built hotels here. The villas in the resort date from this era. Morgat is now administratively part of Crozon, and this has contributed to the latter's development.

Although Morgat has pleasant beaches, today it is the large nature reserves nearby, such as the Marais de l'Aber, that draw visitors. With its population of birds and otters, the Étang de Kerloc'h, covering 110 ha (270 acres) between Camaret and Crozon, is of particular interest to lovers of wildlife. A fascinating feature here are the sea caves carved out of the schist cliffs by the waves.

ENVIRONS: The **Maison des Minéraux** in St-Hernot, on the road to Cap de la Chèvre, contains a splendid collection of local minerals and a rare display of fluorescent rocks.

🏛 **Maison des Minéraux**
St-Hernot, Crozon. [(02) 98 27 19 73. ⬤ Mon–Fri. 🎟 🎫 by arrangement. ♿

CARTULAIRE DE LANDÉVENNEC

This ninth-century book of gospels demonstrates Landévennec's importance in the production of religious texts. Written in Latin, in Carolingian minuscule – the clear calligraphic style introduced by Charlemagne – it contains more than 300 parchment pages. The Four Evangelists are symbolized by animals. St Mark is associated with the horse (*marc'h* means "horse" in Breton), an animal that, in Armorican tradition, replaces the lion. The two feast days honouring St Guénolé, held on 3 March and 28 April, are mentioned. This rare manuscript was presented to the New York Public Library by an American collector in 1929.

Cartulaire de Landévennec, the oldest manuscript created in Finistère

Crozon: Altarpiece of the Ten Thousand Martyrs

THE ÉGLISE ST-PIERRE in Crozon *(see p146)* contains an altarpiece that gives a magnificent visual account of the story of the Ten Thousand Martyrs. It tells the story of the 10,000 soldiers of the Theban Legion who, as punishment for their Christian faith, were put to death on Mount Ararat by Emperor Hadrian during his Armenian campaign in the second century. The soldiers' crucifixion and their composure in the face of death were intended to reflect the Passion of Christ. The altarpiece, made in 1602, is certainly the work of several artists, and it is one of many depictions of the theme that were created during the Renaissance. The story also appears in Anne of Brittany's *Book of Hours*.

Acace Garcère and his troops
The legionnaires, under the command of the orator Acace Garcère, choose death rather than denial of their Christian faith. The Roman soldiers, meanwhile, show their determination as they prepare for war and execute an ostentatious military parade.

Angel
On the eve of battle, the angel invites the martyrs to embrace their faith.

10,000 Legionnaires
During the reign of Emperor Hadrian, an army was raised to put down a revolt by the inhabitants of Armenia.

Confusion of Battle
The future martyrs throw themselves into battle. Despite their entreaties to the gods, fear spreads among the pagan ranks.

Hadrian's soldiers gather stones to throw at those who profess their faith in Christ, but the stones fly back to hit them.

Pagan Soldiers
Hadrian's pagan troops are depicted kneeling before an idol, while the newly converted Christians are shown turning their backs on it.

Grotesque Figure
Kneeling in front of the martyrs, this figure acts out a parody of the Scourging of Christ.

The upper triptych depicts the martyrs receiving communion.

The Crown of Thorns, which was suffered by Christ, is inflicted on the martyrs.

Way to Mount Ararat
The blood that flows from the martyrs' chests is used for their baptism into the Christian faith. They then make their way up to Mount Ararat.

The condemned reassert their faith after they have been led by the angel to the place of their execution.

The Martyrs' Death
The martyrs die on Mount Ararat, at the same hour as Christ died on the Cross.

View from the summit of Ménez-Hom, with the Aulne river below

Ménez-Hom **7**

Road map B2. West of Châteaulin via the D887.

A PEAK ON THE western edge of the Montagnes Noires, Ménez-Hom (*Menez-C'hom* in Breton) rises to a height of 330 m (1,083 ft). It overlooks the Baie de Douarnenez and, in clear weather, Pointe du Van and Cap de la Chèvre can be seen from the summit.

This mountain, which the Celts held to be sacred, is also the land of the *korrigans* (evil spirits) and of the elves of Armorican popular belief and literature. Wildlife here includes Montagu's harrier and warblers, and the marshes of the Aulne estuary at the foot of the mountain are home to herons and ducks, as well as many species of plants. On 15 August each year, during the Festival du Ménez-Hom, the sound of bombards and Breton bagpipes (*see pp20–21*) fills the air.

The chapel in the hamlet of Ste-Marie-du-Ménez-Hom contains a beautiful altarpiece. There is also a parish close and a 16th-century calvary here. In Trégarvan, about 12 km (8 miles) away, an early 20th-century school has been converted into the **Musée de l'École Rurale en Bretagne**.

🏛 **Musée de l'École Rurale en Bretagne**
Trégarvan. 📞 *(02) 98 26 04 72.*
⬛ *all year.* 📷

Châteaulin **8**

Road map B2. 🏘 *5,700.* 🚉
🚏 *Quimper-Cornouaille.*
ℹ️ *Quai Cosmao; (02) 98 86 02 11 (summer only).* 🚌 Thu.
📷 *Boucles de l'Aulne (27 Aug).*

T HE GRAND PRIX des Boucles de l'Aulne that is held here has made this town the Breton capital of cycle racing. The Aulne is the most salmon-rich river in France, so that Châteaulin (*Castellin* in Breton) also attracts large numbers of anglers. Trips along the Aulne on a restored riverboat, the **Notre-Dame-de-Rumengol**, leave from here.

A short walk upriver leads to the Chapelle Notre-Dame, on a wooded hill on the left bank of the Aulne. The church has a 15th-century calvary with a depiction of the Last Judgment.

Port-Launay, where the salmon-rich river attracts many anglers

Port-Launay, on a bend in the Aulne 2 km (1 mile) northeast of Châteaulin, was once the town's port. With low houses lining the riverbank, it offers a timeless picture of Brittany.

In the 16th century, when the plague was taking a heavy toll, a chapel dedicated to St Sebastian, patron saint of healing, was built in St-Ségal, 3 km (2 miles) northwest of Port-Launay. The calvary, monumental entrance and altarpiece are among the finest in southern Finistère.

🚤 *Notre-Dame-de-Rumengol*
Châteaulin. 📞 *(02) 98 86 02 11.*

Pleyben **9**

Road map B2. 🏘 *3,450.* ℹ️ *Place Charles-de-Gaulle; (02) 98 26 71 05.* 📷 *Pardon (1 Aug).* 🚌 Sat.

T HE PARISH OF Pleyben (*Pleiben* in Breton) is mentioned in the 12th-century Cartulaire de Landévennec (*see p147*). Pleyben – a conflation of "Iben", the name of a Breton saint, and the prefix "ple" (*see pp36–7*) – was one of the parishes established when immigrants from Britain arrived in the fifth to seventh centuries.

The **parish close** consists of a calvary – one of the finest in Brittany – an ossuary, a monumental entrance and a church. The latter, dedicated to St Germain of Auxerre, has two belfries. The one on the right is a Renaissance tower, and the one on the left a Gothic spire. Between them is a stair turret with pinnacles and an ornate spire. The nave has a 16th-century painted ceiling with beams carved and painted with sacred and secular scenes. The high altar, dating from 1667, is lit by 16th- and 17th-century stained-glass windows.

The 16th-century ossuary has been converted into a museum of the history of Pleyben. The triumphal entrance, or *porz ar maro* (gate of the dead), through which every deceased member of the parish used to be carried, was built in 1725.

The Pleyben Calvary

THIS GOSPEL IN stone, designed for the edification of illiterate worshippers, was constructed in 1555 and completed in 1650 with the addition of sculptures by Julien Ozanne, of Brest. These, carved in *kersanton*, the dark Breton granite, are on the first tier of the east side of the calvary. They depict The Last Supper, The Entry into Jerusalem, and Christ Washing the Feet of his Disciples. In 1738, the calvary was given the monumental appearance that it has today. There are two curious depictions. One, on the northeastern spur, shows the Devil disguised as a monk who tempts Christ. The other, on the western side, is of Peter weeping for his denial of Christ before a cockerel, of which only the feet survive. The scenes are arranged in sequence, starting with The Visitation, in which the angel appears to Mary. The next scene is The Nativity.

THE PASSION OF CHRIST
The focal point of the parish close, the visual account of the Passion of Christ expresses the fundamental Christian belief in the Death and Resurrection of Christ.

Christ on the Cross

Side cross

Christ Washing the Feet of His Disciples, *on the east side of the calvary, shows Christ in the act of washing Peter's feet. Peter asks: "Lord, do you wash my feet?"*

Peter's Denial *shows Peter lamenting his betrayal of Christ.*

Christ with the Crown of Thorns, flanked by two soldiers.

The *Pietà* shows Mary holding the dead Christ in her arms.

The Flagellation shows the naked Christ tied to a post.

The Last Supper, *on the east side of the calvary.*

CARDINAL POINTS
The scenes on the four sides of the calvary were intended to be read by the faithful as they processed round it. The scenes of the life of Christ are arranged in sequence from west to east, east representing Golgotha and the Resurrection.

North

West

East

South

The plinth of the Pleyben calvary, in a the shape of a cross.

Granite-built house, typical of buildings in Locronan

Locronan ⓾

Road map B2. 🏠 800.
🚉 *Quimper.* 🛈 *Place de la Mairie; (02) 98 91 70 14.*
@ *locronan.tourisme@wanadoo.fr.*

A LEGEND TELLS that Ronan, an Irish monk, came to Cornouaille. He worked tirelessly to evangelize the area, and it became an important place of pilgrimage. In the 15th century, Locronan (*Lokorn* in Breton) developed thanks to the linen and hemp-weaving industry that provided Europe with sailcloth. Old looms and local costumes are displayed in the **Musée d'Art et d'Histoire**.

The **Église St-Ronan**, built in the 15th century, is connected to the 16th-century **Chapelle du Pénity**. The apse of the church is lit by a large 15th-century stained-glass window of the Passion of Christ, and the pulpit (1707) is carved with medallions with scenes from the life of St Ronan. There is also a Rosary altarpiece, dating from the 17th century. The chapel contains a recumbent figure of St Ronan and a magnificent *Descent from the Cross* in painted stone.

The square, in which there is a well, is lined with houses with granite façades. Built in the 17th and 18th centuries,

they were the residences of Locronan's wealthy citizens.

The **Chapelle Bonne-Nouvelle**, in Rue Moal, has a small calvary and an attractive fountain.

🏛 **Musée d'Art et d'Histoire**
📞 *(02) 98 91 70 14.* ◻ *Jun–Sep: daily; Oct–May: Mon–Sat.* ⚝
⛪ **Église St-Ronan and Chapelle du Pénity**
Place de l'Église. ◻ *daily.*
✝ *10:30am Sun.*
⛪ **Chapelle Bonne-Nouvelle**
Rue Moal. ◻ *daily.*

Douarnenez ⓫

Road map B2. 🏠 *15,820.*
🚉 *Quimper.* ✈ *Quimper-Cornouaille.*
🛈 *2 Rue du Dr-Mével; (02) 98 92 13 35.* 🏪 *Halles de la Grande-Place de Tréboul (Mon–Sat, am); central car park (Mon & Fri); Tréboul harbour (Wed & Sat am).* 🎫 *Rosmeur harbour, organized by the tourist office.*

D OUARNENEZ WAS once the largest sardine port in France, and its was here that the first canning factories opened, in 1853. Fishing, in which about 1,000 people are engaged, is no longer sufficient to support the population of Douarnenez, although the fresh fish auction held here is still one of the largest in Brittany.

Remains of a *garum* factory discovered at Les Plomarc'h, a small fishing village next to Douarnenez, indicate that the site was settled in the Gallo-Roman period. *Garum* was a fish sauce highly prized throughout the Roman world. Today, it is the cove at Tréboul and the **Musée du Bateau**, a centre for the preservation of the local seafaring heritage,

that draw visitors to Douarnenez. Salvaged boats can also be seen at the maritime museum of **Port Rhu**. Tours of the harbour and sea fishing trips are offered by **Vedettes Rosmeur**.

Between the quays and the town centre is the 17th-century **Chapelle St-Michel**, which contains a collection of 52 mission pictures created by Michel Le Nobletz (*see p127*).

🚢 **Vedettes Rosmeur**
Harbour. 📞 *(02) 98 92 83 83; tours of the harbour (am), sea fishing.*
🏛 **Musée du Bateau**
Place de l'Enfer. 📞 *(02) 98 92 65 20.*
◻ *mid-Jun–Sep: daily; Mar–mid-Jun & Oct: Tue–Sun.* ⚝
⛪ **Chapelle St-Michel**
Rue du Port-Rhu. 📞 *(02) 98 92 13 35.*
◻ *by arrangement.*

Réserve du Cap Sizun ⓬

Road map A2. 20 km (13 miles) west of Douarnenez via the D7, Chemin de Kérisit. 📞 *(02) 98 70 13 53.* ◻ *Apr–Aug: daily.* **Bretagne Vivante SEPNB** 📞 *(02) 98 49 07 18.*

T HIS NATURE RESERVE, created in 1959 by Michel-Hervé Julien and Bretagne Vivante SEPNB (Société d'Étude et de Protection de la Nature en Bretagne), covers 25 ha (62 acres) on the north coast of Cap Sizun. It attracts many ornithologists, as, from April to the end of August, sea birds come here to breed in their thousands. Migrating birds are also seen here. Visitors may explore the reserve by following marked footpaths. Guided walks are also available.

At Pont-Croix, on the right bank of the Goyen river, which runs along the southern part of Cap Sizun, stands **Notre-Dame-de-Roscudon**, founded in the 13th century. The church's Romanesque vaulting is supported by clustered columns typical of an

Port Rhu, the maritime museum in Douarnenez, with vessels tied up at the quayside

Pointe du Van, with Cap Sizun visible in the far distance

English-influenced architectural style that became known as the school of Pont-Croix style. Le Marquisat, a 16th-century residence, houses the **Musée du Patrimoine**.

The Goyen estuary, with salmon-rich waters and large numbers of birds, offers a walk in an unspoiled environment running for 12 km (8 miles) from Pont-Croix to Audierne.

🏛 **Musée du Patrimoine**
📞 *(02) 98 70 51 86.* ◯ *Sun pm.*

Pointe du Van ⓭

Road map A2. 27 km (17 miles) west of Douarnenez via the D7.

WITH HIGH CLIFFS and the 17th-century Chapelle St-They perching on rocks, the Pointe du Van is a magnificent sight. Although the landscape here is bare, the views of Pointe de Brézellec, Cap de la Chèvre, Pointe St-Mathieu and the rocks known as the Tas de Pois (Pile of Peas) are superb. To the left is Pointe du Raz, the Phare de la Vieille and,

behind it, Île de Sein. A walk along the GR34 long-distance path will reveal several small fishing villages tucked away along the coast here.

Pointe du Raz ⓮

Road map A2. 16 km (10 miles) west of Audierne via the D784.
🚍 *Douarnenez, Audierne, Quimper.*
🅿 *compulsory; pay and display.*

WILD AND MAJESTIC, this spur shaped by the action of waves rises to height of more than 70 m (230 ft). Pointe du Raz (*Beg ar Raz* in Breton) is extended by a spine of submerged rocks, on the most distant of which stands a lighthouse, the Phare de la Vieille.

In fine weather, the Île de Sein and the Ar Men lighthouse are visible from here. On the north side, the sea has carved potholes known as the Enfer de Plogoff, where the legendary Princesse Dahud would cast her unfortunate lovers. The Raz de Sein, a notorious tide race, is much feared by sailors.

Pointe du Raz is now a conservation area with a network of footpaths. There is also a visitor centre, the Maison de la Pointe du Raz, which can be reached on foot or by taking a free ride in an electric-engined boat.

ENVIRONS: The Baie des Trépassés (Bay of the Dead) has a beautiful beach with caves in the cliffs that can be explored at low tide. According to local legend, the bodies of those who had died at sea would be washed up on this beach by strong currents.

The lighthouse on the Île de Sein, seen from Pointe du Raz

THE TROMÉNIE, TOUR OF MONASTERY LAND

Christians processing during the Troménie in Locronan

Some 2,500 years ago, Locronan was a centre of Celtic religion unlike any other in Europe. Here, Celtic astronomical points of reference were used to create a *nemeton*, a quadrilateral circuit 12 km (7.5 miles) long punctuated by 12 markers corresponding to the 12 cycles of the lunar calendar. Although Benedictine monks took over this Celtic site to build a priory, the outline of the sacred itinerary survived the imposition of Christianity. The Celtic astronomical markers became the 12 stations of the Christian procession. The word *troménie* is derived from the Breton words *tro* (tour) and *minihy* (monastery land). The oldest-established *troménie* goes back to 1299. The *grande troménie* secures pilgrims' entry into heaven and equals three *petites troménies*.

Île de Sein **⑮**

🏛 246. 🛈 Mairie; (02) 98 70 90 35.
🚢 Audierne (daily), Brest, Camaret
(summer only). No cars allowed on
the island. 🎭 Pardon de St-Guénolé
(Trinity Sunday, Jun), Pardon de
St-Corentin (first Sun in Aug).

THIS ISLAND, AN EXTENSION of
Pointe du Raz, is no more
than about 2 km (1 mile) long
and 800 m (875 yds) wide,
and its highest point is just
6 m (20 ft) above sea level.
The landscape here is bare
and the small town consists
of a maze of narrow streets
that give welcome shelter
from the wind.
   The Île de Sein (*Enez-Sun*
in Breton) has a few megalithic
monuments, including two
menhirs known as Les Causeurs
(The Talkers) and the Nifran
tumulus. The island may have
been a burial place for druids.
   The islanders' greatest
moment in history came at
the outbreak of World War II,
when they answered the call
of General de Gaulle.
   A track leads to the lighthouse and the Chapelle
St-Corentin. The **Musée Jardin
de l'Espérance** documents
daily life on the island.

ENVIRONS: The **Phare d'Ar
Men**, 12 km (7.5 miles) west
of the island, was built on a
reef that is permanently
battered by the waves. It took
the islanders 14 years to build.
The unmanned lighthouse
protects shipping negotiating
these dangerous waters.

🏛 **Musée Jardin de
l'Espérance**
Quai des Paintolais.
◯ Jun–Sep. 🎟

**Les Causeurs, a pair of menhirs
on the Île de Sein**

Phare d'Ar Men, off the western tip of the Île de Sein

Audierne **⑯**

Road map A2. 🏛 2,470. 🚆
Quimper-Cornouaille. 🚌 Quimper
then by bus. 🛈 8 Rue Victor-Hugo;
(02) 98 70 12 20. 🎭 Pardon (last Sun
in Aug). 🛒 Wed & Sat.

THE SEAFARING TOWN of
Audierne (*Gwaien* in
Breton) still has a busy
harbour, with an inshore
fishing industry specializing in
such highly prized fish as sea
bream and monkfish caught
with seine nets, and sea bass
caught on the line, as well as
crayfish. The fish farms –
Grands Viviers – are open to
visitors. With about 30 pools,
they are the largest in France.
Trips out to sea in a traditional
lobster boat are also on offer
(details from the tourist office).
The boat scrapyard, in the
Anse de Locquéran, where
old lobster boats quietly rot,
is a protected historic site.
   The 17th-century **Église
St-Raymond-Nonnat**, which
overlooks the town, is
decorated with carvings of
ships and has a striking
Baroque belfry.
   The **Planète Aquarium
de la Pointe du Raz**, on
the outskirts of the town,
offers the opportunity to
view marine life.

ENVIRONS: At Primelin, 3 km
(2 miles) west of Audierne on
the D784, is the beautiful
Chapelle de St-Tugen, built
in 1535. While the nave and
square tower are both in the
Flamboyant Gothic style, the
transept and apse date from
the Renaissance.

🐟 **Grands Viviers**
1 Rue du Môle (leading to the beaches).
🕿 (02) 98 70 10 04. ◯ Mon–Fri.

🐟 **Planète Aquarium**
Rue du Goyen. 🕿 (02) 98 70 03 03.
◯ May–Sep: daily; Oct–Apr:
Sun–Thu; school holidays: daily.
🎟 by arrangement. ♿ 🎟
🛈 **Chapelle de St-Tugen**
◯ daily.

**Audierne harbour, with the Église
St-Raymond-Nonnat on the right**

Notre-Dame-
de-Tronoën **⑰**

Road map B2. 9 km (5.5 miles) west
of Pont-l'Abbé, **commune** of St-Jean-
Trolimon. 🕿 (02) 98 82 04 63. ◯
Apr–Sep. 🎟 summer only.

A LANDSCAPE OF BARE dunes
surrounds the chapel and
calvary of Tronoën (*Tornoan*
in Breton). The vaulted
chapel has a rose window,
and two doorways frame an
open belfry set with turrets.
   The calvary (c. 1450–70) is
the oldest in Brittany, and the
detail of its carvings has been
obliterated by the passage of
time. On the platform are
Christ on the Cross, flanked
by the two thieves. The
rectangular base is decorated
by a double frieze illustrating
The Childhood of Christ and
The Passion of Christ.
   The sequence of scenes
begins on the east side with
The Annunciation, continuing
on the north side with
The Visitation and The Nativity.

The scenes are carved in granite from Scaër. This stone is prone to becoming covered in lichen, as can be seen in The Last Judgment and The Last Supper (on the south side). The Visitation, The Nativity and The Three Kings bringing their gifts (north side) are carved in tougher *kersanton* (black granite).

The elegant belfry on the church of Notre-Dame-de-Tronoën

Penmarc'h ⓲

Road map B2. 12 km (7.5 miles) southwest of Pont-l'Abbé via the D785. ✈ Quimper-Cornouaille. 🚍 🏠 6,030. 🚌 Place du Maréchal-Davout; (02) 98 58 81 44. ✪ Festival du Film de la Mer (early May), Pardon de Notre-Dame-de-la-Joie (15 Aug). ⛴ Jun-Sep: Fri am (St-Guénolé harbour) & Wed (Kérity harbour).

THE STORY GOES that the cruel Princess Dahud cast a spell on Marc'h, legendary king of Poulmarc'h, as the result of which his head was turned into that of a horse *(penmarc'h)*.

Penmarc'h consists of three parishes: that of Penmarc'h itself, and those of St-Guénolé and Kérity. St-Guénolé is the second-largest port in the Bigouden and the sixth-largest in France. The computerized fish auction that is held there is the most advanced in Europe.

The **Phare d'Eckmühl** is the pride of the town. Built in 1897 with funds provided by the daughter of Général Davout, Prince of Eckmühl, the lighthouse is in the Breton granite known as *kersanton*. Its beams carry for 50 km

GENERAL DE GAULLE'S CALL TO ARMS

The harsh existence that generations of Sénans (inhabitants of the Île de Sein) had endured gave them a fighting spirit. When, on 18 June 1940, General de Gaulle made his appeal by radio from London, calling on all Frenchmen to fight the German invasion, the men of Sein readily left the island to join other volunteers in England. When the Germans reached Sein, the only people left were women and children. In July 1940, the leader of Free France reviewed the first 600 volunteers, 150 of whom

General de Gaulle with seamen on the Île de Sein

were Sénans. "The Île de Sein therefore represents a quarter of France," exclaimed the general. Of the Sénan seamen who answered the call, only 114 returned. In 1946, de Gaulle came to the island to award it the Croix de la Libération.

(30 miles). The **Musée Pré-Historique Finistérien**, near the Plage de Pors-Carn, documents the region's prehistory.

🗼 **Phare d'Eckmühl**
📞 (02) 98 58 61 17. ⏰ mid-Jun–mid-Sep: daily; mid-Sep–mid-Jun: by arrangement.
🏛 **Musée Préhistorique Finistérien**
Rue du Musée-Préhistorique.
📞 (02) 98 58 60 35. ⏰ Jun–mid-Sep: Wed–Mon. ✔ 📷

Le Guilvinec ⓳

Road map B2. 10 km (6 miles) south of Pont-l'Abbé via the D785 and D57. 🏠 3,040. ✈ Quimper-Cornouaille. 🚍 🚌 ℹ 62 Rue de la Marine; (02) 98 58 29 29. ✪ Les Estivales (Jul–Aug, Fri eve). ⛴ Tue & Sun (summer).

THIS FISHING VILLAGE began to develop in the 19th century when a rail link was built as far as Quimper. It then became Quimper's main supplier of fresh fish. Today, Le Guilvinec (Ar Gelveneg in Breton) is still a large, traditional fishing village, and sea fishing for tourists has been introduced here. The quayside comes to life in the late afternoon when the boats return.

A seaweed oven at Pointe du Men-Meur bears witness to the importance of seaweed-harvesting in the past. Further on is the **Manoir de Kergoz**, an attractive manor built in the 15th century and now restored. It has a 16th-century dovecote. Footpaths lead to Lesconil, a charming fishing village with white houses.

The harbour at Le Guilvinec, where visitors come for sea fishing

The pleasant little fishing port of Île-Tudy

Loctudy ❷

Road map B2. 6 km (4 miles) southeast of Pont-l'Abbé via the D2. 👫 *3,660.* 🚉 *Quimper-Cornouaille.* 🚌 🚌 🛈 *Place des Anciens-Combattants; (02) 98 87 53 78.* 🎉 *Pardon de St-Tudy (Sun after 11 May).* 🛒 *Tue am.*

THE WELL-KNOWN coastal resort of Loctudy (*Loktudi* in Breton) is pleasantly located on the Pont-l'Abbé river, with a fine view of Île Garo and Île Chevalier and of Île-Tudy, a peninsula. Loctudy's fishing port is the foremost provider of live crayfish, the famous "demoiselles de Loctudy". When the trawlers return to the harbour, there is a fish auction on the quay, which is always a high point in daily life everywhere in Armorica. Trips out to sea with rods and bait are organized by the tourist office, and visitors can also learn how to fish with nets and lay lobster pots.

The 12th-century Romanesque Église St-Tudy is in an excellent state of preservation. The capitals are carved with flowers, masks, human figures and animals; the apse has an ambulatory and chapels. Beside the church is the small chapel of Pors-Bihan, and just outside the town, on the road to Pont-l'Abbé, is the pretty Chapelle de Croaziou, with a Celtic cross.

ENVIRONS: When, having sailed from Britain, St Tudy reached Brittany, he founded a monastery on what was, in the early 5th century, an

island. After the saint's death, the monastery was transferred to Loctudy. **Île-Tudy**, now a peninsula, is a small, pleasant fishing village accessible by boat from Loctudy.

Manoir de Kerazan ❷

Road map B2. 4 km (2.5 miles) south of Pont-l'Abbé via the D2. 📞 *(02) 98 87 40 40.* 🕐 *Easter–early Jun & Sep: Tue–Sun pm; mid-Jun–Aug: daily.* 📷 *groups by arrangement.* 🍴 ♿ 🎭 *Soirées Contes et Légendes (Jul–Aug, Thu).*

THIS MAGNIFICENT country residence, built in the 16th century and restored in the 18th, was bequeathed by Joseph Astor to the Institut de France in 1928. The manor, sturdily built in granite, is set in 5 ha (12 acres) of parkland and was obviously designed for a luxurious and sophisti-cated lifestyle.

The Astor family devoted themselves to the develop-ment of Bigouden culture and to local politics. In 1930, a school of embroidery was opened in the house. Later, at the instigation of his father, a

patron of the arts, Joseph Astor assembled a collection of 16th- to 20th-century paintings and drawings, and a large collection of faience from the former faience factory at Porquier. These now form part of a museum collection which also includes costumes and traditional Breton furniture.

Pont-l'Abbé ❷

Road map B2. 👫 *8,425.* 🚉 *Quimper-Cornouaille.* 🚌 *Quimper.* 🚌 🛈 *Place de la République; (02) 98 82 37 99.* 🎉 *Fête des Brodeuses (second Sun in Jul).* 🛒 *Thu.*

THE TOWN is named after the monks (*abbés*) of Loctudy who built the first bridge (*pont*) across the river at this spot. The site had already drawn the attention of the Romans, who built a fortified camp here.

Pont-l'Abbé (*Pont-N'-Abad* in Breton) later became the capital of the Bigouden. During the Middle Ages, the lord of Pont-l'Abbé built a castle surmounted by a huge oval tower. During the Wars of the Holy League (*see p44*), the town's barons converted to Protestantism, and the castle was damaged by attacks, especially during the revolt of the Bonnets Rouges (Red Caps). In 1675, this revolt let to the uprising of hundreds of protestors in Lower Brittany. All wore red hats and all demanded the abolition of the *corvée* (unpaid labour for the feudal lord), of taxation on harvest and of the tithe paid to the clergy, and the universal right to hunt. The repression with which the governor of Brittany responded quelled further attempts at protest.

Granite buildings of the Manoir de Kerazan, built in the 16th century

Église Notre-Dame-des-Carmes, built in 1383

While the main part of the castle contains the town hall, the keep houses the **Musée Bigouden**. This contains an interesting collection of traditional costumes and headdresses, as well as furniture and other objects.

The **Église Notre-Dame-des-Carmes**, built in 1383 and formerly the chapel of the Carmelite convent, has an outstanding 15th-century stained-glass window. It also contains a beautiful representation of the Virgin, embroidered in coloured silks on a banner made by the Le Minor workshop.

Not far from the quays are the ruins of the church of Lambour, which was destroyed by the Duke of

Traditional costume, displayed in the Musée Bigouden

Chaulnes during the Bonnets Rouges uprising. The arches and columns of the church are in the style of the Pont-Croix School *(see pp152–3)*.

The towpath along the Pont-l'Abbé river makes for a pleasant walk. The river flows into an estuary dotted with small islands, Les Rats, Queffen and Garo, which are inhabited by flocks of birds, including common spoonbill and heron. At Pointe Bodillo is the largest colony of herons in Finistère.

🏛 Musée Bigouden
In the castle. **☎** (02) 98 66 09 09.
🕐 Apr–May: Mon–Sat; Jun–Sep: daily.

🔒 Église Notre-Dame-des-Carmes
Place des Carmes. **🕐** 8am–7pm daily
✝ 6:30pm Sat; 11am Sun.

Îles de Glénan ㉓

Road map B3. **ℹ** 49 Rue de Kérourgué, Fouesnant; (02) 98 56 00 93. **🚢** Port-La-Forêt, Beg-Meil, Concarneau.

THIS ARCHIPELAGO, 12 nautical miles (14 miles) off the mainland and opposite the Baie de La Forêt, consists of eight large islands and a dozen islets. Its white sandy beaches, clear water and plant and animal life make the archipelago an exceptionally suitable place for the sailing and deep-sea diving courses that are organized here.

Penfret, the largest island, is where the **Centre Nautique des Glénan** teaches sailing. Established in 1947, the school is world famous for its training in dinghy and catamaran sailing. Students are housed in an 18th-century fort.

The Île St-Nicolas is the base from which the **Centre International de Plongée** holds its diving courses.

The Île Guiautec is a bird sanctuary. A rare flower – the Glénan narcissus, which was brought by the Phoenicians and which flowers in April – also grows on the island.

Centre Nautique des Glénan
Office on Place Pierre-Viannay, Concarneau. **☎** (02) 98 97 14 84.
Centre International de Plongée
Office in Concarneau.
☎ (02) 98 50 57 02.

Port de Cornouailles in Benodet, with the Îles de Glénan in the distance

Street-by-Street: Quimper

Historic costume

FOUNDED BY GAULS on the site of the present Locmaria district, downstream from the present city centre, the town was later named *Aquilonia* (Town of Eagles) by the Romans. For centuries, it was then known as Quimper-Corentin, after Corentine, its first bishop. The city stands at the confluence *(kemper)* of the Steir and the Odet rivers. Rampart walks, projecting towers and walls survive in the old town, although old timber-framed houses now alternate with later mansions and modern architecture. Recent building work has revealed substantial remains of the medieval city.

Musée Departemental Breton
Founded in 1846, the museum is housed in the bishops' palace.

★ Cathédrale St-Corentin
Built in the 13th and 14th centuries, on the site of a Roman temple, the cathedral was later sumptuously renovated.

BOULEVARD AMIRAL DE KERGUÉLEN

ODET

RUE DU ROI GRADLON

RUE DU FROUT

RUE DE LA MAIRIE

PLACE SAINT-CORENTIN

PLACE LAËNNEC

RUE — KÉRÉON

RUE ÉLIE FRÉRON

RUE DU GUÉODET

RUE DES BOUCHERIES

PL. AU BEURRE

RUE DU SALLÉ

RUE

René Laënnec
This statue honours the inventor of the stethoscope, who died in 1826.

★ Musée des Beaux-Arts
Built in 1872 by the Quimper architect Joseph Bigot, it contains collections of Flemish and Italian paintings.

★ **Covered Market**
The market (Les Halles) is open every day except Sunday. It plays a prominent part in the life of the city.

Rue St-François
In the 18th century, crown judges lived in this street, which is lined with tall houses.

Odet River

KEY

– – – Suggested route

Rue Kéréon
The finest and oldest timber-framed houses in Quimper are in Rue Kéréon (Shoemakers' Street), which has a medieval atmosphere.

Place Terre-au-Duc
is lined with timber-framed houses.

The Steir river
runs through the old quarters of the city.

STAR SIGHTS

★ **Cathédrale St-Corentin**

★ **Covered Market**

★ **Musée des Beaux-Arts**

0 m   50
0 yards   50

Exploring Quimper

Listed as a historic town, Quimper (*Kimper* in Breton) has an unusually rich heritage, and great care is being taken to show it to best advantage. The cathedral has been restored and two squares – Places Laënnec and Place St-Corentin – have been totally remodelled. A 12th-century cemetery and 14th-century esplanades have been discovered, and Le Quartier, a newly created cultural district, has opened. Quimper has an illustrious past: it is the birthplace of Fréron (1718–76), Voltaire's famous adversary, of the adventurer René Madec (1738–84), of the poet Max Jacob (1876–1944) and of René Laënnec (1781–1826), inventor of the stethoscope. Yves de Kerguelen, the explorer, is also a native of the Quimper area. The city naturally has a strong Celtic identity, and Celtic culture is celebrated at the Festival de Cornouaille every July. It is also famous for its faience, which has been made here since 1690.

🏚 Old Town

The city's finest medieval streets are those opposite the cathedral, and they are faced with decorative ceramic tiles. Half-timbered houses, slate roofs and cobbled streets also fill this old part of the city.

Faces on the Maison des Cariatides

Rue Kéréon (Shoemakers' Street) is lined with corbelled houses. Other street names, such as Place au Beurre (Butter Square) and Rue des Boucheries (Butchers' Street), also echo the trades that were once practised here.

At No.10 **Rue du Sallé** is the recently restored Minuellou, a former residence of the Mahaut family. Rue des Boucheries is intersected by Rue du Guéodet, which contains the famous 16th-century **Maison des Cariatides**. The faces carved into the stonework of the house are those of Quimpérois who distinguished themselves in the Wars of the Holy League. Further on, the **Rue des Gentilshommes**, which is lined with mansions, leads down to the banks of the Steir, ending at **Rue de la Herse**, which has a projecting turret.

The right bank of the Steir, on the other side of the Pont Médard, was once the

territory of the dukes of Brittany. Half-timbered houses line **Place Terre-au-Duc**. Not far from here is the **Église St-Mathieu**, a church with a particularly fine 16th-century stained-glass window.

The quays along the Odet lead to **Rue St-François** and, further on, to the **Halles du Chapeau-Rouge**, where the

Banner carried in procession during the Grand Pardon

daily market is held. In Rue du Parc, which follows the Odet, is the Café de l'Épée, once patronized by writers and artists from Gustave Flaubert to Max Jacob and now a Quimper institution.

On the opposite side of the Odet, footpaths lead to **Mont Frugy** (70 m/230 ft high), which offers a good view over the city centre.

The Du Plessis distillery, in the Quartier d'Ergué-Armel, contains an interesting collection of antique stills.

🏛 Musée Départemental Breton

1 Rue du Roi-Gradlon. ☎ (02) 98 95 21 60. ☐ Jun–Sep. ● Sun & Mon, am.
The museum is housed in the former bishops' palace on the south side of the cathedral. The palace consists of two wings and, between them, a Renaissance tower containing a spiral staircase. The staircase gives access to all the rooms and is finished with decorative wood carvings. The tower known at the Logis de Rohan, in the Flamboyant Gothic style, was built in 1507 by Bishop Claude de Rohan and restored in the 19th century.

The museum was established in 1846 by the Société d'Archéologie du

Timber-framed houses on Place Terre-au-Duc

Finistère. Devoted to cultural anthropology, it contains an important collection of folk art. Reopened in 1999, it documents 3,000 years of Breton history.

The ground floor contains prehistoric artifacts (spear points, hand axes, Gaulish stele and weapons), a fine collection of painted wooden religious statues and two recumbent figures of knights.

The first and second floors of the museum contain magnificent displays of traditional costumes, 17th- to 19th-century furniture, including chests, box beds and wardrobes, and everyday objects, including an unusual folding spoon.

On the third floor is a collection of 300 pieces of Quimper faience *(see p164)* and stoneware dating from the 17th to the 20th centuries. Medieval and modern religious art is also exhibited. The tour of the museum ends in a room devoted to temporary exhibitions.

***Le Génie à la Guirlande*, by Charles Filiger, Musée des Beaux-Arts**

🏛 Musée des Beaux-Arts

40 Place St-Corentin. 📞 *(02) 98 95 45 20.* ◯ *Jul–Aug: daily.* ● *Oct–Mar: Sun am, Tue & public holidays.*

The gallery was built by the architect Joseph Bigot to house the collection that Jean-Marie Silguy bequeathed to the city. The gallery contains Flemish, Italian and French painting, including works by Sérusier, Denis and Lacombe, members of the Pont-Aven School *(see p169)*.

One room is devoted to the life and work of the poet and painter Max Jacob, a native of Quimper, and that of his friend Jean Moulin. Watercolours and drawings, as well as portraits of Jacob's artist friends, including Cocteau and Picasso, are displayed. Also shown are major works by Rubens, Fragonard and Corot, and 20th-century paintings (by Delaunay and Tal Coat), as well as the work of Breton painters, such as Guillou, Boudin and Noël. There are also some splendid prints and drawings, especially by Charles Filiger.

QUIMPER CITY CENTRE

Cathédrale St-Corentin ①
Église St-Mathieu ④
Hôtel de Ville ②
Musée Départemental Breton ③
Musée des Beaux-Arts ⑤

0 m — 200
0 yards — 200

Locronan

Brest, Morlaix

Douarnenez, Audierne

R. DU CHAPEAU ROUGE
RUE KÉRÉON
RUE ÉLIE FRÉRON
PL. A. MACÉ
RUE LUZEL
R. DE FALKIRK
PLACE LAENNEC
PLACE SAINT-CORENTIN
RUE DU FROUT
RUE ST-FRANÇOIS
R. R. MADEC
R. DU PARC
BOULEVARD DE KERGUÉLEN
JUNVILLE
RUE LAËNNEC
DE L'AMIRAL
ROMARC'H
R. PR. COLIGNON
RUE Odet
BOULEVARD
DUPLEIX
DU
Railway station
PL. DE LA RÉSISTANCE ET DU GÉNÉRAL DE GAULLE
R. STE CATHERINE
RUE
JEAN
JAURÈS
R. TH. LE HARS
R. DE LA DÉESSE
Musée de la Faïence and Faïencerie Henriot
MONT FRUGY

KEY

▨ See pp158–9	🛈 Tourist information
🅿 Parking	⊠ Post office

🏛 Musée de la Faïence

14 Rue Jean-Baptiste-Bousquet. 📞
(02) 98 90 12 72. ⬜ *mid-Apr–Oct: Mon–Sat.* ⚫ *Sun & public holidays.*
The museum is laid out in the Maison Porquier, a former faience factory in the heart of the Locmaria district, where the 18th-century kilns are also located. Recent building work in this district is in keeping with the character of the area.

The museum highlights the elements necessary for making pottery, namely water, clay and fire. The natural occurrence of clay and water in the vicinity is the reason why Quimper became a prime centre of pottery manufac-ture. There is also a display of

Odetta vase with hydrangea motif

Quimper pottery, with work by Alfred Beau, and pieces by major throwers and painters. The creation of the mark Odetta HB Quimper in 1922 and the beginnings of studio pottery are also documented.

Faïencerie HB-Henriot

16 Rue Haute. 📞 *(02) 98 90 09 36.*
⬜ *Mon–Fri.* ⚫ *Sat–Sun & public hols.*
In 1984, two Americans, Paul and Sarah Janssens, acquired the HB-Henriot faience factory. Continuing Quimper's faience-making tradition, the factory is the only one still to produce pieces with freehand decoration.

ENVIRONS: The 16th-century **Calvaire de Quilinen**, in open countryside between Quimper and Châteaulin, is worth a visit. About 1 km (0.5 mile) further on is the Gothic **Chapelle de St-Venec**, dedicated to the brother of St Guénolé, which has a fountain framed by slender twisted columns. The church at **Cast**, 8 km (5 miles) south of Châteaulin, is known for a 16th-century sculpture called *St Hubert's Hunt*. The belvedere at **Griffonez**, on a bend of the Odet 7 km (4 miles) north of Quimper, offers a view of the **Gorges de Stangala**.

Cathédrale St-Corentin

IMPRESSED BY THE religious faith of Corentine, whom he met on Ménez-Hom, so the legend goes, King Gradlon invited the hermit to become Bishop of Quimper and gave him land on which to build a cathedral. History records that in 1239 Bishop Rainaud decided to start building the choir of his projected cathedral. The light and airy building that resulted was achieved by means of new construction techniques: ribbed vaulting supported by flying buttresses. The choir was built out of line with the nave to accommodate an older chapel containing the tomb of Alain Canhiart, who repelled Norman invasions in 913.

★ **Stained-Glass Windows**
The great vertical spaces of the nave, the choir and the transept are lit by superb stained-glass windows made in a local workshop in the 15th century.

Small chapel

The old high altar
beneath a canopy decorated with seraphim, was shown at the Exposition Universelle in Paris in 1867.

The apse of the cathedral and the gardens of the former bishop's residence

VISITORS' CHECKLIST

Place St-Corentin. ☎ *(02) 98 53
04 05.* ✝ *6:30pm Sat;
8:45am, 10am & 6:30pm Sun.*
📷 ♿

★ **Romanesque Nave**
*Rebuilt in the 15th century, the
Romanesque nave and transept are
lit by ten windows in the Flamboyant
Gothic style. The tombs of bishops of
Quimper laid out here and in the
transept are covered by recumbent
figures of the deceased.*

Spires, in the
Pont-Croix style,
were added in 1854.

Twin towers, 76 m
(250 ft) high, are pierced
by double openings.

**St-Guénolé and
St-Ronan Window**,
dating from the 19th
century, depicts the
two saints, one the
founder of the Abbaye
de Landévennec and
the other the hermit
of Locronan.

**Bell turret on
the tower**

Portal
*Seven carved archivolts
frame a rose window
above which runs a
balustrade. Between the
two square galleried
towers is a statue of
King Gradlon.*

West door

Pulpit
*Of painted and gilded wood, the
Baroque pulpit was made in 1679
by Olivier Daniel, of Quimper. It is
decorated with medallions showing
scenes from the life of St Corentine.*

STAR FEATURES

★ **Romanesque Nave**

★ **Stained Glass**

Quimper Faience

THE HISTORY OF Quimper faience began in 1690, when Jean-Baptiste Bousquet settled in the Locmaria district of the town. He came from Moustiers, in Provence, but competition and the lack of wood to fire the kilns had forced him to seek his fortune elsewhere. In Cornouaille, forests were more plentiful and royal permission to cut firewood easier to obtain. Clay in the area was also abundant, and the Odet provided a convenient means of transport.

Faïence by HB Henriot, Quimper

Bousquet's Manufacture de Pipes et Fayences soon prospered, and, thanks to his granddaughter's marriage, he benefited from Italian influence brought by a potter from Nevers, a leading centre of faience manufacture. He was then joined by a manufacturer from Rouen, another prestigious centre of faience production. In the 19th century, Alfred Beau, a photographer and amateur painter from Morlaix, created a new style, based on colourful scenes of daily life.

HISTORY OF FAIENCE

Faience was first made in southern France and in Italy. Faience made in Nevers, in central France, features scenes of daily life and shows a predominant use of yellow. Faience made in Rouen, a major and distinctive centre of production, is remarkably colourful and displays a variety of elaborate motifs, including flowers, trees, birds and cornucopiae. In the 19th century, faience production was dominated by the influence of Alfred Beau and by the distinctive Quimper style, with scenes of daily life depicted in bright colours by the "single stroke" technique, by which shape was defined and colour applied by a single touch of the brush.

View of the Odet at Quimper, overglaze decoration by Alfred Beau, late 19th century

Plate in the Nevers and Moustiers style (1773).

"Single stroke" decoration (early 19th century).

New style Porquier-Beau (late 19th century).

DECORATION

After being removed from the mould and dried, the piece of faience was fired in the kiln and glazed. It was then passed to the decorators. Each design was reproduced on paper, its outline pierced with holes. The paper was applied to the glaze and the outlines transferred with charcoal. The design was then filled in with a fine brush and the piece re-fired.

Piece by Berthe Savigny, a mid-20th century modeller.

Vase with Odetta design (20th century)

Statue of Quillivic (mid-20th century)

POTTING

There are several ways of modelling clay. While circular pieces are shaped on the wheel, more complex pieces are press-moulded. To make highly complex pieces, liquid clay is poured into moulds.

The potter throws a piece on the wheel.

The decorator adds the finishing touches.

Vase by Louis Garin (mid-20th century)

Dish with contemporary decoration

Bénodet 🟤

🏘 2,750. 🚉 ✈ Quimper-Cornouaille. 🛈 29 Avenue de la Mer; (02) 98 57 00 14. 🛒 Place du Meneyer, Mon am.

ON THE BORDER between the Bigouden and the Fouesnant area, Bénodet (*Benoded* in Breton) is a well-known coastal resort on the Odet estuary. Comfortable residences, manor houses and chateaux line the river. The chapel in Le Perguet, just east of Bénodet, was once the parish church. It was rebuilt in the 12th century and has a Romanesque interior and a 15th-century porch.

Penfoul harbour, where boat races and regattas are held, is very lively. Cruises and trips out to sea are offered here. Cruises to Belle-Île, Ouessant, Groix and Seinon aboard the *Le Corentin*, the replica of a 19th-century coastal lugger, are also available. At Le Letty, just south of Bénodet and opposite the Îles de Glénan, is a lagoon known as the **Mer Blanche**, which attracts numerous birds.

🚤 **Vedettes de l'Odet**
Motorboats 📞 (02) 98 57 00 58.
🚤 *Le Corentin*
📞 (02) 98 65 10 00.

The Mer Blanche at Bénodet, a lagoon attracting many birds

Belfry of the Romanesque Église de St-Pierre, in Fouesnant

Fouesnant 🟤

🏘 8,080. 🚉 ✈ Quimper-Cornouaille. 🛈 49 Rue de Kérourgué; (02) 98 56 00 93. 🛒 Wed am in Beg-Meil (summer only); Fri am, Sun am & Tue eve. in La Forêt-Fouesnant (summer only).

AT AN ALTITUDE of 60 m (300 ft) above sea level, Fouesnant (*Fouenant* in Breton) looks across the Baie de La Forêt to the Îles de Glénan. The town is in the centre of an area of lush and fertile valleys. Butter biscuits and the best cider in Brittany have largely made the reputation of the Fouesnant area.

At the Fête du Cidre (Cider Festival), which takes place during the third week of July, the women wear traditional costumes and headdresses with large back-folded wings, waffle collar and lace wimple.

The Romanesque **Église de St-Pierre**, which was restored in the 18th century, has a pitched roof. Inside, tall semi-circular arches rest on capitals carved with acanthus leaves, stars and human figures. The calvary dates from the 18th century, and the war memorial is by the sculptor René Quillivic.

Cap-Coz, on the eastern side of the Anse de Penfoulic at Fouesnant, is a pleasant place for a walk along the coast. From there it is possible to reach the resort of Beg-Meil.

Street-by-Street: Concarneau ㉗

T HE WALLED TOWN *(ville close)*, Concarneau's ancient centre, is set on an islet in the Moros estuary that is just 350 m (380 yds) wide and 100 m (330 ft) long. With narrow paved streets and picturesque houses, the islet is very popular with visitors. It is accessible via two bridges leading to a postern bearing the royal coat of arms. The outer defences here, consisting of a triangular courtyard surrounded by high walls and flanked by two towers, made the town impregnable. Visitors enter this town of medieval streets by crossing an inner moat. At the western end of Rue Vauban, with old, crooked houses, is the Maison du Gouverneur, one of the oldest houses in the *ville close*.

The walled town, Concarneau's historic nucleus, seen from the fishing harbour

★ Logis du Major
Beyond the triangular courtyard, which is defended by the Tour du Major and Tour du Gouverneur at two of its corners, is the Logis du Major, built in 1730.

Musée de la Pêche

RUE MILITAIRE

RUE VAUBAN

RUE THÉOPHILE

RUE

Maison du Gouverneur

Postern

★ Belfry
Fronting the towers, and set at the third corner of the triangle, the belfry was once a watchtower.

Causeway

STAR SIGHTS
★ Belfry
★ Logis du Major
★ Ramparts

Tour de la Fortune
The tower commands a magnificent view of the yachting harbour.

★ **Ramparts**
Beyond the two small bridges at the entrance, a stairway on the left leads to the ramparts. The wall walk gives an impressive view of the ville close.

VISITORS' CHECKLIST

Road map B3. 👥 *19,000.*
🛈 *9 Quai d'Aiguillon; (02) 98 97 01 44.* 🔲 *for the rampart walk.*
📅 *Mon & Fri am.* 🎭 *Fête des Filets Bleus (music and dancing; Aug)* Ⓦ *www.concarneau.org*

PORTE AU VIN

QUAI DE LA

RUE SAINT - GUÉNOLÉ

The Amphitheatre,
facing into the ramparts, the amphitheatre is a venue for summer shows.

PLACE SAINT-GUÉNOLÉ

RUE

DE

L'ÉGLISE

0 m   50

0 yards   50

QUAI DU PASSAGE

KEY

– – – Suggested route

Powder magazine

PLACE DU PETIT CHÂTEAU

Porte du Passage
This gateway leads to the embarkation point for the ferry across the Moros.

Façade of the former hospital
Not far from the amphitheatre, at the eastern end of Rue Vauban, is a fine building that was once a hospital. The façade is in the late Gothic style.

VAUBAN

Sébastien Le Prestre de Vauban (1633–1707), Marshal of France and superintendent of fortifications, is France's most famous military builder. Fascinated by military techniques, he also wrote on the art of warfare and on politics. Brittany's strategic location and new methods of warfare that were developing at the time led Vauban to remodel military defences on Belle-Île and at Concarneau, Port-Louis, Brest and St-Malo, and to build fortifications at Hoëdic and Houat and the Tour Dorée in Camaret.

Sébastien Le Prestre de Vauban

Exploring Concarneau

THE "BLUE TOWN", as it is known, after the blue fishing
nets that were used in the early 20th century, has an
important historic heritage. The islet of Le Conq was inhabited from the 10th century by monks from Landévennec,
and the earliest fortifications date from the 13th century.
By the 14th century, the island settlement had become
the fourth-largest fortified town in Brittany. Briefly
occupied by the English, the town returned to the duchy
of Brittany in 1373, then, with the marriage of Anne of
Brittany and Charles VIII, king of France, in 1491, it
became a royal town. Vauban reinforced its defences in
the 18th century. The first fish cannery opened in 1851,
and 50 years later there were about 30 canning factories
in Concarneau. The disappearance of sardine stocks led
to hardship from 1905, but the Fête des Filets Bleus
helped to raise funds for families in difficulties. The
third-largest fishing port in France, Concarneau
produces 25,000 tonnes of fresh fish a year.

Château de Kériolet, in a recreated Flamboyant Gothic style

Concarneau's attractive walled town, with the Îles de Glénan beyond

🏛 Musée de la Pêche
4 Rue Vauban. 【 (02) 98 97 10 20.
◐ Jul–early Sep: daily; out of season:
closed lunchtime. ◑ third week
in Jan. 🖼
With dioramas and models
complementing the displays
of artifacts, the museum traces
the development of Concarneau
and its seafaring activities
from its beginnings to the
present day. Fishing methods
and the town's maritime
heritage are the main focus
here. There is also an aquarium
containing species of fish
caught in the Atlantic,
and, against the
ramparts, an
open-air maritime
museum with
docks where a
trawler, the
Hémérica, and a
tuna boat are
open to visitors.

Old-style tin of Breton sardines

⚓ Fishing Harbour
Trawlers, tuna boats and
sardine boats are tied up
along the **Quai d'Aiguillon**.
Refrigerator ships that fish in
tropical waters berth along
the **Quai Carnot**. The fish
auction, which has taken
place in Concarneau since
1937, starts at 6am.

➤ Marinarium
Place de la Croix. 【 (02) 98 97
06 59. ◐ phone for details.
Created in 1859, the
Marinarium du Collège de
France was one of
the first maritime
research stations
in Europe. The
flora and fauna of
Brittany's coasts
can be seen in
ten aquariums
and seawater
tanks. The use of

audiovisual facilities, the
opportunity to view certain
species under the microscope,
and guided tours along the
coastline make for a
comprehensive understanding
of marine and coastal life.

♣ Château de Kériolet
Beuzec-Conq, 2 km (1.5 miles) north
of Concarneau. 【 (02) 98 97 36 50.
◐ Easter–Sep. 🖼 groups by
arrangement. 🖼
Built in the 13th century by
the architect Joseph Bigot, of
Quimper, the chateau was
extensively remodelled in the
19th century in a re-creation
of the Flamboyant Gothic
style. Among guests here was
Princess Youssoupova, aunt
of tha last Russian tzar,
Nicolas Romanov.
   The chateau, surrounded by
a lovely garden, is now used
as a venue for artistic events.

🏰 Pointe du Cabellou
Road map B3. 3 km (2 miles) south
of Concarneau via the D783.
On this promontory stands a
17th-century fort with a stone
roof and, at the end of a coast
path leading to the Minaouët
river, there is a 16th-century
tidal mill. **Bretagne Vivante
SEPNB** organizes nature
walks along the coast here, as
it does in the Glénan
archipelago *(see p157)*.

Bretagne Vivante SEPNB
【 (02) 98 50 00 33.

Rosporden 🔢

Road map B3. 10 km (6 miles) north of Concarneau via the D70. 🔢 *6,430.*
🔢 *Quimper.* 🔢 *Quimperlé.*
🔢 *Rue de Bas; (02) 98 59 27 26.*

I N THE MIDST OF lush country-side dotted with picturesque chapels – where pilgrims once called on their *Tro Breiz* (tour of Brittany) – Rosporden stands on the edge of a pond formed by the Aven river. The **Église Notre-Dame**, built in the 14th century and restored in the 17th, has a fine belfry. Inside are a notable altarpiece and several interesting statues.

The many footpaths here, as well as the disused Rosporden-Scaër railway line, allow walkers to explore the area.

Pont-Aven 🔢

Road map B3. 🔢 *2,960.*
🔢 *Quimper.* 🔢 *Quimperlé.* 🔢 *5 Place de l'Hôtel-de-Ville; (02) 98 06 04 70.* 🔢 *Tue am, by the harbour (summer); Place de l'Hôtel-de-Ville (winter).* 🔢 *Pardon des Fleurs d'Ajonc (first weekend in Aug); Pardon de Trémalo (last Sun in Jul).*

P ONT-AVEN WAS originally a small fishing harbour set at the end of a *ria* (ancient flooded valley) and surrounded by mills. Luggers trading eastwards towards Nantes and southwards towards Bordeaux gradually transformed this small town into a busy port. The 17th- and 18th-century granite houses and paved streets that rise in tiers between Rue des Meunières and Place Royale date from this prosperous period in the port's history.

From the 1860s, Pont-Aven owed its renown to the painters who settled here. In the **Bois d'Amour** at the top of the town is the **Chapelle de Trémalo**, where the Christ on the Cross that is the subject of Paul Gauguin's *Christ Jaune* still hangs.

Pont-Aven's Christ on the Cross

The quay at Quimperlé, founded in the 11th century

The **Musée** documents the town's history and contains a collection of paintings by the Pont-Aven School.

Pont-Aven is also famous for its *galettes* (butter biscuits) and traditional costumes.

🏛 Musée
Place de l'Hôtel-de-Ville.
🔢 *(02) 98 06 14 43.* 🔢 *mid-Feb–early Jan: daily.*

Quimperlé 🔢

Road map C3. 🔢 *10,844.*
🔢 *Quimperlé.* 🔢 *Rue Bougneuf; (02) 98 96 04 32.* 🔢 *Fri in Place St-Michel; Tue–Sun, am, in the covered market.* 🔢 *Musiques Mosaïque (third weekend in Jul), Fêtes de la Laïta (mid-Aug).*

T HIS TOWN, at the confluence of the Isole and Ellé rivers, was founded by Benedictine monks in the 11th century,
although it began to develop only in the 17th century. Capuchins and Ursulines also settled here, and nobles built fine residences in **Rue Dom-Morice** and **Rue Brémond-d'Ars**, in the lower town. Other notable buildings are the **Hôtel du Cosquer** and the houses in **Rue Savary**.

Quimperlé (*Kemperle* in Breton) later expanded beyond its old boundaries, developing around the **Église Ste-Croix**, in the lower town, and Place St-Michel, in the higher town. Because of the strongly influential presence of the monks and nuns here, the principal monuments in Quimperlé are religious. They include the Baroque **Chapelle des Ursulines** and the **Église St-Michel** in a combined early and Flamboyant Gothic style.

THE PONT-AVEN SCHOOL

In 1866, a colony of American painters settled in Pont-Aven. Fascinated by the picturesque character of the surroundings, they painted scenes of the daily life that they observed around them. Paul Gauguin arrived in Pont-Aven in 1886, and there he met Charles Laval, Émile Bernard, Ferdinand du Puigaudeau and Paul Sérusier, artists who were later to form part of the Nabis group. Soon after, seeking refuge from the bustle of this coastal town, the group moved to the quieter surroundings of Le Pouldu, east of Pont-Aven. Influenced by primitive art, these painters used colour expressively and evocatively, and imbued images with a symbolic meaning. Their paintings were not intended to reflect reality but to embody reality itself, with line and colour producing a flat image devoid of shading and perspective. Their use of tonal contrasts, their novel approach to composition and their asceticism were at odds with Impressionism.

***La Belle Angèle**, by Paul Gauguin, a leading member of the Pont-Aven School*

MORBIHAN

O CCUPYING THE CENTRAL *southern part of Brittany, the Morbihan, which means "little sea" in Breton, takes its name from the Golfe du Morbihan on the* département's *southeasterly side. With gentle landscapes bathed in sunshine, a deeply indented coastline washed by the Atlantic Ocean, historic towns and cities and harbours thronged with boats, the Morbihan holds many attractions.*

The history of the Morbihan goes back to the remote past. Neolithic people raised an impressive number of large and mysterious standing stones here: the alignments at Carnac and Locmariaquer between them constitute the largest concentration of megalithic monuments in the world.

The Golfe du Morbihan, which is extended inland by the Auray and Vannes rivers, is almost like an inland sea. Marshland and mud flats are home to flocks of birds of various species. The gentle climate, in which a Mediterranean vegetation flourishes, the beauty of a landscape of ever-changing colours, and the soft sand beaches here combine to make the Morbihan a popular tourist destination.

The gulf is dotted with a host of small islands, whose number is said to equal that of the days in the year.

The islands include the Île d'Arz, the aptly named Belle-Île, the Île de Groix and the Île d'Houat, which are a delight for nature-lovers. The Presqu'île de Quiberon, a narrow spit of land protruding out to sea, is almost like a separate region. The peninsula's indented Côte Sauvage (Wild Coast) to the west contrasts with its more sheltered eastern side, where there are many beaches.

Great vitality characterizes towns and cities in the Morbihan, from Vannes, which was established in Gallo-Roman times, to Lorient, which was rebuilt after World War II. In the interior are such monuments to past glories as the Château de Josselin and Château de Pontivy, picturesque houses in Rochefort-en-Terre, and the fine historic covered markets in Questembert and Le Faouët.

The Neolithic alignment of 600 menhirs at Kerlescan, outside Carnac

◁ The calvary at Rochefort-en-Terre, with a carved base and a column crowned by a Crucifixion

Exploring the Morbihan

T HE SOUTH OF THE Morbihan is crossed by the
Vilaine, which flows into the Atlantic just west of
La Roche-Bernard. Vannes, on the far northern side
of the gulf, is the capital of the Morbihan, and a
lively city with an ever-expanding student
population. The Morbihan's two other major
conurbations – Lorient, a port with five harbours,
and Auray, a charming medieval town – are located
further northwest. Water is ubiquitous in
this region; countless rivers have
carved deep canyons, and
rias (ancient valleys
flooded by the sea) go
far inland. The Golfe du
Morbihan is almost closed
and is thus sheltered from
the rigours of the open sea.
Although the Morbihan's
inland region attracts fewer
visitors, it has beautiful
countryside and pretty villages.

SEE ALSO

• *Where to Stay* pp224–6

• *Where to Eat* pp239–41

Basilica at Ste-Anne-d'Auray

SIGHTS AT A GLANCE

The citadel at Port-Louis

GETTING AROUND

From Paris, Vannes can be reached in 3 hours and 10 minutes by TGV (high-speed train), and Lorient in 3 hours 45 minutes. The N24 and its continuation, the N166, link Rennes and Vannes. The fast N165, almost all of it a dual carriageway, links Nantes with Vannes, Auray and Lorient. Several minor roads, including the D780, D781, D199 and D10, run around the edge of the Golfe du Morbihan. The best way of exploring the gulf is, however, by boat, which provides a comprehensive view of the islands and their beautiful coastlines.

KEY

▦	Motorway
▦	Main road
▧	Minor road

Bagpipe-player at the Festival Interceltique held in Lorient

Lorient ❶

Road map C3. 🏛 *61,630*. 🚉 *Rue Beauvais*. 🚌 *Cour de Chazelles.* ⛴ *Rue Gahinet; (08) 20 05 60 00. Sailings to the Île de Groix (all year) and Belle-Île (Jul–Aug).* 🛈 *Quai de Rohan; (02) 97 21 07 84.* 🎫 *Wed & Sat.* 🎭 *Festival de Théâtre (Jul); Festival des Sept Chapelles (classical music, mid-Jul–mid-Aug); Festival Interceltique (Aug).*

IT WAS IN THE 17TH CENTURY, when the French East India Company, based in Port-Louis, needed to expand, that Lorient was created. The new port became the base for trade with the East (*l'Orient*), hence its name, and in 1770 it was chosen as the site of the royal dockyard. Almost completely destroyed during World War II, Lorient has been totally rebuilt.

Today, Lorient is the second-largest port in France on three counts. Not only a large fishing port, it also handles passenger and cargo ships, and is a major boating centre.

Keroman harbour, with a large covered fish market, caters to the fishing industry.

The super-trawler *Victor-Pleven* here allows visitors to learn about life on factory ships. The **Submarine Base**, built by the Germans in 1941, is also open to the public.

The **Quayside Buildings** in the naval dockyard stand on the site of the East India Company. Old cannons are displayed in two pavilions dating from that time. The Tour de la Découverte offers a fine view of the harbour and roadstead (sheltered anchorage).

On Place Alsace-Lorraine is an **Air-Raid Shelter** (*abri*), which could accommodate 400 people and which now gives a flavour of life during the war years (1939–45). In the Quartier de Merville are houses in the Art Nouveau and Art Deco styles that survived the bombing raids.

The tourist office here organizes trips to the roadstead (Rade de Lorient) and along the Blavet river, including a visit to the market at Hennebont (*see p195*).

Teapot, 18th-century, Musée de la Compagnie des Indes

🛥 Victor-Pleven
Port de Keroman. 📞 *(02) 97 88 15 12.* ○ *daily.* 🏛

🏛 Submarine Base
Port de Keroman. 📞 *(02) 97 21 07 84.* 🎫 *Jun–early Sep & school holidays: daily.* 🏛

Painted altarpiece in the choir of the church at Larmor-Plage

🏛 Quayside Buildings
Porte Gabriel. 🎫 *Jul–early Sep & school holidays: daily.* 📞 *(02) 97 21 07 84. Admittance restricted to citizens of the EU (identification required).* 🏛

🏛 Air-Raid Shelter
Place Alsace-Lorraine. 📞 *(02) 97 21 07 84.* 🎫 *Jul–Aug & school holidays: Mon–Sat.* ● *Sun & public holidays.* 🏛

ENVIRONS: Larmor-Plage, to the southwest, has beaches and a fortified Gothic church that is of interest for the painted statues in the north porch and an altarpiece in the Flemish style. To the east, at the mouth of the river, lies the Barre d'Étel, a notorious sandbar. Further north, Belz leads to St-Cado, a small island that is traditionally popular with painters and where there is a Romanesque chapel.

Port-Louis ❷

Road map C3. 12 km (7.5 miles) southeast of Lorient via the D194 then the D781. 🏛 *3,000*. 🚉 *Lorient.* 🛈 *47 Grande-Rue; (02) 97 82 52 93.* 🎫 *Sat.* 🎭 *Regattas (late Jul).*

THE 17TH-CENTURY citadel in Port-Louis, at the entrance to Lorient's roadstead, guards the mouth of the Blavet and Scorff rivers. Begun by the Spaniards, it was completed during the reign of Louis XIII, after whom it is named. Elegant residences dating from this period can be seen in the town, although they suffered damage during World War II.

With maps, models and examples of the highly prized goods that they brought back from the East, the **Musée de la Compagnie des Indes et de la Marine**, within the citadel, describes the illustrious history of the French East India Company.

🏛 Musée de la Compagnie des Indes et de la Marine
Citadelle de Port-Louis. 📞 *(02) 97 82 19 13.* ○ *Apr–May: Wed–Mon; Jun–Sep: daily; Oct–Mar: Wed–Mon.* ● *Dec.* 🏛

Port-Tudy, on the Île de Groix, built in the 19th century

Île de Groix ❸

Road map C3. 🏘 *2,500.* 🚢 *SMNN;*
(08) 20 05 60 00. 🛈 *Mairie, Quai de*
Port-Tudy, (02) 97 86 53 08; in summer:
(02) 97 86 54 96. 🐟 *Tue & Sat, in*
Loctudy. 🎭 *Fête de la Mer (late Jul).*

This picturesque island, with
an area of 24 sq km
(9 sq miles), is best explored
on foot, by bicycle or on
horseback. Between 1870 and
1940, tuna fishing provided
employment for up to 2,000
of the island's seamen. The
harbour at **Port-Tudy** would
then be filled with tuna boats
rather than the pleasure boats
that are moored here today.

The **Écomusée** in Port-Tudy
describes daily life on Groix
as well as its natural environment. The island's interesting
geology is the subject of the
displays in the **Maison de la
Réserve**.

At the end of the road
running south from Créhal, a
coast path leads to the
Trou de l'Enfer, an impressively deep recess in the cliff
face on the southern side of
the island.

On the west coast is the
beautiful Plage des Grands-
Sables, the only convex beach
in Europe, and there is a bird
sanctuary on the north-
westerly Pointe de Groix.

🏛 **Écomusée**
Port-Tudy. 🔴 *mid-Apr–Aug: daily;*
Sep–mid-Apr: Tue–Sun.
🛈 *(02) 97 86 84 60.* 🎟
🌿 **Maison de la Réserve**
Île de Groix. 🛈 *(02) 97 86 55 97.*
🔴 *Jun–Sep & school holidays:*
Mon–Sat; Oct–May: Sat pm.
⬤ *Sun & public holidays.*

Presqu'île
de Quiberon ❹

Road map C4. 🚌 *Auray or Quiberon*
(route served by the Tire-Bouchon
train in Jul–Aug); (08 36 35 35 35).
🚆 *Auray.* 🛈 *14 Rue de Verdun,*
Quiberon; (02) 97 50 07 84.
🌐 *www.quiberon.com* 🐟 *Thu in*
St-Pierre, Sat in Quiberon & Wed in
Port-Haliguen (mid-Jun–mid-Sep).
🎭 *Festival de la Flibuste, Quiberon*
(Apr); concerts (Jul–Aug); Fête de la
Sardine, Port-Maria.

Of all the areas of Brittany
that attract visitors, the
beautiful Presqu'Île de
Quiberon justifiably draws the
greatest number. It is also an
exceptional environment for
sailing and watersports. The
peninsula, 14 km (9 miles)
long, is linked to the mainland by a sandbank, the
Isthme de Penthièvre.

At Plouharnel, just above
the peninsula, visitors can see
the **Galion de Plouharnel**,
the replica of an 18th-century

Plage de Bara, near Quiberon, on
the Côte Sauvage

galleon containing a display
of shell pictures. The **Musée
de la Chouannerie**, in an old
blockhouse nearby, tells the
story of the Chouans *(see p46).*

The Fort de Penthièvre, rebuilt in the 19th century and
now owned by the French
Army, controls access to the
peninsula. To the west,
Portivy, a fishing harbour,
leads to Pointe de Percho,
from where there is a splendid
view of Belle-Île *(see pp176–7)*
and the Île de Groix.

Exposed to the rigours of
the sea, the cliffs of the **Côte
Sauvage** (Wild Coast) are indented with caves and chasms,
and on stormy days the windswept sea at Ber-er-Goalennec
is an impressive sight. Quiberon,
once a busy sardine port, is a
resort now known mainly for
its institute of thalassotherapy.
The town was launched as a
coastal resort in the early
20th century, when silk
manufacturers from Lyon built
villas on the seafront here.

Alignment of menhirs
at St-Pierre-de-Quiberon

From Port-Maria, once a
sardine port, boats sail for
Belle-Île, the Île de Houat and
Île de Hoëdic *(see pp176–7)*.
Pointe du Conguel, with the
Phare de la Teignouse, is the
peninsula's most southerly
point. During the summer,
regattas are regularly held
at Port-Haliguen.

St-Pierre-de-Quiberon, a
family holiday resort on the
eastern side, has good
beaches and interesting
prehistoric standing stones.
There are also many sailing
schools here.

🚢 **Galion de Plouharnel**
Anse de Bégo. 🛈 *(02) 97 52 39 56.*
🔴 *Easter–Sep: daily.* 🎟
🏛 **Musée de la Chouannerie**
Plouharnel. On the D 768. 🛈 *(02) 97*
52 31 31. 🔴 *Apr–Sep: daily.* 🎟

Belle-Île-en-Mer ➎

THE LARGEST ISLAND in Brittany, Belle-Île (Beautiful Island) well deserves its name. Its unspoiled environment, of heathland carpeted in gorse alternating with lush valleys, its beaches and well-kept villages attract numerous holiday-makers. Continually fought over on account of its strategic position south of Quiberon, the island was held by the English in 1761. It was finally exchanged for Minorca in 1763.

Pointe des Poulains
The lighthouse and its setting he great appeal for Sarah Bernhar

Sauzon
The town's colourfully painted houses and the steep-banked inlet here captivated painters and poets, including Victor Vasarely and Jacques Prévert in the 1950s and '60s.

Port-Donnant
is framed by sheer cliffs. The beach here is spectacular.

Grand Phare
commands a view stretching from Lorient to Le Croisic.

Bangor is a small town near some of the wildest stretches of coast.

Port-Goulphar
The cove at Port-Goulphar and the jagged rocks at Port-Coton, where breakers foam furiously, were portrayed by the painter Claude Monet in 1886.

Île de Houat ➏

Road map D4. 👥 *345.* 🚢 *from Quiberon; in summer, also from Port-Narvalo, Vannes & La Trinité; (08) 20 05 60 00.* ℹ️ *Mairie; (02) 97 30 68 04.* 🎉 *gathering of vintage tall ships (Aug); Fête de la Mer (15 Aug).*

LIKE THE NEIGHBOURING Île de Hoëdic, the Île de Houat (Duck Island in Breton) forms part of the Ponant archipelago. Just 5 km (3 miles) long and 1 km (0.5 mile) wide, Houat can be explored easily on foot. A coast path encircles the island, taking in Pointe Beg-er-Vachif, where, at sunset, the mica-rich grey

Cyclists riding through the quiet village of Houat

granite rocks become flecked with red.

Four fifths of the island are covered with heathland. **Houat**, the island's only village, has neat whitewashed houses. The Église St-Gildas, built in 1766, is dedicated to the 6th-century saint who came to live here as a hermit. In **Port-St-Gildas**,

the harbour below Houat, fishing boats come and go.

Vestiges of Houat's former importance as a military base include the Beniguet battery, the En-Tal redoubt and a ruined fort.

The **Éclosarium**, just outside the village, is a plankton research and breeding centre where visitors can see microscopic marine life. The Plage de Treac'h-er-Goured, on the southeastern side, is one of Houat's more sheltered beaches.

🏛 **Éclosarium**
1 km (0.5 mile) from Houat. 📞 (02) 97 52 38 38. 🕐 Easter–Sep: daily.

SARAH BERNHARDT

**Sarah Bernhardt
on Belle-Île**

Born in Rosine Bernard in Paris, the actress known as Sarah Bernhardt (1844–1923) made her debut at the Comédie Française and came to prominence at the Odéon in 1869. From 1870 to 1900, she dominated Parisian theatre and made successful tours abroad. In 1893, she discovered Belle-Île and fell in love with the island. She purchased the Bastion de Basse-Hiot, bought land at Pointe des Poulains, and in 1909 became the owner of the Domaine de Penhoët.

VISITORS' CHECKLIST

Road map C4. 🚶 4,500. 🚢 from Quiberon & Lorient; in summer, also from Port-Narvalo, Vannes & La Trinité. SMNN; (08) 20 05 60 00. 🛈 Quai Bonnelle, Le Palais; (02) 97 31 81 93. 🚢 Tue & Fri in Le Palais; Sun in Locmaria (Jul–Aug) & Thu in Sauzon. 🎉 Regattas (Jun); Festival Lyrique (Jul–Aug); Jazz (Jul); Fête de la Mer (Aug).

Le Palais
The harbour of this town, the capital of Belle-Île, is dominated by a citadel. The museum here documents the island's history.

Pointe e Taillefer

QUIBERON

e Palais

LA TRINITÉ, VANNES

D 25

Pointe de Kerdonis

Locmaria

Plage des Grands-Sables is the island's largest beach.

Pointe du Skeul

Locmaria has several beaches that are ideal for watersports. The town also contains the island's oldest church, built in 1714.

KEY

▬	Main road
▭	Minor road
---	Ferry route
🏛	Museum
⚓	Fort or citadel
⛪	Church
🗼	Lighthouse
⬜	Megalithic site
🌿	Nature reserve
Ⓐ	Camp site
🏖	Beach

0 km _____ 4

0 miles _____ 2

Île de Hoëdic ❼

Road map D4. 🚶 140. 🚢 from Quiberon; in summer, also from Port-Narvalo & Vannes; (08) 20 05 60 00. 🛈 Mairie; (02) 97 30 68 32. 🎉 Fête de la Mer (Aug).

As its breton name suggests, the Île de Hoëdic (Little Duck Island) is smaller than the Île de Houat, its north-westerly neighbour. It is 2.5 km (1.5 miles) long and 1 km (0.5 mile) wide, and like Houat, it is easy to explore on foot.

The island's ubiquitous heathland is scattered with sea pinks and sea bindweed.

Sailing off the Île de Hoëdic, an island with a beautiful coastline

Along the coast, superb beaches alternate with jagged, rocky creeks.

Le Bourg, in the centre of Hoëdic, is a traditional village with long, low houses, white-washed and south-facing. The Église St-Goustan is worth a visit for its attractive blue and gold ceiling and its thanks-giving plaques. Northeast of Bourg, the 19th-century fort contains a short-stay gîte and an **Écomusée** devoted to the island's plants, animals and local history.

🏛 **Écomusée**
Fort d'Hoëdic. 📞 (02) 97 52 48 82. ⭕ Jun–Aug: daily.

Carnac ⓢ

BRITTANY'S BEST-KNOWN prehistoric site is, without doubt,
Carnac. The alignments of 3,000 standing stones –
which may originally have numbered over 6,000 – are
the most extraordinary group of menhirs in the world.
The oldest date from the Neolithic period and the most
recent from the Bronze Age. Although their significance
remains unknown, they were probably connected to
religion. Apart from its famous megaliths, Carnac also
has wide sandy beaches and a lively commercial centre,
making it a popular coastal resort for summer visitors.

The Alignements de Kerlescan, with 240 standing stones

Exploring Carnac

Carnac consists of the town
itself and of Carnac-Plage,
the beach that was created
from scratch out of a lagoon
in 1903.

The Renaissance **Église
St-Cornély**, in the centre of
the town, was built in the
17th century and is dedicated
to the local patron saint of
horned animals. This honour
highlights the importance of
agriculture, and of oxen in
particular, to the local
community. The figure of
St Cornély, framed by oxen,
can be seen above the
pediment of the west door.
The wooden ceiling inside
the church is decorated with
18th-century frescoes, those
over the nave showing scenes
from the life of St Cornély.

Southwest of Carnac,
overlooking the Anse du Pô,
is **St-Colomban**, a
picturesque fishing village
where oysters are farmed.
A few old houses cluster
around the Flamboyant
Gothic chapel, built in 1575.
There is also a 16th-century
fountain with two troughs,
one for washerwomen and
the other for animals.

🏛 Musée de Préhistoire

10 Place de la Chapelle, Carnac-Ville.
📞 (02) 97 52 22 04. 🕐 Jun–Sep:
daily; Oct–May: Wed–Mon. ⬤ Sun
& public holidays. 📷

This important museum
contains a collection of some
500,000 artifacts, although
only 6,000 pieces are shown
at a time. They are presented
in chronological order.

The ground floor is
devoted to the Palaeolithic
(450,000–12000 BC),
Mesolithic (12,000– 5000 BC),
and Neolithic (4500–2000 BC)
periods. The Neolithic period,
when the megaliths were
built *(see p35)*, is particularly
well illustrated. Menhirs
(standing stones), cromlechs
(menhirs in a semicircle),
dolmens (tombs consisting of
two upright stones roofed by
a third), cairns (galleried
graves), tumuli (burial
mounds), and *allées couvertes*
(graves in the form of
covered alleys) are each
explained. Axes made
of polished jadeite (a green
stone), pottery, jewellery,
bone and horn tools, and flint
arrowheads, blades and
handaxes provide a picture of
daily life in Neolithic times.

There are also models and
reconstructions.

The first floor is devoted
to subsequent periods: the
Chalcolithic and the
appearance of the earliest
bronze tools, the Bronze Age
(1800–750 BC), the Iron Age,
and the Gallo-Roman period,
which is fittingly illustrated by
objects found at the Villa des
Bosséno, near Carnac.

🏕 Tumulus St-Michel

On the way out of Carnac-Ville, in the
direction of La Trinité-sur-Mer.
⬤ for excavations.

Built on a natural rise in the
ground that commands a wide
view of the surrounding
megaliths and the Baie de
Quiberon, this tumulus dates
from 4500 BC and is 12 m (40
ft) high. On it stands a chapel
dedicated to St Michael. The
tumulus contains two burial
chambers, which, when they
were investigated in the 19th
century, were found to
contain urns filled with
bones, as well as axes,
jewellery and pottery.

The fountain with two troughs
in St-Colomban

🏕 Alignements de Carnac

Northeast of Carnac-Ville. ℹ️ visitor
centre at Kermario. 📞 (02) 97 52 29
81. 🕐 all year. 📷 Apr–Sep.

Carnac's standing stones, just
outside the town, consist of
three groups, the alignments
at **Ménec**, **Kermario** and
Kerlescan, which are framed
at their eastern and western
limits by cromlechs. To protect
the site from the large number
of visitors that come here,
wire fencing has been erected
all round the alignments.

The precise purpose of the
alignments remains unknown.
The most likely explanation is
that these were places where

regular gatherings took place, and that they were great religious centres, perhaps where rituals connected to a sun god were performed.

Fresco in the Église St-Cornély, Carnac

The Alignements de Kerlescan, in the direction of La Trinité, consist of 555 menhirs arranged in 13 lines. The southwest end is marked by a cromlech of 39 stones. On the heath is the Géant du Manio, a menhir 6 m (20 ft) high.

The Alignements de Kermario consists of 1,029 menhirs laid out in ten rows. This alignment has some of the most beautiful standing stones in Carnac.

The Alignements du Ménec, further west, have the most representative stones. The 1,099 menhirs here are arranged in 11 rows and the tallest stones are 4 m (13 ft) high.

Other megaliths here include the Tumulus de Kercado (east of Kermario), a dolmen dating from 4670 BC with a gallery leading to a burial chamber with engraved walls, and the dolmens at Mané-Kerioned.

The best time to see Carnac's menhirs is at sunrise, when the stones cast extraordinary shadows, and it is best to walk the alignment from east to west.

🏛 Archéoscope

Alignement du Ménec. 📞 (02) 97 52 07 49. ◯ Feb–mid-Nov & Christmas holidays: daily. 🎫

This is a stimulating and realistic reconstruction of various aspects of life during the Neolithic period. The different hypotheses regarding the function and meaning of the alignments are also explained.

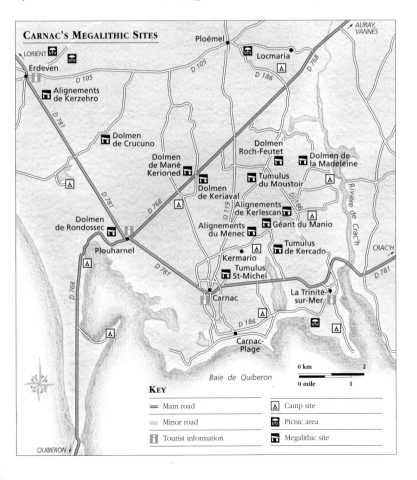

CARNAC'S MEGALITHIC SITES

KEY

━━ Main road

═══ Minor road

ℹ Tourist information

🔺 Camp site

🚻 Picnic area

🔲 Megalithic site

The Grand Menhir Brisé (Great Broken Menhir) at Locmariaquer,
5 m (16 ft) wide and originally 20–30 m (65–98 ft) high

La Trinité-sur-Mer ❾

Road map C3–4. 🏠 *1,450.*
🚌 *Auray.* 🚤 *Navix; (02) 97 55
81 00. Sailings to Belle-Île & Île de
Houat Jul–Aug & cruises in the Golfe
du Morbihan.* 🛈 *Môle Loïc-Caradec
(02) 97 55 72 21).* 🚤 *Tue & Fri.*
🎉 *Spi Ouest France (regattas; Easter);
Fête du Nautisme (May); Fête du
Vieux-Port (Jul); Fête des Vieux
Gréements (Aug); Prix Multicoques
(regattas; late Aug).*

NESTLING IN A sheltered *ria*,
La Trinité-sur-Mer is the
time-honoured meeting place
of sailing enthusiasts. The
town's sailing club, founded
in 1879, is one of the oldest
in France, and it was here
that Éric Tabarly, Peyron
and other yachtsmen began
their careers. From April to
September, regattas take
place in the harbour, which is
large enough to accommodate
1,200 yachts. La Trinité also
has a fishing industry, which
supplies the town's lively
fish market.
    A coast path leads from
the harbour to the beaches,
taking in Pointe de Kerbihan.
The Pont de Kérisper, in the
direction de Carnac, offers a
breathtaking view of the
Crac'h river, which it spans,
the oyster farms further

The Table des Marchands,
a Neolithic galleried grave

upriver, and the marina
further downstream. Trips out
to sea in an old sailing boat
and boat rides on the Crac'h
are available in summer.

Locmariaquer ❿

Road map C–D 3. 10 km (6 miles)
east of La Trinité-sur-Mer via the D 781.
🏠 *1,315.* 🚌 *Auray.* 🚤 *Navix; (02)
97 57 36 78. Trips to Belle-Île & cruises
in the Golfe de Morbihan (Jul–Aug).*
🛈 *Rue de la Victoire; (02) 97 57 33
05.* 🚤 *Tue & Sat (Jul–Aug).* 🎉 *Pardon
(Jun); Randonnée des Mégalithes
(Jun–Sep); Fête de l'Huître (Aug).*

THIS CHARMING coastal resort
also has some of the most
impressive megalithic monuments in Brittany. Just outside
the town is the **Table des
Marchands**, a Neolithic
galleried grave dating from
3700 BC. Its stones are
engraved with scrolls, an axe
shape and depictions of
cattle. Behind the Table des
Marchands, a path leads to
the Mané-Lud tumulus, consisting of 22 engraved stones
forming a corridor. The Er-
Grah Tumulus, 140 m (460 ft)
long, is a burial mound.
    These monuments date
from a time when people
were using polished stone
axes, had learned to make
pottery, and had begun to
keep animals and plant crops.
Having adopted a settled way
of life, they turned to raising
impressive monuments.
    The **Grand Menhir Brisé**,
dating from 4500 BC, is 20 m
(65 ft) long and weighs
350 tonnes. It lies broken
into four pieces, but is the
largest known menhir in the
western world.

🏛 **Megaliths (Grand Menhir
Brisé, Table des Marchands
& Er-Grah Tumulus)**
At the entrance to the town, near the
cemetery. 🎫 *(02) 97 57 37 59.*
🕐 *Apr–Sep: daily; Oct–Mar:
Wed–Mon, pm.* ● *20 Dec–10 Jan.* 🅿

ENVIRONS: The Pointe de
Kerpenhir, opposite Port-
Navalo (*see p184*), southeast
of Locmariaquer, offers a
panoramic view of the Golfe
du Morbihan. The granite
statue of Notre-Dame de
Kerdro protects sailors and
yachtsmen. Behind Plage de
Kerpenhir is the Allé Couverte
des Pierres-Plates (*free access*),
a corridor grave with two
burial chambers engraved
with motifs, which are
connected by a long passage.

Auray ⓫

Road map D3. 🏠 *10,590.* 🚌 *2 km
(1 mile) from the town centre.*
🛈 *Chapelle de la Congrégation,
20 Rue du Lait; (02) 97 24 09 75.*
🚤 *Jul–Aug: Tue–Fri.* 🚤 *Mon on Place
de la République; Fri on Place Notre-
Dame; Sun at the railway station;
Wed eve. (Jul–Aug) at St-Goustan
farm.* 🎉 *Les Not'en Bulles (theatre &
music; Aug).*

TUCKED AWAY at the end of
a *ria*, Auray stands on a
promontory overlooking the
Loch river. With its old houses
and attractive harbour, this is
a delightful town. It also has

Detail of the 17th-century altarpiece
in the Église St-Gildas in Auray

THE IMP OF THE HIGH SEAS

Éric Tabarly (1931–98), once a captain in the French Navy, was the ultimate yachtsman of the second half of the 20th century. Such eulogy would have embarrassed this shy man, who would face cameras with a modest smile. He had a long list of victories to his name. His first came in 1964, sailing in the *Pen Duick II*, when he won the second Solo Transatlantic Race, beating the British. Tabarly became a French yachting legend in the process and, as the newly popular art of sailing gripped the nation, others were inspired to emulate them.

Éric Tabarly aboard the *Côte d'Or*

Timber-framed houses in the Quartier St-Goustan, Auray

its place in the history of Brittany. It was the Battle of Auray, in 1364, that brought an end to the War of the Breton Succession *(see p40)*.

The **Église St-Gildas** has a Renaissance doorway (1636) and contains a remarkable Baroque altarpiece *(see p64)* made by a sculptor from Lavalle in 1657. Place de la République is surrounded by elegant houses, including the Maison Martin and the Hôtel de Trévegat, both dating from the 17th century, and the town hall, built in 1776.

From the belvedere and the promenade above the Loch, where terraced gardens are laid out in tiers below the castle, there is a beautiful view of the river and the harbour.

A 17th-century stone bridge at the bottom of the town leads to **St-Goustan**, which was once Auray's port. Here, medieval timber-framed

houses line the quay, whose peaceful atmosphere has captivated many painters.

The **Goélette-Musée St-Sauveur** is a schooner moored on Quai Martin. Containing displays of sea-faring equipment and models of ships, it is now a museum of coastal shipping. It also traces the seafaring history of St-Goustan. The steep narrow streets behind the harbour are also worth exploring.

🏛 Goélette-Musée St-Sauveur
Quai Martin, St-Goustan harbour.
📞 (02) 97 56 63 38. ⏱ Easter–Sep: daily; Oct–Easter & school holidays: Sat–Sun. 🅰

ENVIRONS: The picturesque fishing village of Le Bono lies 6 km (4 miles) southeast of Auray. The view from the suspension bridge (1840) is magnificent.

The 17th-century cloisters at Ste-Anne-d'Auray

Waxwork of John Paul II in the Musée de Cire, Ste-Anne-d'Auray

Ste-Anne-d'Auray 🕑

Road map D3. 7 km (4 miles) north of Auray via the D17. 🏠 1,760.
🚉 Auray. 🅸 12 Place Nicolazic; (02) 97 57 69 19. 🔄 Wed.
🎪 Grand Pardon (late Jul).

THE SECOND-GREATEST shrine in France after Lourdes, and honoured by a visit from Pope John Paul II in 1999, Ste-Anne-d'Auray became a major place of pilgrimage in the 17th century.

St Anne, mother of the Virgin Mary, appeared to a ploughman, Yves Nicolazic, whom she instructed to build a chapel. When a statue was discovered at the spot that she had indi-cated, a church was built there. It was replaced by the present basilica in 1872. The church contains stained-glass windows depicting scenes from the life of St Anne and of the ploughman. The **Trésor** (Treasury) in the cloisters contains votive plaques, seascapes and model ships, and statues dating from the 15th to the 19th centuries.

The **Musée de Cire de l'Historial**, opposite the basi-lica, traces the origins of the town as a place of pilgrimage and describes the life of Nicolazic. The **Musée du Costume Breton**, on the basilica square, contains displays of local headdresses and costumes, as well as processional banners.

⛪ Trésor de la Basilique
📞 (02) 97 57 68 80. ⏱ Mar–Oct: Tue–Sun. 🅰
🏛 Musée de Cire de l'Historial
6 Rue de Vannes. 📞 (02) 97 57 64 05. ⏱ Mar–mid-Oct: daily. 🅰
🏛 Musée du Costume Breton
On the basilica square. 📞 (02) 97 57 68 80. ⏱ Mar–Oct: Tue–Sun. 🅰

Golfe du Morbihan ⑬

THIS LARGE BAY was created 9,000 years ago, when global warming caused the sea level to rise. About 15,000 years earlier, the sea level was 100 m (330 ft) lower than it is today, and Belle-Île was attached to the mainland. The rising sea gradually created hundreds of islands, the largest of which are the Isle d'Arz and the Île aux Moines. The Golfe du Morbihan consists of two parts: an eastern basin, which is flatter, rather like a lagoon; and a western basin, which is defined by a rocky coastline and where there are strong currents. Here, the sea bed is uneven, particularly around Port-Navalo, where depressions can be as much as 30 m (100 ft) deep. The constant ebb and flow of the tide circulates volumes of water from the Atlantic, encouraging thousands of species of marine plant and animal life to thrive. These in turn provide food for indigenous and migratory birds.

Sailing boat off Île Berder

Île Berder
At low tide, it is possible to walk across the sand to the island.

★ **Port-Navalo**
This small port is also a holiday resort. The coast path offers beautiful views in all directions.

0 km   5

0 miles   3

STAR SIGHTS

★ **Château de Suscinio**

★ **Pointe d'Arradon**

★ **Port-Navalo**

Église St-Gildas-de-Rhuys
Founded in the 11th century, the church still has its original transept and choir.

★ Pointe d'Arradon
*This promontory commands spectacular views of
the Île aux Moines and the Île d'Arz.*

VISITORS' CHECKLIST

Road map D 3-4. 🚃 *Auray &
Vannes.* ℹ️ *Auray (02) 97 24
09 75; Locmariaquer (02) 97 57
33 05; Sarzeau (02) 97 41 82 37;
Vannes (02) 97 47 24 34.*
⛴ *Arradon, Arzon, Baden,
Île aux Moines, Île d'Arz,
Locmariaquer, Sarzeau.* 🚶 🚲

Île d'Arz
*A walk around the island
takes in this old restored
tidal mill.*

KEY

━━	Main road
═	Minor road
- -	Ferry route
ℹ️	Tourist information
♠	Castle
🔲	Megalithic site
🏹	Nature reserve
⛵	Sailing
☀	View point

★ Château de Suscinio
*In the Middle Ages, the castle was the
main residence of the dukes of Brittany. It
was abandoned after the Revolution but, at
the suggestion of the writer Prosper Mérimée,
it was classified as a historic monument in
1835. Now under municipal ownership,
it contains a museum of Breton history.*

Exploring the Golfe du Morbihan

OCAL POINT OF the Morbihan region, the Golfe du Morbihan is 20 km (12 miles) wide and covers 12,000 ha (30,000 acres). The gulf, with its deeply indented coastline and many islands, can be explored by boat from Vannes, Port-Navalo, Auray, La Trinité or Locmariaquer. Tourism, together with shellfish and oyster farming, are major industries here, and, although fishing, sailing and other activities have also developed, the gulf is a haven for bird life. The land around it is dotted with menhirs, dolmens and tumuli.

Detail of the stoup in the Église St-Gildas-de-Rhuys

🏝 Pointe d'Arradon

Road map D3. 9 km (6 miles) south-west of Vannes via the D101 then the D101a. 🛈 *2 Place de l'Église, Arradon; (02) 97 44 77 44.* 🛒 *Tue & Fri.*

The "Riviera of the Gulf", the Pointe d'Arradon can be reached via the D101 west from Vannes. There are some superb houses here and the view takes in the Îles Logoden, Île Holavre and Île aux Moines.

🏝 Île d'Arz

Road map D4. 🚢 *15 mins from Vannes-Conleau, (02) 97 50 83 83; & Navix (02) 97 46 60 00.* 🛈 *Mairie,*

Île d'Arz; (02) 97 44 31 14. 🎉 *Pardon, on Île d'Hur (late Jul); regattas (Aug).*

The Île d'Arz (Bear Island), which attracts fewer visitors than the Île aux Moines, can be explored on foot as it is only 3 km (2 miles) long and 1 km (0.5 mile) wide. The low, whitewashed, slate-roofed houses and lush vegetation here create a typical image of Brittany.

The island is dotted with menhirs and dolmens, with a particular concentration on Pointe de Liouse. The Église Notre-Dame, in the town, has Romanesque capitals

decorated with grotesque figures. Boating enthusiasts will find no fewer than five sailing schools on the island.

⛩ Cairn de Gavrinis

Road map D4. Île Gavrinis. 🛈 *(02) 97 57 19 38.* 🚢 *Larmor-Baden.* 📷 ✔

Discovered in 1832, this single-chambered passage grave is considered to be unusual both on account of its construction – of a type that makes it one of the oldest in the region – and because of its engravings. When the writer

---

CAIRN DE GAVRINIS

Measuring 16 m (52 ft), the Cairn de Gavrinis is the longest dolmen in France. The gallery leading to the burial chamber consists of 29 stones, some of which are engraved with symbolic motifs including shields, scrolls, axes, horn shapes and other signs. Inferences about the significance of these signs gives an insight into the meaning of such inscriptions.

Carved Stone No. 8 has engravings in which the central motif is a shield. This is usually a schematic depiction of an anthropomorphic deity.

The cairn, still an impressive 6 m (20 ft) high, is almost intact.

Gallery

The stones forming the gallery were carefully selected and positioned so as to minimize the gaps between each of them.

Prosper Mérimée visited it in 1835, he was struck by what he saw: "stones covered in peculiar drawings...curved, straight, broken and wavy lines combined in a hundred different ways".

🏛 Île aux Moines

Road map D4. 🚢 from Port-Blanc, (02) 97 57 23 24, or Vannes-Conleau, (02) 97 46 60 00. 🅸 The harbour; (02) 97 26 32 45. 🅰 summer: daily; winter: Wed & Fri. 🎫 Semaine du Golfe (gathering of old sailing ships, Ascension, 40th day after Easter); Festival de Voile (Aug).

This cruciform island, 6 km (4 miles) long and 3 km (2 miles) wide, once belonged to the Abbaye de St-Sauveur in Redon (see p64). The largest island in the Golfe du Morbihan, it has been in-habited since Neolithic times, and it has several megalithic sites. The most notable are the cromlech at Kergonan, the largest in France, and, further south, the dolmen of Pen-Hap.

Like the neighbouring Île d'Arz, the Île aux Moines has fine 17th- and 18th-century houses. Its mild microclimate supports a vegetation asso-ciated with more southerly climes. Eucalyptus, mimosa, camellia and fig all thrive here. As for the island's forests – Bois d'Amour (Wood of Love), Bois des Soupirs (Wood of Sighs) and Bois des Regrets (Wood of Regrets) – their names alone are conducive to gentle reverie.

Each of the promontories on the island's indented coastline offers spectacular views of the gulf.

🏛 Presqu'île de Rhuys

Road map D4. South of the Golfe du Morbihan, via the D780 from Vannes. 🅸 Sarzeau, (02) 97 41 82 37; St-Gildas-de-Rhuys, (02) 97 45 31 45; Port du Crouesty, (02) 97 53 69 69. 🅰 Sun in St-Gildas-de-Rhuys); Tue in Port du Crouesty; Mon in Port du Crouesty (Jul–Aug). 🎫 Fête de l'Huître (Apr); Semaine du Golfe (gathering of old sailing boats; Ascension, 40 days after Easter); Fête Médiévale (Château de Suscinio, Jul); Festival de Théâtre (Château de Suscinio, Aug); Fête de la Mer (Aug).

Like Quiberon (see p175), this peninsula has two different aspects: a sheltered

An attractive 18th-century house on the Île aux Moines

north-facing side, and a southern side that is exposed to the rigours of the Atlantic.

The Italianate **Château de Kerlévenan** dates from the 18th century. Only its park is open to visitors. The **Château de Suscinio**, on the south side, is surrounded by marshland. Built as a hunting lodge in the 13th century, it was converted into a fortress in the 14th century. It has a drawbridge flanked by towers, its walls are set with watchtowers, and it is surrounded by a moat fed by the sea. In the 15th century, Francis II and his daughter, Anne of Brittany, chose Nantes rather than Suscinio as their place of residence, and the castle fell into neglect. It now houses a museum devoted to the history of Brittany.

St-Gildas-de-Rhuys, further west, is named after an English monk who established a monastery here in the 6th century. The **Musée des Arts et des Métiers**, at the Le Net

roundabout, contains recon-structions of workshops and shops dating from the 1600s to the 1950s. Between here and Arzon stands the Tumulus de Tumiac, also known as Caesar's Mound because the future Roman emperor is reputed to have used it as a lookout.

At the western tip of the peninsula, Port-Navalo and Port du Crouesty are modern coastal resorts. The coast path here commands impressive views of the gulf. It is also worth calling at the pretty little port of Le Logeo, opposite the Îles Branec.

Sarzeau, in the centre of the peninsula, has fine 17th- and 18th-century residences with ornate dormer windows. The chapel at Penvins, nearby, dates from 1897.

Migratory birds can be observed from footpaths on the peninsula's north coast.

⚜ Château de Kerlévenan

On the D780. 🅲 (02) 97 26 46 79. **Park** 🅾 Jul–mid-Sep: daily, pm; Nov–Jun: by arrangement. ⬤ mid-Sep–Oct. 🅿

⚜ Château de Suscinio

From Sarzeau, take the D198. 🅲 (02) 97 41 91 91. 🅾 Apr–Sep: daily; Oct–Mar: Thu, Sat–Sun & public holidays; Mon, Wed & Fri, pm. ⬤ 20 Dec–Jan & Mar outside school holidays. 🔳

🏛 Musée des Arts et Métiers

Le Net roundabout. 🅲 (02) 97 53 68 25. 🅾 high season: 10am–noon & 2–7pm daily; low season: 2–7pm daily. ⬤ Sun am. 🔳

The chapel at Penvins, near Sarzeau, in the form of a Greek cross

Street-by-Street: Vannes

THE MEDIEVAL CENTRE of Vannes is a honeycomb of narrow streets which, like those around the Cathédrale St-Pierre, are lined with well-restored timber-framed houses. The main entrance into the walled town, a busy commercial district, is Porte St-Vincent, near Place Gambetta. The walls on the eastern side offer a fine view of the town, with formal gardens laid out below, and also pass the city's old wash houses. The harbour, to the south, is a lively centre of activity.

★ City Walls and Gardens
Part of the Gallo-Roman walls around the old town survives.

Place Gambetta
This square, opposite the marina, is always busy. It is a central meeting place for the inhabitants of Vannes, who fill the café terraces here.

The fish market takes place twice a week, on Wednesdays and Saturdays

Château de l'Hermine
The chateau was built in the 18th century on the site of the residence of the dukes of Brittany. It is fronted by extensive formal gardens, where it is pleasant to walk.

The new market was opened in 2001.

Porte Poterne leads to the gardens beneath the city walls.

STAR SIGHTS

★ City Walls and Gardens

★ Doorway of the Cathédrale St-Pierre

★ Place des Lices

Wash Houses
Located beside the Marle river, the city's wash houses date from 1820. They were still in use after World War II.

Place Henri-IV
The square is lined with timber-framed houses dating from the 15th and 16th centuries, the oldest in Vannes. In the Middle Ages, a popular bird market was held here.

VISITORS' CHECKLIST

Road map D3. 🚶 48,455.
🛈 Office du Tourisme du Pays de Vannes, 1 Rue Thiers, (02) 97 47 24 34. 🗓 Wed & Sat am.
🎭 Fêtes Historiques (Jul); Festival de Jazz (Jul); Nuits Musicales du Golfe (Jul–Aug); Fêtes d'Arvor (traditional dancing and music, Aug).

Musée Archéologique

Musée de la Cohue is an art gallery that also contains displays of artifacts relating to seafaring.

★ Doorway of the Cathédrale St-Pierre
Built in the 16th century in the Flamboyant Gothic style, the doorway is lined with niches that, in keeping with Breton tradition, contain statues of the Apostles.

Porte St-Jean was the home of executioners, whose profession passed from father to son.

RUE SAINT SALOMON

RUE BURGAULT

RUE DES HALLES

PLACE HENRI IV

RUE BILLAUT

PLACE DE ALENCIA

RUE DES ORFÈVRES

PLACE SAINT-PIERRE

RUE DES CHANOINES

RUE DE LA MONNAIE

RUE SAINT GUENAËL

RUE BRIZEUX

PLACE LAROCHE

PLACE BRÛLÉE

RUE PORTE PRISON

PARTS

RUE DES VIERGES

★ Place des Lices
The square is surrounded by well-kept timber-framed houses, the most recent dating from the 17th century.

Porte Prison, dating from the 13th and 15th centuries, was the main gateway into Vannes. Criminals were imprisoned there.

Tour des Connétables
The tower, the highest in Vannes, was built in the 16th century and is now owned by the city authorities, who have restored it. It is has a pointed roof and mullioned windows.

0 m   100
0 yards   100

KEY

– – – Suggested route

Exploring Vannes

THE HISTORY OF VANNES goes back to Roman times, when it was known as Darioritum. In the 5th century, it was a diocese and, in the Middle Ages, a city of major importance. Vannes expanded during the 14th century, when it became the capital of Brittany. As a university town, an administrative centre and the capital of the Morbihan, it is again expanding rapidly today. The city also attracts large numbers of sightseers and holiday-makers.

Porte Poterne, the city's postern gate, built in the 17th century

🏰 Town Walls

Vannes was once completely surrounded by defensive walls. Two thirds of these remain, and some have been incorporated into more recent buildings. Part of the Gallo-Roman walls survive on the north side of the city.

Vannes' finest gateway is on its southern side, opposite the harbour. This is Porte St-Vincent, built in 1624. It was restored in 1747, when the gate's existing arrow slits and machicolation were replaced by niches with shell motifs and columns with capitals.

From here to Porte Prison, on the north side of the town, the wall walk overlooks formal gardens laid out in the former moat. It also passes Porte Poterne (1678), and the historic wash houses nearby. Other towers in the town walls include Tour de la Trompette, Tour de la Poudrière, Tour de la Joliette, and Tour du Bourreau. The highest is Tour du Connétable.

🛐 Cathédrale St-Pierre

⬜ May–Oct: Mon–Sat & public holidays; Nov–Apr: daily pm during school holidays. 🖼️

From a vantage point on the Colline du Mené, the Cathédrale St-Pierre dominates the old town. It was built in the Flamboyant Gothic style, but has neo-Gothic additions dating from the 19th century.

A rotunda chapel dedicated to the Holy Sacrament is built into the north aisle. A jewel of Renaissance architecture, it has a double tier of niches with pediments and high windows framed by semicircular arches. It contains the tomb of St Vincent-Ferrier, a Spanish monk renowned for his preaching. A Gobelins tapestry decorates the wall.

The cathedral treasury contains some fine metalwork.

🏰 Old Town

Place Henri-IV, at the heart of the old town, is lined with 15th- and 16th-century half-timbered houses, the oldest in Vannes. Many of the houses in the area around the square have unusual decoration. The house at No. 13 Rue Salomon has animal carvings and, on the corner of Rue Noé, is the famous inn sign in the form of "Vannes et sa Femme", the couple who ran the tavern.

In the 17th century, when the Breton parliament was exiled in Vannes, many fine granite or stone town houses (hôtels) were built here. The Hôtel de Lannion, in Impasse de la Psalette, flanked by a projecting turret, was once the residence of the governors of Vannes and Auray. The Hôtel de Limur, in Rue Thiers, with a Neo-Classical façade, is a three-storey residence with a courtyard and a garden.

🏛️ Musée de la Cohue

9 & 15 Place St-Pierre. 📞 (02) 97 47 35 86. ⬜ Jun–Sep: daily; Oct–May: Mon, Wed–Sat & Sun pm. ● public holidays.

The museum is laid out in a restored covered market (cohue) whose origins go back to the 13th century. While market stalls occupied the ground floor, the first floor housed the ducal courts of the Breton parliament, when the latter was exiled to Vannes in 1675 on the orders of Louis XIV. The building was then used as a theatre until the 1950s.

The Musée de la Cohue is an art gallery whose most highly prized exhibit is Delacroix's *Crucifixion*. Millet, Corot and Goya are also represented. The work of Breton painters, including Maufra, Henri Moret, Paul Helleu, and of engravers native to Vannes, such as Frélaut and Dubreuil, are also displayed, as is that of contemporary artists, including Tal Coat, Soulages and Geneviève Asse. Two other rooms in the museum are devoted to pieces relating to seafaring.

Statue of the Virgin in the Cathédrale St-Pierre

🏛 Musée Archéologique
Château Gaillard, 2 Rue Noé.
(*(02) 97 47 35 86.* **●** *for renovation, except in summer.*
Housed in the 15th-century Château Gaillard, which once accommodated the Breton parliament, this archaeological museum contains prehistoric artifacts from sites in the Morbihan. These include axes of polished jadeite and jewellery made of variscite (a kind of turquoise). Coins struck by the Veneti, a local Gaulish tribe, pieces from Roman Gaul, and medieval and Renaissance artifacts are also displayed.

🏮 Place Gambetta
This semicircular square, lined with the white façades of residential blocks, was laid out in the 19th century and is today one of the liveliest parts of Vannes. The harbour lies immediately to the south, so that pleasure boats can sail right up into the heart of the city.

From the square, Promenade de la Rabine, a wide walkway which is continued by a coast

The marina in Vannes, just south of Place Gambetta

road, leads to the Presqu'île de Conleau, 4 km (3 miles) downstream.

ENVIRONS: The **Forteresse de Largoët d'Elven**, 14 km (9 miles) northeast of Vannes, is an example of medieval Breton architecture. The fortress has two towers and a curtain wall dating from the 13th century, a 14th-century keep, a gatehouse and a 15th-century circular tower.

The surrounding **Landes de Lanvaux**, heathland with lakes and woods, is traversed by footpaths and cycle tracks.

♟ Forteresse de Largoët d'Elven
From Vannes, take the N166 then the D135 at St-Nolff. The fortress is about 3 km (2 miles) further north.
(*(02) 97 53 35 96.* **◯** *Jun–Sep: daily; 20 Mar–May, Oct, Sat–Sun, school holidays & public holidays: pm only.* 🎫

VANNES CITY CENTRE

Cathédrale St-Pierre ①
Musée Archéologique ④
Musée de la Cohue ③

Old Town ②
Place Gambetta ⑤

Railway station

Lorient

RUE HOCHE

PLACE M. MARCHAIS

R. J. LE BRIX   RUE   DU   MÈNE

RUE SAINT PATERN

RUE BURGAULT

R. DES CHANOINES   PLACE BRÛLÉE

R. A. LEGRAND

Rennes

R. DU POT D'ÉTAIN

② PLACE HENRI IV

R. SAINT SALOMON   ①   R. SAINT GUÉNAEL

③

RUE DE LA MONNAIE

RUE   F.   DECKER

JARDINS DE LA PRÉFECTURE

RUE NOÉ

④

PLACE L. LAROCHE

PLACE DE LA RÉPUBLIQUE

P ⊠

RUE LE HELLEC

P
PLACE DES LICES

R. DE LA PORTE POTERNE

PARC DE LA GARENNE

RUE RICHEMONT

THIERS

RUE SAINT VINCENT

la Marle

R. A. LE PONTOIS

→ *Nantes*

KEY

P Parking

i Tourist information

⊠ Post office

🏛 Church

▢ *See pp186–7*

⑤

P

0 m   100

0 yards   100

The 16th-century town hall in
La Roche-Bernard

La Roche-Bernard ⓯

Road map D3. 34 km (21 miles)
southeast of Vannes on the N165.
🚇 Ponchâteau. 🏩 14 Rue du
Docteur-Cornudet; (02) 99 90 67 98.
🖴 Thu. 🎭 Fest-noz in St-Jean (14 Jul);
concerts (weekends, mid-Aug).

PERCHED ON a rocky spur,
La Roche-Bernard stands
at an important intersection
on the estuary of the Vilaine.
In the 11th century, a village
grew up around the fortress
and, six centuries later,
Richelieu ordered naval
dockyards to be installed. It
was here that the three-decker
La Couronne, pride of the
French navy, was built in 1634.
   The port consists of a marina,
along the Vilaine, and of the
old harbour that was later
abandoned in favour of the
Quai de la Douane. Salt, corn,
wine, quicklime and chestnut
wood once passed through the
docks here. In the old town,
which rises in tiers, is the
16th-century Maison du Canon,
which houses the town hall,
and the Auberge des Deux
Magots, on Place du Bouffay.
There are former salt ware-
houses in Rue de la Saulnerie.
   The **Musée de la Vilaine
Maritime** is laid out in the
16th-century Maison des
Basses-Fosses, where the
ground floor is carved out of
the living rock. The museum
traces the history of navigation
on the Vilaine and documents
the rural life of the region.

ENVIRONS: The **Parc
Zoologique de Branféré**,
20 km (12 miles) northwest
of La Roche-Bernard, has
over 100 species of animals
that roam in relative freedom.

🏛 **Musée de la
Vilaine Maritime**
6 Rue Ruicard. 📞 (02) 99 90 83 47.
🕐 May: Sat–Sun; early Jun: daily pm;
mid-Jun–mid-Sep: daily; mid–end Sep
& school holidays: daily pm.
🐾 **Parc Zoologique
de Branféré**
Le Guerno, via the N165.
📞 (02) 97 42 94 66. 🕐 Apr–Sep:
daily; Oct–Mar: daily pm (phone
in advance).

Questembert ⓰

Road map D3. 28 km (17 miles) east
of Vannes, via the N166, the D775
and the D5. 🚇 Bel Air. 🏩 15 Rue
des Halles; (02) 97 26 56 00. 🖴 Mon.
🎭 Pardon in Bréhardec (15 Aug);
Soirées Estivales (fest-noz, songs of
the sea, Sat in Jul–Aug).

THIS SMALL TOWN, whose
name means "chestnut-
tree land" in Breton, owes its
former prosperity to the fairs
that took place here, in the
covered market (1675).
Nearby is the former
Hostellerie Jehan le Guenego,
built in 1450 and the oldest
house in the town. The
16th-century Hôtel Belmont
next door, now the tourist
office, is enlivened by some
remarkable wooden caryatids.
There are many producers of
duck foie gras in the area.

Rochefort-
en-Terre ⓱

Road map D3. 33 km (20 miles)
east of Vannes via the N166, the
D775 and the D774. 🚇 Bel Air.
🏩 Place des Halles; (02) 97 43 33
57). 🎭 Pardon (mid-Aug); Festival
de Musique (late Aug).

BUILT ON A promontory
above the Gueuzon river,
this village has a medieval
atmosphere. Because of its
strategic position, the site
has been fortified since
Roman times.
   A keep overlooking
Rochefort was built in the
12th century, and in the 15th
the town was enclosed by
walls. Demolished on three
previous occasions, the **castle**
was again destroyed during
the Revolution. In 1907,
Alfred Klots, an American
painter, restored it and moved
into the castle's 17th-century
outbuildings. The castle
museum contains antique
furniture, paintings by Alfred
Klots and various items
illustrating life in the area.
The moat walk offers a good
view of the surroundings.
   The finest houses in
Rochefort, with granite or
schist façades, carved with
decorative motifs, are in
Grande-Rue and Place du
Puits. The Église Notre-Dame-
de-la-Tronchaye, built on the
hillside and dating from the
15th and 16th centuries, has a
façade in the Flamboyant
Gothic style. Features of
interest within include beams

Wooden roof of the 17th-century covered market in Questembert

Place du Puits, in the flower-filled village of Rochefort-en-Terre

decorated with monsters, woodcarvings on the theme of death (left of the pulpit) and a Renaissance altar-piece. A 16th-century calvary stands on the church square.

♣ **Castle and Museum**

(02) 97 43 31 56. ☐ Apr–May: Sat–Sun & public holidays, pm; Jun: daily pm; Jul–Aug: daily; Sep: daily pm. ● Oct–Mar.

Ploërmel ⓲

Road map D3. ☐ Vannes. ⚑ 7,200. ⓘ 5 Rue du Val; (02) 97 74 02 70. ♨ Jul–Aug: Mon, Wed & Fri. ☐ Mon & Fri. ⚑ Songs of the sea (late Jul); Semaines Arthuriennes (late Jul–early Aug).

THIS TOWN WAS one of the places of residence of the dukes of Brittany. The tombs of John II and Jean III lie in the 16th-century Église St-Armel, near the tomb of Philippe de Montauban. The fine stained-glass window with the Tree of Jesse is the work of Jehan le Flamand. The north entrance is decorated with some strikingly expressive reliefs depicting the vices and the Last Judgment.

The **Maison des Marmousets** (1586), opposite the tourist office in Rue Beaumanoir, has some unusual reliefs. Next door is the Hôtel des Ducs de

Bretagne, which, built in 1150, is the town's oldest building. The astronomical clock (1855), near the Lycée Lamennais, was made by a member of the Ploërmel brotherhood, which was founded by the older brother of the writer Félicité de Lamennais (see pp23 & 47).

ENVIRONS: The Circuit de l'Hortensia is a walk around the Lac au Duc, 1 km (0.5 mile) northwest of Ploërmel. The lake is bordered by 2,000 hydrangeas representing 12 different types of these colourful flowering shrubs.

Josselin ⓳

Road map D3. ☐ Vannes. ⚑ 2,500. ⓘ Place de la Congrégation; (02) 97 22 36 43. ☐ Sat. ⚑ Fair & Fest-noz (Whitsun, every two years); Festival Médiéval (14 Jul); Pardon (8 Sep).

LINEN WEAVING and the linen trade created Josselin's wealth. The town has at least two important buildings: the **Château de Josselin** (see pp192–3) and the **Basilique Notre-Dame-du-Roncier**, with legendary origins.

A miraculous statue of the Virgin was found under brambles (ronces) and a church was built on the holy spot. The basilica that now stands on this legendary site

Figure, Maison des Marmousets

is in the Flamboyant Gothic style, with typically Gothic gargoyles, but Romanesque columns survive in the choir. Recumbent statues of Olivier de Clisson (see p192) and of his wife, Marguerite de Rohan, lie near the miraculous statue.

Rues des Vierges, Olivier-de-Clisson and Trente are lined with fine 16th- and 17th-century houses. The **Musée des Poupées**, at No. 3 Rue Trente, contains some 600 wax, wooden and porcelain dolls dating from the 17th and 18th centuries. Chapelle Ste-Croix (1050), on the banks of the Oust, is the oldest chapel in the Morbihan.

Marguerite de Rohan, Basilique Notre-Dame-du-Roncier, Josselin

ENVIRONS: From the Middle Ages, the Forêt de Lanouée, 10 km (6 miles) north of Josselin, provided firewood for the ironworks where cannon balls were made. They were at their most productive in the 18th century.

The parish close at Guéhenno, 11 km (7 miles) southwest of Josselin, is the only complete example in the Morbihan. Two statues of soldiers guard the entrance to the ossuary, where there is a figure of the resurrected Christ. The calvary is the most spectacular part of the close. It dates from 1550 but was badly damaged in the Revolution. Eventually a parish priest undertook its restoration. A column with the symbols of the Passion of Christ stands in front of it.

🏛 **Musée des Poupées**

3 Rue Trente. ☐ Apr–May & Oct: Wed pm, Sat & Sun; Jun, Sep & school holidays: daily pm; Jul–Aug: daily. ● Nov–Mar.

Château de Josselin

PERCHED ON ROCKS opposite the Oust river, the Château de Josselin, once the stronghold of the Rohan dynasty, is an impressive sight. It is defended by four towers built by Olivier de Clisson in the 14th century. The castle's military severity is softened by the more delicate inner façade, dating from the early 16th century and looking onto gardens. A fine Flamboyant Gothic building, the castle has delicately carved granite galleries, pinnacles, balustrades and chimneypieces, and is decorated with a range of motifs, including fleurs-de-lis, stoats and lozenges.

Detail of the chimneypiece, with the Rohans' motto, "A Plus"

Ten dormer windows rising through two storeys cover almost half the façade.

★ Library
Containing 3,000 volumes, the library was remodelled in the neo-Gothic style in the 19th century.

★ Interior North Façade
This side of the castle has dormer windows with ornamental pediments. Each window is different, and together they embody the decorative repertoire of the time.

Prison tower

OLIVIER DE CLISSON

One of the most illustrious owners of the Château de Josselin was Olivier de Clisson (1336–1407). He married Marguerite de Rohan and in 1370 acquired the castle. De Clisson harboured a long hatred of the king of France, who had ordered his father's execution because of his support of the English. During the War of the Breton Succession, de Clisson sided with the English. However, he later transferred his allegiance to the French, befriending Bertrand du Guesclin and succeeding him as constable of France. De Clisson finally gave his daughter in marriage to the son of Charles of Blois, his erstwhile enemy.

Equestrian statue of Olivier de Clisson

STAR FEATURES

★ **Grand Salon**

★ **Interior North Façade**

★ **Library**

★ Grand Salon
The room has a chimneypiece decorated with garlands and hunting scenes, as well as 18th-century furniture and a portrait of Louis XIV painted by Rigaud.

VISITORS' CHECKLIST

Place de la Congrégation. [
(02) 97 22 36 45. **Ground floor:**
○ Apr–May: 2–6pm Wed, Sat–Sun;
Jun: 2–6pm daily; Jul–Aug: 10–6pm
daily; Sep: 2–6pm daily; Oct:
2–6pm Wed, Sat–Sun; school
hols: 2–6pm daily. ● Nov–Mar.

The main courtyard is an ideal place from which to take in this fine Gothic building.

Façade over the Oust
The fortress stands on an outcrop of schist at the foot of which runs the Oust river. Only four of the nine towers raised by Olivier de Clisson survive.

Entrance gate

Entrance Gate
Beyond the entrance gate is an inner façade with a wealth of intricate carving.

Dining Room
The neo-Gothic furniture in the dining room is the work of a local cabinetmaker and the design of the chimneypiece echoes that in the Grand Salon.

Machicolated defences at the Château des Rohan in Pontivy

Baud ⑳

Road map D3. 24 km (15 miles) north of Auray via the D768. 🚉 *Auray.* 🏠 *4,600.* 🚌 *Place Mathurin-Martin; (02) 97 39 17 09.* 🚏 *Sat.*

THE SMALL TOWN of Baud overlooks the Evel valley. In the upper town is the Chapelle Notre-Dame, with an interesting 16th-century apse.

Fontaine Notre-Dame-de-la-Clarté in Baud

In the lower town, is the 16th-century **Fontaine Notre-Dame-de-la-Clarté**, which provides water for the old wash houses here.

Also of interest is the **Conservatoire de la Carte Postale**, with a collection of 20,000 old postcards depicting the crafts of the past and local history.

ENVIRONS: about 2 km (1 mile) southwest of Baud, near a ruined castle, is a statue known as the Vénus de Quinipily. Standing about 2 m (7 ft) high, the almost naked figure is inscribed with the mysterious letters "LIT". Either Egyptian or Roman, it may represent Isis, a fertility goddess revered by Roman legionaries.

Public footpaths traverse the woods around Baud. The Blavet valley also contains a large number of interesting calvaries, fountains and chapels. In summer, exhibitions of contemporary art are held in many of the villages.

🏛 **Conservatoire de la Carte Postale**
Rue d'Auray. 📞 *(02) 97 51 15 14.* 🕐 *mid-Jun–mid-Sep: daily; mid-Sep–mid-Jun: Wed, Thu, Sat & Sun pm.*

Pontivy ㉑

Road map D3. 🚉 🚌 *Rue d'Iéna.* 🏠 *13,300.* 🚌 *Rue du Général-de-Gaulle; (02) 97 25 04 10.* 🚏 *Tue.* 🎭 *Kan ar Bol (Breton tales and songs, late Mar); Festival de Musique Classique (Apr); concerts (Jul–Aug).*

THIS TOWN, the capital of the Rohan dynasty, consists of two distinct parts: the medieval town, with timber-framed houses and a great castle; and an imperial town, with straight avenues arranged around Place Aristide-Briand. This latter district was laid out on the orders of Napoleon, who aimed to make Pontivy a base from which to fight back against the Chouans (see p46).

The **Château des Rohan,** which was begun in 1479 by John II de Rohan, is a fine example of military architecture. The seignorial living quarters overlooking the courtyard were remodelled in the 18th century. Exhibitions and shows take place at the castle in summer.

The old town spreads out around the castle. Of the old town walls, only la Porte de Carhaix survives. The finest houses here, built in the 16th and 17th centuries, are those on Place du Martray and along Rue du Fil and Rue du Pont.

A canal runs alongside Pontivy, making the town an important intersection for river traffic. The towpath also offers the chance of walks through beautiful countryside.

⚓ **Château des Rohan**
📞 *(02) 97 25 12 93.* 🕐 *Easter–mid-Sep: daily; mid-Sep–Easter: Wed–Sun.*

NAPOLÉON-VILLE

In 1790, Pontivy sided with the Republicans and the town became the focus of the Chouan royalists' war (see p46). In March 1793, 10,000 recalcitrant peasants attacked the town. Napoleon chose Pontivy as a base from which to lead a counter-attack. He also decided to canalize the Blavet river between Brest and Nantes and built a new town. When the Napoleonic Empire collapsed, the project was still unfinished. An imperial district was, however, built during the reign of Napoleon III.

Mairie de Pontivy, built during the Napoleonic period

Guéméné-sur-Scorff ❷

Road map C–D3. 19 km (12 miles) west of Pontivy via the D782.
🚉 *Lorient.* 👥 *1,500.* ℹ️ *Rue Bisson; (02) 97 51 20 23 & (02) 97 39 33 47 (Jun–Sep).* 🛒 *Thu.* 🎭 *Fête de l'Andouille (late Aug).*

NOW A CENTRE of *andouille* (sausage) production, the town was the object of bitter dispute during the War of the Breton Succession *(see p40)*. The houses on Place Bisson reflect its former prosperity.

Frescoes in the choir of the church in Kernascléden

Kernascléden ❷❸

Road map D3. 30 km (19 miles) southwest of Pontivy via the D782.

IT IS WORTH stopping at this little village to visit the 15th-century church, which contains frescoes that are among the finest of their period. The choir is decorated with scenes of the life of the Virgin and of the childhood of Christ. In the crossing is a chillingly realistic depiction of the Dance of Death, similar to that in the Chapelle Kermaria-an-Iskuit *(see p101)*, in the Côtes d'Armor.

Le Faouët ❷❹

Road map C3. 35 km (22 miles) north of Lorient via the D769.
🚉 *Quimperlé.* 👥 *3,000.* ℹ️ *1 Rue de Quimper; (02) 97 23 23 23.* 🛒 *first and third Wed in the month.* 🎭 *Pardons (last Sun in Jun, third Sun in Aug); folk festival (mid-Aug).*

ISOLATED IN undulating wooded landscape, the village of Le Faouët has a fine 16th-century covered market.
The **Musée des Peintres du Faouët**, in a former convent, contains 19th-century paintings of country life in Brittany and Breton landscapes. In the **Musée de l'Abeille Vivante**, visitors can observe bees in glass-sided hives.

ENVIRONS: The chapels in the vicinity of Le Faouët – St-Nicolas, Ste-Barbe and St-Fiacre – are each worth a visit. The most interesting is the Chapelle St-Fiacre, 3 km (2 miles) southeast of Le Faouët, in the Flamboyant Gothic style and with a gabled belfry. It also contains a beautiful rood screen.
The **Parc Aquanature Le Stérou**, 6 km (4 miles) southeast of Le Faouët, is a 70-ha (170-acre) nature park with a population of deer.

🏛 **Musée des Peintres du Faouët**
1 Rue de Quimper. 📞 *(02) 97 23 23 23.* ⏰ *Apr & Jun–Sep: daily. daily.*
🏛 **Musée de l'Abeille Vivante**
Kercadoret, Le Faouët. 📞 *(02) 97 23 08 05.* ⏰ *Apr–Oct: daily.*
🦌 **Parc Aquanature Le Stérou**
Route de Priziac. 📞 *(02) 97 34 63 84.* ⏰ *Easter–Nov & school holidays: daily; Dec–Easter: Sun & school holidays.*

The stud at Hennebont, housed in a former Cistercian abbey

Hennebont ❷❺

Road map C3. 13 km (8 miles) northeast of Lorient, via the D769 then the D769 bis. 🚉 👥 *14,000.* ℹ️ *9 Place du Maréchal-Foch; (02) 97 36 24 52.* 🛒 *Thu.* 🎭 *Medieval festivals (late Jul); Pardon (late Sep).*

OVERLOOKING the steep banks of the Blavet river, Hennebont was once one of the largest fortified towns in the area. On Place Foch, with a central well (1623), is the Basilique Notre-Dame-du-Paradis, built in the 16th century. The walled town, damaged during World War II, is defended by the Porte du Broërec'h. This 13th-century gatehouse contains a **museum** of local history. A view of the gardens and the river can be enjoyed from the rampart walk.
The **Haras National** (National Stud), where 75 thoroughbreds (including Breton post-horses, Arabs and Selle Français) are kept, is housed in a former Cistercian abbey. Visitors can see the farrier's forge, the tack room, the stables, the school and a collection of carriages.
The Forges d'Hennebont, at Inzinzac, are ironworks that operated from 1860 to 1966, and were important to the local economy. The **Écomusée Industriel** here describes metalworking techniques, as well as worker's living and working conditions at the time.

🏛 **Musée des Tours Broërec'h**
Rue de la Prison. 📞 *(02) 97 36 29 18.* ⏰ *Jun–mid-Sep: daily.*
🐴 **Haras National**
Rue Victor-Hugo. 📞 *(02) 97 89 40 30.* ⏰ *Jul–Aug: daily; Sep–Jun: Mon–Fri & Sun pm.*
🏛 **Écomusée Industriel**
Inzinzac, Zone Industrielle des Forges. 📞 *(02) 97 36 98 21.* ⏰ *Jul–Aug: daily; Sep–Jun: Mon–Fri & Sun pm.*

The Oratoire St-Michel, attached to the Chapelle Ste-Barbe, near Le Faouët

LOIRE-ATLANTIQUE

BETWEEN ANCENIS *in the east and St-Nazaire in the west, the great Loire river winds lazily, cutting through verdant lands and flowing through Nantes, the region's capital, before broadening into an estuary as it empties into the Atlantic. While the north of the Loire-Atlantique is a region of lakes and woodland, the south is characterized by mud flats, especially on the Guérande peninsula to the west.*

Both in historical and in geographical terms, the Loire-Atlantique is assuredly Breton. Yet, incorporated into the Pays de la Loire in 1969, the region is also oriented towards the south and the Vendée, to the southwest.

The central axis of the Loire-Atlantique is the Loire estuary, which provides a link with the Atlantic. On it stands Nantes, the former capital of the dukes of Brittany, and today not only the capital of the Pays de la Loire but also the largest city in western France. Until the mid-19th century, the Loire was a major artery for the transport of commercial goods: salt from Guérande and fish from the Atlantic were transported inland by boat.

The Loire-Atlantique is made up of a mosaic of distinct areas. While the Presqu'île de Guérande and the coastal town of Le Croisic grew rich long ago from salt-panning, La Baule and the surrounding coastal resorts came into their own in the late 19th century. The industrial city of St-Nazaire enjoyed a golden age in the first half of the 20th century.

While the Pays de Retz, to the west, is a land of pasture, beaches and mud flats fringed by the sea, the Pays d'Ancenis, to the east, is a major wine-producing area, where hillsides are dotted with terracotta-roofed houses. The Forêt de Gâvre and the countryside around Châteaubriant, to the north, offer yet more lush landscapes.

Le Croisic, with the former residences of wealthy merchants lining the quay

◁ Interior of the 9th-century Carolingian abbey church of St-Philibert-de-Grand-Lieu

Exploring the Loire-Atlantique

NAMED AFTER THE RIVER that traverses it from east to west, flowing into the Atlantic Ocean at St-Nazaire, the Loire-Atlantique is Brittany's most southerly region. The northwest of this *département*, consisting of the Presqu'île de Guérande and the great nature reserve of La Brière, is dominated by heathland with outcrops of granite, by marshland and by a rocky coastline. Slate-roofed or thatched houses are ubiquitous here. The area around Châteaubriant, in the north, contains a central expanse of woodland with outcrops of blue-grey schist. This is good walking country. South of the Loire, vineyards where Muscadet and Gros Plant are grown stretch as far as the eye can see. In the Pays de Retz, which borders the Atlantic in the west, wide sandy beaches alternate with marshes where salt has been gathered since ancient times.

Villa Ker Souveraine in Pornichet

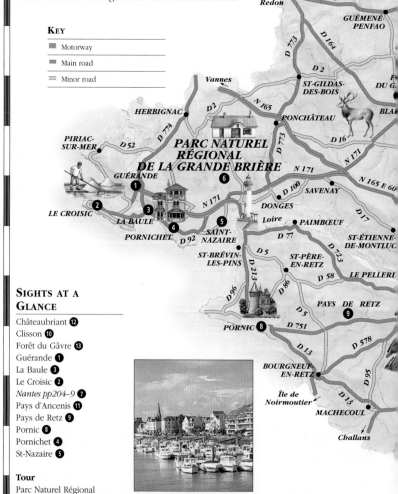

KEY

≡ Motorway

≡ Main road

≡ Minor road

SIGHTS AT A GLANCE

Châteaubriant ⑫
Clisson ⑩
Forêt du Gâvre ⑬
Guérande ①
La Baule ③
Le Croisic ②
Nantes pp204–9 ⑦
Pays d'Ancenis ⑪
Pays de Retz ⑨
Pornic ⑧
Pornichet ④
St-Nazaire ⑤

Tour

Parc Naturel Régional de la Grande Brière ⑥

The harbour at Le Croisic

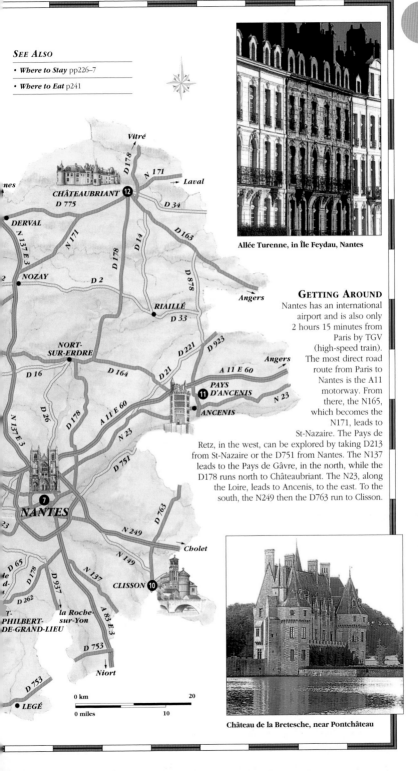

SEE ALSO

- *Where to Stay* pp226–7
- *Where to Eat* p241

Vitré

CHÂTEAUBRIANT ⑫

DERVAL

NOZAY

RIAILLÉ

NORT-SUR-ERDRE

Laval

Angers

Angers

PAYS D'ANCENIS ⑪

ANCENIS

NANTES ⑦

Cholet

CLISSON ⑩

la Roche-sur-Yon

T-PHILBERT-DE-GRAND-LIEU

Niort

LEGÉ

Allée Turenne, in Île Feydau, Nantes

GETTING AROUND

Nantes has an international airport and is also only 2 hours 15 minutes from Paris by TGV (high-speed train). The most direct road route from Paris to Nantes is the A11 motorway. From there, the N165, which becomes the N171, leads to St-Nazaire. The Pays de Retz, in the west, can be explored by taking D213 from St-Nazaire or the D751 from Nantes. The N137 leads to the Pays de Gâvre, in the north, while the D178 runs north to Châteaubriant. The N23, along the Loire, leads to Ancenis, to the east. To the south, the N249 then the D763 run to Clisson.

0 km 20
0 miles 10

Château de la Bretesche, near Pontchâteau

Porte St-Michel, the main entrance into the walled town of Guérande

Guérande ❶

Road map D4. 🏯 *12,000.*
🚉 *La Baule.* ✈ *Nantes-Atlantique.*
ℹ *1 Place du Marché-aux-Bois;*
(02) 40 24 96 71. 🏪 *Wed & Sat.*
🎭 *Remontée du Sel de Guérande*
(Apr–May), Fête du Sel et de l'Oiseau
(May), La Salicorne (Mar & Jun).

OVERLOOKING EXTENSIVE salt marshes on the Presqu'Île de Guérande, this town has long depended on the salt-panning industry. Although this industry began in Roman times, it became important only in the 15th century.

The old town is enclosed within 14th- and 15th-century ramparts. The Porte St-Michel, the gatehouse and main entrance on the eastern side, contains a **Château-Musée**, in which local furniture, costumes, faïence and religious art are displayed. The Collégiale St-Aubin, the collegiate church in the centre of the old town, was built in the 13th century and later

remodelled. The interior has 14th- and 15th-century stained-glass windows, and Romanesque capitals carved with scenes of martyrdom and fantastic animals. The **Musée de la Poupée et du Jouet Ancien** contains dolls and toys dating from 1830 to the present day.

ENVIRONS: The D99 running northwest out of Guérande leads to La Turballe, the largest sardine port on the Atlantic coast. The market where the fish auction takes place has an exhibiton on fishing. Past Pointe du Castelli, the roadreaches the coastal resort of Piriac-sur-Mer, where a granite-built church stands amid narrow streets.

The D774 south from Guérande winds through salt marshes, leading to Saillé, a typical salt-panning village. The **Maison des Paludiers** here documents the history of the salt-panning industry on the peninsula.

♟ **Château-Musée**
Porte St-Michel. 📞 *(02) 40 42 96 52.*
🕐 *Apr–Oct: daily.* ⬤ *Mon am*
(outside school holidays). 🎫
🏛 **Musée de la Poupée**
23 Rue de Saillé. 📞 *(02) 40 15 69 13.*
🕐 *May–mid-Nov & school hols: daily.*
⬤ *Mon; mid-Jan–mid-Feb & Nov–Apr.*
🏚 **Maison des Paludiers**
18 Rue des Prés. Garnier, Saillé.
📞 *(02) 40 62 21 96.* 🕐 *Mid-Feb–Oct*
& school hols: daily. 🎫

Le Croisic ❷

Road map D4. 🏯 *4,450.* 🚉
🚌 *La Baule.* ✈ *Nantes-Atlantique.*
ℹ *Place du 18 Juin-1940; (02) 40 23*
00 70. 🏪 *Thu & Sat.* 🎭 *Fête de la*
Mer (Aug), Les Vieux Métiers de la
Mer (Jun–Sep).

SET ON A peninsula reaching 5 km (3 km) into the Atlantic, Le Croisic is both a an active fishing port and a popular holiday resort. The old town, once the base of privateers, has some fine houses dating from the time when salt was shipped from Le Croisic to destinations as distant as the Baltic. In the **Océarium,** one of the largest private aquariums in France, the marine life of the Atlantic coast can be observed.

The Flamboyant Gothic Église St-Guénolé has a high tower from which Batz-sur-Mer can be seen. The granite Chapelle Notre-Dame-du-Mûrier, built in the 15th century, is now in ruins.

ENVIRONS: The **Musée des Marais Salants** in Batz-sur-Mer, 5 km (3 miles) southeast of Le Croisic, documents the history of the salt marshes and the lives of salt panners in the 19th century.

🏛 **Océarium**
Avenue de St-Goustan, Le Croisic.
📞 *(02) 40 23 02 44.* ⬤ *Three weeks*
in Jan. 🎫
🏛 **Musée des Marais Salants**
29 bis, Rue Pasteur, Batz-sur-Mer.
📞 *(02) 40 23 82 79.* 🕐 *Jun–Sep &*
school holidays: daily; Oct–May:
Sat–Sun. 🎫

The harbour at Le Croisic, with active fishing and shellfish-farming industries

The beautiful 8-km (5-mile) beach at La Baule

La Baule **❸**

Road map D4. 🏠 15,000.
🚉 🚌 🛈 8 Place de la Victoire; (02)
40 24 34 44. 🏪 Apr–Sep & school
holidays: daily am; Oct–Mar: Tue–Sun,
am. 🎭 Pardon d'Escoublac (Aug).

THIS RESORT IS famous for
its exceptionally long
beach, which stretches
for some 8 km (5 miles).
It became a holiday
resort when the rail link
with the interior opened
in 1879. Residential
districts were then
created, and a multitude of
villas and luxury hotels
sprang up. The seafront
promenade was opened in
1929. Later, however,
apartment blocks replaced the
seaside villas, although a few
fine examples survive, particularly in the resort's eastern
extension, La Baule-les-Pins.
About 10 km (7 miles) inland
from La Baule is the large
Forêt d'Escoublac, which
is traversed by footpaths.

Pornichet **❹**

Road map D4. 🏠 8,160.
🚉 🚌 La Baule. 🛈 3 Boulevard
de la République; (02) 40 61 33 33.
🏪 Wed & Sat.

OCCUPYING THE eastern third
of a wide bay, Pornichet
is extended on its eastern side
by several beaches and

smaller bays. "Port Niché"
(Nestling Harbour) began to
grow into a fashionable resort
in 1860, when publishers and
other literary people came to
enjoy the coast here. The

Detail from an elegant
villa in Pornichet

Plage des Libraires (Booksellers'
Beach) recalls those days.
   This smart resort, which has
now grown into a small town,
boasts elegant villas built
between 1880 and 1930.

St-Nazaire **❺**

Road map E4. 🏠 66,000.
🚉 🚌 ✈ Nantes-Atlantique.
🛈 Boulevard de la Légion-d'Honneur;
(02) 40 22 40 65. 🏪 Tue, Fri & Sun.
🎭 Les Escales, Festival de Musiques
du Monde (Aug), Consonances
(chamber music; Sep).

THE GREAT PORT of St-Nazaire
began to develop in the
19th century, when ships too
large to sail up the Loire to
Nantes would dock here.
The port is still a major
industrial and shipbuilding
centre today.
   The **Écomusée**, in the
harbour, illustrates the wildlife
and history of the Loire
estuary. It also gives access
to *L'Espadon*, a French
submarine built in 1957, in
which the life of submariners
is re-created. A monument
commemorating the abolition
of slavery stands near the
ecomuseum.
   The **Chantiers de
l'Atlantique**, shipyards from
which such legendary liners
as *Normandie* (1932) and
France (1960) were launched,
and where impressive cruise
liners are still built today, are
open to visitors.
   Escal-Atlantic, an
exhibition tracing the history
of ocean liners, is laid out in
a huge Nazi blockhouse in
the submarine base here.

🏛 **Chantiers de
l'Atlantique, Ecomusée,
Escal'Atlantic, *L'Espadon*
submarine**
Port de St-Nazaire.
📞 (08) 10 88 84 44. ☐ Apr–Oct:
daily. ● Nov–Mar: Mon–Tue &
three weeks in Jan. 📷

Pont de St-Nazaire over the Loire estuary, the longest bridge in France

Tour of the Parc Naturel Régional de la Grande Brière ❻

Consisting of a landscape of reed beds crossed by canals, the Parc Naturel Régional de la Grande Brière occupies the centre of the Presqu'île de Guérande. This natural environment of 40,000 ha (99,000 acres) was made a protected area in 1970. It has an abundant population of birds, and also contains about 2,000 traditional stone-built, thatched houses. One way of exploring the park is by boat, accompanied by local guide. Alternative ways to enjoy it are on foot, by bicycle, on horseback or by horse-drawn carriage.

Château de Ranrouet ①
The origins of this imposing fortress, now in ruins, go back to the 13th century.

Les Fossés-Blancs ②
This is Grande Brière's most northerly barge port. The botanical nature walk that has been created here follows the canal and then penetrates deep into the reed beds. Boats, with a guide, can be hired here.

St-Lyphard ③
From the belfry of the church in the village of St-Lyphard, there is a stunning view of Grande Brière.

Kerhinet ④
This village came to life again when Grande Brière was declared a protected area. It consists of a cluster of 18 thatched houses, one of which contains a restored bread oven. About 1 km (0.5 mile) further west is a well-preserved Neolithic galleried grave.

LA ROCHE-BER
VANNES

Herbignac

D 51

D 774

Kerbourg

D 51

D 47

Guérande

LE CROIZIC

N 171

LA BAULE

St-André-des-Eaux

D 127

D 127

PORNICHET

Bréca ⑤
This barge port is located at the western extremity of the Bréca Canal, which opened in 1937–8 and which crosses Grande Brière from east to west, starting at Rozé.

La Barbière ⑩
The Dolmen de la Barbière at Crossac testifies to human habitation of this area 5,000 years ago. There are also megaliths at Herbignac and St-Lyphard.

Chapelle-des-Marais ⑪
The Maison du Sabotier (Clogmaker's House) here is open to visitors. The church contains a statue of St Cornély, protector of horned animals, and in the village hall *(mairie)* the fossilized stump of a tree that grew in the marshes is on display.

Île de Fédrun ⑨
The centre of the island, inhabited since ancient times, was reserved for growing staple crops. A road running around the edge links the island's houses. The Maison de la Mariée (Bride's House), at No. 30, displays bridal headdresses.

Rozé ⑧
This port, with a lock on its west side, is the point from which the water level is controlled. It was through Rozé that peat, Grande Brière's "black gold", was transported. The Maison de l'Éclusier (lock-keeper's cottage) and Parc Animalier (small animal park) are open to the public.

Pont de Paille at Trignac ⑦
With its locks and pounds (holding areas for barges), Trignac is the largest barge port in Grande Brière. It is also known for its excellent fishing. The bridge spans the Canal de Rozé, one of the major canals across the reserve.

La Chaussée-Neuve ⑥
This barge port, which once handled consignments of peat, now attracts people who come to the park to fish and shoot. At the beginning of each year, reed-cutters land their harvest here. The reeds are used to roof the houses in Grande Brière.

*Map labels:*
D 50
Ste-Reine-de-Bretagne
⑪
D 33
PONTCHÂTEAU
D 4
D 50
Crossac
⑩
D 16
Canal du Nord
St-Joachim
⑨
Canal de Rozé
⑧
Canal de Trignac
St-Malo-de-Guersac
D 50
Montoir-de-Bretagne
SAVENAY, NANTES
⑦
D 971
ST-BRÉVIN-LES-PINS
N 171

0 km   5
0 miles   3

KEY
━━ Suggested route
⋯ Other roads
🔆 Viewpoint

Nantes

Cicada motif at La Cigale

Hᴵꜱᴛᴏʀᴵᴄ ᴄᴀᴘᴵᴛᴀʟ of the dukes of Brittany, Nantes is today capital of the Pays de la Loire. Such dual importance enhances the cultural diversity of this vibrant city. Connected to the Atlantic via the wide lower reaches of the Loire, Nantes is a port city, and historically the slave trade ensured its prosperity. But, in the heart of vegetable-growing country, Nantes is now focused on a land-based economy. A stately city but also a modern metropolis, an industrial and cultural centre with a well-respected university, Nantes is one of the most dynamic towns in France, with a steadily growing population and pleasant, well-kept districts.

Doorway and balcony in Rue Kervégan

🏛 Place du Bouffay

This is the heart of Nantes, where the founders of the future city settled, near the confluence of the Loire and the Erdre. In the Middle Ages, a fortress (destroyed in the 18th century) was built to serve as a prison and law tribunal, and executions took place on the square.

The street names in the vicinity echo the past: Rue de la Bâclerie (Bolt Street), with 15th-century timber-framed houses, Rue de la Juiverie (Jewry Street), Rue des Halles (Market Street), Place du Pilori (Stocks Square). The Église Ste-Croix, on Place Ste-Croix, was begun in the 17th century and completed 200 years later. The clock and bell were transferred from the destroyed Tour du Bouffay in 1860. This pedestrianized area is a part of Nantes that has been least affected by the city's rapid development.

🏛 Quartier Graslin

Place Royale links the medieval quarter of Nantes with the Neo-Classical Quartier Graslin. Laid out by the architect Mathurin Crucy in 1790, the square is lined with tall residential buildings of elegant restrained design. The blue granite fountain, dating from 1865, is decorated with personifications of the Loire and its tributaries.

Statue in Passage Pommeraye

Place Graslin, nearby, is named after Jean Graslin, a Parisian barrister who came to seek his fortune in Nantes in 1750. A shrewd speculator, he purchased land and commissioned Crucy to develop the district. Part of this development was the Neo-Classical **theatre**, centrepiece of the square. The building, fronted by eight Corinthian columns crowned with eight muses, is a focal point of cultural life in Nantes.

Opposite stands **La Cigale**, a famous brasserie that opened in 1895. The decoration of the interior, by Émile Libaudière, is in the Art Nouveau style: large areas of dark wood carvings are surrounded by motifs in ceramic, wrought iron, mosaic and plaster, featuring stylized cicadas (*cigales*). This is somewhere to go as much to feast the eyes as to enjoy good food.

🏛 Île Feydeau

This district, a former island, was created when branches of the Loire were filled in the 1930s and 1940s, and it is here that the wealth generated by a profitable trade in slaves and sugar is most evident. The luxurious private residences here were built in the 18th century by traders who bought slaves with cheap jewellery, sold them and then returned from Africa with vessels loaded with sugar.

Allée Turenne, Allée Duguay-Trouin, Allée Brancas, **Rue Kervégan** and Place de la Petite-Hollande are lined with houses decorated with masks, shells, the faces of bearded spirits and ears of corn, and faced with wrought-iron balconies – all outward signs of wealth.

🏛 Passage Pommeraye

Opened in 1843, this unusual arcade is named after the man who built it. Pommeraye, a lawyer, joined forces with Guilloux, a restaurateur, to create the arcade, designed on the model of those that were built in Paris at the time.

The Neo-Classical theatre on Place Graslin

The shops, cafés and restaurants that opened here soon attracted Nantes' wealthy inhabitants. The film-maker Jacques Demy, who was born in Nantes, chose the arcade as the location for two of his films, *Lola* and *Une Chambre en Ville*. An elegant wooden staircase, decorated with lamps and statues, gives access to the arcade's three galleries, on different levels. Between those on the upper floor is a Neo-Classical porch decorated with medallions.

⛫ Musée Dobrée

18 Rue Voltaire. 🗣 *(02) 40 71 03 50.* 🕐 *Tue–Sun.* ⬤ *Mon & public holidays.* 🖾 *except Sun.*

At the age of 28, Thomas Dobrée (1810–95), heir to a family business going back 300 years, turned down a career as a shipowner to concentrate on collecting art. In time, his collection came to encompass painting, sculpture and drawings, tapestries, furniture and porcelain, arms and armour, and religious art.

Louis XII and Anne of Brittany, a painting in the Musée Dobrée

From 1862 until his death, Dobrée devoted himself to creating a suitable building in which to house the 10,000 pieces that his collection by then comprised. For this he commissioned the architect Viollet-le-Duc, who built the Neo-Gothic chateau that is now the Musée Dobrée.

Among the finest pieces on display here are a gold reliquary with a crown containing the heart of Anne of Brittany (1514), enamels, such as the 12th-century Reliquary of the True Cross, and the 13th-century Reliquary of

St Calminius. Engravings by Dürer, Schongauer, Rembrandt, Ruysdael and Jacques Callot are among the museum's masterpieces.

Two other buildings stand in the palace precinct. One is the Musée Archéologique is devoted to prehistory, ancient Egyptian and Greek artifacts and local Gaulish and Gallo-Roman history. The other is the Manoir de la Touche, which documents local history during the Revolution, especially the Vendée Wars.

NANTES CITY CENTRE

Cathédrale St-Pierre-et-St-Paul ⑦
Château des Ducs de Bretagne ⑥
Île Feydeau ③
Jardin des Plantes ⑪
Musée des Beaux-Arts ⑧
Musée Dobrée ⑤
Musée Jules-Verne ⑩
Passage Pommeraye ④
Place du Bouffay ①
Quartier Graslin ②
Usine LU ⑨

KEY

🚉 Railway station
🚌 Bus station
🅿 Parking
ℹ Tourist information
⊠ Post office
⛪ Church

0 m   400
0 yards   400

Around the Chateau and Beyond

LU logo of
c. 1930

THE CHÂTEAU DES DUCS de Bretagne
(see pp208–9), with Place du Bouffay
and the Cathédrale St-Pierre-et-St-Paul, once
formed the hub of Nantes. This nucleus is
on the eastern side of the present city.
The Jardin des Plantes, the Musée des
Beaux-Arts and the picturesque Lieu Unique
are other landmarks. The Musée Jules-
Verne, devoted to this famous native of Nantes, is on
the western side of the city, well beyond the port.

The Musée des Beaux-Arts,
late 19th-century façade

⌂ Cathédrale St-Pierre-et-St-Paul

Place St-Pierre. ◯ daily.
Standing on the site of a
Roman building, vestiges of
which remain in the crypt, the
Flamboyant Gothic cathedral
was begun in 1434. Its
construction continued until
the 19th century, when the
apse was completed.
   The cathedral has richly
decorated doorways and an
impressively lofty nave, 37 m
(120 ft) high. The choir and
ambulatory are lit by
contemporary stained-glass
windows. A fine example of
the Renaissance style, the
black and white marble tomb
of Francis II and his wife
Marguerite de Foix was carved
by Michel Colombe in 1507. It
is surrounded by allegorical
statues; that of Justice is
thought to portray their
daughter, Anne of Brittany.
   Porte St-Pierre, next to the
cathedral and once part of the
walls that surrounded Nantes,
leads to Cours St-Pierre, a
walkway where there are
remains of the 13th-century

ramparts. Impasse St-Laurent,
on the left of the cathedral,
leads to La Psalette, a
charming Gothic house dating
from the 15th century.

🏛 Musée des Beaux-Arts

10 Rue Georges-Clemenceau. ☎ (02)
40 41 65 65. ◯ Wed–Mon. ● Tue
& public holidays. 🎫 except Sun.
Built by the architect Josso, a
native of Nantes, in the late
19th century, this is one of
best designed museums of its
period. The building is
arranged around a large
courtyard lit by natural light.
   The ground floor, of simple
design, is devoted to modern
and contemporary art, from
Impressionism to the present
day, and including abstract art
of the 1950s. Besides
paintings by the Fauves and
the Nabis, there are two
Monets (Waterlilies and
Gondolas in Venice),
Lighthouse at Antibes by

Statue of Marguerite de Foix,
Cathédrale St-Pierre-et-St-Paul

Signac, and works by Dufy,
Émile Bernard, Mauffra and
the Pont-Aven School (see
p169), as well as 11 paintings
by Kandinsky. Works by
Manessier, Soulages and
Bazaine represent more
recent developments.
   The first floor is devoted to
major periods in the history
of art from the 13th century
to the first half of the 19th.
The collection of early Italian
painting includes a Virgin in
Majesty by the Master of
Bigallo (13th century), a
Madonna with Four Saints
(c. 1340) by Bernardo Daddi
and St Sebastian and a
Franciscan Saint (15th–16th
century) by Perugino. A
typically full-blooded
Rubens, Judas Maccabaeus

THE REVOLUTION IN NANTES

During the civil war fought between royalists and
republicans during the French Revolution, one man in
particular stood out in the political climate that prevailed in
Nantes. Jean-Baptiste Carrier, a member of the Convention
(revolutionary assembly), was sent to Brittany on a mission
to pacify the region. After the royalist Chouans were defeated
at Savenay, he inflicted on the citizens of Nantes a cruel
repression. He designed boats with a hull that could be
opened when the vessel reached the middle of the Loire,
drowning as many as 100 people at a time. "Republican
weddings" consisted of tying a man and a woman together
and tossing them
into the river.
Some 5,000
people lost their
lives under this
regime. Executions
of royalists also
took place on
Place Viarme,
in Nantes.

Mass drownings organized by Jean-Baptiste
Carrier in Nantes in June 1793

Praying for the Dead (1635), provides a dramatic and strong contrast to peaceful Dutch and Flemish landscapes and still-life paintings.

French painting of the 17th century is represented by

Le Gaulage des Pommes, by Émile Bernard, Musée des Beaux-Arts

three works by Georges de la Tour, a master of the depiction of light: *The Hurdy-Gurdy Player*, *St Peter's Denial* and *Apparition of the Angel before St Joseph*.

Highlights of the 19th-century collections include works by Ingres, particularly his beautiful portrait of *Madame de Senonnes* (1814), by Delacroix (*Caïd, Moroccan Chief*), and by Corot (*Democrites and the Abderitans*), as well as paintings by the Barbizon School. In the room devoted to Courbet, the subject-matter and compo-sition of *The Gleaners* demonstrates his skill as a realist.

🏛 Usine LU, Lieu Unique

Rue de la Biscuiterie, Quai Ferdinand-Favre. 🄲 (02) 40 12 14 34 (ticket office) & (02) 51 72 05 55 (restaurant). ⭘ daily.

The history of Nantes is inseparable from that of the almost legendary biscuit, the Petit-Beurre LU, which people have enjoyed for over a century.

In 1846, the Lefèvre-Utile, a couple from Lorraine who settled in Nantes, opened their first pâtisserie. To challenge competition from British imports, they began making biscuits on an industrial scale and in 1885 built a factory. The Petit-Beurre was launched, followed by the Paille d'Or. From 1913, LU turned out 20 tonnes of biscuits per day. When the factory became too small, it was abandoned.

Threatened with demolition in 1995, the factory was rescued and, since 1999, what became known as the Lieu Unique (Unique Place) has become a cultural centre where festivals, shows and exhibitions take place. It is very popular with the people of Nantes.

🌿 Jardin des Plantes

Boulevard Stalingrad & Place Sophie-Trébuchet. ⭘ daily.

Opened in the early 19th century, the botanical garden – the second-largest in France after the Jardin des Plantes in Paris – covers 7 ha (17 acres) and contains 12,000 species of plants. It was originally a garden of mostly medicinal plants, but sea captains brought back exotic specimens that rapidly broadened its scope. Today, the garden contains over 200 varieties of camellia,

which flourish beneath the oldest magnolias in Europe. In the tropical greenhouses flourish a great many species of orchid.

🏛 Musée Jules-Verne

3 Rue de l'Hermitage. 🄲 (02) 40 69 72 52. ⭘ Wed–Mon. ⬤ Tue, Sun am & public holidays. ▨

This small house at the top of a steep street is the birthplace of the writer Jules Verne. The museum that it now contains gives a detailed account of his life and work, and of the peculiar world that he created in his novels. Books, souvenirs, quotations, humorous drawings,

Jules Verne, born in Nantes in 1828

cards, magic lanterns and models draw the visitor into the imaginary world created by the writer. There is also furniture from his house in Amiens, where Verne spent most of his life.

ENVIRONS: The 11th-century **Château de Goulaine**, 13 km (8 miles) southeast of Nantes, contains a collection of tropical butterflies, and an exhibition documenting the history of the LU biscuit factory. The reception rooms are sumptuously decorated.

🏰 Château de Goulaine

Haute-Goulaine. 🄲 (02) 40 54 91 42. ⭘ Easter–Nov: Sat–Sun & public holidays; mid-Jun–mid-Sep: Wed–Mon. ▨ 🄲 for groups, all year round by arrangement.

The Jardin des Plantes, botanical gardens laid out as a park in the English style

Château des Ducs de Bretagne

O N THE BANKS of the Loire, the Château des Ducs de Bretagne was founded in the 13th century, and served both as a residential palace and military fortress. Anne of Brittany was born here in 1477, and it is here that Henry IV is supposed to have signed the Edict of Nantes in 1598. Over the centuries, the castle was continually remodelled. The sturdy towers and drawbridge, part of the fortifications, are counterbalanced by delicate Renaissance buildings facing onto the courtyard. Converted into barracks in the 18th century, the castle passed into state ownership after World War I and now contains a museum. A restoration programme to return the buildings to their original appearance was launched in 1993. A major museum of the history of Nantes is also projected.

★ Grand Logis
The façade bears the coat of arms of Louis XII and Anne of Brittany.

Tour du Port was hidden by a bastion for 200 years. The bastion was demolished in 1853.

Courtine de la Loire, the wall linking Tour de la Rivière and Tour du Port, was built in the 15th and 16th centuries.

Petit Gouvernement
Built in the 16th century, during the reign of Francis I, the king's apartments are now known as the Petit Gouvernement (Governor's Small Palace). The dormer windows are typical of the Renaissance.

ILLUSTRIOUS GUESTS

**Henry IV
(1553–1610)**

Many famous people have passed through the gates of the Château des Ducs de Bretagne. The wedding of Francis II of Brittany and Marguerite de Foix took place here in 1471, and it was also here that their daughter, Anne, Duchess of Brittany, was married to Louis XII in 1499. In 1532, Francis I of France came here to mark the "permanent union of the duchy and country of Brittany with the kingdom of France", as an inscription in the courtyard recalls. Henry II, then Charles IX, also stayed in the castle. In 1598, Henry IV thrashed out the terms of the Edict de Nantes, which legalized Protestantism. He may even have signed the edict at the castle. Louis XIV also stayed here when he came to Nantes in 1661, during a gathering of the States of Brittany.

Tour de la Rivière
Forming part of the castle's system of defences, the Tour de la Rivière consists of two floors with a terrace above.

Grand Gouvernement
The ducal palace, known since the 17th century as the Grand Gouvernement (Governor's Great Palace), has been restored to its original splendour. The double staircase leads up to a single row of steps beneath a porch.

VISITORS' CHECKLIST

4 Place Marc-Elder.
(02) 40 41 56 56.
10am–6pm Wed–Mon during temporary exhibitions. The castle is currently undergoing restoration. Tue & public holidays. Sun for groups by arrangement.

The castle museum is devoted to regional folk art of the 16th to 20th centuries.

★ Vieux Donjon
The polygonal keep, built in the 14th century on the orders of John IV de Montfort, is the oldest part of the castle. It is attached to the 18th-century caretaker's lodge.

Bastion St-Pierre, built in the 16th century, was levelled off in 1904.

★ Tour du Fer-à-Cheval
This shield decorates the keystone of the vaulting inside the Tour du Fer-à-Cheval (Horseshoe Tower). Guarding the northwest corner of the castle, it is a fine example of 15th-century military architecture.

STAR FEATURES

★ **Grand Logis**

★ **Tour du Fer-à-Cheval**

★ **Vieux Donjon**

The Harness Room was built by the army in the 17th and 18th centuries.

The thalassotherapy centre on Plage de l'Alliance, in Pornic

Pornic ❽

Road map E5. 🏘 9,900. 🚌 🚃 ⛴
ℹ *Place de la Gare; (02) 40 82 04
40.* 🕑 *Thu & Sun.* 🎭 *spring carnival
(Apr), Fête de la Mer et du Goût (Aug).*

A SMALL FISHING harbour,
Pornic is also a coastal
resort with yachting harbours
and a **thalassotherapy
centre**. The lower town, with
brightly painted fishermen's
houses, is dominated by the
outline of the castle, which
was owned by Gilles de Rais
(see p41) in the 15th century.
It was remodelled by Viollet-
le-Duc in the 19th century.
The coast road beyond Pornic
is lined with 19th-century villas
where the writers Michelet
and Flaubert, as well as the
painter Renoir, once stayed.
   St-Michel-Chef-Chef, 9 km
(5 miles) further north, is
renowned for its biscuits
made with salted butter, and
for its wide beach.

Pays de Retz ❾

Road map E5. Machecoul. Between
the D751 and the D13. 🚌 🚃 *Nantes.*
ℹ *14 Place des Halles, Bourgneuf-en-
Retz, (02) 40 31 42 87), & Route de
Boin, Machecoul, (02) 40 21 93 63).*

M ACHECOUL, ONCE the capital
of the Pays de Retz, was
the fiefdom of Gilles de Rais,
the local Bluebeard *(see p41)*.
The ruins of one of his castles
still stand here.
   The **Musée du Pays de Retz**
at Bourgneuf-en-Retz, 12 km
(9 miles) further west on the
D13, describes the local salt-
panning and fishing industries,
as well as the crafts of the past.

Les Moutiers-en-Retz, on the
coast, owes its name to two
11th-century monasteries.
Vestiges of these buildings
can be seen in the Église
St-Pierre, built in the 16th
century in the Gothic style.
Near the church is an 11th-
century lantern whose flame
was intended to light the
darkness for the dead.
   The Lac de Grand-Lieu, to
the east, is an unusually rich
bird sanctuary. The **Maison
du Lac** here documents the
local wildlife, including 225
species of birds, among which
are heron and teal. Built in the
9th century, the Carolingian
abbey church of **Abbaye de
St-Philbert**, at St Philbert-de-
Grand-Lieu, is one of the
oldest churches in France. In
the crypt lies the tomb of St
Philbert, the abbey's founder.

🏛 **Musée du Pays de Retz**
Rue des Moines, Bourgneuf-en-Retz.
📞 *(02) 40 21 40 83.*
⭕ *Apr–Nov: Tue–Sun.* ⚫ *Dec–Mar.*
🏯 **Maison du Lac**
St-Philbert-de-Grand-Lieu.
📞 *(02) 40 78 73 88.* ⭕ *May–Sep:
daily; Oct–Apr: Mon–Sat, Sun pm.*
⛪ **Abbaye de St-Philbert**
ℹ *St-Philbert de Grand-Lieu;
(02) 40 78 73 88*

Clisson ❿

Road map F5. 20 km (12 miles) south
of Nantes via the D59. 🏘 *5,550.*
🚌 *Place du Minage; (02) 40 54 02
95.* 🕑 *Tue, Wed & Fri.* 🎭 *Les
Italiennes de Clisson (theatre, music
& film, Jul), Les Médiévales (Aug).*

A ROMANTIC DREAM led to the
development of Clisson.
In the 19th century, the Cacault
brothers, natives of Nantes who
loved Italy, built themselves a
Tuscan-style villa here. This
set a trend, and ochre-walled,
red-roofed houses, in striking
contrast to those roofed in the
more customary slate, soon
sprang up all around.
   Although it is in ruins, the
Château de Clisson here,
built in stages between the
13th and the 16th centuries,
well illustrates the evolution
of military architecture.
   La Garenne Lemot, an
estate on the eastern exit
from the town, has two
further examples of the
Italianate style: the estate
office, by the architect Crucy
(1815), and the Villa Lemot,
designed by the sculptor
Lemot (1824). The surrounding parkland is decorated with
antique columns, obelisks,
follies and other ornaments.
   Muscadet and Gros Plant
vines are grown in the vineyards between Clisson and
the Loire.

🏰 **Château de Clisson**
Place du Minage. 📞 *(02) 40 54 02 22.*
⭕ *Wed–Mon.* 🈸
🌿 **La Garenne Lemot**
Gétigné. 📞 *(02) 40 54 75 85.*
⭕ **Park**: *daily.* **Estate office:**
*Apr–Sep: Wed–Mon, Tue pm:
Oct–Mar: Tue–Sun.*
Villa Lemot:
*temporary
exhibitions.*

The Carolingian abbey at St-Philbert-de-Grand-Lieu

Pays d'Ancenis ⑪

Road map F4. Ancenis. 30 km
(19 miles) east of Nantes via the A11
or the N23. 🚶 *7,000*. 🚉 ✈ *Nantes-Atlantique*. ℹ *27 Rue du Château;
(02) 40 83 07 44*. 🎭 *Fête de la Loire
et des Vins (May)*. 🛒 *Thu*.

Tʜɪs ᴀʀᴇᴀ ᴏғ countryside,
whose focal point is the
town of Ancenis, flanks a
stretch of the Loire that in
places runs between high cliffs.

Ancenis, set in the midst of
vineyards, has some elegant
wine merchants' houses and a
16th-century **chateau**.

Further downstream is the
Donjon d'Oudon, a 14th-
century keep. Overlooking
Ancenis, the keep is also
ideally situated to survey the
Loire, once the main traffic
artery in western France.
Further upstream is the
hillside town of Varades. The
elegant 19th-century Italian-
style **chateau** here was built
by an engineer who had
made his fortune during the
reign of Napoleon III.

🏰 **Château d'Ancenis**
Rue du Pont. ☎ *(02) 40 83 87 00*.
🎟 *exterior of the castle, Jul–Aug*.
🏰 **Donjon d'Oudon**
Rue du Pont-Levis. ☎ *(02) 40 83
60 17*. ☐ *Easter holidays: daily;
May–mid-Jun: Sat–Sun & public
holidays; mid-Jun–mid-Sep:
daily*. 🎟
🏰 **Château de Varades**
Palais Briau. ☎ *(02) 40 83 45 00*.
☐ *Apr–Jul: Sat–Sun & public holidays;
Aug: daily pm; Sep–Oct: Sat–Sun &
public holidays*. 🎟

The Nantes–Brest Canal at Blain, just south of the Forêt du Gâvre

Châteaubriant ⑫

Road map F3. 🚶 *13,380*.
🚉 🚌 ℹ *22 Rue de Couëré;
(02) 40 28 20 90*. 🛒 *Wed am*.
🎭 *Foire de Béré (Sep), Journées
Gastronomiques (Nov)*.

Tʜᴇ ғᴇᴡ sᴜʀᴠɪᴠɪɴɢ schist-
built medieval houses
here give the walled town of
Châteaubriant a historic
atmosphere. Two **chateaux**
stand in close proximity on a
hill overlooking the Chere

**South gallery of the Renaissance
chateau in Châteaubriant**

river: a medieval fortress,
with a keep, and an elegant
Renaissance chateau with a
main building flanked by wings.

The Romanesque Église
St-Jean-de-Béré, built in
contrasting blue schist and
red granite, contains a 17th-
century Baroque altarpiece.

🏰 **Chateaux**
Access via Place Charles-de-Gaulle.
☎ *(02) 40 28 20 90*. ☐ *mid-Jun–
mid-Sept: Mon, Wed–Sat, Sun pm*.
🎟 *interiors of the castles*. 🎟

Forêt du Gâvre ⑬

Road map E4. Blain. 35 km (22 miles)
north of Nantes via the N137 then the
D164. 🚶 *7,450*. ℹ *2 Place Jean-
Guilhard; (02) 40 87 15 11*. 🛒 *Tue &
Sat am*. 🎭 *Festival Anne de Bretagne
(Jun), St-Laurent (Aug)*.

Cᴏᴠᴇʀɪɴɢ ᴀ ʟᴀʀɢᴇ massif
enclosed by the Don, Isac
and Brivet rivers, the forest is
good walking country. There
is also an interesting museum
and a chateau to explore here.

The **Musée des Arts et
Traditions Populaires**, in
Blain, on the D164, is devoted
to daily life in the early 20th
century. The **Château de la
Groulais**, in the direction of
St-Nazaire, was the residence
of the Clisson and Rohan
families during the Middle
Ages. Temporary exhibitions
are held here.

🏛 **Musée des Arts et
Traditions Populaires**
2 Place Jean-Guilhard, Blain.
☎ *(02) 40 79 98 51*. ☐ *Tue–Sun,
pm*. 🎟
🏰 **Château de la Groulais**
South exit from Blain. ☎ *(02) 40 79
07 81*. ☐ *Apr–Oct: Tue–Sun*. ⛔ *Nov–
Mar: groups only, by arrangement*. 🎟

VENDÉE WARS

In 1793, the persecution of the clergy, the execution of
Louis XVI and a rise in taxation provoked an anti-republican
uprising in the Vendée. Royalists soon followed up with acts
of barbarism, and the execution of republicans in Machecoul
began on 11 March. Catelineau, a carter, and Stofflet, a
gamekeeper, joined by various
aristocrats, stirred up revolt
among the peasantry. In June,
the Armée Catholique et Royale
Vendée seized control of the
Vendée, as well as the towns of
Saumur and Angers, but it was
defeated by the republicans at
Cholet on 17 October. On the
orders of General Turreau, the
latter led punitive expeditions
in the Vendée in 1794–5.

**Republican prisoners being
given their freedom**

TRAVELLERS' NEEDS

WHERE TO STAY

OR MANY DECADES, Brittany has been among the most popular tourist destinations in France. As a result, the region is well equipped to cater for the needs of visitors. From grand chateaux to basic camping sites, and including establishments in the familiar hotel chains, there is accommodation to suit every taste and budget, and even in individual locations the choice is wide.

Accommodation in Brittany's coastal resorts is, of course, more varied and plentiful than that available inland, even though there is much to interest visitors in areas away from Brittany's coasts. While the resorts are oriented towards holiday-makers' enjoyment of beaches, watersports and sailing, a warm welcome at a guesthouse inland brings visitors closer to the soul of Brittany.

RESERVATIONS

IN THE SUMMER holiday season, Brittany, like any other area that attracts large numbers of visitors, becomes very crowded. This particularly applies during school holidays and over long holiday weekends, and also when local festivals and other events take place.

It is therefore essential to book your accommodation well in advance. Branches of the French Tourist Office hold a list of hotels in Brittany and can make a reservation for you. Outside the busiest periods, it is best to make a reservation by contacting your chosen hotel direct. Whether you would like to stay in a hotel of character and atmosphere, or prefer guesthouse accommodation *(chambres d'hôtes)*, and whether you have in mind a particular area of Brittany or simply need a suggestion for a weekend break, the **Maison de la Bretagne** can provide all the necessary information.

HOTEL CATEGORIES

THE FRENCH MINISTRY of Tourism grades hotels into five categories, with a rating of one to five stars. This

The Hôtel Castel Marie-Louise in La Baule *(see p227)*

rating gives an idea both of the size of the rooms on offer, and also of the facilities available.

A two-star hotel, for example, will have a lift if there are four or more floors, and there will be a telephone in each room. Some of the more modest establishments have a no-star rating.

PRICES

IN BRITTANY, as in the rest of France, advertised prices include tax and service. Charges are per room rather than per person, except when board or half-board is offered. In country areas, half-board may be compulsory, or indeed may even be the sole option when the hotel is the only place in the town or village where visitors can have a meal.

Most establishments through all categories make a small charge for a third person or a child sharing a double room.

A room with shower is usually about 20 per cent cheaper than one with bath.

Some establishments may close during the winter. However, those that stay open may offer advantageous rates during the low season. Information on off-season rates and deals is available from travel agents or directly from the hotels themselves.

CHAIN HOTELS

The large hotel chains have establishments all over Brittany. Among them is **Groupe Envergure**, which includes hotels forming part of the Balladins, Campanile, Climat de France, Kyriad, Bleu Marine, Première Classe, Nuit d'Hôtel, Clarine and Côte à Côte sub-chains.

As with those in the older-established **Ibis**, **Mercure** and **Novotel** chains, strict controls ensure that these establishments offer a high standard of comfort and cleanliness and an excellent range of facilities. **Formule 1**, by contrast, is a chain of hotels designed to provide basic facilities at a low price.

Château de Locguénolé, in Hennebont *(see p225)*

TRADITIONAL FAMILY-RUN HOTELS

Establishments affiliated to **Logis de France**, the leading independent association of hotels in Europe, will suit visitors who prefer smaller hotels with local character. Identifiable by a green and yellow logo *(see p217)*, hotels in this chain offer a more personal welcome and an authentic flavour of their particular locality. The hotels themselves are usually buildings of character that are very much in keeping with their surroundings.

Relais du Silence is an affiliation of distinguished hotels with a friendly atmosphere and where peace and relaxation are a prime consideration. They have a two-star to five-star rating.

LUXURY HOTELS

THOSE WHO LIKE a little luxury and a memorable gastronomic experience will not be disappointed by the finest hotels in Brittany. A number of chateaux and listed buildings have been converted into upmarket hotel-restaurants, some of which employ the services of prestigious chefs. Such hotels are ideal for visitors seeking the very best in French hospitality and cuisine.

Establishments of this type belong to either of two main associations. One is **Relais et Châteaux**, with eight hotel-restaurants in Brittany, including the Château de

The Hôtel Reine Hortense in Dinard *(see p218)*

The Grand Hôtel des Thermes in St-Malo *(see p219)*

Locguénolé in Hennebont *(see p225)*, the Auberge Bretonne in La Roche-Bernard *(see p226)* and Le Castel Marie-Louise in La Baule *(see p227)*. The other is **Châteaux et Hôtels de France**, with nine establishments in Brittany, including the Hôtel Reine Hortense in Dinard *(see p218)*.

THALASSOTHERAPY

THIS THERAPEUTIC treatment uses the curative powers of sea water, which is rich in iodine and trace elements, and whose curative effects and revitalizing properties are widely known. Between St-Malo in the north and La Baule in the south, there are 11 thalassotherapy centres along the coasts of Brittany. Among the best known are the Institut de Thalassothérapie de Quiberon *(see p175)* and the Thermes Marins in St-Malo, where there are six sea-water swimming pools.

Thalassotherapy centres offer several options that also include accommodation. There are, for instance, anti-stress treatments, cures to combat the effects of smoking, and post-natal courses. Full details on thassalotherapy in Brittany is available from the **Comité Régional du Tourisme de Bretagne** *(see p216)*.

CHAMBRES D'HÔTES

PRIVATE HOUSES with rooms to let *(chambres d'hôtes)* are becoming increasingly numerous in Brittany. This option has many advantages. Staying in a private house provides the opportunity to meet local people and to experience Breton culture at a more authentic level than is possible when staying in a hotel.

When guesthouses provide meals, this is also an opportunity to enjoy local specialities in informal surroundings and for considerably less than the price of a restaurant meal.

A list of private houses offering *chambres d'hôtes* is available from local tourist offices. *Chambres d'Hôtes en Bretagne*, a full listing giving all details, is published by **Gîtes de France**.

The Hôtel Ker Moor in St-Quay-Portrieux *(see p221)*

COUNTRY GÎTES

O FTEN ON FARM premises, country gîtes (*gîtes ruraux*) are fully furnished, fully equipped houses or apartments built in the local rural style. Their setting and immediate surroundings are far superior to that of most other types of rented accommodation.

One of the best-known organizations to which country gîtes are affiliated is **Gîtes de France**, which has several local offices in Brittany and which publishes four handbooks, listing gîtes in the Côtes d'Armor, the Morbihan, Finistère and Ille-et-Vilaine respectively.

Gîtes de France also issues lists of specific types of accommodation in Brittany: these are *gîtes de caractère* (picturesque houses), *gîtes de pêche* (for fishing), *gîtes d'étape* (dormitory accommodation for groups), *gîtes Panda* (in the Parc Naturel Régional d'Armorique; *see pp140–1*), *chalets loisirs* (for outdoor activities), gîtes for people with disabilites and gîtes suitable for elderly people.

The association also issues a free guide, *Bienvenue à la Ferme en Bretagne*.

SELF-CATERING ACCOMMODATION

L OCAL ESTATE and letting agents hold lists of houses and apartments that can be rented for holidays. Rental is by the week, usually starting on Saturdays. Weekend bookings may also be possible, except in the high season. Local tourist offices in Brittany will provide lists of self-catering accommodation with contact details for booking. It is advisable to obtain full information, including the name of the local organization in charge of self-catering accommodation.

DIRECTORY

French Government Tourist Offices

UK: 178 Piccadilly, London W1V OAL 090 6824 4123 (within UK only).
w www.franceguide.com
w www.en-france.com

US (east coast): 444 Madison Avenue, New York 10022.
(212) 838 7800.

US (mid-west): 676 North Michigan Ave, Suite 3360, Chicago, IL 60611.
(312) 751 7800.

US (west coast): 9454 Wilshire Bd, Suite 715, Beverly Hills, CA 90212.
(310) 271 2693.

Comité Régional de Tourisme de Bretagne
1 Rue Raoul-Ponchon, 35069 Rennes.
(02) 99 36 25 25.
w www.brittanytourism.com

Maison de la Bretagne
203 Bd St-Germain, 75007 Paris.
(01) 53 63 11 50.
w www.tourisme bretagne.com

YOUTH HOSTELS

Youth Hostel Association (YHA)
Trevelyan House, 8 St Stephen's Hill, St Albans, Herts AL1 2DY.
01727 845 047.
w www.yha.org.uk

Hostelling International-American Youth Hostels (HI-AYH)
733 15th St NW, Suite 840, PO Box 37613, Washington DC 20005.
202 783 6161.
w www.hiay.org

CROUS
2 Avenue Le Gorgeu, BP 88710, 29287 Brest.
(02) 98 03 38 78.

7 Place Hoche, BP 115, 35002 Rennes Cedex.
(02) 99 84 31 31.

CAMPING

Fédération Française de Camping et de Caravaning
78 Rue de Rivoli, 75004 Paris.
01 42 72 84 08.
w www.campingfrance.com

CHAIN HOTELS

Destination Bretagne
26 Rue du Maréchal-Leclerc, 35800 Dinard. (02) 99 16 40 31. w destination-bretagne.com

Groupe Envergure
01 64 62 46 46.
w www.envergure.fr

Formule 1
0892 685 685.
w www.hotelformule1.com

Ibis, Novotel, Sofitel, Mercure
020 8283 4500 UK.
w www.accorhotels.com

TRADITIONAL HOTELS

Logis de France
(01) 45 84 83 84.
w www.logis-de-france.fr

Relais du Silence
(01) 44 49 90 00.
w www.silencehotel.com

LUXURY HOTELS

Relais et Châteaux
0825 32 32 32.
w www.relaischateaux.com

Châteaux et Hôtels de France
12 Rue Auber, 75009 Paris

(01) 40 07 00 20.
w www.chateauxhotels.com

GÎTES DE FRANCE
59 Rue St-Lazare,75009 Paris. (01) 49 70 75 75.
w www.gites-de-france.fr

Côtes d'Armor
7 Rue St-Benoît, BP 4536, 22045 St-Brieuc.
(02) 96 62 21 73.

Finistère
5 Allée Sully, 29322 Quimper.
(02) 98 64 20 20.

Ille-et-Vilaine
8 Rue de Coëtquen, BP 30645, 35160 Rennes.
(02) 99 78 47 57.

Loire-Atlantique
1 Allée Baco, BP 93218, 44032 Nantes.
(02) 51 72 95 65.

Morbihan
42 Avenue Wilson, BP 30318, 56403 Auray.
(02) 97 56 48 12.

Gîtes de France brochures are obtainable from French Government Tourist Offices.

SELF-CATERING

Brittany Centre
Wharf Road, Portsmouth, PO2 8RU.
0990 360 360.

YOUTH HOSTELS

SOME OF THE least expensive accommodation is provided by youth hostels (auberges de jeunesse). This is available to everyone, regardless of age, as long as they have a **Youth Hostel Association** or **Hostelling International** card. A full list of youth hostels is available from the association. During the summer, students may also stay in rooms in student lodgings at universities. These rooms can be booked through **CROUS (Centre Régional des Oeuvres Universitaires)**.

Logis de France logo

CAMPSITES

MANY CAMPSITES in Brittany have exceptionally fine locations, perhaps beside the sea or, inland, deep in a forest. Lists of campsites are available from the tourist offices of each *département* of Brittany. Advance booking is advised.

The **Fédération Française de Camping et de Caravaning** publishes an official guide of approved campsites. The Association des Gîtes de France also provides a guide to campsites on farms and publishes *Campings Verts en Bretagne (Green Campsites in Brittany)*.

Campsites are subject to an official classification system, which runs from a one-star to a four-star rating according to

toilet, washing and facilities such as public telephones, swimming pools and television. It is sometimes possible to hire tents and camper vans, or rent bungalows.

Camping rough at one of the unofficial camp sites along the coast also has its attractions. Such sites often have stunning locations and campers may pitch their tents in return for a very small payment.

DISABLED TRAVELLERS

VARIOUS organizations provide information on holidays and establishments with facilities for disabled people. The **GIHP** (Groupement pour l'Insertion des Personnes Handicappés Physiques), the **Association des Paralysés de France** and its travel branch, APF Evasion, **Voyages ASA** and the **EPAL** (Association Évasion en Pays d'Accueil et de Loisirs) all organize holidays for disabled people. The **CNRH** (Comité National pour la Réadaptation des Handicapés) and the Association des Paralysés de France have local offices that issue lists of establishments adapted for people with disabilities. **Gîtes de France** publish a list of gîtes with wheelchair access and special equipment.

The **CIDJ** (Centre d'Information et de Documentation Jeunesse) has information for young disabled travellers. For details, *see p256*.

USING THE LISTINGS

The hotels on pages 218–227 are listed according to region and price category. The symbols summarize the facilities at each hotel.

🛏 All rooms have bath or shower unless otherwise indicated

� Rooms with a view

▤ Air-conditioning in all rooms

24 24-hour room service

TV Television in all rooms

🏊 Swimming pool or beach

♿ Wheelchair access

🛗 Lift

💪 Gym/fitness facilities

🗂 Business facilities

@ Email address

W Website

FAX Fax number

✤ Affiliation to Relais et Châteaux *(see p215)*

● Closed

💳 Credit cards accepted

Price categories
For a standard double room per night with shower, breakfast, service and taxes included:

€ under 25 euros
€€ 25 to 45 euros
€€€ 45 to 65 euros
€€€€ 65 to 80 euros
€€€€€ over 80 euros

※ **Camper vans at a site on Pointe de l'Arcouest, on the Côtes d'Armor** *(see p99)*

Choosing a Hotel

THE HOTELS LISTED below have been selected on the basis of their location or facilities, across a broad price range. Some also have a restaurant. They are listed by region, the coloured thumb tabs corresponding with those by which the regions of Brittany are identified in each section. For a list of restaurants, see pp232–41.

	NUMBER OF ROOMS	FACILITIES FOR CHILDREN	PRIVATE PARKING	RESTAURANT	TERRACE
ILLE-ET-VILAINE					
CANCALE: *Château Richeux* ✤ €€€€ Le Point-du-Jour, 35350 St-Méloir-des-Ondes. ((02) 99 89 64 76. FAX (02) 99 89 88 47. @ bricourt@relaischateaux.fr The chateau is, in fact, a magnificent 1920s villa overlooking the Baie du Mont-St-Michel. With a relaxing and sophisticated atmosphere, it has a large garden and rooms with period furniture. The restaurant, Le Coquillage, offers seafood specialities, and diners can enjoy a superb view of the bay. TV ⬛⬛⬛⬛⬛⬛	16	●	■	●	■
COMBOURG: *Château de la Ballue* €€€€ Bazouges-la-Pérouse, 35560. ((02) 99 97 47 86. w www.la-ballue.com An elegant 17th-century chateau set in idyllic parkland. Laid out in the style of an Italian Baroque garden, the park contains contemporary works of art. The hotel has beautiful rooms, and meals (which must be pre-ordered) are prepared by the chateau's owner, who uses 17th-century methods and recipes. ⬛⬛	5		■	●	■
DINARD: *Hôtel Printania* €€ 5 Avenue. George-V, 35800. ((02) 99 46 13 07. FAX (02) 99 46 26 32. @ printania.dinard@wanadoo.fr The hotel commands one of the finest views of Dinard and the bay. The rooms and communal areas are furnished with antique Breton furniture, including box beds. The staff in the restaurant are dressed in traditional Breton costume. TV 24 ⬛⬛ *mid-Nov–mid-Mar.*	57	●		●	■
DINARD: *Hôtel Reine Hortense* €€€€ 19 Rue Malouine, 35800. ((02) 99 46 54 31. FAX (02) 99 88 15 88 @ reine.hortense@wanadoo.fr This charming Belle Époque villa, decorated with many pieces that once belonged to Queen Hortense of the Netherlands, offers a beautiful view of St-Malo. There is also a beach for the exclusive use of the hotel residents. TV ⬛⬛⬛⬛⬛ *mid-Nov–Mar.*	8	●	■		■
DOL-DE-BRETAGNE: *Hôtel de Bretagne* € 17 Place Chateaubriand, 35120. ((02) 99 48 02 03. FAX (02) 99 48 25 75. This centrally located, well-kept hotel has the atmosphere of a family guest house. The rooms are clean, light and airy, and the restaurant offers simple dishes that are good value for money. TV ⬛⬛⬛ *Oct.*	27	●		●	
FOUGÈRES: *Grand Hôtel des Voyageurs* € 10 Place Gambetta, 35300. ((02) 99 99 08 20. FAX (02) 99 99 99 04. @ hotel-voyageurs-fougeres@wanadoo.fr Located near the tourist office, in the heart of the upper town, this is a fine 1900s hotel with tastefully decorated and completely renovated rooms. There is also a billiard room. TV 24 ⬛⬛⬛⬛ *two weeks over Christmas–New Year.*	37		■		
LOHÉAC: *Hôtel Gibecière* € 22 Rue de la Poste, 35550. ((02) 99 34 06 14. FAX (02) 99 34 10 37. This small, family-run hotel, located in the centre of the village, has spacious, well-furnished rooms. Not far from the Manoir de l'Automobile *(see p64)*, it is convenient for those with an interest in car, 4-x-4 and go-kart circuit racing. TV ⬛⬛⬛⬛	23	●	■		
MONT-ST-MICHEL: *Hôtel de la Digue* €€ At the dyke, 2 km (1 mile) from Mont-St-Michel. ((02) 33 60 14 02. FAX (02) 33 60 37 59. @ hotel-de-la-digue@wanadoo.fr A fine hotel, built on an elongated plan, with pleasant rooms. The breakfast room offers a view of the mount. TV ⬛⬛⬛⬛ *mid-Nov–Mar.*	36		■	●	■

Price categories for a double room per night with bath or shower, including breakfast and VAT.			NUMBER OF ROOMS	FACILITIES FOR CHILDREN	PRIVATE PARKING	RESTAURANT	TERRACE

Price categories for a double room per night with bath or shower, including breakfast and VAT.
€ under 25 euros
€€ 25 to 45 euros
€€€ 45 to 65 euros
€€€€ 65 to 80 euros
€€€€€ over 80 euros

FACILITIES FOR CHILDREN
Such facilities include cradles, cots and a baby-sitting service. Some hotels provide high chairs and offer children's menus.
PRIVATE PARKING
The hotel has its own car park or parking spaces. These may not be on the same premises.
RESTAURANT
This is not necessarily recommended, although particularly good hotel restaurants are also listed in the restaurant section.
TERRACE
The hotel has a terrace, interior courtyard or garden, and meals may be served outdoors.

	Rooms	Children	Parking	Restaurant	Terrace
MONT-ST-MICHEL: *Terrasses Poulard* — €€€ Grande Rue (within the walls). ((02) 33 89 022 02. FAX (02) 33 60 37 31. The best hotel on Mont-St-Michel, with tastefully decorated rooms and a warm welcome. The hotel's two smallest rooms, the Chambre Maupassant and Chambre Du Guesclin, are inexpensive. TV 🌿 🔒 ⚏	29	●	■	●	
PAIMPONT: *Le Relais de Brocéliande* — € 5 Rue des Forges, 35380. ((02) 99 07 84 94. FAX (02) 99 07 80 60. W www.le-relais-brocéliande.fr Located in the Forêt de Paimpont *(see p62)*, near a lake where guests may fish with tackle hired from the hotel. Catches are cooked for guests in the restaurant. The hotel has a fine terrace with a beautiful fountain. TV 🌿 🔒 ⚏ ● *mid-Dec–early Jan.*	23	●	■	●	■
REDON: *Hôtel Jean-Marc Chandouineau* — €€ 1 Rue Thiers, 35600. ((02) 99 71 02 04. FAX (02) 99 71 08 81. An establishment with attractive, comfortable attic rooms and an excellent restaurant, which offers specialities based on local produce. 🔒 🍴 🔒 ⚏	7	●	■	●	
RENNES: *Hôtel Angelina* — € 1 Quai Lamennais, 35000. ((02) 99 79 29 66. FAX (02) 99 79 61 01. @ angelina-rennes@aol.com Just ten minutes' walk from the railway station, this 2-star hotel is centrally located. Although it appears somewhat austere, it has large, comfortable rooms and a pleasant breakfast room. TV 🔒 📶 ⚏	30	●			
RENNES: *Lecoq-Gadby* — €€€€ 156 Rue Antrain, 35000. ((02) 99 38 05 55. FAX (02) 99 38 53 40. @ lecoqgadby@chateauxhotels.com Established 100 years ago, this hotel is located in a residential quarter near Mont-Thabor. It has a garden with box trees and roses, a summer dining room and, in the new wing, pleasant, thoughtfully furnished and tastefully decorated rooms. TV 🔒 🍴 📶 🔒 ⚏	11	●	■	●	■
ST-MALO: *Le Grand Hôtel des Thermes* — €€ Grande Plage du Sillon, 35401. ((02) 99 40 75 75. FAX (02) 99 40 76 00. W www.thalassosaintmalo.com Looking onto the sea, this is a comfortable, classic seaside hotel that also offers thalassotherapy. The large rooms are light and airy. TV 🔒 📶 🌿 🍴 🔒 ⚏ ● *two weeks in Jan.*	21		■		■
ST-MALO: *La Villefromoy* — €€€ 7 Boulevard Hébert, 35400. ((02) 99 40 92 20. FAX (02) 99 56 79 49. @ villefromoy@chateauxhotels.com Ideally located near the seafront promenade that is the hub of life in St-Malo, this elegant late 19th-century hotel looks onto the sea. The rooms have sophisticated décor and there is a warm welcome. TV 🔒 🌿 📶 🔒 ⚏	21		■		■
ST-MALO: *Le Beaufort* — €€€€ 25 Chaussée du Sillon, 35400. ((02) 99 40 99 99. FAX (02) 99 40 99 62. W www.hotel-beaufort.com This comfortable hotel, built in 1850, was thoroughly renovated in 2001. Just 3 minutes' walk from the walled town, it stands on the seafront promenade linking St-Malo and Paramé, facing the sea. TV 🔒 🌿 📶 🔒 ⚏	22	●			■
ST-MÉLOIR-DES-ONDES: *Tirel Guérin* — €€€ Gare de la Gosnière (next to Cancale), 35350. ((02) 99 89 10 46. FAX (02) 99 89 12 62. @ tirelguerin@chateauxhotels.com Located in open countryside 10 km (6 miles) from St-Malo and Cancale, this hotel is a haven of peace. The restaurant is known for its classic, light cuisine. TV 🔒 🌿 ≣ 🍴 📶 🔒 🔒 ⚏ ● *mid-Dec–mid-Jan.*	50	●	■	●	■

		NUMBER OF ROOMS	FACILITIES FOR CHILDREN	PRIVATE PARKING	RESTAURANT	TERRACE
Price categories for a double room per night with bath or shower, including breakfast and VAT. € under 25 euros €€ 25 to 45 euros €€€ 45 to 65 euros €€€€ 65 to 80 euros €€€€€ over 80 euros	**FACILITIES FOR CHILDREN** Such facilities include cradles, cots and a baby-sitting service. Some hotels provide high chairs and offer children's menus. **PRIVATE PARKING** The hotel has its own car park or parking spaces. These may not be on the same premises. **RESTAURANT** This is not necessarily recommended, although particularly good hotel restaurants are also listed in the restaurant section. **TERRACE** The hotel has a terrace, interior courtyard or garden, and meals may be served outdoors.					

CÔTES D'ARMOR

BRÉHAT (ÎLE DE): *Hôtel-Restaurant Bellevue* €€€ Port-Clos, 22870. ((02) 96 20 00 05. FAX (02) 96 20 06 06. A large hotel with splendid views of the sea, and 5 minutes' walk from the beach. Although this is a busy establishment, there is always a pleasant welcome. The rooms are modern and comfortable. The dining room is on a veranda and there is also a large terrace. Bicycles for exploring the island can be hired. TV ⛄ 🔲 🖉 ● *three weeks in Nov & Jan–mid-Feb.*	17	●		●	
BRÉLIDY: *Château de Brélidy* €€€ 22140. ((02) 96 95 69 38. FAX (02) 96 95 18 03. @ brelidy@chateauxhotels.com This imposing 16th-century manor house, with a view of the Méné-Bré river, is one of the best places to stay in the Côtes d'Armor, and an ideal base from which to explore the region. The comfortable rooms are decorated in a sophisticated style. Private fishing. TV 🔲 ⛄ 🍽 🔲 🖉 ● *Nov–Apr.*	10	●	■	●	■
CAP FRÉHEL: *Le Fanal* €€€ On the road Cap-Fréhel, then turning off to Plévenon, 22240. ((02) 96 41 43 19. In the style of a modern chalet, this hotel, 400 m (450 yds) from the cliffs, blends well into the heath landscape of Cap Fréhel. The rooms are small but very clean, and there is a large and beautiful garden. ⛄ 🖉 ● *Oct–Mar.*	9		■		■
DINAN: *Hôtel Avaugour* €€€ 1 Place Champ, 22100. ((02) 96 39 07 49. FAX (02) 96 85 43 04. @ Avaugour.Hotel@wanadoo.fr Located in the historic centre of Dinan, the hotel backs onto the ramparts. The newly renovated rooms overlook the garden. A very comfortable place to stay. TV 🔲 🔳 ⛄ 🔲 🔲 🖉 ● *mid-Nov–mid-Dec; mid-Jan–mid-Mar.*	24	●		●	■
DINAN: *Hôtel Le Jerzual* €€€€ 26 Quai des Talards, 22100. ((02) 96 87 02 02. FAX (02) 96 87 02 03. A modern hotel in the old harbour, on the banks of the Rance. There is a swimming pool, sauna, steam room and jacuzzi. TV 🔲 🏊 🔲 🔲 🖉	54	●	■	●	■
GUINGAMP: *Le Relais du Roy* €€€ 42 Place du Centre, 22200. ((02) 96 43 76 62. FAX (02) 96 44 08 01. This 17th-century building retains its original porch. Inside, a fine granite staircase leads up to the comfortable rooms. The hotel restaurant has a good reputation in the region. TV 🔲 🖉 ● *early Jan.*	7			●	
LAMBALLE: *Manoir du Vaumadeuc* €€€€ Pleven, 22130. ((02) 96 84 46 17. FAX (02) 96 84 40 16. This beautiful 15th-century house, a listed building, has an idyllic setting amid formal gardens, with wooded parkland beyond. The interior has exposed beams, original stonework and stately chimneypieces. 🔲 🔲 🖉 ● *Dec–Easter; restaurant (reservation only): Oct–Jun.*	13	●	■	●	■
MÛR-DE-BRETAGNE: *Auberge Grand'Maison* €€ 1 Rue Léon-le-Cerf, 22530. ((02) 96 28 51 10. FAX (02) 96 28 52 30. @ grandmaison@armoinet.tm.fr An inviting hotel with nine newly renovated rooms and a restaurant that is renowned for its delectable foie gras profiteroles. The Lac de Guerlédan (see p90) is 3 km (2 miles) to the west. TV 🔲 🔲 🖉 ● *two weeks in Feb; three weeks in Oct.*	9			●	
PAIMPOL: *Le Repaire de Kerroc'h* €€ 29 Quai Morand, 22500. ((02) 96 20 50 13. FAX (02) 96 22 07 46. @ repairedeuxkerroch@aol.com This *malouinière (see p84)* dominates the Baie de Paimpol. Each room is named after one of the islands beyond the bay and restaurant offers refined seafood cuisine. For more informal dining, there is also a bistro. TV 🔲 ⛄ 🔲 🖉	13	●	■	●	

PERROS-GUIREC: *Manoir du Sphinx* €€€ 20
67 Chemin de la Messe, 22700. **(** *(02) 96 23 25 42.* **FAX** *(02) 96 91 26 13.*
@ manoirdusphinx@wanadoo.fr
In this 1900s manor house on the edge of the cliff, all rooms have a sea view.
The garden, planted with hydrangeas, stretches down to the beach 100 m
(110 yds) below the hotel. **TV** 🛏 🌱 🏊 ⬆ 🚻 🚻 🗐 ● *early Jan–late Feb.*

PLANCOËT: *Jean-Pierre Crouzil* €€€€ 7
20 Les Quais, 22130. **(** *(02) 96 84 10 24.* **FAX** *(02) 96 84 01 93.*
@ ecrin@chateauxhotels.com
A traditional establishment redolent of Brittany, with meticulously
decorated rooms. The high-class restaurant *(see p235)* attracts many
connoisseurs. **TV** 🛏 ▤ 🍴 🚻 🗐 ● *early Jan–early Feb.*

PLANCOËT-PLOREC: *Château le Windsor* €€€ 23
Le Bois-Billy, 22130. **(** *(02) 96 83 04 83.* **FAX** *(02) 96 83 05 36.*
@ lewindsor@chateauxhotels.com
Located between the coast and woodlands, the chateau is
20 km (12 miles) from the beaches of the Côte d'Émeraude.
Among its attractions are fine period furniture, an 11-ha (27-acre)
park and a restaurant serving delicious seafood dishes.
TV 🛏 🌱 🏊 🏋 🍴 🚻 🗐 ● *mid-Nov–end Nov; mid-Jan–mid-Feb.*

PLANGUENOUAL: *Domaine du Val* €€€ 53
22400. **(** *(02) 96 32 75 40.* **FAX** *(02) 96 32 71 50.*
@ val@chateauxhotels.com
A superb hotel and leisure complex, the Château du Val is located
800 m (870 yds) from the sea. It is set in 11 ha (27 acres) of parkland,
with tennis and squash courts, a swimming pool and saunas.
TV 🛏 🏊 🍴 🚻 🗐

SABLES-D'OR-LES-PINS: *La Voile d'Or* €€€ 25
22240. **(** *(02) 96 41 42 49.* **FAX** *(02) 96 41 55 45.*
@ la-voile-dor@wanadoo.fr
Located on the edge of the resort and about 100 m (110 yds) from the sea,
this hotel has very comfortable rooms. The restaurant has a good reputation
locally. 🛏 🌱 🚻 🚻 🗐 ● *mid-Nov–mid-Mar.*

ST-BRIEUC: *Hôtel Clisson* €€ 24
36 Rue Gouët, 22000. **(** *(02) 96 62 19 29.* **FAX** *(02) 96 61 06 95.*
A very comfortable hotel, located away from the bustle of St-Brieuc.
The rooms are pleasantly furnished and some have a jacuzzi bath.
TV 🛏 🌱 ⬆ 🚻 🗐 ● *mid-Dec–early Jan.*

ST-CAST-LE-GUILDO: *Les Dunes* €€ 27
Rue Primauguet, 22380. **(** *(02) 96 41 80 31.* **FAX** *(02) 96 41 85 34.*
A well-maintained 1930s hotel. The most modern rooms are those
at the back of the building. The renowned restaurant serves fish and
seafood specialities. **TV** 🛏 🏊 🗐 ● *Oct–mid-Apr.*

ST-QUAY-PORTRIEUX: *Ker Moor* €€€ 29
13 Rue Prés-le-Sénécal, 22410. **(** *(02) 96 70 52 22.* **FAX** *(02) 96 70 50 49.*
A hotel in a fine Moorish-style villa built by a Breton diplomat in the
early 20th century. The more recent part of the building has attractive
rooms. The restaurant, with a panoramic view, serves excellent fish and
seafood dishes, including scallops. **TV** 🌱 ⬆ 🗐 ● *mid-Dec–early Jan.*

TRÉBEURDEN: *Manoir de Lan-Kerellec* ✤ €€€€ 19
Central street in Lan-Kerellec, 22560. **(** *(02) 96 15 47 47.*
FAX *(02) 96 23 66 88.*
@ lankerellec@relaischateaux.com
A hotel in a tastefully renovated 19th-century Breton manor house.
All the rooms have a sea view and some have a balcony. Imaginative
cuisine is served in a dining room designed in the form of a ship's hull.
TV 🌱 🏊 🚻 🗐 ● *mid-Nov–mid-Mar.*

NORTHERN FINISTÈRE

BATZ (ÎLE DE): *Grand Hôtel Morvan* € 32
Pors-Kernoc, 29253. **(** & **FAX** *(02) 98 61 78 06.*
A small, basic hotel with simply furnished, well-lit rooms. Fish and seafood
dishes are served in a dining room with 1950s-style décor.
🛏 🏊 🌱 🚻 **TV** 🗐 ● *mid-Nov–Feb.*

Price categories for a double room per night with bath or shower, including breakfast and VAT. € under 25 euros €€ 25 to 45 euros €€€ 45 to 65 euros €€€€ 65 to 80 euros €€€€€ over 80 euros	**FACILITIES FOR CHILDREN** Such facilities include cradles, cots and a baby-sitting service. Some hotels provide high chairs and offer children's menus. **PRIVATE PARKING** The hotel has its own car park or parking spaces. These may not be on the same premises. **RESTAURANT** This is not necessarily recommended, although particularly good hotel restaurants are also listed in the restaurant section. **TERRACE** The hotel has a terrace, interior courtyard or garden, and meals may be served outdoors.	NUMBER OF ROOMS	FACILITIES FOR CHILDREN	PRIVATE PARKING	RESTAURANT	TERRACE

Hotel	Rooms	Children	Parking	Restaurant	Terrace
BREST: *Hôtel Bellevue* € 53 Rue Victor-Hugo, 29200. ((02) 98 80 51 78. FAX (02) 98 46 02 84. @ hbellevue@wanadoo.fr The hotel is located in the centre of Brest, in a quiet street near the railway station. The rooms have a sea view and the welcome is warm and cheerful. TV 🖥 24 ❄ 🔊 🛏 🗐	26	●	■		
CARANTEC: *Hôtel de Carantec-Patrick Jeffroy* €€€€ 20 Rue de Kelenn, 29660. ((02) 98 67 00 47. FAX (02) 98 67 08 25. @ carantec@chateauxhotels.com This elegant Breton house is perched on the cliff edge, and the rooms have a view of the Baie de Morlaix and Presqu'île de Carantec. The reception is not always the friendliest, but the restaurant serves imaginative cuisine. The beach is 100 m (110 yds) away. TV 🖥 ❄ 🔊 🛏 🗐 ● *Jan.*	12	●	■	●	■
CONQUET (LE): *Hôtel de la Sainte-Barbe* €€ Pointe de la Ste-Barbe, 29217. ((02) 98 89 00 26. This seaside hotel is located above the fishing village and near the boarding point for boats to Île d'Ouessant and Île Molène. The restaurant specializes in fish and seafood. TV 🖥 ❄ 🌊 🔊 🛏 🗐 ● *mid-Nov–mid-Dec.*	49	●	■	●	■
LANDÉDA: *La Baie des Anges* €€€ 350 Route des Anges, 29870. ((02) 98 04 90 04. FAX (02) 98 04 92 27. @ anges@chateauxhotels.com This elegant 19th-century house facing onto the sea has comfortable rooms. The breakfasts are copious. ● *early Jan–mid-Feb.*	20	●	■		■
LANDERNEAU: *L'Amandier* € 55 Rue de Brest, 29800. ((02) 98 85 10 89. FAX 02 98 85 34 14. This hotel offers excellent value for money. The comfortable rooms have sophisticated décor, and the restaurant serves tasty cuisine based on local ingredients. TV 🗐	8			●	
LOCQUIREC: *Le Grand Hôtel des Bains* €€€€ 15 bis Rue de l'Église, 29241. ((02) 98 67 41 02. FAX (02) 98 67 44 60. @ grand-hotel-des-bains@wanadoo.fr Renovated in 1996, this imposing establishment is the archetypal family hotel. It is set in extensive parkland, and the most expensive rooms have a sea view. Facilities include a covered swimming pool, steam room, jacuzzi and balneotherapy (spa bath treatment). TV 🖥 ❄ 🌊 🔊 🛏 🗐 ● *Jan.*	36		■	●	■
MORLAIX: *Hôtel de l'Europe* €€ 1 Rue Aiguillon, 29600. ((02) 98 62 11 99. FAX (02) 98 88 83 38. @ reservations@hotel-europe.com.fr This late 19th-century building is located in the centre of Morlaix. The hall is decorated with 17th-century woodcarvings. TV 🖥 24 🔊 🛏 🗐 ● *Christmas–New Year.*	60	●		●	
OUESSANT (ÎLE D'): *Le Ti Jan Ar C'Hafe* €€ Kernigou, 29242. ((02) 98 48 82 64. FAX (02) 98 48 88 15. A colourful, meticulously renovated house (whose name means "Joan of Arc's Little Café") with a lot of character. It has beautiful rooms, a neat garden and a wooden terrace. TV 🖥 ❄ 🗐 ● *Jan–Mar.*	8				■
PLOUGASTEL-DAOULA: *Hôtel Kastel Roc'h* € 91 Avenue du Général-de-Gaulle, 29470. ((02) 98 40 32 00. FAX (02) 98 04 25 40. @ castelroch@wanadoo.fr A Breton villa with rooms that have been completely renovated. Those looking onto the open countryside are particularly quiet. TV ❄ 🔊 🛏 🗐 ● *first week in Jan.*	46	●	■	●	■

ROSCOFF: *Le Brittany*   €€€   25
Boulevard Ste-Barbe, 29680. ☎ *(02) 98 69 70 78.* FAX *(02) 98 61 13 29.*
@ hotel.brittany@wanadoo.fr
This fine Breton manor house has a stunning location on the seafront
immediately opposite the Île de Batz. The restaurant is renowned for its
fine cuisine. TV ☷ ☰ ☝ ♿ ☷ ☷ ● *20 Oct–20 Mar.*

ST-POL-DE-LÉON: *Hôtel de France*   €   23
29 Rue Minimes, 29250. ☎ *(02) 98 29 14 14.* FAX *(02) 98 29 10 57.*
@ hotel.de.france.finistere@wanadoo.fr
Completely renovated in 1999, this elegant house has a quiet
location in extensive parkland, yet it is within easy reach of the town
centre. Pleasant rooms and a relaxed, family atmosphere. TV ☷ ☷

ST-THÉGONNEC: *Auberge de Saint-Thégonnec*   €€€   19
6 Place de la Mairie, 29410. ☎ *(02) 98 79 61 18.* FAX *(02) 98 62 71 10.*
@ auberge@wanadoo.fr
This *auberge* has very comfortable, well-decorated rooms. Breakfast is
copious and the restaurant serves good cuisine based on fresh local
ingredients. TV ☷ 24 ♿ ☷ ☷ ● *mid-Dec–early Jan.*

STE-ANNE-DU-PORTZIC: *Belvédère*   €€€   30
Via the D789, towards Ste-Anne-du-Portzic, 29200 Brest.
☎ *(02) 98 31 86 00.* FAX *(02) 98 31 86 39.* W www.belvedere.brest.com
This modern building, located on the beach, has comfortable, light
and airy rooms overlooking the entrance to the roadstead (Rade de Brest).
TV 24 ☷ ☰ ☝ ♿ ☷ ☷

SOUTHERN FINISTÈRE

AUDIERNE: *Au Roi Gradlon*   €€   19
3 Avenue Emmanuel-Brusq, 29770. ☎ *(02) 98 70 04 51.* FAX *(02) 98 70 14 73.*
W www.auroigradlon.com
A modern hotel with an unusually fine location right on the beach.
From the rooms, which have all been renovated, and the restaurant,
there is a splendid view of the Atlantic Ocean. TV ☷ ☷ ☷ ☷
● *mid-Dec–early Jan.*

BÉNODET: *Hôtel-restaurant Le Minaret*   €€€   20
Corniche de l'Estuaire, 29950. ☎ *(02) 98 57 03 13.* FAX *(02) 98 66 23 72.*
@ leminaret@wanadoo.fr
This 1920s Moorish-style villa was owned by a doctor who ministered
to the pasha of Marrakech, and fell in love with Morocco. The mosaic-
decorated room known as the Chambre du Pacha is stunning. The
garden is a simplified replica of the gardens of the Alhambra in Granada.
TV ☷ ☷ ☰ ☝ ☷ ☷ ● *mid-Oct–early Apr.*

CAMARET: *Thalassa*   €€   47
Quai du Styvel, 29570. ☎ *(02) 98 27 86 44.* FAX *(02) 98 27 88 14.*
W www.hotel-thalassa.com
This modern hotel consists of two parts. The rooms are modern and well-
furnished, and some have a view of the harbour. Facilities include a heated
seawater swimming pool, a steam room and a fitness centre. The hotel has a
good fish restaurant. Buffet breakfast. TV ☷ ☷ ☰ ☝ ☝ ☷ ● *Oct–mid-Apr;*
restaurant: Oct–Apr.

CONCARNEAU: *KerMoor*   €€   12
Plage des Sables-Blancs, 29900. ☎ *(02) 98 97 02 96.* FAX *(02) 98 97 84 04.*
This early 20th-century seaside villa has an ideal location on Plage des Sables-
Blancs. All the rooms, which are decorated as the interior of a ship, have a
sea view. An excellent establishment. TV ☷ 24 ☷ ☷ ☷

DOUARNENEZ: *Le Clos de Vallombreuse*   €€€   26
7 Rue d'Estienne-d'Orves, 29100. ☎ *(02) 98 92 63 64.* FAX *(02) 98 92 84 98.*
@ clos.vallombreuse@wanadoo.fr
This early 20th-century town house overlooking the sea stands in a small,
quiet park in the centre of Douarnenez. The light and airy rooms are
smartly decorated. Good restaurant. TV ☷ ☷ ☰ ♿ ☷

FORÊT-FOUESNANT: *Le Manoir du Stang*   €€€   24
29940. ☎ FAX *(02) 98 56 97 37.* @ stang@chateauxhotels.com
Built in the 15th and 17th centuries, this elegant country house stands
in 40 ha (100 acres) of parkland. The rooms, with period furniture,
look onto formal gardens or lakes. ☷ ☷ ☝ ☷ ● *Oct–Apr.*

			FACITIES FOR CHILDREN	PRIVATE PARKING	RESTAURANT	TERRACE

Price categories for a double room per night with bath or shower, including breakfast and VAT.

€ under 25 euros
€€ 25 to 45 euros
€€€ 45 to 65 euros
€€€€ 65 to 80 euros
€€€€€ over 80 euros

FACILITIES FOR CHILDREN
Such facilities include cradles, cots and a baby-sitting service. Some hotels provide high chairs and offer children's menus.
PRIVATE PARKING
The hotel has its own car park or parking spaces. These may not be on the same premises.
RESTAURANT
This is not necessarily recommended, although particularly good hotel restaurants are also listed in the restaurant section.
TERRACE
The hotel has a terrace, interior courtyard or garden, and meals may be served outdoors.

	NUMBER OF ROOMS	FACITIES FOR CHILDREN	PRIVATE PARKING	RESTAURANT	TERRACE
MOËLAN-SUR-MER: *Le Manoir de Kertalg* €€€ Route de Riec-sur-Belon, 29350. [(02) 98 39 77 77. FAX (02) 98 39 72 07. @ kertalg@free.fr This old ivy-covered manor house stands in extensive woodland. The converted outbuildings contain spacious, well-decorated rooms. TV 🛏 ♨ ✍ ● *15 Nov–Easter.*	9	●	▦		▦
MORGAT: *Grand Hôtel de la Mer* €€ 17 Rue d'Ys, 29160. [(02) 98 27 02 09. FAX (02) 98 27 02 39. The décor of this grand 1920s hotel is quite basic but the rooms have a view either of the Baie de Douarnenez or of the wooded park. TV 🛏 ♨ ↥ ♿ 🔥 ✍ ● *Nov–late Mar; restaurant: Mon–Tue.*	78	●	▦	●	▦
PLONÉOUR-LANVERN: *Le Manoir de Kerhuel* €€ Route de Quimper, 29720. [(02) 98 82 60 57. FAX (02) 98 82 61 79. @ manoir-kerhuel@wanadoo.fr A 10-minute drive from Quimper, this 15th-century manor house, set in 6 ha (15 acres) of parkland, is an ideal base from which to explore southern Finistère. TV 🛏 ♨ ≈ 🍴 ♿ ✍ ● *early Jan–late Mar; mid-Nov–mid-Dec.*	26	●	▦	●	▦
PLONEVEZ-PORZAY: *Le Manoir de Moëllien* €€€ 29550. [(02) 98 92 50 12. FAX (02) 98 92 56 54. @ moellien@aol.com About 3 km (2 miles) from the beaches of Douarnenez and the medieval town of Locronan, this granite manor house has a timeless atmosphere. Some rooms have been made in the converted outbuildings. TV 🛏 ♨ ♿ 🔥 ✍ ● *mid-Nov–late Mar.*	18	●	▦	●	▦
PONT-AVEN: *Roz-Aven* €€ 11 Quai Théodore-Botrel, 29930. [(02) 98 06 13 06. FAX (02) 98 06 03 89. @ roz-aven@wanadoo.fr In the harbour, on the edge of the Aven river, this hotel is a 16th-century thatched house with a modern extension. TV ♨ ♿ ✍ ● *Nov–late Feb.*	24	●	▦		▦
PONT-L'ABBÉ: *Hôtel de Bretagne* €€ 24 Place République, 29120. [(02) 98 87 17 22. FAX (02) 98 95 61 25. A family hotel in the centre of Pont-l'Abbé with pleasant, plainly furnished rooms. The largest are at the front of the building. TV 🛏 ✍ ● *mid-Jan–early Feb.*	18	●		●	▦
QUIMPER: *La Mascotte* €€ 6 Rue Th.-Le-Hars, 29000. [(02) 98 53 37 37. FAX (02) 98 90 31 51. @ mascotte-quimper@hotel-sophiebra.com A modern, functional hotel with a central location. The rooms are small, with basic décor. Buffet breakfast. TV 24 ↥ ♿ 🔥 ✍	63	●		●	
QUIMPER : *Le Dupleix* €€€ 34 Boulevard Dupleix, 29000. [(02) 98 90 53 35. FAX (02) 98 52 05 31. @ hotel-dupleix@wanadoo.fr A centrally located hotel with a view of the Odet river and the cathedral towers. The rooms are large and quiet. TV 🛏 24 ↥ ♿ 🔥 ✍	29		▦		▦
TREGUNC: *Les Grands Roches* €€€ Northeast of Tregunc, 29910. [(02) 98 97 62 97. FAX (02) 98 50 29 19. The hotel consists of a group of converted farm buildings set in 8 ha (20 acres) of parkland with dolmens and menhirs. The rooms are furnished in a country style. TV ≈ 🍴 ✍ ● *early Nov–late Mar.*	21	●	▦	●	▦

MORBIHAN

	NUMBER OF ROOMS	FACITIES FOR CHILDREN	PRIVATE PARKING	RESTAURANT	TERRACE
AURAY: *Hôtel Le Branhoc* € 5 Route du Bono, 56400. [(02) 97 56 41 55. FAX (02) 97 56 41 35. @ le.branhoc@wanadoo.fr A basic hotel with newly renovated rooms, almost all of which look onto surrounding parkland. TV 🛏 ♿ 🔥 ✍ ● *mid-Dec–mid-Jan.*	35	●	▦		▦

BELLE-ÎLE-EN-MER: *Hôtel Vauban* €€ 16
1 Rue des Remparts, Le Palais, 56360. ((02) 97 31 45 42. FAX (02) 97 31 42 82.
W www.hotelvauban.com
A small hotel overlooking the town from its location above the ramparts.
Commanding a panoramic view of the harbour and the bay, it is five minutes'
walk from the beach. TV ⬛ ❄ ⬛ ⬛ ⬤ *mid-Nov–early Feb.*

BILLIERS: *Domaine de Rochevilaine* €€€€€ 38
On Pointe de Pen-Lan-Sud, 56190. ((02) 97 41 61 61. FAX (02) 97 41 44 85.
@ rochevilaine@chateauxhotels.com
A hotel complex consisting of converted buildings on the estate and
including a balneotherapy (water treatment) centre. The rooms have
sophisticated décor and the restaurant is renowned. TV ⬛ ❄ ⬛ ⬛ ⬛ ⬛ ⬛

CARNAC: *Hôtel Celtique* €€€ 56
17 Avenue Kermario/82 Avenue des Druides, 56340. ((02) 97 52 14 15.
FAX (02) 97 52 71 10. @ hotel.celtique.bw.carnac@wanadoo.fr
This hotel is 500 m (550 yds) from one of the most beautiful beaches
in the bay. The well-lit rooms look onto an extensive garden with ancient
pine trees. The open-air swimming pool is converted into a covered pool
during the winter. TV ⬛ 24 ❄ ⬛ ⬛ ⬛ ⬛ ⬛ ⬛

BONO (LE): *Le Manoir de Kerdréan* €€€ 69
Just outside Le Bono, 56400. ((02) 97 57 84 00. FAX (02) 97 57 83 00.
@ contact@abatial.com
Hidden away in an oasis of greenery and looking onto a golf course, this
hotel has an exceptionally good location. There are rooms in the main
house itself as well as in the newer annexe. The facilities include a tennis
court, swimming pool and billiard room. TV ⬛ 24 ❄ ⬛ ⬛ ⬛ ⬛ ⬛

GROIX (ÎLE DE): *Hôtel de la Marine* €€ 22
7 Rue du Général-de-Gaulle, 56590. ((02) 97 86 80 05. FAX (02) 97 86 56 37.
@ hotel-de-la-marine@wanadoo.fr
A fine old house very near the pier. The welcome is friendly and the
rooms clean and pleasant. Simple, tasty dishes are served in a rustic
dining room. ⬛ ❄ ⬛ ⬛
⬤ *restaurant: Oct–Mar & Sun eve & Mon (outside school holidays).*

HENNEBONT: *Château de Locguénolé* ✤ €€€€ 22
On the road to Port-Louis, 1 km (0.5 mile) south of Hennebont, 56700.
((02) 97 76 76 76. FAX (02) 97 76 82 35.
A chateau and manor house in 120 ha (300 acres) of parkland lining a wide
coastal inlet. Antique furniture, woodcarvings and tapestries create an
authentic décor. TV ⬛ ❄ ⬛ ⬛ ⬛ ⬛ ⬤ *Jan–last week in Feb.*

HOUAT (ÎLE DE): *L'Ezenn Bar-Hôtel* €€ 6
On the road leading to Plage de Treac'h-Er-Goured, 56170.
((02) 97 30 69 73. @ ezenn@free.fr
Clean, comfortable, well-furnished rooms in a hotel that gives good value
for money. Four of the rooms have a sea view and look onto the hotel's small
garden. Canoes can be hired in summer. ⬛ ❄ ⬛ ⬛

LORIENT: *Hôtel Victor-Hugo* € 30
36 Rue Lazare-Carnot, 56100. ((02) 97 21 16 24. FAX (02) 97 84 95 13.
@ hotel-victorhugo.lorient@wanadoo.fr
The hotel is located in the new town, next to the embarkation point
for boats to the Île de Groix marina. The rooms are clean and comfortable
and the welcome friendly. TV ⬛ ⬛

MOINES (ÎLE AUX): *Le San Francisco* €€€ 8
Le Port, 56780. ((02) 97 26 31 52. FAX (02) 97 26 35 59. @ le-san-francisco@worldline.fr
This building, which belongs to Franciscan sisters, was modernized and
converted in 2001, and some rooms are in the attic. Breakfast is served
in the former chapel. TV ⬛ ❄ ⬛ ⬛ ⬤ *Nov–Easter.*

PÉNESTIN: *Hôtel Loscolo* €€€ 15
Southwest of Pointe de Loscolo, 56760. ((02) 99 90 31 90. FAX (02) 99 90 32 14.
This appealing establishment near La Roche-Bernard has rooms with
a sea view. TV ⬛ 24 ❄ ⬛ ⬛ ⬤ *Nov–late Apr.*

PONTIVY: *Hôtel de l'Europe* € 20
12 Rue François-Mitterrand, 56300. ((02) 97 25 11 14. FAX (02) 97 25 48 04.
Located in the centre of the town, this stately 19th-century house has
pleasant, well-kept rooms. TV ⬛ ❄ ⬛ ⬛ ⬛ ⬛

For key to symbols, see back flap

	Price categories for a double room per night with bath or shower, including breakfast and VAT. € under 25 euros €€ 25 to 45 euros €€€ 45 to 65 euros €€€€ 65 to 80 euros €€€€€ over 80 euros	**FACILITIES FOR CHILDREN** Such facilities include cradles, cots and a baby-sitting service. Some hotels provide high chairs and offer children's menus. **PRIVATE PARKING** The hotel has its own car park or parking spaces. These may not be on the same premises. **RESTAURANT** This is not necessarily recommended, although particularly good hotel restaurants are also listed in the restaurant section. **TERRACE** The hotel has a terrace, interior courtyard or garden, and meals may be served outdoors.	NUMBER OF ROOMS	FACILITIES FOR CHILDREN	PRIVATE PARKING	RESTAURANT	TERRACE

PORT-CROUESTY: *Le Crouesty*   €€
Rue du Crouesty, 56640 Arzon. (02) 97 53 87 91. FAX (02) 97 53 66 76.
A quiet, modern hotel built in traditional Breton style and located opposite the harbour. The rooms are functional but attractively decorated.
TV ⬛ ⬛ ⬛ ● *mid-Nov–first week in Feb.*

| 26 | ● | | | ■ |

PORT-NAVALO: *Hôtel Glann Ar Mor*   €
27 Rue des Fontaines, 56640. (02) 97 53 88 30. @ glannarmor@aol.com
Located near Port-Navalo's roadstead, this is a small, friendly establishment with just eight rooms. The restaurant serves basic fish and seafood dishes.
⬛ ⬛ ● *two weeks in winter.*

| 8 | | ■ | ● | ■ |

QUESTEMBERT: *La Bretagne et sa Résidence* ❖   €€€€
13 Rue St-Michel, 56230. (02) 97 26 11 12. FAX (02) 97 26 12 37.
@ bretagne@relaischateaux.com
The rooms in this beautiful country house have sophisticated décor. Delicious breakfasts and excellent cuisine. TV ⬛ ⬛ ⬛ ● *three weeks in Jan.*

| 9 | ● | ■ | ● | ■ |

QUIBERON (PRESQU'ÎLE DE): *Roch Priol*   €
5 Rue Sirènes, 56170. (02) 97 50 04 86. FAX (02) 97 30 50 09.
@ info@hotelrochpriol.com
Located 500 m (550 yds) from the sea in a residential quarter of Quiberon, this is a welcoming hotel with a family atmosphere. It is built in Breton style, and the rooms are basic but clean. TV 24 ⬛ ⬛ ⬛ ⬛ ● *15 Nov–15 Feb.*

| 45 | ● | ■ | ● | |

ROCHE-BERNARD (LA): *L'Auberge Bretonne* ❖   €€€€
2 Place Du Guesclin, 56130. (02) 99 90 60 28. FAX (02) 99 90 85 00.
@ aubbretonne@relaischateaux.fr
This small *auberge* in the centre of the village has been converted into a luxury hotel complex. The rooms are light and airy. Excellent restaurant.
TV ⬛ ⬛ ⬛ ⬛ ● *three weeks in Jan; mid-Nov–mid-Dec.*

| 8 | ● | ■ | ● | ■ |

ROCHEFORT-EN-TERRE: *Château de Talhouët*   €€€€
56220. (02) 97 43 34 72. FAX (02) 97 43 35 04.
The rooms in this imposing 16th-century chateau are unusually large and very tastefully decorated. The peace of the location is enhanced by the surroundings, a 20-ha (50-acre) park. TV ⬛ ⬛ ⬛ ● *restaurant, winter.*

| 8 | ● | ■ | ● | ■ |

SARZEA: *Le Mur du Roy*   €€
Penvins, 56370. (02) 97 67 34 08. FAX (02) 97 67 36 23.
This hotel has direct access to the beach. The rooms, some with sea view, are very clean. The restaurant offers excellent value for money. TV ⬛ ⬛ ⬛ ⬛

| 10 | | ■ | ● | ■ |

TRINITÉ-SUR-MER (LA): *Petit Hôtel des Hortensias*   €€€
Place de la Mairie, 56470. (02) 97 30 10 30. FAX (02) 97 30 14 54.
@ leshortensias@aol.com
A hotel 50 m (50 yds) from the beach and looking onto the harbour, but also within easy reach of the town centre. The tastefully furnished rooms are named after Breton islands. TV ⬛ ⬛ ⬛ ⬛ ● *Dec–Jan.*

| 5 | | | ● | ■ |

VANNES: *Le Roof Hôtel-Restaurant*   €€€
At the end of the Presqu'île de Conleau, 56000. (02) 97 63 47 47.
FAX (02) 97 63 48 10.
This hotel is located virtually on the water's edge. Some of the rooms have a superb view of the Golfe du Morbihan. TV ⬛ ⬛ ⬛ ⬛ ⬛ ⬛

| 40 | ● | ■ | ● | ■ |

LOIRE-ATLANTIQUE

BAULE (LA): *Saint-Christophe*   €€€
Place Notre-Dame, 44500. (02) 40 60 35 35. FAX (02) 40 60 11 74.
@ deck@saintchristophe.com
The rooms here are arranged in three early 20th-century villas. The atmosphere is more like that of a family house than a hotel. Half-board available in July and August. TV ⬛ ⬛ ⬛ ⬛

| 32 | ● | ■ | ● | ■ |

BAULE (LA): *Castel Marie-Louise* ✤ €€€€ | 31
1 Avenue Andrieu, 44500. 【 *(02) 40 11 48 38.* FAX *(02) 40 11 48 35.*
@ marielouise@relaischateaux.com
This superb 1910s manor house, in a quiet location a stone's throw
from the casino, overlooks the bay. The rooms are furnished with antiques.
TV ≈ ♦ 🅱 🖉 ● *early Jan–mid-Feb.*

BERNERIE-EN-RETZ: *Château de la Gressière* €€€ | 15
Rue Noue-Fleurie, 44500. 【 *(02) 51 74 60 06.* FAX *(02) 51 74 60 02.*
@ legressiere@wanadoo.fr
A small 19th-century manor house. The luxuriously appointed rooms
have a view of the beach and the sea. TV 🛏 ≈ 🅱 🖉

CROISIC (LE): *Fort de l'Océan* €€€€ | 9
Pointe du Croisic, 44490. 【 *(02) 40 15 77 77.* FAX *(02) 40 15 77 80.*
@ contact@fort-océan.com
This 17th-century fortified residence overlooks the sea, offering
an exceptionally fine view of the Côte Sauvage.
TV 🛏 ≈ 🍴 ♦ 🅱 🖉 ● *restaurant: mid-Nov–mid-Dec & Jan.*

MISSILLAC: *La Bretesche* ✤ €€€€ | 32
Domaine de La Bretesche, 44780. 【 *(02) 51 76 86 96.* FAX *(02) 40 66 99 47.*
@ hotel@bretesche.com
Some unusually attractive rooms have been created in the converted
outbuildings opposite the majestic crenellated castle, which stands near
a lake. There is an 18-hole golf course on the estate.
TV 🛏 24 ≈ ♦ 🅱 🖉 ● *late Jan–early Mar.*

NANTES: *Hôtel Duchesse Anne* €€ | 69
3–4 Place de la Duchesse-Anne, 44000. 【 *(02) 51 86 78 78.* FAX *(02) 40 74 60 20.*
@ contact@hotel-duchesse-Anne.com
Located behind the Château des Ducs de Bretagne, this characterful old
building has rooms to suit all budgets. Most of the rooms have a view of
the castle. The hotel is also near the cathedral and Musée des Beaux-Arts, and
300 m (330 yds) from the railway station. TV 🛏 24 ≈ ♦ 🅱 🖉

NANTES: *L'Hôtel* €€ | 31
6 Rue Henri-IV, 44000. 【 *(02) 40 29 30 31.* FAX *(02) 40 29 00 95.*
@ hotel@mageos.com
This hotel, opposite the Château des Ducs de Bretagne, has soundproofed
rooms, providing welcome relief from the city bustle. Breakfast is generous
and the establishment offers excellent value for money. TV 🛏 24 ≈ ♦ 🅱 🖉

NANTES: *La Pérouse* €€€ | 47
3 Allée Duquesne, 44000. 【 *(02) 40 89 75 00.* FAX *(02) 40 89 76 00.*
W www.hotel-la-perouse.fr
A plain white granite building, this newly built hotel is a striking
example of modern architecture. The rooms contain designer furniture.
TV 🛏 24 🍴 ♦ 🖉

PORNIC: *Hôtel Beau Soleil* €€ | 18
70 Quai Leray, 44210. 【 *(02) 40 82 34 58.* FAX *(02) 40 82 43 00.*
Located in the harbour, this hotel has small but well-kept rooms,
most of them with a sea view. TV 🛏 ≈ 🖉

PORNICHET: *Le Régent* €€€ | 15
150 Boulevard des Océanides, 44210. 【 *(02) 40 61 05 68.* FAX *(02) 40 61 25 53.*
W www.le-regent.fr
The rooms in this early 20th-century house are decorated with a marine
theme and have sea views. The restaurant offers tasty fish dishes.
🛏 ≈ 🍴 🖉 ● *mid-Nov–early Feb.*

PORNICHET: *Villa Flornoy* €€€ | 21
7 Avenue Flornoy, 44210. 【 *(02) 40 11 60 00.* FAX *(02) 40 61 86 47.*
@ hot-flornoy@aol.com
Set in a well-kept garden, this large period house has been converted
into a hotel with clean, attractive rooms. It is 500 m (550 yds) from the
beach. TV 🛏 🅱 🖉 ● *Nov–late Jan.*

ST-MARC-SUR-MER: *Hôtel de la Plage* €€ | 33
97 Rue du Commandant-Charcot, 44600. 【 *(02) 40 91 99 01.*
FAX *(02) 40 91 92 00.* W www.hotel-de-la-plage-44.com
Located on the beach near La Baule, this quiet, comfortable hotel
commands some stunning views. TV 🛏 ♦ 🖉

WHERE TO EAT

Logo of Coreff beer, brewed in Morlaix

THE FOREMOST agricultural region of France, Brittany abounds in produce that is the basis of the region's cuisine. Brittany is best known for its fish and shellfish, but locally produced cooked meats and free-range poultry are also on the menu. Excellent fruit and vegetables, including strawberries and artichokes, are grown in Brittany. Breton cider and prized Muscadet from the vineyards around Nantes are other specialities. From the finest meals served in some of the most highly reputed establishments in France to a plate of pancakes enjoyed in a simple *crêperie*, Brittany's restaurants cater for all tastes and all pockets.

The Auberge Bretonne in La Roche-Bernard *(see p240)*

TYPES OF RESTAURANTS

BRETONS ARE fond of good food, and locally grown produce provides plenty of opportunity for creating excellent dishes. Away from the coasts, especially, there are restaurants that offer genuine Breton cuisine at reasonable prices. Some hotels, particularly those affiliated to **Logis de France** *(see p215)*, serve high-quality regional food. The *fermes-*

Art Nouveau interior of La Cigale in Nantes *(see p241)*

auberges (farmhouse inns) and *tables d'hôtes* offer the opportunity of enjoying simple, inexpensive dishes made with local produce.

On the coasts, the choice is wider but the quality may not be the highest. There are fast-food outlets, pizzerias, snack bars and *crêperies* (pancake houses) as well as upmarket restaurants.

Balades Gourmandes is an association of 22 restaurants in Ille-et-Vilaine that offer original cuisine based on local produce. Information is available from the **Comité Départemental du Tourisme d'Ille-et-Vilaine**.

LOCAL PRODUCE

SUCH IS THE abundance and variety of Brittany's fish and seafood and of locally grown fruit and vegetables that it is impossible to mention any more than the most popular.

Breton cuisine is renowned chiefly for its fish dishes. Because of the freshness of local catches, the grilled mackerel and sardines served in Brittany are particularly delicious. Monkfish, sea bass, yellow pollack, turbot, red mullet, sole or sea bream, gently baked or served with *beurre blanc* (a butter, vinegar and shallot sauce), are succulent dishes. In the Loire-Atlantique, shad, elvers and lamprey also appear on the menu. Seafood, such as oysters from Cancale, Paimpol, Aven-Belon, Quiberon and Croisic, and mussels from Vivier and Pénestin, as well as whelks, winkles, shrimps, spider crabs and lobsters, are piled high in almost every market near the coast. Lovers of seafood never tire of scallops, that highly prized delicacy, while top chefs are beginning to use edible seaweed and samphire in their dishes.

According to the season, Brittany's inland areas also offer a range of culinary

DIRECTORY

FERMES-AUBERGES

Chambre d'Agriculture de Bretagne
111 Boulevard Mal-de-Lattre-de-Tassigny, 35042 Rennes Cedex.
(*(02) 99 59 43 33.*

Comité Régional du Tourisme
Information on
Tables et Saveurs de Bretagne
(*(02) 99 28 44 30.*

Comité Départemental du Tourisme d'Ille-et-Vilaine
Information on Balades Gourmandes
(*(02) 99 78 47 47.*

Les Forges, a restaurant near the Forêt de Brocéliande *(see p232)*

delights. Potatoes, a basic ingredient in all Breton cuisine, artichokes, cauliflowers, beans (such as those known as *coco de Paimpol*), lamb's lettuce from the Nantes area, asparagus, onions from Roscoff, turnips and leeks are all popular ingredients. Locally grown fruit includes apples, pears and kiwi fruit, and succulent melons from the Rennes area.

BRETON SPECIALITIES

BRITTANY IS famous for its traditionally made butter biscuits and delicious pancakes *(see pp230–31)*, as well as for the tempting *plateau de mer* (seafood platter) and *homard à l'armoricaine* (lobster served in a hot garlic and tomato sauce). Another great classic, albeit in a different league, is a dish of mussels, such as *moules marinière* (mussels cooked in wine).

Because it is a prime producer of pork, Brittany also offers a range of products made from pig meat. Two of the most prominent are *andouilles* (chitterling sausages made with lard) from Guéméné-sur-Scorff, and, from Baye, sausages and pâté (including the famous Hénaff brand).

As for meat dishes, there is the succulent *agneau de pré-salé* (salt-pasture lamb) from

Mont-St-Michel, roast duckling and cold duck galantine.

Breton salted butter (French butter is otherwise unsalted) is also highly prized. In the days before refrigerators existed, salt was added to butter as a preservative, and to this day salted butter is an essential ingredient in Breton cuisine. Salt from Guérande, meanwhile, is recognized as the best in the region.

Breton cakes include *kouign amann*, a delicious cake made with wheat flour, butter and sugar, which is eaten warm. *Far*, Breton prune flan, and *quatre-quarts*, a rich fruit cake, are other deservedly famous specialities, along with Traou-Mad de Pontaven (cookies), Pleyben or St-Michel *galettes* (butter biscuits) and the wafer-thin *crêpes-dentelles* from Quimper.

As for liquid refreshment, cider is the most popular drink in Brittany. Although many people like sweet cider *(cidre doux)*, connoisseurs prefer dry *(cidre brut)*. The best cider-producing regions of Brittany are the areas around Dol-de-Bretagne and the Arguenon, Rance, Messac, Fouesnant and Domagné valleys. *Chouchen*, a kind of mead (or hydromel) is also worth sampling, as is the locally brewed beer. Among the best brands are Coreff, of Morlaix, and Telenn Du, a wheat beer. Muscadet from the Loire-Atlantique is a delicate, crisp, dry wine.

Sign outside the Auberge Bretonne in La Roche-Bernard

PRACTICALITIES

IN THE HIGH SEASON, it is always advisable to book a restaurant table in advance. While informal dress is perfectly acceptable in most restaurants, such casual wear as shorts is likely to attract disapproval in higher-class establishments. Swimming costumes are definitely unacceptable, except in beach-side restaurants.

Most restaurants offer children's menus, and almost all accept the main bankers' cards. However, in country areas, a wise precaution is to bring cash should any other form of payment not be accepted.

WHEELCHAIR ACCESS

UNFORTUNATELY, few restaurants have proper wheelchair access. When booking, inform the restaurant staff that extra space for a wheelchair will be needed. Organizations providing information for disabled travellers are listed on page 217.

CHILDREN

CHILDREN ARE welcomed in Brittany, and many restaurants, such as creperies, are suitable for families. Most establishments offer special menus for children, and some provide highchairs for toddlers.

USING THE LISTINGS

Key to the symbols in the restaurant listings on pages 232–41:

C telephone number
FAX fax number
Q excellent wine list
● closed

Price categories for a three-course meal with half a bottle of house wine, including service and VAT.
€ under 25 euros
€€ 25 to 45 euros
€€€ 45 to 65 euros
€€€€ 65 to 80 euros
€€€€€ over 80 euros

What to Eat in Brittany

**Connétable
sardines**

ISCERNING GOURMETS once despised Breton cuisine. For them, such filling dishes as boiled meat with cabbage lacked refinement, and they were dismissive of the humble pancakes that, together with fat bacon, oatmeal gruel and buckwheat, once constituted the staple diet of Bretons. Times have changed. By using fresh produce – free-range poultry and freshly picked vegetables, excellent seafood and locally caught fish – in simple but flavoursome dishes, this fertile and abundant region has risen to the highest ranks of culinary excellence.

***Buckwheat pancakes**,
served with a cheese, ham,
salmon or other filling.*

SEAFOOD

Fish, shellfish and crustaceans have pride of place on restaurant tables all along the coasts of Brittany. They are invariably of the highest quality and can be served in different ways, from the simplest to the most refined – in *beurre blanc* (a butter, vinegar and shallot sauce), steamed in seaweed, or *à l'armoricaine* (in a garlic and tomato sauce).

**Shallot
vinegar**

**Buttered
bread**

***Stuffed clams**, served
hot with a knob of slightly
salted butter.*

***Scallops**, served in their shells
with a salad of samphire and a
dash of cider brandy.*

***Cancale oysters**, served
raw, with shallot vinegar
and rye bread.*

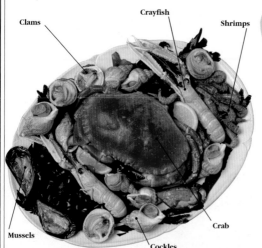

Crayfish

Clams

Shrimps

Mussels

Cockles

Crab

***Pike with
beurre blanc**,
sprinkled with
parsley, a
speciality of Nantes*

SEAFOOD PLATTER

The ingredients of a seafood platter (*plateau de mer*) vary with the season, the daily catch and the coastal location. In good restaurants, the shellfish and crustaceans are served on a bed of seaweed, with bread, homemade mayonnaise, shallot vinegar, wedges of lemon and salted butter.

SPECIALITIES

Pancakes and butter biscuits are perhaps the best-known Breton specialities. But there are others: local cooked meats such as chargrilled streaky bacon, home-cooked tripe, chitterling sausage, chicken in Fouesnant cider, oat-meal soup, and most especially *kig ha fars*, a stew prepared by traditional methods.

Carrots / Cabbage / Buckwheat cakes cooked in muslin / Streaky bacon / Beef / Knuckle of pork / Cooked sausages / Stock

KIG HA FARS

This is a stew served with white or black *far*, buckwheat cakes cooked in muslin parcels that are plunged into the hot stew.

Andouillette de Géméné, handmade, oak-smoked chitterling sausage, can be served hot or cold.

Monkfish à l'Armoricaine, served in a tomato sauce and flambéed, is a speciality of the Bigouden region.

Agneau de pré-salé (salt-pasture lamb), shown here with beans and artichoke hearts, is roasted in a hot oven.

DESSERTS

It is the local salted butter that gives Brittany's nourishing and flavoursome desserts their unique flavour. It is used in rich fruit cakes, flans *(fars)*, pancakes *(krampouez)* and the famous *kouign amann*, a cake that originated in Douarnenez.

Far aux pruneaux, a prune flan baked in an earthenware dish, is a speciality of Lower Brittany.

Sweet pancakes, made with wheat, are best enjoyed with a glass of chilled cider or buttermilk.

VEGETABLES

Grown in greenhouses or in open fields, Brittany's spring vetegables can be served in various ways. They are delicious *au gratin* or in a chive sauce.

Breton cauliflower / Artichoke, the pride of Brittany

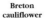

Kouign amann is a light cake painted with egg and sprinkled with sugar before it is baked in the oven.

Choosing a Restaurant

THE RESTAURANTS, cafés and bars in this guide
have been selected for their good value,
interesting location or exceptional food. They are
listed by region, the coloured thumb tabs
corresponding to those by which the regions of
Brittany are identified throughout this guide.

	CREDIT CARDS ACCEPTED	FIXED-PRICE MENU	OPEN LUNCHTIME	OPEN LATE	OUTSIDE TABLES

ILLE-ET-VILAINE

CANCALE: *Le Saint-Cast* €€	MC V	●	■		■
Route de la Corniche, 35260. **(** (02) 99 89 66 08. **FAX** (02) 99 89 89 20. This excellent fish and seafood restaurant is located above the coast road that runs around the bay. The dishes served here reflect the chef's travels abroad; one speciality is a lobster *tajine* with pasta, inspired by Moroccan cuisine. ● *Tue, Wed (out of season); mid-Nov–mid-Dec; Feb school holidays.*					
CANCALE: *Maison de Bricourt* €€€€€	AE DC V	●	■		
1 Rue du Guesclin, 35260. **(** (02) 99 89 64 76. **FAX** (02) 99 89 88 47. This converted *malouinière (see p84)* serves imaginative dishes with an international flavour. The sea bass in flavoured oil and spider crab with wild sorrel are especially recommended. The establishment's own oyster beds are open to visitors from September to April. ● *Tue, Wed (except eves in Jul–Aug); mid-Dec–mid-Mar.*					
COMBOURG: *L'Écrivain* €	MC V	●	■		■
Place St-Gilduin, 35270. **(** (02) 99 73 01 61. **FAX** (02) 99 73 01 61. Imaginative and flavoursome cuisine based on local produce. Specialities include fish smoked on the premises and *millefeuille de foie gras* with artichokes. Excellent value for money. ● *Sun eve (out of season); Wed eve–Thu; 1–15 Oct; Feb school holidays.*					
DINARD: *Le Prieuré* €	MC V	●	■		■
1 Place du Général-de-Gaulle, 35800. **(** (02) 99 46 13 74. **FAX** (02) 99 46 81 90. Delicious fish and seafood dishes are served in a dining room with a magnificent sea view. ● *Mon eve (Jul–Aug); Sun eve–Mon (out of season).*					
DINARD: *Didier Méril* €€	AE MC V	●	■	●	■
6 Rue Yves-Verney, 35800. **(** (02) 99 46 95 74. **FAX** (02) 99 16 07 75. This restaurant, formerly known as La Palmeraie, serves traditional cuisine, fish and seafood in pleasant surroundings. 🍴 ● *Wed (Oct–Mar); Dec, Jan.*					
FOUGÈRES: *Les Voyageurs* €€	AE V	●	■	●	
10 Place Gambetta, 35300. **(** (02) 99 99 14 17. **FAX** (02) 99 99 28 89. A gourmet restaurant offering exquisite and imaginative dishes, including pan-fried *escargot* profiteroles and grilled swordfish. Delectable desserts. ● *Sat lunchtime, Sunday eve.*					
FOUGÈRES: *Le Haute-Sève* €€€	V	●	■		
37 Boulevard Jean-Jaurès, 35300. **(** (02) 99 94 23 39. This excellent gourmet restaurant serves traditional cuisine based on local produce. Friendly welcome. Reservation is compulsory on weekdays, before 3pm. ● *Sun eve–Mon.*					
PAIMPONT: *Les Forges* €	DC MC V	●	■	●	■
Les Forges, 35380. **(** (02) 99 06 81 07. **FAX** (02) 99 06 92 15. In a magical location on the edge of the Forêt de Brocéliande, this restaurant serves traditional dishes perfected by the chef over three decades. The specialities are fish and game. ● *Mon eve; early Sep.*					
PAIMPONT (FORÊT DE): *L'Auberge du Presbytère* €€	V	●	■		
Preffendel, 35380. **(** (02) 99 61 00 76. **FAX** (02) 99 61 00 48. A relaxing establishment with a good reputation. It is housed in a former presbytery and, in fine weather, meals are served outdoors. ● *Sun eve, Mon.*					

		CREDIT CARDS ACCEPTED	FIXED-PRICE MENU	OPEN AT LUNCHTIME	OPEN LATE	OUTSIDE TABLES

Price categories are for a three-course meal for one without wine, including service and VAT. Meals are often cheaper at lunchtime than in the evenings.
€ under 25 euros
€€ 25–45 euros
€€€ 45–65 euros
€€€€ 65–80 euros
€€€€€ over 80 euros

CREDIT CARDS ACCEPTED
The following credit cards are accepted:
American Express (AE), Diners Club (DC),
Japan Credit Bureau (JCB), MasterCard (MC), Visa (V).

FIXED-PRICE MENU
Set meals, usually consisting of three courses, are served.

OPEN LATE
The establishment admits customers up to 10pm.

OUTSIDE TABLES
Meals can be served outdoors, in a courtyard or garden, from which there is often a fine view.

Restaurant	Price	Credit Cards	Fixed-Price Menu	Open at Lunchtime	Open Late	Outside Tables
RENNES: *L'Auberge Saint-Sauveur* 6 Rue du St-Sauveur, 35000. ((02) 99 79 32 56. FAX (02) 99 78 27 93. A restaurant in a converted 16th-century canons' residence. The grilled Breton lobster and duck foie gras are recommended. ● Sat lunchtime, Sun, Mon lunchtime.	€€	AE V	●	●		
RENNES: *L'Ouvrée* 18 Place des Lices, 35000. ((02) 99 30 16 38. FAX (02) 99 30 16 38. A restaurant with a splendid location on a square lined with timber-framed houses. A picturesque market takes place on the square. ● ● Sat lunchtime; Sun eve; first two weeks in Aug.	€€	AE V	●	●	●	
RENNES: *L'Escu de Runfao* 11 Rue du Chapitre, 35000. ((02) 99 79 13 10. FAX (02) 99 79 43 80. A gourmet fish restaurant in a 16th-century house. The dishes are prepared with scrupulously fresh ingredients. ● Sat lunchtime, Sun.	€€	AE V	●	●	●	●
ST-MALO: *Le Chalut* 8 Rue Corne-de-Cerf, 35400. ((02) 99 56 71 58. FAX (02) 99 56 71 58. A restaurant serving refined and inventive cuisine. Among the fish and seafood specialities, the braised John Dory with wild mushrooms is especially recommended. ● Tue lunchtime (Jul–Aug); Sun eve–Mon (Sep–Jun).	€€	AE V	●	●	●	
ST-MALO: *Le Chasse-Marée* 4 Rue du Grout-St-Georges, 35400. ((02) 99 40 85 10. FAX (02) 99 56 49 52. Sophisticated gourmet cuisine, based on fish and seafood. ● Sat lunchtime, Sun.	€€	AE DC V	●	●	●	
ST-MALO: *Delaunay* 6 Rue Ste-Barbe, 35400. ((02) 99 40 92 46. FAX (02) 99 56 88 91. Excellent regional specialities served in a light and airy dining room. ● Sun–Mon (Oct–Jun); mid-Nov–mid-Dec; mid-Jan–mid-Feb.	€€	V	●	●		●
ST-MALO: *À La Duchesse Anne* 5 Place Guy-la-Chambre, 35400. ((02) 99 40 85 33. FAX (02) 99 40 00 28. Such dishes as grilled lobster Duchesse Anne and succulent foie gras are served in the appealingly nostalgic setting of this long-established restaurant. ● Mon lunchtime (Jul–Aug); Sun eve, Wed (Sep–Jun); Dec, Jan.	€€€	DC MC V		●		●
ST-MÉLOIR-DES-ONDES: *Tirel Guérin* 35350. ((02) 99 89 10 46. FAX (02) 99 89 12 62. A restaurant in the countryside 10 km (6 miles) from St-Malo and Cancale. It is renowned for its light classic dishes. ● Sun eve (early Oct–early Apr).	€€€	AE DC JCB MC V	●	●		
MONT-ST-MICHEL: *Hôtel-Restaurant de la Mère Poulard* 50116. ((02) 33 60 14 01. FAX (02) 99 89 88. The *Omelette de la Mère Poulard* served here is something of an institution, but the restaurant makes a little too much of this reputation. The welcome is lukewarm and the prices prohibitive.	€€€	AE DC JCB MC V	●	●	●	
MONT-ST-MICHEL: *L'Escale* About 2 km (1 mile) from the mount, on the causeway, 35260. ((02) 33 89 32 00. FAX 02 33 89 32 01. This restaurant, in the same chain as the Hôtel-Restaurant de la Mère Poulard *(see above)*, is the only one with a superb view of Mont-St-Michel. Traditional and regional cuisine, simple and tasty, at reasonable prices. Specialities include seafood and lamb dishes.	€€	AE DC MC V	●	●	●	●

Price categories are for a three-course meal for one without wine, including service and VAT. Meals are often cheaper at lunchtime than in the evenings.
€ under 25 euros
€€ 25–45 euros
€€€ 45–65 euros
€€€€ 65–80 euros
€€€€€ over 80 euros

CREDIT CARDS ACCEPTED
The following credit cards are accepted: American Express (AE), Diners Club (DC), Japan Credit Bureau (JCB), MasterCard (MC), Visa (V).

FIXED-PRICE MENU
Set meals, usually consisting of three courses, are served.

OPEN LATE
The establishment admits customers up to 10pm.

OUTSIDE TABLES
Meals can be served outdoors, in a courtyard or garden, from which there is often a fine view.

	CREDIT CARDS ACCEPTED	FIXED-PRICE MENU	OPEN LUNCHTIME	OPEN LATE	OUTSIDE TABLES

CÔTES D'ARMOR

BELLE-ÎLE-EN-TERRE: *Le Relais de l'Argoat* €€ 9 Rue de Guic, 22810. **(** (02) 96 43 00 34. **FAX** (02) 96 43 00 76. This former post house has two welcoming dining rooms. It offers flavoursome dishes and an excellent choice of cheeses. ● *Sun eve, Mon.*	MC V	●	■		
DINAN: *Le Bistrot du Viaduc* €€ 22 Rue du Lion-d'Or, 22100 Lanvallay. **(** (02) 96 85 95 00. **FAX** (02) 96 85 95 01. Local dishes served in a pleasant setting, with a splendid view of the Rance valley. The specialities here are crispy pig's trotter and cod *à la bretonne.* ● *One week in late Dec & two weeks in Jun.*	V	●	■		■
DINAN: *Chez la Mère Pourcel* €€ 3 Place des Merciers, 22100. **(** (02) 96 39 03 80. **FAX** (02) 96 39 49 91. A restaurant in a former merchant's house on the finest square in Dinan. High-quality fish and seafood dishes are served and the wine list includes excellent Loire wines. 🍴 ● *Sun eve–Tue (Oct–Mar); Sun eve–Mon (Apr–Jun).*	AE DC MC V	●	■		■
DINAN: *Les Grands Fossés* € 2 Place du Général-Leclerc, 22100. **(** (02) 96 39 21 50. **FAX** (02) 96 39 42 60. A fish and seafood restaurant in a 19th-century town house 300 m (330 yds) from the town hall. The atmosphere is friendly and convivial, and the menu varies according to the season and to daily fish catches.	MC V	●	■		
ERQUY: *L'Escurial* €€ Boulevard de la Mer, 22430. **(** (02) 96 72 31 56. **FAX** (02) 96 63 57 92. This restaurant, with a dining room offering a splendid view of the sea, is renowned for its scallops and pan-fried John Dory with foie gras. Only local produce is used. ● *Sun eve–Mon; Mon (Jul–Aug); mid-Nov–mid-Jan.*	DC MC V	●	■		
GUINGAMP: *Le Relais du Roy* €€ 42 Place du Centre, 22000. **(** (02) 96 43 76 62. **FAX** (02) 96 44 08 01. High-quality traditional cuisine served in a sophisticated dining room. ● *Sun; first two weeks in Jan.*	AE V	●	■		
LAMBALLE: *Le Connétable* € 9 Rue Paul-Langevin, 22400. **(** (02) 96 31 03 50. Gourmet cuisine served in a smart town house. Specialities are ostrich in a mushroom *jus* and salmon smoked on the premises. ● *Sun eve–Mon.*	MC V	●	■	●	
LANNION: *La Ville Blanche* €€€ 3 km (2 miles) from Lannion, on the road to Tréguier, 22300. **(** (02) 96 37 04 28. **FAX** (02) 96 46 57 82. A restaurant with an excellent and unusual menu devised by two brothers. The monkfish in cider served with fresh young vegetables and the caramelized apple *millefeuille* are recommended. Reservation essential. ● *Sun eve (except Jul–Aug); Mon & Wed eve (Jan–Feb); third week in Oct.*	AE DC V	●	■		
NOTRE-DAME-DU-GUILDO: *Le Gilles de Bretagne* € On the harbour, 22380. **(** (02) 96 41 07 08. A fish and seafood restaurant. Try the spectacular seafood platter for two, followed by grilled lobster, cheeses and dessert. Reservation advisable in summer. ● *Tue (except in summer); Jan–early Feb.*	MC V	●	■		
PAIMPOL: *Hôtel-Restaurant de la Marne* €€€ 30 Rue de la Marne, 22500. **(** (02) 96 20 82 16. **FAX** (02) 96 20 92 07. The many local specialities include roast monkfish tournedos with bacon, crayfish and foie gras. 🍴 ● *Sun eve–Mon (except Jul–Aug); public holidays; Feb school holidays.*	AE MC V	●	■		

PAIMPOL: *Le Repaire de Kerroc'h* €€ JCB MC V ● ■
29 Quai Morand, 22500. [(02) 96 20 50 13. FAX (02) 96 22 07 46.
The restaurant is located beside the marina. Divided into two parts –
one is a bistro and the other a high-class restaurant – it caters for all
tastes and budgets. ● Tue, Wed lunchtime.

PERROS-GUIREC: *Le Suroît* € V ● ■   ■
81 Rue Ernest-Renan, 22700. [(02) 96 23 23 83. FAX (02) 96 91 18 32.
Located on the harbour, opposite the fresh fish auction. Enjoyable
cuisine, focusing on fish and seafood, is served in a welcoming
dining room with a wood fire. ● Sun eve, Mon.

PLANCOËT: *Jean-Pierre Crouzil* €€€€ AE DC JCB MC V ● ■ ● ■
20 Les Quais, 22130. [(02) 96 84 10 24. FAX (02) 96 84 01 93.
High-quality, imaginative regional cuisine, including Breton lobster and
oysters in Vouvray zabaglione. ● Sun eve, Mon, Tue lunchtime (except Jul–Aug).

PLÉNEUF-VAL-ANDRÉ: *Au Biniou* € AE DC MC V ● ■ ●
121 Rue Clemenceau, 22370. [(02) 96 72 24 35. FAX (02) 96 63 03 23.
Near the beach at Val-André, this restaurant offers high-quality cuisine:
braised sea bass in fennel, braised calves' sweetbreads with apples and
mushrooms. ⛶ ● Tue eve (Feb); Wed lunchtime (Jul–Aug).

ST-BRIEUC: *Aux Pesked* €€€ AE DC MC V ● ■ ● ■
59 Rue du Légué, 22000. [(02) 96 33 34 65. FAX (02) 96 33 65 38.
This restaurant, the best in St-Brieuc, serves light, sophisticated
dishes in delightful surroundings. Fish specialities.
● Sat lunchtime, Sun eve, Mon; late Aug–mid-Sept; late Dec–mid-Jan.

ST-BRIEUC: *L'Amadeus* € MC V ● ■
22 Rue Gouët, 22000. [(02) 96 33 92 44. FAX (02) 96 61 42 05.
The dining room here has a fine ceiling with original beams. The fillet of
sole with duck-liver pâté is outstanding and the desserts are varied and
original. ● Sat lunchtime–Sun (Jul); mid-Feb–early Mar; Aug.

ST-BRIEUC: *La Croix Blanche* €€ MC V ● ■
61 Rue de Geneve, 22000.
This gourmet restaurant offers such unusual fish and seafood dishes as
crab lasagne with grapefruit, and John Dory with shrimps and grilled
streaky bacon. ● Sun eve. and Mon; first three weeks in Aug and Feb school hols.

ST-QUAY-PORTRIEUX: *Le Mouton Blanc* € V ● ■
52 Quai République, 22410. [(02) 96 70 58 44. FAX (02) 96 70 58 44.
Delicious seasonal specialities are served in a dining room on the first floor,
with a fine view of the harbour. ⛶ ● Wed eve, Thu eve (except during school holidays);
mid-Nov–first week in Dec; third week in Feb.

TRÉBEURDEN: *Ker An Nod* €€ AE V ● ■ ●
2 Rue de Porz-Termen, 22560. [(02) 96 23 50 21. FAX (02) 96 23 63 30.
The specialities here are fish and seafood. The warm oysters in
Muscadet butter and the Trégor chicken with crayfish are
recommended. ● early Jan–late Mar.

TRÉBEURDEN: *La Tourelle* € AE DC MC V ● ■ ●
Rue du Trouzoul. [(02) 96 23 62 73.
A good range of delicious fish and seafood dishes are served in this
restaurant, located opposite the harbour. ● Tue–Wed; Jan.

TRÉGASTEL: *Auberge de la Vieille Église* €€ MC V ● ■   ■
Place de l'Église, in the old town, 22730.
[(02) 96 23 88 31. FAX (02) 96 15 33 75.
A flower-covered Breton inn offering exceptionally good cuisine.
Specialities include scallop tagliatelle and fish *pot-au-feu*. ● Mon
(except Jul–Aug), Tue eve, Sun; March.

TRÉGUIER: *Les Trois Rivières* € AE V ● ■   ■
Restaurant of the Hôtel Aigue-Marine, beside the marina, 22220.
[(02) 96 92 97 00. FAX (02) 96 92 44 48.
The talented young chef here prepares dishes that are good value for
money. The striped mullet and the fish with cheese are recommended.
● Mon (out of season); Sat lunchtime, Sun eve; mid-Jan–mid-Feb.

For key to symbols, see back flap

	CREDIT CARDS ACCEPTED	FIXED-PRICE MENU	OPEN LUNCHTIME	OPEN LATE	OUTSIDE TABLES

Price categories are for a three-course meal for one without wine, including service and VAT. Meals are often cheaper at lunchtime than in the evenings.
€ under 25 euros
€€ 25–45 euros
€€€ 45–65 euros
€€€€ 65–80 euros
€€€€€ over 80 euros

CREDIT CARDS ACCEPTED
The following credit cards are accepted:
American Express (AE), Diners Club (DC),
Japan Credit Bureau (JCB), MasterCard (MC), Visa (V).

FIXED-PRICE MENU
Set meals, usually consisting of three courses, are served.

OPEN LATE
The establishment admits customers up to 10pm.

OUTSIDE TABLES
Meals can be served outdoors, in a courtyard or garden, from which there is often a fine view.

NORTHERN FINISTÈRE

		Credit Cards	Fixed-Price	Open Lunch	Open Late	Outside
Batz (Ile de): *Grand Hôtel Morvan* In the harbour, 29253. ((02) 98 61 78 06. FAX (02) 98 61 78 06. Tasty fish and seafood served in a dining room with 1950s décor. ● *Dec–mid-Feb.*	€	V	●	■		■
Brest: *Océania* 82 Rue Siam, 29200. ((02) 98 80 66 66. FAX (02) 98 80 65 50. This gourmet restaurant offers fish and seafood specialities. The chef usually devises a new menu every day, which varies according to fresh local produce. ● *Sat lunchtime–Mon lunchtime.*	€	AE MC V	●	■	●	
Brest: *Ma Petite Folie* Plage du Moulin, next to the marina, 29200. ((02) 98 42 44 42. FAX (02) 98 41 43 68. A restaurant on a ship serving some of the finest cuisine in Brest. Reservation essential at weekends and in high season. ● *last two weeks in Aug.*	€	DC MC V	●	■		
Brest: *La Fleur de Sel* 15 bis Rue de Lyon, 29200. ((02) 98 44 38 65. FAX (02) 98 43 38 53. Good traditional cuisine served in an Art Deco dining room. Exceptionally good wine list. ▼ ● *Sat lunchtime; late Jul–late Aug, first week in Jan.*	€	AE DC MC V	●	■		
Carantec: *Cabestan* 7 Rue du Port, 29660. ((02) 98 67 01 87. FAX (02) 98 67 90 49. A restaurant serving traditional cuisine, with a dining room and veranda that overlook the harbour. ● *mid-Nov–mid-Dec.*	€€	V	●	■		
Carantec: *Hôtel de Carantec* 29660. ((02) 98 67 00 47. FAX (02) 98 67 08 25. A large hotel *(see p222)* with a restaurant specializing in fish and seafood. ● *Sun eve–Mon (except public holidays); two weeks in Jan.*	€€	AE MC V	●	■	●	■
Landerneau: *Le Clos du Pont* Rue du Pontic, 29800. ((02) 98 21 50 91. FAX (02) 98 21 34 33. Cuisine with a touch of sophistication, such as brill with rhubarb and a red chilli and garlic mayonnaise, served in comfortable surroundings. Reservation compulsory. ● *Sat lunchtime, Sun eve–Mon lunchtime (winter).*	€	MC V	●	■		■
Lannilis: *Auberge des Abers* 5 Place Auditoire, 29870. ((02) 98 04 00 29. While lunch here takes place in a convivial dining room on the ground floor, dinner is served in more refined surroundings on the first floor. ● *Sun eve–Mon; first week in Mar; mid-Sep–early Oct.*	€€€	AE MC V	●			
Locquirec: *Le Grand Hôtel des Bains* 15 Rue de l'Église, 29241. ((02) 98 67 41 02. FAX (02) 98 67 44 60. This hotel restaurant offers sophisticated cuisine, including crab *millefeuille* and Breton lobster. ▼ ● *Mon–Sat lunchtimes (Sep–Jun); Jan.*	€€	AE DC MC V	●			
Morlaix: *L'Europe* Place Émile-Souvestres, 29600. ((02) 98 88 81 15. FAX (02) 98 88 81 15. The menu here features fish, seafood and other fine produce. The dining room has superb 18th-century woodcarvings. ● *Christmas & New Year.*	€	MC V	●			■
Morlaix: *Brocéliande* 5 Rue des Bouchers, 29600. ((02) 98 88 73 78. A restaurant with a friendly atmosphere and offering simple, tasty dishes such as filet mignon with rhubarb compote. ● *Tue lunchtime.*	€	MC	●		●	

MORLAIX: *La Marée Bleue* €€ MC V
3 Rampe Ste-Mélaine, 29600. ((02) 98 63 24 21.
In pleasant surroundings, this good fish restaurant offers dishes
prepared with fresh seasonal produce. ● *Sun eve–Mon; Sep–Mar.*

PLOUGASTEL-DAOULAS: *Le Chevalier de l'Auberlac'h* € AE DC MC V
5 Rue Mathurin-Thomas, 29470. ((02) 98 40 54 56. FAX (02) 98 40 65 16.
The best restaurant on the peninsula. Good traditional cuisine, such as
baked fish sauerkraut with duck foie gras. ● *Sun eve, Mon eve.*

PLOUDIER: *La Butte* €€ MC V
10 Rue de la Mer. ((02) 98 25 40 54. FAX (02) 98 25 44 17.
A restaurant with a stunning view of the Baie de Goulven. The menu
features such refined fish dishes as salmon in sorrel fondue, and meat
dishes such as young pigeon *pot-au-feu.* ● *Sun, Mon.*

ROSCOFF: *L'Écume des Jours* € MC V
Quai d'Auxerre, 29680. ((02) 98 61 22 83. FAX (02) 98 61 22 83.
Imaginative dishes, such as roasted scallops with magret of smoked
duck, are served in a comfortable and intimate setting.
🍷 ● *Tue–Wed (except July–Aug); Dec–Jan.*

ROSCOFF: *Le Temps de Vivre* €€€ V
Place de l'Église, 29680. ((02) 98 61 27 28. FAX (02) 98 61 19 46.
The imaginative menu includes cabbage stuffed with crab, and
turbot casserole. Elegant dining room with a sea view.
● *Mon–Tue lunchtime (Jul–Aug); Sun eve (Sep–Jun); Mar; three weeks in Oct.*

ST-POL-DE-LÉON: *La Pomme d'Api* €€ MC V
49 Rue Verdrel, 29250. ((02) 98 69 04 36.
Good traditional cuisine served in a fine mid-16th-century Breton house.
The menu includes roast lamb and seaweed-steamed sea bass.
● *Sun eve–Mon; Tue (out of season); last two weeks in Nov; Feb school holidays.*

ST-THÉGONNEC: *L'Auberge de Saint-Thégonnec* €€ AE MC V
6 Place de la Mairie, 29410. ((02) 98 79 61 18. FAX (02) 98 62 71 10.
An excellent restaurant with a menu based on fresh local produce.
Dishes include braised veal with mushrooms. 🍷 ● *Mon; Sat lunchtime
(out of season); Sun eve (mid-Sep–mid-Jun); mid-Dec–first week in Jan.*

SOUTHERN FINISTÈRE

AUDIERNE: *Le Goyen* €€ AE MC V
Place Jean-Simon, 29770. ((02) 98 70 08 88. FAX (02) 98 70 18 77.
Dedicated to Breton cuisine, this restaurant has its own oyster and
lobster farms. Portions are generous. ● *Mon (out of season, except
public holidays); Easter.*

BÉNODET: *Les Bains de Mer* €€€ AE MC V
11 Rue de Kerguélen, 29950. ((02) 98 57 03 41. FAX (02) 98 57 11 07.
This hotel restaurant, with a relaxed atmosphere, offers traditional
seafood dishes as well as Italian specialities, including pizzas.
● *mid-Nov–Feb.*

BÉNODET: *Ferme du Letty* €€€ AE DC MC V
5 Rue du Letty, 29950. ((02) 98 57 01 27. FAX (02) 98 57 25 29.
One of the best restaurants in Finistère. Although the service is a little
over-formal, the imaginative, slightly exotic dishes are excellent.
● *Tue (Jul–Aug); Mon–Tue & Thu–Sat lunchtimes; mid-Nov–late Feb.*

CONCARNEAU: *À l'Ancre* € MC V
22 Rue Dumont-d'Urville, 29900. ((02) 98 60 58 68.
Meat and fish are grilled in the large hearth in front of guests.
● *Mon; Tue lunchtime (out of season).*

CONCARNEAU: *Chez Armande* € AE MC
15 bis Avenue du Dr-Nicolas, 29900. ((02) 98 97 00 76. FAX 02 98 97 00 76.
The restaurant is located opposite the walled town. Good traditional fish
and seafood dishes. ● *first week in Sep; Christmas holidays.*

For key to symbols, see back flap

Price categories are for a three-course meal for one without wine, including service and VAT. Meals are often cheaper at lunchtime than in the evenings.
€ under 25 euros
€€ 25–45 euros
€€€ 45–65 euros
€€€€ 65–80 euros
€€€€€ over 80 euros

CREDIT CARDS ACCEPTED
The following credit cards are accepted:
American Express (AE), Diners Club (DC),
Japan Credit Bureau (JCB), MasterCard (MC), Visa (V).

FIXED-PRICE MENU
Set meals, usually consisting of three courses, are served.

OPEN LATE
The establishment admits customers up to 10pm.

OUTSIDE TABLES
Meals can be served outdoors, in a courtyard or garden, from which there is often a fine view.

	CREDIT CARDS ACCEPTED	FIXED-PRICE MENU	OPEN LUNCHTIME	OPEN LATE	OUTSIDE TABLES

CONCARNEAU: *Coquille* €€
Quai Moros, 29900. ((02) 98 97 08 52. FAX (02) 98 50 69 13.
Fish and seafood specialities are served in a dining room looking onto the fishing harbour. The paintings by local artists exhibited here attract a large clientele. ● *Sun eve–Mon; three weeks in Jan; first two weeks in May.*
AE V — ● ■ — ■

CROZON: *Le Mutin Gourmand* €€
Place de l'Église, 29160. ((02) 98 27 06 51. FAX (02) 98 26 11 97
At this well-regarded restaurant, located in a former post office, the menu changes with the seasons. Local specialities are complemented by a wide choice of wines from southern France. ♥ ● *Jan.*
MC V — ● ■

DOUARNENEZ: *Le Doyen* €€
4 Rue Jean-Jaurès, 29100. ((02) 98 92 00 02. FAX (02) 98 92 27 05.
The restaurant of the Hôtel de France offers tasty dishes, mostly fish and seafood. ● *Sun eve–Mon; Tue (Oct–May); early Jan.*
AE MC V — ● ■ ●

FOUESNANT: *Restaurant de l'Armorique* €
33 Rue de Cornouaille, 29170. ((02) 98 56 63 63. FAX (02) 98 56 65 36.
Good Breton dishes, such as knuckle of pork in cider or sea bass with leeks. ● *two weeks in Feb.*
V — ● ■ ● ■

LOCRONAN: *Manoir de Moëllien* €€
Northwest of Locronan, Plovénez-Porzay, 29550.
((02) 98 92 50 40. FAX (02) 98 92 55 21.
A restaurant in a 17th-century manor house, with an attractive dining room filled with Breton furniture. Renowned fish and seafood cuisine, including salmon smoked on the premises. ● *Wed (mid-Nov–mid-Mar).*
AE DC MC V — ● ■

LOCTUDY: *Relais de Lodonnec* €€
3 Rue des Tulipes, 2 km (1 mile) south of Loctudy, 29750. ((02) 98 87 55 34.
This restaurant, in an old fisherman's cottage 50 m (55 yds) from the beach, offers excellent seafood dishes. ♥ ● *Mon (Jul–Aug); Tue eve–Wed (out of season); mid-Jan–mid-Feb.*
MC V — ● ■ ●

PONT-AVEN: *Le Moulin de Rosmadec* €€€
Venelle de Rosmadec, 29930. ((02) 98 06 00 22. FAX (02) 98 06 18 00.
In a 15th-century mill on the banks of the Aven, this restaurant has a good reputation locally. The menu includes grilled lobster, sautéed crayfish in a potato *millefeuille* and, for dessert, pancakes with a hint of lemon and a blackberry coulis. ● *Wed; Feb; two weeks in Nov.*
MC V — ● ■ — ■

PONT-L'ABBÉ: *Le Relais de Ty-Boutic* €€
Ty-Boutic, 29120. ((02) 98 87 03 90. FAX (02) 98 87 30 63.
The dishes here, skillfully prepared from local products, include succulent coley fillet with cabbage and sausage, and crayfish with leeks.
● *Sun eve, Mon.*
V — ● ■ — ■

QUIMPER: *Les Acacias* €€
Boulevard Creac'h-Gwen, 29000. ((02) 98 52 15 20. FAX (02) 98 10 11 48.
Located in verdant surroundings on the banks of the Odet, this restaurant has a menu based on such local produce as fish, pigeon, Baye snails and Plougastel strawberries. ● *Sat lunchtime, Sun eve, Mon eve; Aug.*
V — ● ■

QUIMPER: *L'Ambroisie* €€
49 Rue Élie-Fréron, 29000. ((02) 98 95 00 02. FAX (02) 98 95 88 06.
A restaurant with a modern dining room decorated with prints by Francis Bacon. The menu features seafood dishes such as lobster or shellfish *jus* and leek fondue, and excellents desserts. ● *Mon (winter); Feb; late Jun–mid-July; 30 Nov.*
MC V — ● ■

QUIMPER: *Le Stade*
12 Avenue Georges-Pompidou, 29000. **(** (02) 98 90 22 43. **FAX** (02) 98 90 39 99.
This restaurant deserves its excellent reputation. It offers gourmet
dishes such as scallop risotto with truffles, grilled supreme of young roast
pigeon with liver cooked in Armagnac, and chestnut *millefeuille*.
Y ● *one week in Feb; one week in late Jul–early Aug; early Sep.*

€€ | AE DC MC V | ● ■ ●

QUIMPER: *Le Capucin Gourmand*
29 Rue Réguaires, 29000. **(** (02) 98 95 43 12. **FAX** (02) 98 95 13 34.
Tasty Breton specialities, such as warm truffle and shellfish salad, and
St Malo turbot tart with rosemary. The equally good desserts include
Bigouden-style prune flan with apple wine sauce. ● *Sun, Mon lunchtime.*

€€ | AE MC V | ● ■ ●

QUIMPERLÉ: *Le Bistro de la Tour*
2 Rue Don-Morice, 29300. **(** (02) 98 39 29 58. **FAX** (02) 98 39 21 77.
This restaurant, with a tastefully decorated dining room, is well-known
both for the quality of its cuisine and its unusually good wines. The cellar
contains over 600 vintages. **Y** ● *Sat lunchtime & Sun eve.*

€€ | AE MC V | ● ■

MORBIHAN

ARZ (ILE D'): *Les Îles*
In the town centre, 56840. **(** (02) 97 44 30 95. **FAX** (02) 97 44 33 61.
A convivial restaurant with a menu including oysters au gratin and
chargrilled lobster. ● *Sat–Sun; Mon–Fri eves (except during school holidays).*

€ | V | ● ■ ■

AURAY: *L'Églantine*
17 Place St-Sauveur, 56400. **(** (02) 97 56 46 55.
A small auberge with a warm welcome. Good Breton specialities,
including monkfish and salmon in a chive and horseradish sauce.
● *Wed (out of season).*

€ | MC V | ● ■ ■

AURAY: *La Closerie de Kerdain*
20 Rue L.-Billet, 56400. **(** (02) 97 56 61 27. **FAX** (02) 97 24 15 79.
A fine 18th-century dining room with woodcarvings and a large
Breton chimneypiece. The refined dishes include cream of crayfish
soup and squid with artichokes and hazelnuts. ● *Mon; three weeks in Mar;
late Nov–mid-Dec.*

€€€ | AE DC MC V | ● ■ ■

BELLE-ILE-EN-MER: *Castel Clara*
Port-Goulphar, Bangor, 56360. **(** (02) 97 31 84 21. **FAX** (02) 97 31 51 69.
Excellent fish and seafood cuisine served in a restaurant with an
impressive view of the cliffs at Port-Goulphar. ● *mid-Nov–mid-Feb.*

€€ | AE DC MC V | ● ■ ■

BILLIERS: *Domaine de Rochvilaine*
On Pointe de Pen-Lan-Sud, 56190. **(** (02) 97 41 61 61. **FAX** (02) 97 41 44 85.
A restaurant located at the tip of a rocky promontory. The imaginative
cuisine includes crayfish with citrus fruits and brioche.

€€€ | AE DC MC V | ● ■ ■

BONO (LE): *Hostellerie Abbatiale de Kerdréan*
56400. **(** (02) 97 57 84 00. **FAX** (02) 97 57 83 00.
A restaurant in a beautifully verdant setting, offering high-quality cuisine.
Specialities include roast crayfish with paprika butter.

€ | AE DC MC V | ● ■ ■

CARNAC: *Auberge Le Râtelier*
4 Chemin du Douet, 56340. **(** (02) 97 52 05 04. **FAX** (02) 97 52 76 11.
This restored farmhouse, with original stonework, offers traditional fish
dishes. ● *Tue; Wed (during school holidays).*

€€ | AE DC MC V | ●

GROIX (ILE DE): *Les Courreaux*
47 Rue du Général-de-Gaulle, 56590. **(** (02) 97 86 82 66.
An excellent restaurant very near the harbour serving imaginative fish
and seafood dishes. ● *Mon lunchtime; late Nov–mid-Feb.*

€ | AE V | ● ■ ● ■

HENNEBONT: *Château de Locguénolé*
Route de Port-Louis, 56700. **(** (02) 97 76 76 76. **FAX** (02) 97 76 82 35.
A restaurant set in 120 ha (300 acres) of parkland. The sophisticated
menu includes meat *millefeuille*, grilled lobster and potato ravioli with
suckling pig. **Y** ● *early Jan–first week in Feb.*

€€€ | AE DC MC V | ● ■ ■

For key to symbols, see back flap

	CREDIT CARDS ACCEPTED	FIXED-PRICE MENU	OPEN LUNCHTIME	OPEN LATE	OUTSIDE TABLES

Price categories are for a three-course meal for one without wine, including service and VAT. Meals are often cheaper at lunchtime than in the evenings.
€ under 25 euros
€€ 25–45 euros
€€€ 45–65 euros
€€€€ 65–80 euros
€€€€€ over 80 euros

CREDIT CARDS ACCEPTED
The following credit cards are accepted:
American Express (AE), Diners Club (DC),
Japan Credit Bureau (JCB), MasterCard (MC), Visa (V).

FIXED-PRICE MENU
Set meals, usually consisting of three courses, are served.

OPEN LATE
The establishment admits customers up to 10pm.

OUTSIDE TABLES
Meals can be served outdoors, in a courtyard or garden, from which there is often a fine view.

Restaurant	Price	Cards	FPM	OL	OLt	OT
LORIENT: *Le Jardin Gourmand* 46 Rue Jules-Simon, 56100. ((02) 97 64 17 24. FAX (02) 97 64 15 75. One of the best restaurants in Lorient, with a flavoursome menu that changes with the seasons. Reservation strongly advised. ● Sun–Mon; early Aug; two weeks in Feb.	€€	DC JCB MC V	●	■		
LORIENT: *L'Amphitryon* 127 Rue du Colonel-Muller, 56100. ((02) 97 83 34 04. FAX (02) 98 97 37 02. This restaurant, with modern décor, is one of the best in Lorient. The menu includes potatoes in sardine butter, eggs with caviar, and calves' sweetbreads with truffles. Reservation essential. 🍷 ● Sun, Mon.	€€€	AE MC V	●	■		
QUESTEMBERT: *La Bretagne* 13 Rue St-Michel, 56230. ((02) 97 26 11 12. FAX (02) 97 26 12 37. One of the best restaurants in France. Meals are served in an elegant dining room or in the beautiful conservatory. Specialities include oysters in foaming tarragon butter and Breton-style pigs' trotters. 🍷 ● Mon, except eves in Jul–Aug; three last weeks in Jan.	€€€	AE DC MC V	●	■		
QUIBERON: *La Chaumine* 36 Place du Manémeur, 56170. ((02) 97 50 17 67. FAX (02) 97 50 17 67. A small, family-run inn located in the heart of the fishermen's quarter. Simple, well-cooked dishes, such as crayfish in mayonnaise and lambs' sweetbreads. ● Sun–Mon (out of season).	€€	AE V	●	■		■
QUIBERON: *Le Verger de la Mer* Boulevard Goulvars, 56170. ((02) 97 50 29 12. Located next to the Institut de Thalassothérapie, this restaurant serves generous, tasty dishes such as shellfish *pot-au-feu* with herbs, and sole in shrimp *jus*. ● Tue eve, Wed; early Jan–late Feb.	€	AE V	●	■		■
QUIBERON: *Le Relax* 27 Boulevard Castero, Plage de Kermovan, 56170. ((02) 97 50 12 84. FAX (02) 97 50 12 84. A restaurant with a dining room offering views of the sea and the garden. The fish menu changes with the seasons. ● Sun eve, Mon (Oct–Mar); early Jan–mid-Feb.	€	AE DC MC V	●	■		■
ROCHE-BERNARD (LA): *L'Auberge Bretonne* Place du Guesclin, 56130. ((02) 99 90 60 28. FAX (02) 99 90 85 00. One of the best restaurants in Brittany, with a dining room in a gallery looking onto the vegetable garden. The many specialities include a delicate shellfish jelly, casserole of lobster with lime-flowers and apples, and chocolate macaroon. ● Mon lunchtime, Thu, Fri lunchtime; mid-Nov–mid-Dec; three weeks in Jan.	€€€€	AE DC MC V	●	■		
ROCHEFORT-EN-TERRE: *La Petite Bretonne* Opposite the church, 56220. ((02) 97 43 37 68. This restaurant offers delicious and unusual pancake specialities. In winter the dining room is heated by a large open fire. ● Wed & Sun lunchtime.	€	MC V		■		■
STE-ANNE-D'AURAY: *L'Auberge* 56 Route de Vannes, 56400. ((02) 97 57 61 55. FAX (02) 97 57 69 10. The dining room contains old wooden furniture and is decorated with a collection of Breton costume. The generous dishes served here include pumpkin soup and a light mussel *feuilleté*, plaice tart with tomato and whisked butter, and *kouign amann* (Breton tart) with pears and honey sauce. ● Tue (out of season), Wed; mid-Nov–early Dec; Feb school holidays.	€€	AE V	●	■		

SARZEAU: *Le Mur du Roy* €€ | DC MC V
Penvins, 56370. ((02) 97 67 34 08. FAX (02) 97 67 36 23.
A fish and seafood restaurant offering good value for money. The menu
consists of a choice of four main dishes and a dessert. ● *two weeks in Jan.*

TRINITÉ-SUR-MER (LA): *L'Azimut* €€ | DC MC V
1 Rue du Men-Dû, on the coast road, 56470. ((02) 97 55 71 88. FAX (02) 97 55 80 15.
A restaurant with an elegant dining room and an attractive terrace. The
meticulously prepared fish and seafood dishes include chargrilled lobster
and scallops stuffed with foie gras. ● *Tue eve; Wed (except during school hols).*

VANNES: *Restaurant de Roscanvec* €€ | MC V
17 Rue des Halles, 56000. ((02) 97 47 15 96. FAX (02) 97 47 86 39.
A restaurant in the centre of town, with dining areas on several floors.
Gourmet dishes include oysters *à la nage* and coconut-milk blancmange
with chopped nuts. ● *Sun eve (Oct–Jun); late Dec–early Jan.*

VANNES: *Régis Mahé* €€ | MC V
24 Place de la Gare, 56000. ((02) 97 42 61 41. FAX (02) 97 54 99 01.
Dishes here include lobster and pigeon tart with honey glaze, and
ice cream with butter caramel. The dining room has medieval décor.
● *Sun–Mon; Feb school holidays; one week in Jun; last two weeks in Nov.*

LOIRE-ATLANTIQUE

BAULE (LA): *Le Rossini* €€ | AE MC V
13 Avenue Evens, 44500. ((02) 40 60 25 81. FAX (02) 40 42 73 52.
The restaurant of the Hôtel Lutétia, with decoration in the International
Modern style, serves such gourmet dishes as fillet of beef Rossini and
roast salmon in red butter. ● *Sun eve; Mon (out of season and during school
holidays); Tue lunchtime; Jan.*

NANTES: *Lou Pescadou* €€ | AE CB V
8 Allée Baco, 44000. ((02) 40 35 29 50. FAX (02) 51 82 46 34.
One of the best fish restaurants in Nantes. A fresh catch is delivered
daily. Reservation advised. ● *Sat lunchtime–Sun, Mon eve; two weeks in Aug.*

NANTES: *Le Gavroche* €€ | AE MC
139 Rue des Hauts-Pavés, 44000. ((02) 40 76 22 49. FAX (02) 40 76 37 80.
An elegant restaurant serving imaginative dishes that vary according to the
season. The desserts are particularly recommended.
● *Sun eve–Mon; late Jul–late Aug.*

NANTES: *L'Atlantic* € | AE DC MC V
26 Boulevard Stalingrad, 44000. ((02) 40 74 00 72. FAX (02) 40 14 08 47.
Located near the railway station, this restaurant has a menu featuring
traditional cuisine as well as its own tasty specialities. ● *Sat.*

NANTES: *La Cigale* €€ | MC V
4 Place Graslin, 44000. ((02) 51 84 94 94. FAX (02) 51 84 94 95.
An excellent brasserie with an Art Nouveau interior (*see pp204 & 228*),
opposite the Théâtre Graslin. Nantes high society is the clientele here.

PORNIC: *Beau Rivage* €€ | AE V
Plage de la Birochère, 44210. ((02) 40 82 03 08. FAX (02) 51 74 04 24.
A restaurant with a fine location, looking onto the beach. The menu,
based on fish and seafood, includes bouillabaisse (fish soup) and lobster
salad with herbs. ● *Sun eve–Mon; Wed (out of season); Jan; 10–26 Dec.*

ST-JOACHIM: *La Mare aux Oiseaux* €€€ | AE DC MC V
162 Île de Fédrun, 44720. ((02) 40 88 53 01. FAX (02) 40 91 67 44.
Highly imaginative cuisine prepared by a skilled young chef. The
chopped eels with herbs and the crisp frogs' legs with Breton seaweed
are recommended. ■ ● *Sun eve; Mon (out of season); late Feb–Mar.*

ST-NAZAIRE: *L'An II* €€ | AE V
2 Rue Villebois-Mareuil, 44600. ((02) 40 00 95 33. FAX (02) 40 53 44 20.
A good fish restaurant with a view of the estuary. The marinated Turballe
sardines in olive oil and fine Guérande salt are recommended. ■

SHOPS AND MARKETS

Tin of Breton sardines

FROM THE STALLS laid out on a Saturday in Vitré to the great covered market in Plouescat, Brittany's weekly food markets are key events in the region's gastronomic life. It is here that the best and freshest local produce – crisp young vegetables, glistening seafood, farm-produced cheeses, cider and charcuterie – is to be found. There are also many fascinating shops to be explored, offering other Breton goods, among the most distinctive being striped sailors' sweaters, Quimper faience and craft items, such as ship models, with a marine theme.

Artichokes, sold in every market in Brittany

MARKETS

THE REGULAR WEEKLY markets are the major outlet for local produce and local, or even family, specialities. But they are not the only choice. To promote their own produce, certain growers have set up small farmers' markets on their own farm premises, where they sell goat's cheese, buttermilk and other produce from local farms.

There are farmers' markets in Planguenoual, Milizac, Plouzélambre and Notre-Dame-du-Guildo. *Circuits gourmands* (gastronomic tours) are also organized by local producers in an initiative to promote local delicacies. A list of these markets and the addresses of the relevant producers are available from tourist offices.

LOCAL DRINKS

THANKS TO A small group of cider-makers, such as **Éric Baron**, who use traditional methods, cider has undergone a revival in popularity since the 1980s. The Cornouaille region produces an excellent cider, which has an AOC classification. Robust and with an orange hue, it goes very well with seafood.

Some producers, such as **Fisselier** and **Dassonville**, also offer a wide range of liqueurs made from strawberries and other suitable kinds of fruit, as well as coffee liqueurs made with cider brandy, *chouchenn*, a mead made with cider and honey, *pommeaux* (sparkling apple wines) and Breton whisky. There is also *lambig*, made by distilling cider brandy and ideal for lobster flambé.

There were once 75 breweries in Brittany, and, following a decline, there has been a resurgence of small independent breweries since 1985. The beers that they produce – such as Coreff, a pale ale, Blanche Hermine and Telenn Du, a wheat beer – easily equal more famous brands.

PRODUCE OF THE SEA

FRESH FISH auctions are held in many harbours all along the coast of Brittany. If the idea of attending one does not appeal, there are

Coreff beer

alternatives. Oysters can be bought at oyster farms, such as that at the **Château de Belon**. Fish and seafood can also be bought from wholesalers and from fish farms *(viviers)*, such as those in Audierne, Camaret and **Roscoff**. Although wholesale prices fluctuate, they are always sure to be lower than retail prices.

The best kinds of oysters are Nacre des Abers and Morlaix-Penzé, which have a sweet taste; Aven-Belon, which are crisp and sweet; Cancale, firm with a nutty aftertaste; Paimpolaise, salty with a flavour of the sea; and the plump Ria d'Étel.

Easier to take home are sardines, mackerel fillets, slices of tuna and traditionally cured sprats, which are canned in factories, such as **Gonidec**, on the south coast of Brittany. Guérande salt, jars of samphire and seaweed products are also good buys. With 800 different varieties, the coast of Finistère is one of the largest seaweed-growing areas in the world. The benefits of seaweed are many and varied. **Thalado**, for example, makes seaweed bath salts, soap, tonic lotions and nutritional supplements.

Oysters on a stall in Vivier-sur-Mer

SAILORS' CLOTHING

IN MOST HARBOURS there is a fishermen's cooperative where traditional sailors' clothing, labelled "Made in Breizh" is on sale. This ranges from thick pullovers, indigo-and-cream striped sweaters and smocks, to waxed jackets and seamen's watch jackets with double waterproof collars. Perfectly suited for sailing and for fishing trips, these tough, weatherproof clothes are derived from traditional Breton clothing. The *kabig*, a jacket made of heavy cloth, evolved from the *kab an aod* that Breton seaweed-gatherers once wore.

The best-known brands of seamen's clothing are Captain Corsaire, **Armor Lux** and **Guy Cotten**, the leading manufacturer of clothes for professional seamen.

Stall selling *Kouign amann*, the traditional Breton cake

Retail outlet of the Faïencerie Henriot in Quimper

HANDICRAFTS

COLOURFUL QUIMPER faience *(see pp164–5)*, particularly that produced by the **Faïencerie Henriot**, is without doubt Brittany's best known hand-crafted product. The Île de Bréhat is also renowned for its glassware and Pont-l'Abbé for its embroidered linen, such as that offered for sale in **Le Minor**.

There are also craftsmen's workshops that are open to the public in Brasparts *(see p140)*, in Locronan *(see p152)*, in Guérande *(see p200)*, in the villages around Pont-Scorff, 7 km (4 miles) from Lorient, and in St-Méloir, 17 km (10 miles) from Dol-de-Bretagne.

Browsing in shops selling marine antiques may also turn up some interesting finds, as may a visit to woodworkers such as **Thierry Morel** in Plouvien, **Frères Douirin** in Plozévet, and Francis Tirot in Fougères, all of whom make wooden ship models.

Most shops are open from 9am to 12.30pm and 2.30 to 7pm, Monday to Saturday.

DIRECTORY	

REGIONAL SPECIALITIES

FINISTÈRE
Brasserie Corref
1 Place de la Madeleine, Morlaix.
(02) 98 63 41 92.
Strong, traditionally brewed beers.

Château de Belon
On the right bank of the river, Riec-sur-Bélon.
(02) 98 06 90 58.
Oysters.

Dassonville
Pen-ar-Ros, Plouegat-Moysan.
(02) 98 79 21 25.
Chouchenn (mead) & honey.

Éric Baron
Kervéguen, Guimaec.
(02) 98 67 50 02.
Cider made by traditional methods.

Gonidec
2 Rue Bisson, Concarneau.
(02) 98 97 07 09.
Canned fish.

Thalado
5 Avenue Victor-Hugo, Roscoff.
(02) 98 69 77 05.
Edible seaweed and seaweed for use in thalassotherapy.

Viviers de Roscoff
Pointe Ste-Barbe, Roscoff.
(02) 98 61 19 61.
Crustacean farms.

ILLE-ET-VILAINE
Fisselier
56 Rue du Verger, Rennes-Chantepie.
(02) 99 41 00 00.
Liqueurs made by traditional methods.

CLOTHES & HANDICRAFTS

FINISTÈRE
Bonneterie d'Armor
60 bis Rue Guy-Autret, Quimper.
(02) 98 52 25 54.
Head office of Armor Lux (for sailors' clothing).

Faïencerie H-B Henriot
Place Bérardier, Quimper.
(02) 98 52 22 52.
Quimper faience

Frères Douirin
9 Impasse Poste, Plozevet.
(02) 98 91 42 65.
Ship models.

Guy Cotten
Pont Minaouët, Trégunc.
(02) 98 97 66 79.
www.guycotten.com
Sailors' clothing.

Le Minor
3 Quai St-Laurent, Pont-l'Abbé.
(02) 98 87 07 22.
Embroidery, lace & tulle.

Thierry Morel
47 Rue du Général-de-Gaulle, Plouvien.
(02) 98 40 99 24.
Ship models.

What to Buy in Brittany

**Quimper faience
seated figure**

BRITTANY PROJECTS a distinctive image. This is reflected in the seamen's striped sweaters and yellow oilskins and the pretty Quimper faience that are the staple of so many souvenir shops. But there is, in fact, far more to Breton craftsmanship than this. Not only are there countless delicacies – butter made in the churn, local pâtisserie, cooked meats and traditionally made cider – but also many high-quality items with a marine theme. Ranging from seaweed balm to antique sextants and sailors' chests, these are redolent of the high seas and, of course, of Brittany itself.

Handmade toy boat

SOUVENIRS

In the most popular coastal resorts, a little discrimination is sometimes needed to distinguish good-quality pieces from cheap souvenirs. It is best to choose locally made items, or to look round old chandlers' shops. CDs of traditional Breton songs are another reliable buy.

almanach
du
marin breton

2001

**The sailor's
almanac,** *giving the times of tides, is an essential accessory for anglers and yachting enthusiasts.*

Pipe

Nautilus shells *make attractive ornaments and, like other souvenirs with a marine theme, they bring a taste of the sea to any décor.*

Plaster figures *of a Breton couple, sold in many local shops.*

Lighthouse

Bowl

Breizh

Breton pennant

FAIENCE

Continuing a tradition established in the 17th century *(see pp164–5)*, Quimper's faience factories produce wares in a range of shapes, decorated with patterns such as *petit breton* and *à bords jaune*, painted in various colours.

Quimper faience tray

Quimper faience salt cellar and pepper pot

Faience pitcher
decorated with a classic Quimper floral pattern.

Quimper faience,
like this colourful plate with floral border, is decorated entirely freehand, without the use of transfers. Good-quality pieces are signed by the decorator.

CLOTHES

Sturdy and weather-resistant, traditional sailors' clothing
conjures up images of the open sea and ocean spray.
With the rise in popularity of sailing and water sports,
it has become essential wear both for yachting
enthusiasts and for casually chic town-dwellers.

**Seaman's woolly
hat**, ideal for keeping
out a sea fret.

Kabig, a hooded jacket made
of heavy waterproofed cloth.

Sailors' sweaters

SWEETS AND BISCUITS

Among Breton specialities are many kinds of sweets and biscuits,
some owing their distinctive taste to Brittany's excellent butter.
These treats include pancakes (packaged in foil), butter toffees,
butter biscuits, especially *petits-beurre* made in Nantes, and
berlingots, handmade sweets also from Nantes.

Butter toffees

Traou Mad,
butter
biscuits,
made in
Pont-Aven

Box of Leroux toffees

Berlingots
*are twisted
sweets made
by traditional
methods.*

Tins of coloured *berlingots*, made in Nantes

SKINCARE PRODUCTS

A wide range of skincare products,
including seaweed-based cosmetics
and creams made with extracts of oyster,
are on sale in thalassotherapy centres all
along the coasts of Brittany.

Phytomer for skincare   **Bath salts**

**Traditional
Breton cider**

**Fleur de
caramel**

**Fraise de
Plougastel**

ALCOHOLIC DRINKS

Brittany is renowned for its ciders
and liqueurs, including *fleur de
caramel* liqueur and *fraise de
Plougastel*, a strawberry liqueur.

ENTERTAINMENT IN BRITTANY

B RETONS ARE FOND of festivals and celebrations, and they are also enthusiastic communicators. Music, film and cartoon festivals, as well as live performances, take place all over Brittany throughout the year. The region also has a

Musician at the Festival des Vieilles Charrues

great variety of museums, art galleries and other cultural centres. Those who do not wish to spend all their time on the beach will find more than enough to entertain them. For details of local festivals, see Brittany Through the Year *(pp28–31)*.

GENERAL INFORMATION

T HE REGIONAL newspapers and magazines *(see p255)* are the best source of information regarding festivals and other events *(see pp28–31)*. Lists of upcoming events are also available from the Comité Régional du Tourisme, for the whole of Brittany, and the relevant Comité Départemental, for each region of Brittany. Local tourist offices are another convenient source of information.

BUYING TICKETS

T ICKETS FOR shows and festivals for which there is an admission charge are usually available direct from the organizers. Shops run by FNAC (Fédération Nationale d'Art et de Culture), which can be found in large towns, also have ticket offices.

It is worth bearing in mind that most major events usually draw very large crowds, and it may be necessary to book tickets several months in advance.

MUSIC

T HE PASSIONATE enthusiasm that Bretons have for music *(see pp20–1)* goes back to their ancient roots. Many solo musicians and groups who began their careers in Brittany have gone on to achieve much wider fame. In this respect, **Ubu**, the arts centre in Rennes, stands out for its policy of promoting avant-garde musicians.

Brittany also hosts many major music festivals. Among the greatest is the Festival des Vieilles Charrues in Carhaix *(see p29)*, the Route du Rock in St-Malo *(see p29)*, the Rencontres Transmusicales in Rennes *(see p31)*, the Festival Astropolis in Concarneau, and the Festival Art Rock in St-Brieuc *(see p28)*. For jazz enthusiasts there is the Festival du Jazz in Vannes *(see p29)*.

Traditional Breton music is celebrated at the Festival Interceltique in Lorient *(see p29)*, which draws 4,500 performers and 450,000 spectators each year. The focus of the Festival de Cornouaille in Quimper is world music.

THEATRE

B ESIDES THE high-quality programme of plays performed by the **Théâtre National de Bretagne** in Rennes, theatre in Brittany comes to the fore at the annual Festival Tombées de la Nuit *(see p28)*, which takes place in the city in July. Other theatres with dynamic programmes are in Nantes and Brest.

CINEMA

S EVERAL ANNUAL FILM festivals take place in Brittany. Established over ten years ago, the **Festival du Film Britannique** in Dinard *(see p30)* shows feature films and organizes retrospectives. Prominent people from the world of film, including actors, directors, producers and distributors, attend.

Travelling, a week-long film festival that takes place in Rennes in January, highlights the work of filmmakers from a particular city, such as London, Berlin or Tokyo. This is an opportunity to see some

Dancers at the Rencontres Transmusicales in Rennes

unusual productions. The **Festival de Cinéma de Douarnenez**, meanwhile, shows films on the theme of various civilizations.

EXHIBITIONS

BRITTANY HAS a wealth of museums and art galleries, with interesting or unusual permanent collections and temporary exhibitions.

Some of the best temporary exhibitions can be seen at two venues in Rennes – the Musée des Beaux-Arts *(see p59)* and **La Criée**, a centre for modern art. There are also the **Centre d'Art Passerelle** in Brest, the Musée des Jacobins in Morlaix *(see p117)*, the contemporary art centre in Kerguehennec, the **Galerie Dourven** in Trédrez-Locquémeau, the Musée de La Cohue in Vannes *(see pp187–8)* and the Musée des Beaux-Arts in Quimper *(see pp158 and 161)*.

Participants in the Festival Interceltique in Lorient

DIRECTORY

VENUES

CÔTES D'ARMOR

Le Masque en Mouvement
(theatre)
13 Rue de la Gare,
22250 Broons.
((02) 96 84 75 19.

La Passerelle
(theatre)
Place de la Résistance,
22000 St-Brieuc.
((02) 96 68 18 40.

Théâtre des Jacobins
Rue de l'Horloge,
22100 Dinan.
((02) 96 87 03 11.

FINISTÈRE

Le Quartz de Brest
(theatre, music and dance)
4 Avenue Clemenceau,
29200 Brest.
((02) 98 33 70 70.

Théâtre de Cornouaille
(regional theatre in Quimper)
4 Place de la Tour-d'Auvergne,
29000 Quimper.
((02) 98 55 98 55.

ILLE-ET-VILAINE

Opera
Place de l'Hôtel-de-Ville,
35000 Rennes.
((02) 99 78 48 68.

Salle de la Cité
(music and dance)
10 Rue St-Louis,
35000 Rennes.
((02) 99 79 10 66.

Théâtre National de Bretagne
1 Rue St-Hélier,
35000 Rennes.
((02) 99 31 12 31.

Théâtre de la Parcheminerie
23 Rue de la Parcheminerie,
35000 Rennes.
((02) 99 79 47 63.

Le Triangle
(music and dance)
30 Boulevard de Yougoslavie,
35000 Rennes.
(02 99 22 27 27.

Ubu
(music and dance)
10–12 Rue Jean-Guy,
35000 Rennes.
((02) 99 31 12 10.

LOIRE-ATLANTIQUE

Cité des Congrès de Nantes-Atlantique
(theatre, music and dance)
5 Rue Valmy,
44000 Nantes.
((02) 51 88 20 00.

L'Espace 44
(theatre, music and dance)
84 Rue du Général-Buat,
44000 Nantes.
((02) 51 88 25 20.

Lieu Unique
(theatre, music and dance)
Quai Ferdinand-Favre,
44000 Nantes.
((02) 40 12 14 34.

Théâtre Graslin
(opera)
1 Rue Molière,
44000 Nantes.
((02) 40 41 90 60.

MORBIHAN

Plateau des 4 Vents
(theatre)
2 Rue du Professeur-Mazé,
56100 Lorient.
((02) 97 37 53 05.

Théâtre de Lorient
11 Rue Claire-Droneau,
56100 Lorient.
((02) 97 83 51 51.

ART GALLERIES

CÔTES D'ARMOR

Galerie Dourven
Domaine Départemental du Dourven,
22300 Trédez-Locquémeau.
((02) 96 35 21 42.

FINISTÈRE

Centre d'Art Passerelle
41 bis Rue Charles-Berthelot,
29200 Brest.
((02) 98 43 34 95.

ILLE-ET-VILAINE

La Criée
Halles Centrales,
Place Honoré-Commeurec,
35000 Rennes.
((02) 99 78 18 20.

MORBIHAN

Domaine de Kerguehennec
Centre d'Art Contemporain
Bignan, 56500 Locmine
((02) 97 60 44 44.

LOIRE-ATLANTIQUE

Forum
10 Passage Pommeraye,
44000 Nantes.
((02) 51 88 25 25.

CINEMA

Festival du Film Britannique
Organizer's office:
2 Bd Féart, 35800 Dinard.
((02) 99 88 19 04.
FAX (02) 99 46 67 15.
@ fest.film.britan.dinard@wanadoo.fr
W festivaldufilm-dinard.com

Festival Travelling de Rennes
Clair Obscur, Université Rennes 2, 6 Avenue Gaston-Berger,
35043 Rennes Cedex.
((02) 99 14 11 43.
W www.travelling-festival.com

Festival de Cinéma de Douarnenez
20 Rue du Port-Rhu, BP 206,
29172 Douarnenez Cedex.
((02) 98 92 09 21.
FAX (02) 98 92 28 10.
@ fdz@wanadoo.fr
W www.kerys.com/festival

OUTDOOR ACTIVITIES

WITH BEAUTIFUL BAYS and beaches, dramatic promontories and cliffs, and picturesque islands, Brittany is well endowed with areas of natural beauty. The region's coast is its best-known feature, and many watersports are available *(see pp250–51)*.

Brittany's spectacular coastline should not, however, obscure the attractions of the interior. These include the Monts d'Arrée and the Montagnes Noires, as well as heathland, forests, lakes, rivers, canals, valleys and marshland. These landscapes can be explored on foot, by bicycle or on horseback. Brittany's nature reserves and coastal areas offer plenty of opportunities for bird-watching, and, with more than 30 fine golf courses, the region is also attractive to keen golfers.

Cyclists at Fort de La Latte, a 13th-century fortress on Cap Fréhel

WALKING

RUNNING BOTH along coastlines and inland, France has over 60,000 km (37,000 miles) of long-distance footpaths (Sentiers de Grande Randonnée, or GR) and 80,000 km (50,000 miles) of Promenade et Randonnée (PR) routes. These are maintained and marked out by volunteers of the **Fédération Française de la Randonnée Pédestre**.

Most of the best footpaths in Brittany are mentioned in the appropriate entries in this guide. Various organizations, such as **Rando Breiz** and the Comité Régional du Tourisme, offer walking programmes with overnight stays in *gîtes* (some of which have received an award for their standards of comfort), or in *chambres d'hôtes* (guest rooms) or small, family-run hotels.

CYCLING

THE BLAVET VALLEY, the Cornouaille region and the Baie du Mont-St-Michel have been identified as prime areas for mountain biking (Sites VTT) by the **Fédération Française de Cyclotourisme de Bretagne**.

As with long-distance walking *(see above)*, gîte and other en-route accommodation can be arranged through local cycling organizations or the Comité Régional du Tourisme.

Walkers near the Phare du Paon, Isle de Bréhat

HORSEBACK RIDING

THOSE WHO prefer to explore Brittany on horseback will enjoy following Équibreizh, a long-distance bridleway that traverses Brittany. It is clearly marked and covers over 2,000 km (1,250 miles) of varied and scenic terrain. The *Topo-Guide Équibreizh*, published by **ARTEB** (Association Régionale pour le Tourisme Équestre de Bretagne), includes detailed maps indicating routes, overnight stopping places, riding centres, farriers and horse transporters. Accommodation can also be arranged through the **Comité Régional** in the revelant area of Brittany.

BIRD-WATCHING

BRITTANY IS one of the best places in Europe for birdwatching. The diversity of the region's landscapes attracts a great variety of birds *(see pp14–15)*, from the ubiquitous herring gull and crested cormorant, to the marsh harrier and ringed plover. There is much for nature-lovers to see, and almost 20 bird sanctuaries and other protected areas to explore.

Bretagne Vivante-SEPNB (Société pour l'Étude et la Protection de la Nature en Bretagne) and **Vivarmor Nature** both organize a variety of bird-watching trips, in winter as well as in summer. Useful information is also available from **LPO (Ligue pour la Protection des Oiseaux)**.

GOLF

THERE ARE 32 golf courses in Brittany, providing golfing enthusiasts with a wide choice. The **Ligue de Golf de Bretagne** and the Comité Régional du Tourisme publish a guide listing all the golf courses in the region. Many options, from a day's play to a full week, are available. The association **Formule Golf** offers tailor-made golfing programmes spread over several days.

SPORT AND TOURISM FOR DISABLED PEOPLE

BRITTANY HAS several organizations that arrange holidays and sports activities for people with disabilites. Founded in 1982 by UFCV (Union Francaise des Centres de Vacances et de Loisirs),of which it is a member, the **Association EPAL** (Évasion en Pays d'Accueil et de Loisirs, *see p255)* organizes sightseeing and sporting holidays for disabled people.

Golf course at Les Rochers-Sévigné in Vitré

Two other organizations – **RADAR**, based in London, and **Handitour** *(see pp256),* based in Canada – offer a similar service.

Comprehensive information relevant to activities organized in Brittany is available from the **Comité Régional de Sport Adapté de Bretagne** and the **Comité Régional de Handisport de Bretagne**. The names and contact details of other organizations that arrange a variety of sports and holidays for people with disabilities is given on p256.

Bird-watching at Cap Sizun, in southern Finistère

DIRECTORY

WALKING

Fédération Française de la Randonnée Pédestre
13 bis Avenue de Cucillé,
35000 Rennes.
((02) 99 54 67 61.
w www.ffrp.asso.fr

Rando Breiz
1 Rue Raoul-Ponchon
35000 Rennes
((02) 99 27 03 20.
@ info@randobreizh.com

CYCLING

Fédération Française de Cyclotourisme de Bretagne
11 Rue Alphonse-Guérin,
35000 Rennes.
((02) 99 36 38 11.

HORSEBACK RIDING

ARTEB
101 Chemin Randreux,
22700 Perros-Guirec.
((02) 96 91 43 84.

Comité Régional de Bretagne
5 bis Rue Waldeck-Rousseau, BP 307,
56103 Lorient.
((02) 97 84 44 00.
@ creb@wanadoo.fr

Tourisme Équestre des Pays de la Loire
3 Rue Bossuet,
44000 Nantes.
((02) 40 48 12 27.

BIRD-WATCHING

Bretagne Vivante-SEPNB (Société pour l'Étude et la Protection de la Nature en Bretagne)
186 Rue Anatole-France,

BP 32,29276
Brest cedex.
((02) 98 49 07 18.
w www.bretagne-vivante.asso.fr/

LPO (Ligue pour la Protection des Oiseaux)
11 Rue De Lattre-de-Tassigny,
56100 Lorient.
((02) 97 37 50 36.
w http://perso.wanadoo.fr/lpo. bretagne/

Vivarmor Nature
10 Boulevard Sévigné,
22000 St-Brieuc.
((02) 96 33 10 57.
w www.assoc.wanadoo.fr/vivarmor/

GOLF

Formule Golf
1 Place de Galarne,
BP 36213,
44262 Nantes Cedex 2.
((02) 40 12 55 95/
(02) 40 12 55 99.
w www.formule-golf.com

Ligue de Golf de Bretagne
130 Rue Pottier,
35000 Rennes.
((02) 99 31 68 80.

VISITORS WITH DISABILITIES

RADAR
12 City Forum, 250 City Road. London EC1V 8AF.
(020 7250 3222.
w radar.org.uk

Comité Régional de Handisport de Bretagne
Rue Auguste Fresnel,
29490 Guipavas.
((02) 98 42 61 05.

Comité Régional de Sport Adapté de Bretagne
26 Rue La Landelle,
29200 Brest.
((02) 98 02 37 76.

Watersports

FROM THE ILLUSTRIOUS seafaring traditions of the past to the prestigious regattas that take place in its major coastal harbours today, Brittany has a close association with the sea. This, together with a spectacular coastline, makes it an ideal environment in which to enjoy watersports. Of the variety of watersports practised in Brittany, yachting, canoeing, scuba-diving, sand yachting and surfing are by far the most popular. For beginners and experienced alike, the opportunities for enjoying them are many, and each in its different ways reveals the power and beauty of the sea.

Sailing boat bear Phare de la Vieille, off southern Finistère

SAILING

WITH HUNDREDS of sailboards, catamarans, dinghies and traditional sailing boats invading its coastal waters each summer, Brittany is one of the best places in the world for sailing. It has more than 70 marinas and mooring for a total of 22,120 pleasure boats. Sailing courses and cruises are also available.

Brittany's sailing schools, of which there are over 70, together with several dozen watersports associations, have high standards of tuition and safety. The only conditions for joining are the ability to swim 50 m (55 yds), which can be proved either by showing a certificate or by completing a test, and the production of a medical certificate of fitness.

The main sailing centres are St-Malo, St-Cast-Le Guildo, Pléneuf-Val-André, Perros-Guirec, Rade de Brest, Crozon-Morgat and Lorient. Information on sailing schools is available from the **Ligue de Voile de Bretagne** or the Comité Départemental in the relevant area of Brittany.

For coastal and ocean sailing, there are schools that offer high standards of tuition in a friendly atmosphere. Groups are organized according to participants' ability, and the schools cater for all levels, including introductory tuition for children, and theory and competitions for more experienced sailors. Information is available from **Formules Nautiques Bretagne**. During school holidays, this organization also offers residential courses for children aged six to 17, running from six days to one month. Parents wishing to accompany their children may stay in gîtes, apartments or hotels.

SURFING

CAP FRÉHEL, Le Dossen, Le Petit-Minou, La Palue, La Torche, Guidel, the Presqu'île de Quiberon and other places along the coasts of Brittany attract some 15,000 surfers each year.

Catering for all abilities, Brittany's eight surfing schools offer tuition in long-boarding, body-boarding, skim-boarding and body-surfing. They are located in Dinard, Brest, Crozon-Morgat, Audierne, La Torche, Larmor-Plage, Guidel and Plouharnel. The **ESB (École de Surf de Bretagne)** and **WSA (West Surf Association)** jointly constitute the regional surfing federation.

DIVING

ABOUT 190 diving clubs in Brittany and the Loire area are affiliated to the **Comité Inter-Régional de Plongée de Bretagne et des Pays de la Loire**.

The organization Plongée Label Bretagne has eight diving centres. Catering for children, families, individuals and groups, they offer tuition for beginners as well as tailor-made dives, underwater photography sessions, and visits to local shipwrecks. These centres are based in St-Malo, Erquy, Trébeurden, Brest, Camaret, Audierne, Lorient and Concarneau. Their details are available from the Comité Inter-Régional de Plongée.

Kayaks around the Île de Batz, in northern Finistère

Sand yachts in Plestin-les-Grèves, on the Côtes d'Armor

CANOEING

NEITHER CANOEING nor kayaking require a particularly high degree of skill. The boats are easy to manoeuvre and are ideal for exploring small bays and inlets that are accessible only from the sea.

To ensure good standards of equipment and safety, the **Comité Régional de Bretagne** has set up Point Kayak de Mer, an affiliation which now has 15 centres. These are based in St-Malo, St-Pierre de Quiberon, St-Armel, La Roche-Derrien, Paimpol, Loguivy, Plestin-les-Grèves, Ploudalmezeau, Perros-Guirec, Crozon, St-Lunaire, Pontrieux, Plouhinec, Erdeven and Moelan-sur-Mer. Brittany's canals and rivers are also worth exploring by canoe. Special kayaking and rafting centres have been set up in Lannion, Cesson-Sévigné and Inzinzac-Lochrist. The canoeing centres in Pont-Réan and Quimper-Cornouaille have both been made a Point Canoë Nature, a mark of quality bestowed by the Comité Régional de Bretagne.

SAND YACHTING

NOW A SPORT with an international following, sand yachting has several sub-disciplines, which are distinguishable by the type of equipment used.

There are over 15 sand-yachting clubs in Brittany. Most bear the name "École de Char à Voile", indicating that they are affiliated to the **Ligue de Char à Voile de Bretagne**.

Full information on sand yachting is available from this organization.

SAFETY AT SEA

SAILING IS NOT a sport for the uninitiated. A lack of knowledge or plain negligence is responsible for several accidents every year. Before setting out on a sailing trip, it is essential to obtain a local weather forecast, as weather conditions can change rapidly. Novice sailors must be supervised by professionals at all times.

The *Almanach du Marin Breton*, an annual navigational handbook for amateur yachtsmen and professional seamen, is available from all good newsagents. Published by **Œuvre du Marin Breton**, a non-profit-making association, it contains information aiding the safety of vessels, a map of local currents, tidetables, astral and radio navigation, details of weather conditions at sea and of lighthouses and beacons, administrative information, maps of harbours and nautical instructions. In case of difficulties at sea, contact **CROSS** (Centre Régional Opérationnel de Surveillance et de Sauvetage), a coastguard and sea-rescue organization.

DIRECTORY

SAILING

Formules Nautiques Bretagne
1 Rue de Kerbriant, BP 39, 29281 Brest Cedex.
((02) 98 41 59 43.

Ligue de Bretagne
1 Rue de Kerbriant, BP 39, 29281 Brest Cedex.
((02) 98 02 49 67.
W http://asso.ffv.fr/ligue-bretagne

Ligue des Pays de la Loire
44 Rue Romain-Rolland, 44000 Nantes.
((02) 40 58 61 23.

SURFING

ESB & WSA (École de Surf de Bretagne & West Surf Association)
Galerie Marchande, 56520 Guidel-Plages.
((02) 97 05 93 00.
W www.ecole-surf-bretagne.com

Comité Régional Pays de la Loire
14 Rue de la Félicité, 85800 St-Gilles.
((02) 51 54 63 16.

Fédération Française de Surf
W www.surfingfrance.com/federation.php

DIVING

Comité Inter-Régional de Plongée de Bretagne et des Pays de la Loire
39 Rue de Villeneuve, 56100 Lorient.
((02) 97 37 51 51.
W www.ffessm-cibpl.asso.fr

CANOEING

Comité Régional de Bretagne
Base Nautique, Plaine de Baud, 35 Rue Jean-Marie-Huchet 35000 Rennes.
((02) 23 20 30 14.
W www.crbck.dhs.org

Comité Régional Pays de la Loire
75 Avenue du Lac-de-Maine, 49000 Angers.
((02) 41 73 86 10.
W paysdeloire@ffcanoe.asso.fr

SAND YACHTING

Ligue de Char à Voile de Bretagne
Kervily, 56330 Pluvigner.
((02) 97 24 71 24.

USEFUL NUMBERS

CROSS Corsen (northern coast)
((02) 98 89 31 31.

CROSS Étel (southern coast)
((02) 97 55 35 35.

Œuvre du Marin Breton (publisher of *Almanach du Marin Breton*)
((02) 98 44 06 00.

SURVIVAL
GUIDE

PRACTICAL INFORMATION

A PRIME TOURIST destination, Brittany attracts large numbers of visitors during the summer. At the height of the holiday season, which runs from 14 July to 15 August, the population of Brittany's coastal resorts can triple or even quadruple. This does not detract from its appeal, as Brittany has much to offer, especially a wide range of watersports, and is well geared to the needs of visitors. However, those who choose to visit at quieter times of the year will experience more intimate aspect of the region. Out of season, Brittany's beaches are almost deserted; its prehistoric monuments seem even more mysterious; and the region's towns and cities, with their fine architecture and strong historical associations, can more easily be appreciated.

Breton headdress

The Hôtel Keraty in Dinan, which houses the tourist office

WHEN TO GO

O UTSIDE FRENCH school holidays, Brittany is reasonably quiet. The best times to come are just before the summer holiday season, and just after. These times are in June, when the season is just starting to get under way, and September, by which time many holiday-makers have gone home.

September is, in fact, the best time to come to Brittany. By then, Bretons have more time to welcome visitors, historic monuments and other places of interest are no longer crowded, and the long autumn tides create sights of unforgettable beauty.

Sign for a local tourist office

Nevertheless, Brittany in the summer offers all the pleasures of the beach, as well as walking and cycling through lush countryside. Restaurants, bars, nightclubs and festivals are then also in full swing.

VISAS

T HERE ARE NO visa requirements for EU nationals, or for visitors from the United States, Canada, Australia or New Zealand who plan to stay in France for less than three months. For trips of over three months, visas should be obtained prior to departutre from the French consulate in your own country.

Visitors from most other countries require a tourist visa. Anyone planning to study or work in France should apply to their local French consulate several months in advance.

TOURIST INFORMATION

M OST TOWNS and even some villages in Brittany have some kind of tourist information bureau. *Offices de tourisme* (tourist offices in larger towns), *syndicats d'initiative* (tourist information centres in smaller towns and villages, often located in the *mairie*) and tourist spots pool information and dispense leaflets listing local attractions and outlining sightseeing tours as well as town maps, calendars of events and information on all types of accommodation. Of course, greater tourist information facilities will be found in the coastal resorts than in small villages in the interior of Brittany. Some tourist offices can also book hotel rooms for visitors.

It is also perfectly acceptable to ask passers-by for information. Bretons are obliging and are keen to help visitors appreciate the attractions of their region. The addresses and telephone numbers of tourists offices are given at the start of each entry throughout this guide.

ANIMALS

V ISITORS MAY bring their pets into France as long as the animal is not younger than three months old, that it has been microchipped, and that it has been vaccinated against rabies. You may be required to show your pet's vaccination certificate. It is advisable to obtain up-to-date information from a veterinary practice in your own country before leaving.

TAX-FREE GOODS

V ISITORS RESIDENT outside the EU can reclaim the sales tax TVA, or VAT, on French goods if more than 175€ is spent in one shop in one day.

The Plage de l'Anse sur Suscinio at Sarzeau, in the Golfe du Morbihan

Obtain a *détaxe* receipt and take the goods (unopened) out of the country within three months. The form should be presented to customs when leaving the country. The reimbursement will be sent on to you.

Exceptions for *détaxe* rebate are food and drink, medicines, tobacco, cars and motorbikes, although tax can be reimbursed for bicycles. More information and advice are available from the **Centre des Renseignements des Douanes** (*see p256*).

DUTY-PAID AND DUTY-FREE GOODS

T HERE ARE NO longer any restrictions on the quantities of duty-paid and VAT-paid goods you can take from one EU country to another, as long as they are for your own use and not for resale. You may be asked to prove the goods are for your own use if they exceed the EU suggested quantites. If you cannot do so, the entire amount of the goods (not just the deemed excess) may be confiscated and destroyed. The suggested limits are: 10 litres of spirits, 90 litres of wine, 110 litres of beer and 800 cigarettes. Visitors under the age of 17 are not allowed to import duty-paid tobacco or alcohol.

WEBSITES

W IDE-RANGING information on Brittany, whether from a cultural, tourist or practical

point of view is available on the internet. There are general websites on Brittany (*www. toutelabretagne.com*), and others describing each region of Brittany, such as *www. centrebretagne.com*. Still others suggest tours of the region (*www.bretagne-evasions.com*) and gives lists of accommodation (*www. hotels-de-bretagne.com*). For more websites, see the Directory.

The website of the local daily newspaper *Ouest France* also gives comprehensive information on tourism in Brittany (*www.france-ouest.com*).

Bretagne Magazine and ArMen, two local magazines

ADMISSION CHARGES

F OR MUSEUMS and historic monuments, admission charges range from €1.5 to €6. Concessions are offered to students (bearing a valid student card), to people under the age of 26 (bearing an international youth card), and to people over the age of 65. There is sometimes no admission charge for children. Full details of youth and student reductions are available from youth information centres.

OPENING HOURS

M OST MUNICIPAL museums are closed on Mondays, and most national museums on Tuesdays. In the high season, many of them are open every day and do not close for lunch. It is, however, always best to telephone in advance to check a museum's opening times.

Some country churches are kept locked. By inquiring at local information centres or even by asking passers-by, you can usually find out who holds the key. Admission is usually free, except for church treasuries, crypts and cloisters.

Most shops have longer opening hours during the summer. Outside the high season, shop opening times are usually 9am–noon and 3–7pm, Tuesday to Saturday.

MEDIA

T HE MAIN NATIONAL French dailies are, from right to left on the political spectrum, *Le Figaro*, *France Soir*, *Le Monde*, *Libération* and *L'Humanité*. Like every region of France, Brittany also has good local newspapers. The daily *Ouest France* has the largest circulation. Regional magazines include the monthly *Ar Men* and the quarterly *Bretagne Magazine*. Both contain information on cultural events in Brittany.

The major nationwide TV channels are *TF1* and France 2. *TV Breizh* concentrates on Breton culture. News bulletins broadcast by *France 3* (at noon and 7pm) cover local events. For English-language media, *see p261*.

TV Breiz, focused on Breton culture

Ouest France and Le Télégramme, two local newspapers

TRAVELLING WITH CHILDREN

ALTHOUGH CHILDREN are welcome in most hotels and restaurants, it is best to check in advance that facilities are available. Hotels offering facilities for children, such as cots and baby-sitting services, are indicated in the hotels listing on pp218–27. Many restaurants provide highchairs and offer children's menus or smaller portions for children.

Family tickets on public transport and for admission to museums, chateaux and other attractions are also available. Most activities for children are organized in school holidays.

As in other countries, children in cars are legally required to travel in child car seats.

DISABLED TRAVELLERS

UNFORTUNATELY, few hotels, restaurants and tourist sites in Brittany have adequate provision for disabled visitors. However, several organizations offer assistance to disabled travellers in Brittany and can arrange holidays especially adapted to people with disabilities (see p 216 and Directory, below).

SMOKING

IN FRANCE, smoking is forbidden on public transport and in public places such as museums, historic monuments and cinemas. Although restaurants theoretically have smoking and non-smoking areas, it is rare for this to be rigidly enforced.

ELECTRICITY

THE CURRENT in France is 220v-AC with two-pin, round-pronged plugs. While some hotels provide adaptors on request, it is best to take some with you to be on the safe side, especially if you are staying in self-catering accommodation.

FRENCH TIME

FRANCE IS ONE HOUR ahead of Greenwich Mean Time (GMT) in winter, and two hours in summer. The French use the 24-hour clock; for example, 7pm is expressed as 19:00.

DIRECTORY

TOURIST INFORMATION

CIDJ (Centre d'Information et de Documentation pour la Jeunesse)
101 Quai Branly, 75015 Paris.
((01) 44 49 12 00.

CIJB (Centre Information Jeunesse Bretagne)
Maison du Champ-de-Mars,
6 Cours des Alliés,
35043 Rennes Cedex.
((02) 99 31 47 48.

CRIJ (Centre Régional Information Jeunesse)
28 Rue Calvaire, 44000 Nantes.
((02) 51 72 94 50.

Customs (Douane)
(general information)
(0825 30 82 63.

Ministère de l'Éducation Nationale
w www.education.gouv.fr

Comité Régional du Tourisme de Bretagne
1 Rue Raoul-Ponchon,
35000 Rennes.
((02) 99 36 15 15.

Comité Régional du Tourisme des Pays de la Loire
2 Rue Loire, 44200 Nantes.
((02) 40 48 24 20.

Maison de la Bretagne
203 Boulevard St-Germain,
75007 Paris.
((01) 53 63 11 50.

Secrétariat d'État au Tourisme
w www.tourisme.gouv.fr

WEBSITES

w www.bretagneworld.com
(general information on Brittany as a tourist destination)
w www.touelabretagne.com
w www.brittanytourism.com
w www.visit-bretagne.com
w www.region-bretagne.fr
(culture, current affairs, tourism and related subjects)
w www.bretagne-evasion.com
w www.france-ouest.com
w www.centrebretagne.com
w www.pays-de-dol.com
w www.morbihan.com

COMITÉS DÉPARTEMENTAUX DU TOURISME

Côtes d'Armor
29 Rue des Promenades,
22000 St-Brieuc.
((02) 96 62 72 00.

Finistère
11 Rue Théodore-Le-Hars,
29000 Quimper.
((02) 98 76 20 70.

Ille-et-Vilaine
4 Rue Jean-Jaurès, 35000 Rennes.
((02) 99 78 47 47.

Loire-Atlantique
2 Allée Baco, 44000 Nantes.
((02) 51 72 95 30.

Morbihan
P.I.B.S. Kerino, Allée Nicolas-Le-Blanc, 56000 Vannes.
((02) 97 54 06 56.

DISABLED TRAVELLERS

Association des Paralysés de France
17 Boulevard Auguste-Blanqui,
75013 Paris.
((01) 40 78 69 00.

CNRH (Comité National pour la Réadaptation des handicapés)
236 bis Rue de Tolbiac,
75013 Paris.
((01) 53 80 66 66.

EPAL
11 Rue d'Ouessant, BP 2,
29801 Brest.
((02) 98 41 84 09.
w www.epal-association.com

Handitour
4815 de Mentana,
Montréal, QC H2J-3C1,Canada.
((00) 514 598 5685
or (00) 1 800 361 4541.

Voyages ASA
21 Rue Richard Lenoir, Paris 75011
((01) 40 09 0 65

Personal Security and Health

WITH COMPETENT local authorities and efficient public services, Brittany is a safe as well as a pleasant place to visit. However, to guard against petty crime, take a few simple precautions: do not flaunt valuable possessions and never leave them in full view in a parked car; also take care in crowds, where there may be pickpockets.

PERSONAL SECURITY

LIKE THE REST of France, Brittany is not an area where violent crime is a problem, although you should take the precautions that you would at home.

If you are the victim of theft or assault, report this to the police immediately or, in small towns or villages, go to the *mairie* (town hall). If you are involved in a car accident, avoid confrontation. In potentially difficult situations, try to stay calm and speak French if you can, as this may help to defuse the situation.

EMERGENCIES

IF YOU ARE involved in, or witness, an emergency at sea, call CROSS (Centre Régional Opérationnel de Surveillance et de Sauvetage), an organization that coordinates sea rescue in Brittany. **CROSS Corsen** covers the north coasts of Brittany, and **CROSS Étel** the south coasts. These centres in turn call on the services of the French Navy or of SNSM (Société Nationale de Sauvetage en Mer), a voluntary lifeboat organization.

In the case of an accident or emergency on land, call **SAMU** (Service d'Aide Médicale d'Urgence) by dialling 15, or the **Sapeurs Pompiers** (fire brigade) by dialling 18.

Military lifeboatmen answering an emergency call

MEDICAL TREATMENT

ALL EUROPEAN UNION nationals are entitled to French social security coverage. However, medical treatment must be paid for and hospital rates vary widely. Collecting an E111 form (from post offices in the UK) before you travel will allow you to claim reimbursement. But as this does not cover all treatments, all travellers should purchase health insurance. Non-EU nationals are obliged to carry medical insurance, taken out before they arrive.

For minor health problems, go to a pharmacy (identifiable by a green cross), where the staff will give appropriate medication, or will refer you to a doctor. A card in the window will give details of the nearest duty pharmacy *(pharmacie de garde)* for night openings.

In the case of serious illness or injury, go to the casualty department *(services des urgences)* of the nearest hospital. Your consulate should also be able to recommend an English-speaking doctor.

BY THE SEA

MANY OF Brittany's beaches are patrolled by life-guards, and most are marked with flags indicating whether it is safe to swim. A green flag indicates that swimming is safe, orange that it is dangerous, and red that it is forbidden. It is absolutely crucial to respect these indications, and also to be aware of weather forecasts. Most accidents are caused by ignorance of the power of winds, currents and tides.

As elsewhere in the European Union, a blue flag indicates that the beach and the water are clean.

DIRECTORY

EMERGENCY NUMBERS

CROSS Corsen
(sea rescue, north coast)
℡ (02) 98 89 31 31.

CROSS Étel
(sea rescue, south coast)
℡ (02) 97 55 35 35.

Fire (Sapeurs Pompiers)
℡ 18.

Police and Gendarmerie
℡ 17.

Ambulance
℡ 15.

Local Weather Station
℡ 08 36 68 02 XX
(for XX, dial the number of the relevant département: Côtes d'Armor: 96; Finistère: 98; Ille-et-Vilaine 99; Loire-Atlantique: 40; Morbihan: 97.)

MAIN HOSPITALS

CÔTES D'ARMOR
Centre Hospitalier (CH)
10 Rue Marcel-Proust,
22000 St-Brieuc.
℡ (02) 96 01 71 23.

FINISTÈRE
Centre Hospitalier de Cornouaille
14 Avenue Yves-Thépot,
29000 Quimper.
℡ (02) 98 52 60 60.

Centre Hospitalier Universitaire (CHU)
5 Avenue Foch, 29200 Brest.
℡ (02) 98 22 33 33.

ILLE-ET-VILAINE
Centre Hospitalier Régional et Universitaire (CHRU)
2 Rue Henri-Le-Guilloux,
35000 Rennes.
℡ (02) 99 28 43 21.

LOIRE-ATLANTIQUE
Centre Hospitalier Régional (CHR)
1 Place Alexis-Ricordeau,
44000 Nantes.
℡ (02) 40 08 22 22.

MORBIHAN
Centre Hospitalier Bretagne Atlantique
20 Boulevard Maurice-Guillaudot,
56000 Vannes.
℡ (02) 97 01 41 41.

Banking and Local Currency

YOU MAY BRING any amount of currency into France, but anything over 7,500 euros (in cash or cheques) must be declared on arrival. The same applies when you leave. Travellers' cheques are the safest way to carry money abroad, but credit and debit cards, both of which can be used to withdraw local currency, are by far the most convenient. Bureaux de change are located at airports, large railway stations, and in some hotels and shops, but banks usually offer the best rates of exchange.

USING BANKS

MOST FRENCH BANKS have a bureau de change, but rates can vary. Most banks, even in rural areas, also now have ATMs (automatic teller machines) outside, or an indoor area that is open 24 hours a day. ATMs accept credit cards in the Visa/Carte Bleue or MasterCard groups, and debit cards (Switch, Maestro, Delta and Cirrus).

This is the quickest and easiest way of obtaining money in local currency, although a small charge will be deducted from your account for this service. Also bear in mind that ATMs may quickly run out of notes over public holidays and also before the end of ordinary weekends.

If there is no ATM, you can withdraw up to €300 per day on a Visa card at the foreign exchange counter of a bank showing the Visa sign. The bank may need to obtain telephone authorization for such withdrawals.

BUREAUX DE CHANGE

AS IN OTHER areas of France except Paris, independent bureaux de change are rare. They are, however, to be found in most major railway stations and in areas with a high density of tourists. These privately owned bureaux de change do not usually offer rates as favourable as banks. Also check their commission and any minimum charge.

Machine for reading credit cards

TRAVELLERS' CHEQUES AND CREDIT CARDS

TRAVELLERS' CHEQUES can be obtained from **American Express** and **Thomas Cook**, or from your bank. If you know that you will spend most of them, it is best to have the cheques issued in euros. American Express cheques are widely accepted in France. If cheques are exchanged at an Amex office, no commission is charged. In the case of theft, cheques are replaced at once.

Because of the high commissions charged, many French businesses do not accept the American Express credit card. The most widey used credit card is Carte Bleue/ Visa. Eurocard/MasterCard is also widely accepted.

Credit cards issued in France are now "smart cards", which means that, instead of having a magnetic strip on the back, they have a *puce* (a microchip capable of storing data). Many retailers have machines designed to read both smart cards and magnetic strips. Conventional non-French cards cannot be read in the smart card slot. Persuade the cashier to swipe the card through the magnetic reader *(bande magnétique)*. You may also be asked to tap in your PIN code *(code confidentiel)* and press the green key *(validez)* on a small keypad by the cash desk. Retailers accept payment by credit cards only for amounts above a certain figure.

BANKING HOURS

MOST BANKS in France are open for business from 8.30 or 9am to 5pm, Tuesday to Saturday, closing for lunch from noon to 2pm. Banks usually close at noon on the day before public holidays *(see p31)*.

THE EURO

Since the beginning of 2002, the euro, the European single currency, has been in use in 12 of the 15 countries of the European Union. Austria, Belgium, Eire, Finland, France, Germany, Greece, Italy, Luxembourg, the Netherlands, Portugal and Spain have all gone over to the single currency. Only the United Kingdom, Denmark and Sweden have retained their respective currencies, with an option to review their decision in the future.

Euro notes are identical across all 12 countries. Euro coins, by contrast, have one side identical (the value side), and one side unique to each country. Both notes and coins are valid and interchangeable within each of the 12 countries now using the euro.

Banknotes

Euro banknotes have seven denominations. The 5€ note (which is grey) is the smallest, followed by the 10€ (red), 20€ (blue), 50€ (orange), 100€ (green), 200€ (yellow) and 500€ (purple). All notes show the stars of the European Union.

5 euros

10 euros

20 euros

50 euros

100 euros

200 euros

500 euros

Coins

Euro coins have eight denominations: 1€ and 2€; and 50 cents, 20 cents, 10 cents, 5 cents, 2 cents and 1 cent. The 1€ and 2€ coins are silver and gold. The 50-cent, 20-cent and 10-cents coins are gold. The 5-cent, 2-cent and 1-cent coins are bronze.

2 euros

1 euro

50 cents

20 cents

10 cents

5 cents

2 cents

1 cent

Communications

FRENCH TELECOMMUNICATIONS, run by France Télécom, are reliable and efficient. Public telephones are located in most public places – frequently in the central squares of towns and villages – and post offices *(bureaux de poste)* are identified by the blue-on-yellow La Poste sign. La Poste used to be called PTT *(postes, télégraphes, téléphones)*, so road signs often still indicate "PTT".

Foreign-language newspapers are available in most large towns and major resorts in Brittany. Some national television channels and radio stations broadcast foreign-language programmes.

A distinctive yellow French mailbox

TELEPHONING IN FRANCE

TO USE A payphone *(cabine)*, you usually need a phonecard *(télécarte)*. Sold in newsagents *(maisons de la presse)* and tobacconists *(tabacs)*, these are available in 50 or 120 telephone units, and are simple to use. For local calls, a unit lasts up to six minutes. Many public telephones now also accept credit cards (with a PIN number). Few payphones take coins.

Cheap rates, giving 50 per cent lower call charges, operate from 7pm to 8am Monday to Friday, from midnight to 8am and from noon to midnight on Saturday, and all day Sunday. In cafés, payphones are token-operated and are reserved for the use of the café's customers.

Post offices have telephone booths *(cabines)* where you make the call first then pay at the counter. Long-distance calls made in this way are much cheaper than from hotels, where hefty surcharges are often added.

The Home Direct, or *pays directe,* calling service allows you to book a call through an operator in your own country, and to pay by credit card or by reversing the charges (collect call). Sometimes, you can also call a third country by this method.

All French telephone numbers have 10 digits. The first two digits indicate the region: 01 indicates Paris and the Île de France; 02 the northwest (Brittany falls into this region); 03, the northeast; 04, the southeast (including Corsica); and 05, the southwest. When phoning from outside France, do not dial the initial zero.

USING A PHONECARD TELEPHONE

1 Lift the receiver and wait for the dialling tone.

2 Insert the *télécarte,* arrow side up.

3 The display will show how many units are stored on the card and will then tell you to dial.

4 Key in the number and wait to be connected.

5 If you want to make another call, do not replace the receiver; simply press the green follow-on call button.

6 When you have finished the call, replace the receiver. The card will emerge from the slot.

FRANCE TELECOM
600 AGENCES
PARTOUT
EN FRANCE

TELECARTE 50

FRANCE TELECOM

MOBILE PHONES

MOST NEW MOBILE phones brought in from another European or Mediterranean country can be used in France exactly as at home. However, US-based mobiles (cell phones) need to be "triple band" to be usable in France. Mobile phones are also readily available for hire in France.

Remember that making or receiving international calls via a mobile phone is very expensive for both parties.

USING LA POSTE

THE POSTAL SERVICE in France is fast and reliable. However, it is not cheap, especially for sending parcels abroad, since all surface-mail services have been discontinued.

At La Poste, postage stamps (timbres) are sold singly or in books (carnets) of ten. Stamps for ordinary letters within the EU are also sold in newsagents and tobacconists. Letters are posted in yellow mail boxes, which often have separate slots for the town you are in, the département and other destinations (autres destinations).

For a small collection fee, post offices also provide a mail-holding service (poste restante), so that you can receive mail care of post offices anywhere in France.

Post offices are usually open from 8am to 7pm Monday to Friday, often closing at lunchtime, and 8am to noon on Saturdays. Some of the larger post offices also have ATMs from which cash can be withdrawn with a banker's card (see p 258).

USING MINITEL

MINITEL, USE OF which is free in post offices, provides a variety of services through a screen and keyboard connected to the

A cybercafé, one of a growing number in Brittany's larger towns

telephone line. To use Minitel, press the telephone symbol and enter the Minitel number and code. For directory information, press the telephone symbol and key in 3611. When beeping starts, press Connexion/Fin. Specify the service or name of the supplier required. Enter the town or area. Press Envoi to search. To disconnect, press Veille or Connexion/Fin.

INTERNET ACCESS

AS ELSEWHERE in France, the internet is widely accessible in Brittany, in internet cafés and in many hotels. The French modem socket is incompatible with US and UK plugs. Although adaptors are available, it is cheaper to buy a French modem lead.

NEWSPAPERS

IN RESORTS AND large cities, many British newspapers are available on the day of publication. Some, like Financial Times Europe and Guardian Europe, are European editions. Others may arrive slightly later. English-language publications include The Weekly Telegraph, Guardian International, USA Today, Economist, Newsweek and International Herald Tribune. For details of French newspapers, see p255.

TV AND RADIO

THE POPULAR subscription and satellite channels in France (collectively known as TPS, or télévision par satellite) include English-language

An automatic teller machine at a post office

MTV, CNN, Sky and BBC World. English-language films on French television are generally subtitled when first shown; dubbed versions appear later.

UK radio stations can be picked up in France, including Radio 4 during the day (648 AM or 198 Long Wave). On the same wavelength, BBC World Service broadcasts through the night. Voice of America can be found at 90.5, 98.8 and 102.4 FM. Radio France International (738 AM) gives daily news in English from 3 to 4pm. For details of French television, see p255.

USEFUL NUMBERS

Emergencies: 17

Directory enquiries: 12.

International directory enquiries: 32 12.

International telegrams: 0800 33 44 11.

Home Direct: 0800 99, followed by the country code (preceded by 00 in most cases).

Calling France: from the UK and US: 00 33; from Australia: 00 11 33. Omit the first 0 of the French area code.

International calls: dial 00 (wait for dialling tone) + country code + area code (omit initial 0) + the number. Country codes: Australia: 61; Canada & USA: 1; Eire: 353; New Zealand: 64; UK 44.

TRAVEL INFORMATION

RITTANY CAN easily be reached by air or, via the Channel Tunnel, by train, car or coach. There are flights from London direct to Brittany's two international airports, Rennes and Nantes. An alternative, with more frequent services, is to fly to Paris and catch a connecting flight

A Brit'Air plane, from a fleet serving Brittany

or train to a choice of destinations in Brittany. The whole region is served by fast rail connections from Paris, and, linked by the Autoroute de l'Ouest, it is no more than three hours' drive from the French capital. There are also regular ferry services direct to Brittany from the UK.

Passengers in the check-in hall at Nantes-Atlantique airport

ARRIVING BY AIR

RITTANY HAS two international airports – Nantes and Rennes – and seven domestic airports, including an aerodrome. From the UK, there are flights direct to Rennes, Nantes and Dinard, and flights to Paris with onward connections to Nantes, Rennes, Dinard, Brest, Quimper, Lannion, St-Brieuc, Morlaix and Lorient.

British Airways operates four flights a day from London-Heathrow to Nantes.

AIRPORT	INFORMATION	DISTANCE FROM CITY	TAXI TO CITY
CÔTES D'ARMOR			
Lannion	((02) 96 05 82 22	12 km (7 miles)	8€ to Lannion
FINISTÈRE			
Brest-Guipavas	((02) 98 32 01 00	5 km (3 miles)	15€ to Brest
Morlaix-Ploujean	((02) 98 62 16 09	3 km (2 miles)	9€ (weekdays), 12€ (weekends) to Morlaix
Quimper-Cornouailles	((02) 98 94 30 30	7 km (4 miles)	15€ to Quimper
ILLE-ET-VILAINE			
Dinard-Pleurtuit-St-Malo	((02) 99 46 18 46	10 km (6 miles) from Dinard 15 km (9 miles) from St-Malo	11€ (weekdays), 14€ (weekends) to Dinard 15€ (weekdays), 23€ weekends to St-Malo
Rennes	((02) 99 29 60 00	8 km (5 miles)	11–12€ (weekdays), 15€ (weekends)
LOIRE-ATLANTIQUE			
Nantes-Atlantique	((02) 40 84 80 00	12 km (7 miles)	23€ to Nantes
MORBIHAN			
Aérodrome de Belle-Île-en-Mer	((02) 97 31 83 09	5 km (3 miles)	9–14€ to Le Palais
Lorient-Lan-Bihoué	((02) 97 87 21 50	10 km (6 miles)	12–14€ (weekdays), 20€ (weekends) to Lorient

Ryanair's daily flights from London-Heathrow and London-Gatwick to Dinard-Pleurtuit-St-Malo also take in the Channel Islands.

Many direct flights from London to Paris are provided by British Airways, **British Midland**, **Ryanair**, **buzz**, **easyJet** and **Air France**.

From the US, there are flights direct to Paris from about 20 cities, mainly with **American**, **Delta**, United, Northwest, Continental, Virgin and British Airways. From Canada, Air France and Air Canada fly direct to Paris. During the summer, **Air Transat** also operates flights from Toronto and Montreal to Nantes. **Qantas** provides connecting flights from Australia and New Zealand.

CONNECTIONS FROM PARIS

FROM PARIS-ORLY and Paris-Roissy-Charles-de-Gaulle, there are several flights a day to Brest, Lorient, Quimper, Lannion, Rennes, St-Brieuc and Nantes. They are operated by **Air France** via **Brit'Air** and **Regional** (the parent company that runs Regional Air Lines, Flandre Air and Proteus).

From Brussels, it is also possible to travel to Rennes on a combined Air France-Thalys (flight and high-speed-train) ticket.

Finist'Air flies from Brest to the Île d'Ouessant. **Air Lib** flies from Lille and Mulhouse to Nantes, and from Paris to Lannion.

Brittany is also served by rail links from Paris, including a TGV (high-speed-train) service to Rennes and Nantes (see pp264–5).

AIR FARES

WHETHER THEY are provided by the no-frills budget airlines or the classic, full-service major airlines, flights to France are usually more expensive during school holidays and at half-terms, especially in summer. However, APEX (Advance Purchase) fares give substantial savings. APEX fares can be ideal for a vacation, as they require you to pre-book outward and return flights that cannot be changed or cancelled.

Competition between airlines has resulted in other advantageous reductions. All airline companies usually give reductions to families, to people under the age of 25, to students under the age of 27, to retired people over the age of 60, and to groups of at least six people.

Through its range of *Tempo* fares, Air France offers four levels of reduction: the further ahead you book (up to 15 days before departure), the greater the reduction offered. Children under the age of two travel free, although they are not allocated a seat of their own, and fares for children under 12 are subject to a 60 per cent reduction.

AIRPORT CONNECTIONS

NONE OF BRITTANY's airports are further than 15 km (9 miles) from the centre of the city that they serve, and

most are much nearer. All the airports are connected to the city centre by regular bus services.

It is also possible to travel from the airport by taxi. The table opposite gives distances between airports and town centres, as well as average taxi fares.

AIRPORT CAR HIRE

AVIS, BUDGET, Europcar, Hertz and other major international car hire companies have offices either in Brittany's airports themselves, or in the nearest town. The central-booking contact details of car hire companies operating in Brittany are given on p267.

Terminal at Rennes-St-Jacques airport

Travelling by Train

IT IS EASY and enjoyable to travel in France by train, and this is also one of the best ways both of reaching and of travelling around Brittany. While both Nantes and Rennes are served by TGVs (high-speed trains) from Paris, *trains corail* (intercity trains) link Brittany's main towns, and TER (local express trains) provide connections to smaller towns and villages in the region. Areas of Brittany without a rail service can be reached by bus (SNCF runs a fleet of modern buses, which are free to rail-pass holders) and sometimes by boat.

Automatic ticket machine

ARRIVING BY TRAIN

FOR TRAVELLERS arriving from Britain, **Eurostar** gives access to the entire French rail network. At Lille, two hours by Eurostar from London, passengers can change to onward TGVs (high-speed trains), which bypass Paris and continue southwest to Brittany.

Three hours from London Waterloo, Eurostar arrives at Paris Gare du Nord. This is also the terminus for high-speed Thalys trains from Brussels, Amsterdam and Cologne.

Trains for Brittany leave from Gare Montparnasse, in the southwest of Paris.

HIGH-SPEED TRAINS

TRAINS RUNNING on new high-speed lines are the pride of the SNCF (the national rail company). Note that in some towns, the new TGV station is separate from the main station, and can be out of the town centre.

Journey times by TGV from Paris are 2 hours to Rennes or Nantes, 2 hours 35 minutes to St-Nazaire, 2 hours 50 minutes to St-Brieuc, 3 hours to Vannes, 3 hours 30 minutes to Lorient, and 4 hours 10 minutes to Brest or Quimper. The journey time from Paris to St-Malo by ordinary train is 3 hours. Other direct TGV links are Lille–Rennes (3 hours 50 minutes), Lille–Nantes (3 hours 50 minutes) and Lyon–Nantes (4 hours 30 minutes).

Advance booking is compulsory on TGV trains, and is available up to five minutes before departure time. The inspector will then allocate you a seat.

Special family coaches (*Espace Famille*), located in second-class, non-smoking coaches of TGVs, consist of four facing seats with a table in the middle, separated off by half-doors. The nursery nearby is equipped with a changing mat and facilities for heating babies' bottles.

BOOKING WITHIN FRANCE

AUTOMATIC TICKET and reservation machines (*billeterie automatique*) are found at main stations. They take credit cards or coins. You can also check train times and fares and make reservations by phoning **SNCF**, by using the Minitel system (see p261), or via the SNCF website (see p265). Tickets may be purchased by credit card, then collected at the station.

As with all travel by TGV, reservations are compulsory for all train journeys on public holidays, and for a *couchette* or *siège inclinable* (reclinable seat). Both reservation and rail tickets must be validated in a *composteur* machine before boarding the train. Failure to do so can result in a fine.

BOOKING OUTSIDE FRANCE

TICKETS AND PASSES for rail travel (including Motorail) in France can be booked and paid for in advance direct from SNCF. Book online on their website (allow 7 days for ticket delivery), or by phone on 00 33 836 353 539, a special **SNCF** bookings line for English speakers (7am to 10pm daily). You can pay for your tickets by credit card. Online booking is also possible on the **Eurostar** website.

A TGV train, providing swift and comfortable passenger transport

TRAVEL INFORMATION

Foreign rail travel agents like **Rail Europe** can take bookings by post, by phone, online, or in person at their London shop. Rail Europe bookings must be made between 14 and 60 days in advance, and a small charge is made for credit card bookings. Note that reservations made in another country may be difficult or impossible to change in France; any alterations to your booking should be made by the original issuing company.

Pontrieux railway station, served by a steam train during the summer

TICKETS AND PASSES

THERE IS A basic fare for each rail journey, but numerous discounts are available on French trains. These reduced fares and travel passes are for certain categories of passengers. Substantial fare discounts are offered to people over 60 (*Découverte Senior*), to those under 26 (*Découverte 12–25*), for up to four adults travelling with a child under 12 (*Découverte Enfant Plus*), or anyone booking more than 30 days or more than 8 days in advance (*Découverte J30* or *J8*).

Rail passes give even larger fare reductions. Strictly for non-residents, the France Railpass can only be bought outside France. It gives unlimited travel for 3 to 7 days. If you are planning to travel in other countries too, choose Eurodomino passes for individual countries, allowing travel between 3 and 8 days, or Interail, which gives 12-, 22- or 30-day travel for under-26s (or, for a higher price, over 26s) in different zones of Europe. When purchasing a rail ticket – whether in France or abroad – it is also possible to pre-book a car (*Train + Auto*) or bike (*Train + Vélo*)

to await you at your destination, or even a hotel (*Train + Hôtel*).

Discounts and passes are not valid on certain dates and at certain times. The SNCF *Calendrier Voyageurs* (Travellers' Calendar), available at all stations, shows blue and white periods. Almost all fare reductions are valid only in blue periods. The white period is normally only Monday 5–10am and Friday and Sunday 3–8pm.

For 9€ the Pass Bretagne allows unlimited travel in Brittany on TER trains and SNCF buses on Saturdays, mid-June to mid-September.

TIMETABLES

FRENCH RAILWAY timetables change twice a year, in May and September. Stations

sell the SNCF's *Ville-à-Ville* timetable, which details main-line routes nationwide. SNCF also sells regional timetables and issues free leaflets giving information on travelling with children, reduced fares, train travel for disabled people and the TGV network.

DIRECTORY

Eurostar
London Waterloo International
08705 186 186.
www.eurostar.com

Rail Europe
179 Piccadilly, London W1V 0BA
08705 848 848.
(020) 7647 4900.
www.raileurope.co.uk

www.britcities.com
(non UK European travel)

Rail Europe Group
Westchester One, 44 South Broadway, White Plains, New York, NY 10601.
08705 848 848.

SNCF France
(00 33 0) 836 353 539 (English) Minitel: 3615 SNCF.
www.sncf.fr.com

Passengers in the ticket hall at Rennes railway station

The railway station at Brest

2 6 5

Brittany by Road

B RITTANY HAS an excellent road network. Roads linking its major towns and cities consist both of motorways, which are toll-free, and of fast dual carriageways. By following Brittany's major roads and more especially its minor roads, visitors will discover picturesque villages and remote places of interest. Many of the coast roads command spectacular views.

Road sign for a roundabout

A minor road in Brittany with a magnificent view of the sea

GETTING TO FRANCE BY CAR OR COACH

T HERE IS A GOOD choice of car-ferry services from various destinations in the UK *(see pp268–9)*. You can profit from discount fares for short breaks, a flat rate for a car with up to five passengers. You can take your car on the **Eurotunnel** shuttle through the Channel Tunnel. **Eurolines** provides a coach service to Brittany direct from the UK or via Paris.

THE CHANNEL TUNNEL

T HE CHANNEL Tunnel is a 52-km (31-mile) rail tunnel that runs beneath the English Channel between Britain and France. Its English terminal is at Folkestone, in Kent, and the French terminal is at Sangatte, 3 km (2 miles) from Calais. The terminal leads directly onto motorways – the M20 in England and the A16 in France.

MOTORING IN BRITTANY

M OTORWAYS *(autoroutes)* lead directly into Brittany from Caen, in the north, Rennes in the east and Nantes in the south. The main route into Brittany from Paris is the A11 motorway to Le Mans, followed by the A81 motorway, then the M157 to Rennes (see road map on inside back cover).

Once off the motorways, drivers can use the efficient network of major roads *(routes nationales)*, which link Brittany's major towns, as well as the more scenic minor roads *(routes départementales)*. Roads from Paris can become congested at weekends and at the beginning and end of summer holidays. The worst times are from mid-July to the end of August. In Brittany itself, congestion on the roads is rare. However, traffic can sometimes build up in coastal resorts towards the end of the day, when people start to leave the beaches and when offices close.

D 50
CALLAC
KALLAG

D 31
MOUSTÉRU
MOUSTERUZ

Road signs in French and Breton

WHAT TO TAKE

M ANY MOTOR INSURERS now offer a green card (which gives full cover abroad) as a free extension with fully comprehensive policies. The AA, RAC and Europ Assistance also have special policies providing a rescue and recovery service.

It is compulsory to take the original registration document for the car, a current insurance certificate, or green card, and a valid driving licence. You should also carry a passport or National ID card. A sticker showing the car's country of registration must be displayed near the rear number plate. The head-lights of right-hand-drive cars must be adjusted for left-hand driving or have deflectors fitted (kits are available at most ports). You must also carry spare headlight bulbs and a red warning triangle if your car does not have hazard warning lights.

RULES OF THE ROAD

U NLESS ROAD signs indicate otherwise, *priorité a droite* means that you must give way to vehicles joining the road from the right, except on roundabouts or from private property. Most major roads outside built-up areas have the right of way indicated by a *passage protégé* sign.

Contrary to convention in the UK, flashing headlights in France means that the driver is claiming the right of way.

Other French motoring rules include the compulsory wearing of seat belts, the use

One of several fast dual carriageways in Brittany

of booster seats for children under 10, and the obligation to carry a valid driving licence or identification papers at all times. For further details, consult the **RAC** website.

SPEED LIMITS AND FINES

SPEED LIMITS in France are as follows:

On *autoroutes*: 130 km/h (80 mph); 110 km/h (70 mph) when it rains.

On dual carriageways: 110 km/h (70 mph); 90–100 km/h (55–60 mph) when it rains.

On other roads: 90 km/h (55 mph); 80 km/h (50 mph) when it rains.

In towns: 50 km/h (30 mph), unless marked otherwise. In some places it may be lower. Normal limits may not always be indicated.

On-the-spot fines of around 150€ are summarily levied for not stopping at a Stop sign, for overtaking where forbidden, or other driving offences. Drink-driving can lead to confiscation of the vehicle or even imprisonment.

BUYING PETROL

DIESEL FUEL (*gazole* or *gasoil*) is comparatively cheap in France and is sold everywhere. Leaded petrol (*super*) and unleaded petrol (*sans plomb*) are more expensive, and leaded is now sometimes hard to find. Large supermarkets sell all of them at a discount. Filling up the tank is known as *faire le plein*. Petrol stations in rural areas may be closed on Sundays.

Logos of three major car hire companies

AUTOROUTE TOLLS

WHEN YOU join an *autoroute à péage* (tolled motorway), collect a ticket from the machine as you pass through the toll point. This identifies your starting point on the *autoroute*. You do not pay

until you reach an exit toll. You are charged according to the distance travelled and the type of vehicle. While at least two booths per toll point are

A pay-and-display ticket machine, widely used in town car parks

always manned by attendants, automatic machines can also be used. These take coins, and will give change, and also accept credit cards.

CAR HIRE

ALL THE MAIN international car-hire companies operate in France. They have offices either in Brittany's main airports or in the centre of major towns.

It is worth ringing round before you leave for France as there are many special offers for rentals booked and prepaid in the UK or USA.

For car hire booked in combination with flights, your travel agent can usually organize a good deal. SNCF (the French state railway) offers combined train and car-hire fares. Phone **Rail Europe** for information *(see p265)*.

For non-EU residents planning to drive in France for a minimum of three weeks, the best option is the short-term tax-free purchase-and-buy-back service (TT leasing) offered by Citröen, Peugeot and Renault.

PARKING

FINDING A PARKING space in coastal towns in Brittany during the summer can be difficult. However, almost all large towns have car parks with a pay-and-display system (*horodateur*). Villages have free, usually very central, parking areas.

Brittany by Boat

Breton motorboat

WITH FREQUENT FERRY crossings from the UK to Roscoff, St-Malo and Cherbourg, as well as destinations further north along the French coast, Brittany is easy to reach by sea. As with the rail shuttle through the Channel Tunnel, travelling by ferry allows you the convenience of bringing your own car.

With Belle-Île, the Île d'Ouessant and the Golfe du Morbihan among its most picturesque attractions, Brittany also invites exploration by boat. A wide range of boat trips are on offer. There are regular sea links to Brittany's many islands, and trips out to sea in old sailing ships. Sailing along Brittany's rivers and canals, which are now reserved for pleasure boats, is a particularly pleasant way of experiencing the riches and variety of Brittany's cultural heritage.

Motorboat approaching the landing stage at Roscoff

Passengers disembarking on the Île de Sein

CHANNEL FERRIES

IN ADDITION TO the Eurotunnel vehicle-carrying rail shuttles *(see p264)*, there are several ship or catamaran crossings between the UK and Continental ports.

P&O Stena runs between Dover and Calais, with frequent crossings (1 hr 30 mins). **P&O Portsmouth** runs between Portsmouth and Le Havre (5 hrs). **Condor** has a fast ferry from Poole to St-Malo (4 hrs 30 mins). **Brittany Ferries** runs a service from Portsmouth to St-Malo (9 hrs), a service from Portsmouth to Caen (6 hrs), and a service from Plymouth to Roscoff (6 hrs). From Poole to Cherbourg, Brittany Ferries

---

DIRECTORY

LINKS TO THE ISLANDS

Compagnie des Îles
(Arz)
☎ *(02) 97 46 18 19.*

Compagnie Navix (Arz)
☎ *(02) 97 46 60 00.*

Vedettes de Bréhat
(Bréhat)
☎ *(02) 96 55 73 47.*

Armein (Batz)
☎ *(02) 98 61 77 75.*

Finistérienne (Batz)
☎ *(02) 98 61 78 87.*

Penn-Ar-Bed Brest
(Molène, Ouessant, Sein)
☎ *(02) 98 80 80 80.*

Vedette Biniou-II
(Sein)
☎ *(02) 98 70 21 15.*

SMNN
(Belle-Île, Île de Groix, Île de Hoëdic, Île de Houat)
☎ *0820 056 000.*

Vedettes de l'Odet
(Îles de Glénan)
☎ *(02) 98 57 00 58.*

Izenah Croisière
(Île aux Moines)
☎ *(02) 97 26 31 45.*

CANAL & RIVER TRIPS

CÔTES D'ARMOR
Vedettes de Guerlédan
22530 Caurel.
☎ *(02) 96 28 52 64.*

Vedette Jaman 4
22108 Dinan.
☎ *(02) 96 39 28 41.*

FINISTÈRE
Aulne Loisirs-Plaisance
29520 Châteauneuf-du-Faou.
☎ *(02) 98 73 28 63.*

ILLE-ET-VILAINE
Péniche St-Christophe
35600 Redon.
☎ *(02) 99 71 46 03.*

Cotre Corsaire Le Renard
35408 St-Malo.
☎ *(02) 99 40 53 10.*

LOIRE-ATLANTIQUE
Bateaux Nantais
44000 Nantes.
☎ *(02) 40 14 51 14.*

MORBIHAN
L'Étoile du Blavet
56650 Inzinzac-Lochrist.
☎ *(02) 97 85 37 01.*

FERRIES

Brittany Ferries
☎ *0825 828 828.*
W *www.brittany-ferries.fr*

Condor Ferries
☎ *(02) 99 200 300.*
W *www.condorferries.co.uk*

Hoverspeed
☎ *0820 0035 55.*
☎ *01304 865 000 in the UK.*
W *www.hoverspeed.co.uk*

P&O Portsmouth
☎ *0825 013 013.*
W *www.poportsmouth.com*

P&O Stena
☎ *03 21 46 10 10.*
W *www.posl.com*

has a conventional ship (4 hrs 30 mins), and a fast ferry, the *Condor Vitesse* (2 hrs 15 mins).

Hoverspeed operates Super Seacat high-speed catamarans from Dover to Calais (45 minutes) and from Newhaven to Dieppe.

BOAT AND CANAL TRIPS

THERE ARE many opportunities for visitors to take boats trips out to sea, usually in an old restored sailing boat and usually lasting either a full day or half a day. **Cotre Corsaire Le Renard** organizes trips in the Baie de St-Malo of one or several days. Various suggestions for boat trips out to sea appear at the head of the relevant entries in this guide. Information on other boat trips and cruises is available from tourist offices.

Brittany has 600 km (375 miles) of canals and navigable rivers. There are several major routes. One, an 85-km (53-mile) trip along the Ille-et-Rance canal and the Vilaine river, goes from St-Malo, in the north, to La Roche-Bernard, in the south. Others are the Nantes–Brest canal (360 km/225 miles long), which joins the Erdre, Oust and Aulne rivers, the Blavet valley (Lorient to Pontivy), and St-Nazaire to Nantes, along the Loire.

The small harbour at Dinan, on the Rance river

SEA LINKS TO THE ISLANDS

BRITTANY'S LARGEST islands all have sea links with the nearest harbour on the mainland. The routes are: Vannes–Île d'Arz (15 mins); Pointe de l'Arcouest–Île de Bréhat (15 mins); St-Quay-Portrieux–Île de Bréhat (1 hr 15 mins); Roscoff–Île de Batz (15 mins); Le Conquet/Brest–Île d'Ouessant (1 hr/ 2 hrs 30 mins); Le Conquet/Brest–Île Molène (30 mins/1 hr 45 mins); Crozon/Audierne–Île de Sein (1 hr); Lorient–Belle-Île (1 hr 30 mins); Quiberon–Belle-Île (45 mins); Lorient–Groix (45 mins); Concarneau–Îles de Glénan (1 hr); Bénodet/Loctudy–Îles de Glénan (1 hr 30 mins); Quiberon–Houat (45 mins) Quiberon–Hoëdic (1 hr 10 mins/ 1 hr 25 mins); Port-Blanc–Île aux Moines (5 mins).

General Index

Acknowledgments

DORLING KINDERSLEY would like to thank the
following people and institutions whose
contributions and assistance have made the
preparation of this book possible.

MAIN CONTRIBUTORS

GAËTAN DU CHATENET
Entomologist, ornitholist, corresponding
member of the Muséum National d'Histoire
Naturelle de Paris, draughtsman and miniature
painter, Gaëtan du Chatenet is the author of
many works published by Delachaux & Niestlé
and Gallimard.

JEAN-PHILIPPE FOLLET
Jean-Philippe Follet, who was born and
brought up in the Morlaix area, studied at the
Faculté de Celtique in Rennes and at the Centre
de Recherches Bretonnes et Celtiques in Brest.
He works as a writer and translator.

JEAN-YVES GENDILLARD
The son of Breton parents, Jean-Yves
Gendillard is a teacher. He has a special
interest in Brittany and in religious art. He has
spent a considerable amount of time in southern
Finistère, and has a particular knowledge of
the chapels and calvaries of that area.

ÉRIC GIBORY
Born in St-Malo, Éric Gibory spent his childhood
and adolescence there. He has helped to
organize cultural events, is the author of four
Guides Bleus published by Hachette and has
contributed to several travel magazines.

RENÉE GRIMAUD
A specialist in tourism, Renée Grimaud has
contributed to many travel guides and has
edited several illustrated books on the regions
of France, notably on the Loire and its
chateaux. A native of the Vendée, she has a
detailed knowledge of the Loire region and of
Brittany, which she visits regularly.

GEORGES MINOIS
A senior history teacher at the Lycée Renan in
St-Brieuc and the holder of a doctorate, George
Minois is also the author of 30 books, including
several on Brittany, such as *Nouvelle Histoire
de la Bretagne, Anne de Bretagne* and *Du
Guesclin*, published by Fayard.

OTHER CONTRIBUTORS
Sophie Berger, Vanessa Besnard, Isabelle
De Jaham, Marie-Christine Degos, Mathilde
Huyghes-Despointes, Sonia Rocton, Sarah
Thurin and Sébastien Tomasi.

PHOTOGRAPHY
Philippe Giraud.

**STUDIO PHOTOGRAPHY AND
ADDITIONAL PHOTOGRAPHY**
Anne Chopin.

PICTURE RESEARCH
Marie-Christine Petit.

CARTOGRAPHY
Fabrice Le Goff.

ADDITIONAL CARTOGRAPHY
Quadrature Créations.

ILLUSTRATIONS
FRANÇOIS BROSSE
Architectural drawings, Street-by-Street maps
and drawings pp56–7, 78–9, 108—9, 116–17,
158–9, 166–7, 184–5, 186–7.

ANNE DELAUNAY-VERNHES
Architectural drawings pp60–1, 104–5, 122–3,
162–3, 192–3, 208–9.

ÉRIC GEOFFROY
Illustrations on "Exploring" and "At a Glance"
maps, on small town plans and tour maps
pp50–1, 54–5, 59, 76, 81, 88–9, 98, 103, 114–15,
126–7, 133, 140–1, 144–5, 161, 172–3, 182–3,
189, 198–9, 202–3, 205.

EMMANUEL GUILLON
Façades, perspectives and artwork pp16–17,
18–19, 104–5, 122–3, 151, 192–3, 208–9.

GUÉNOLA DE SANDOL
Artwork pp60–1, 162–3.

PROOFREADERS
Cate Casey, Emily Hatchwell.

INDEX
Lucilla Watson.

SPECIAL ASSISTANCE
M. Alexandre and M. Tournaire at Service
Départemental de l'Architecture et du Patrimoine
du Finistère; Mme Delmotte, M. Charles-Tanguy
Leroux and M. Christian Gerardot of DRAC de
Bretagne; Marie Godicheau of the Service
Météorologique de Rennes; M. Guillet, Château
des Ducs de Bretagne; M. Job an Irien of Éditions
Minihi-Levenez; M. le Curé Louis Le Bras and
M. Paul Nemar of the church at Crozon; Henri
Le Roux (butter toffees, Quiberon); Philippe Le
Stum, curator at the Musée Départemental Breton
in Quimper; Mathieu Lefèvre of the festival
Étonnants Voyageurs, St-Malo; the mayor of
St-Malo; Florent Patron of Éditions Coop Breizh;
M. Alain-Charles Perrot (Parlement de Bretagne);
Mme Marie-Suzanne de Ponthaud (head archi-
tect, Cathédrale St-Tugdual, Tréguier);
Océanopolis, Brest; public relations
department, Banque de France; information
service, *Bretagne Magazine*; public relations
department, La Poste; public relations
department of the city of St-Malo for the
Quai des Bulles festival; press office, Air
France; press office, *Transmusicales*, Rennes;
ADA; Musée des Vieux Outils, Tinténiac;
Musée des Terre-Neuvas, Fécamp. Armor Lux
(clothing, Quimper); Saint-James (clothing,
Saint-James); Phytomer (beauty products, St-
Malo); Thalado (beauty products, Roscoff);
Verreries de Bréhat; the shop Quimper-Faïence
de Paris; Fisselier (traditionally made liqueurs,
Chantepie).

PHOTOGRAPHY PERMISSIONS
THE PUBLISHER would like to thank those individuals who gave permission to photograph on their premises:

Mme Martine Abgrall, for the alignments at Carnac; Mme Martine Becus, at the Château des Rochers Sévigné in Vitré; Florence and Marc Benoît, at the Hôtel La Reine Hortense in Dinard; Mme Burnot, curator at the Musée du Château de Dinan; M. de Calbiac, at the Manoir de Kerazan; Mme Caprini and Lan Mafart, at the Librairie Caplan in Guimaec; Mme Gaillot, at the Musée de la Pêche in Concarneau; M. and Mme Gautier, in Plouezoc'h; M. Bernard Guillet and Christelle Goldet, at the Château des Ducs de Bretagne in Nantes; M. Hommel, of the Musée de l'Automobile in Lohéac; M. Patrick Jourdan, curator at the Musée des Jacobins in Morlaix; M. Le Goff, of the Musée du Léon in Lesneven; M. Bernard Lefloc'h, of the Musée Bigouden in Pont-L'Abbé; Mme Lilia Millier, at the Hôtel Castel Marie Louise in La Baule; Mme Françoise Louis, for the Château de Suscinio; M. Mézin, curator at the Musée de la Compagnie des Indes in Port-Louis; Mme Quintin, at the Musée de la Fraise in Plougastel-Daoulas; Mme Riskine, curator at the Musée de la Préhistoire in Carnac; Mme de Rohan, at the Château de Josselin; Mme de Sagazan, at the Manoir de Traonjoly in Cléder; Mme Michèle Sallé, at the Château de la Hunaudaye; M. Sanchez, at the Parlement de Bretagne in Rennes; M. Jacques Thorel, at the Auberge Bretonne in Roche-Bernard; M. Bernard Verlingue, curator at the Musée de la Faïence in Quimper; Faïencerie H. B. Henriot in Quimper. The staff at the Château de Kerjean; the staff at the brasserie La Cigale in Nantes; the director at the Parc Animalier de Menez-Meur; Camac Harps in Mouzeil; the staff at the Maison de la Mariée on the Île de Fédrun; the owner of the Château de Goulaine; the shop L'Épée de Bois in Paris. The publisher would also like to thank all those who gave permission to photograph at various other shops, restaurants, cafés, hotels, churches and publics places too numerous to mention individually.

PICTURE CREDITS
Every effort has been made to trace the copyright holders and we apologize in advance for any unintentional omissions. We would be pleased to insert the appropriate acknowledgments in any subsequent edition of this publication.

t = top; tl = top left; tlc = top left centre; tc = top centre; trc = top right centre; tr = top right; cra = centre right above; cl = centre left; c = centre; cr = centre right; clb = centre left below; cb = centre below; crb = centre right below; bl = below left; b = below; bc = below centre; bcl = below centre left; bcr = below centre right; br = below right.

The publisher would like to thank the following individuals, companies and picture libraries for permission to reproduce their photographs:

6–7: RMN/R.-G. Ojeda. *Port Breton,* Paul Bellanger-Adhémar. Château-Musée, Nemours. 7: Hachette/drawing by F. Benoist et Sabatier. 11a: Musée Départemental Breton. *Souvenirs de la Bretagne,* Louis Caradec (1850). 12c: Béghin-Say. 14tl: Jacana/S. Chevalier. 14tr: Jacana/S. Cordier. 14cl: Jacana/C. Bahr. 14cr: Jacana/M. and A. Boet. 14bcl: Jacana/H. Brehm. 14bcr: Jacana/M. and A. Boet. 14bl: Jacana/S. Cordier. 14br: Jacana/W. Wisniewski. 15a: Jacana/G. Ziesler. 15cl: Jacana/B. Coster. 15cml: Jacana/P. Prigent. 15cmr: Jacana/C. Nardin. 15cr: Jacana/S. Cordier. 15bl: Jacana/P. Prigent. 15br: Jacana/P. Prigent. 20tr: R. Viollet. 20bl: M. Thersiquel. 20br: R. Viollet/Viollet Collection. 21t: Darnis. 21c: Darnis. 21b: Andia Presse/Betermin. 22al: A. Chopin. 22tr: Éditions Minihi Levenez/Y. Le Berre, B. Tanguy, Y. P. Castel. 22c: Éditions Coop. Breizh. 22b: Keystone Illustration. 23tl: Corbis/Sygma/S. Bassouls. 23tr: Scope/B. Galeron. 23c: J. L. Charmet. *La Revue Illustrée.* Bibliothèque des Arts Décoratifs, Paris. 23b: Rue des Archives. 24c: J. L. Charmet/M. Mehent. 24br: J. L. Charmet. 24–25c: G. Dagli Ortl/Louis Garneray. Musée des Beaux-Arts, Rouen. 25tl: ADAGP, Paris 2002/M. Dupuis. *Pardon des Terre-Neuvas,* P. Signac (1928). Musée d'Histoire, St-Malo. 25tr: RMN/G. Blot. *Combat Naval,* Théodore Gudin (1802–80). Château de Versailles et Trianon. 25bl: Gamma/G. Philippot, T. Goisque. 25br: Corbis/Sygma/D. Aubert. 26–7c: M. Thersiquel. Fête des Brodeuses, Pont-l'Abbé. 26tr: G. Dagli Orti. *Femmes de Plougastel au Pardon de Ste-Anne,* C. Cottet. Musée des Beaux-Arts, Rennes. 26cl: Michael Thersiquel, brooch by P. Toulhoat. 26cr: R. Viollet. 26bl: M. Thersiquel. 26bc: Éditions Jos Le Doaré. 26br: Éditions Jos Le Doaré. 27al: Gernot. Brest. 27 tr: Éditions Jos Le Doaré. 27c: Musée Départemental Breton, Quimper. 27bl, bc, br: Éditions Jos Le Doaré. 28b: Étonnants Voyageurs festival, Rennes. *Whales in the Ice in the Arctic,* William Bradford, Brandywine, Calgary, Canada. 29t: A.-L. Gac. 30b: G. Cazade, public relations, St-Malo. 31b: A.-L. Gac. 32tr: Scope/B. Galeron. 32tl: R. Viollet. 32c: Hachette/C. Boulanger. 32bl: Scope/B. Galeron. 32br: Andia Presse/Le Coz. 33ar: Scope/B. Galeron. 33br: Y. Boëlle. 34: AKG Paris. *Chronique de Bretagne,* Pierre Le Beau. Bibliothèque Nationale, Paris. 37t: Leemage/L. de Selva. Morlaix church. 37c: Archbishopric of Rennes. Cartulaire de Redon No. 9, 11th century. 38t: Josse. *Capture of Dinan and Rendering the Keys.* Musée de la Tapisserie, Bayeux. 38c: Josse, BN, Paris. 38b: Hachette. 39a: Leemage/L. de Selva. 39c: AKG Paris/J. P. Dumontier. Église St-Yves, La Roche Meurice. 39b: RMN/J.G. Berizzi. Musée des Traditions Populaires, Paris. 40t & 40c: AKG Paris. *Chronique de Bretagne,* Pierre Le Beau. Bibliothèque Nationale, Paris. 41t: G. Dagli Orti. *Chronique en Prose de Bertrand Du Guesclin.* Bibliothèque Municipale, Rouen. 41c: Josse. *Procès de Gilles de Rais.* Bibliothèque Nationale,

Paris. **41bl**: G. Dagli Orti. Detail of Dance of Death fresco. La Ferté Loupière church. **41bl**: Hachette. **42tl**: RMN. Miniature of Anne of Brittany (1499). Musée de la Renaissance, Écouen. **42tr**: Leemage/ L. de Selva. Coat of arms of Anne of Brittany (1514). Bibliothèque Municipale, Rennes. **42–3c**: G. Dagli Orti. *Marriage of Charles VIII and Anne of Brittany*, St-Èvre. Château de Versailles. **42cl**: *Chroniques et Histoires de Bretons*, Pierre Le Beau, Bibliothèque Nationale, Paris. **43tl**: Josse. *Louis XII and Anne of Brittany*. Musée Condé, Chantilly. **43tr**: G. Dagli Orti. *Vie des Femmes Célèbres*, A. du Four. Musée Dobrée, Nantes. **43c**: Bridgeman/Giraudon. *Claude de France*. Pushkin Museum, Moscow. **43bl**: G. Dagli Orti. Biblioteca Marciana, Venice. **43br**: Charles Hémon. Gold reliquary with the heart of Anne of Brittany. Musée Dobrée, Nantes. **44tl**: Marine Nationale, Service Historique de la Marine, Brest. *Carte Britanniae*. **44c**: RMN/F. Raux. *François d'Argouges* (1669), J. Frosne. Château de Versailles et Trianon. **44bl**: Hachette. Engraving by the Rouargues brothers. **45t**: AKG Paris/ S. Domingie. *Campaign of the Holy League in Brittany*. Uffizi, Florence. **45c**: G. Dagli Orti. Lollain, private collection, Paris. **45b**: Hachette. **46a**: AKG Paris. *Jean Cottereau*, A.F. Carrière. Bibliothèque Nationale, Paris. **46c**: G. Dagli Orti. Musée Dobrée, Nantes. **46bl**: Hachette. Engraving by Berthault after Swebach-Desfontaines. **46br**: Hachette. Lithograph by Bernard-Romain Julien. **47t**: RMN/Arnaudet. Opening of the railway line from Paris to Brest. Musée de la Voiture, Château de Compiègne **47b**: A. Chopin. **49**: Hachette. Engraving by Y. M. Le Gouaz. Bibliothèque Nationale, Paris. **51bl**: Andia Presse/Diathem. **57b**: Robien Collection. *Head of an Angel*, Botticelli. Musée des Beaux-Arts, Rennes. **58b**: RMN. *Effet de Vagues*, Georges Lacombe. Musée des Beaux-Arts, Rennes. **61c**: Inventaire Général-ADAGP/C. Arthur/Lambart, 1998. *La Félicité Publique*. Centre de Documentation du Patrimoine, Rennes. **63t**: G. Dagli Orti. *The Romance of Tristan* (11th century). Musée Condé, Chantilly. **63cl**: AKG Paris. *Histoire de Merlin*, R. de Boron. Bibliothèque Nationale, Paris. **63cr**: Hachette. *The Holy Grail Appears before the Knights of the Round Table*. Bibliothèque Nationale, Paris. **63bl**: J. L. Charmet. *King Arthur and the Knights of the Round Table*, fresco by Viollet-Le-Duc. Bibliothèque des Arts Décoratifs, Paris. **63br**: J. L. Charmet. *Merlin and Vivien*, Gustave Doré. Bibliothèque des Arts Décoratifs, Paris. **67b**: Hachette. **68c**: D. Provost. clogs, 1928. Musée de l'Outil et des Métiers, Tinténiac. **69b**: Hachette. Lithograph by Lardereau. **72**: Dorling Kindersley except **72b**: Hachette/Musée de Bayeux. **73–5**: Dorling Kindersley. **77t**: Jacana/M. Willemeit. **82a**: Lee Miller. **94br**: Gaulish village, Pleumeur Bodou. **95b**: Jacana/J. T. Guillots. **97b**: Bertrand Brelivet Collection/carte-postale.com. **99br**: RMN/P. Bernard. *Rue à Bréhat*, Henri Dabadie. Musée des Beaux-Arts, Lille. **101a**: G. Dagli Orti. Engraving from *Petit Journal*. **102bl**:

Alain Grenier, private collection. **104b**: Quintin town hall. Musée-Atelier des Toiles de Lin. **105c**: Musée Mathurin Méheut, Lamballe. **119t**: P. Seitz/Caplan and Co. café-bookshop, Morlaix. **121t**: Office Municipal de Tourisme, Roscoff. Musée des Johnnies. **127t**: Musée Départemental Breton/P. Sicard. *Le Miroir du Monde*, Michel le Nobletz. See of Quimper. **127br**: Écomusée des Goémoniers et de l'Algue/S. Allançon, Plouguerneau. **129c**: Jacana/B. Coster. **133t**: RMN/J. de la Baume. *La Mer Jaune*, Georges Lacombe. Musée des Beaux-Arts, Brest. **135tl**: Georges Perrot, Brest. **135tr**: Océanopolis/T. Joyeux. **147b**: Abbaye de Landevennec. Frontispiece of the Évangéliaire de Landevennec (c. 870). **148–9**: Louis Le Bras, parish priest at Crozon. **153b**: SCOPE/B. Galeron. **155t**: Keystone. **158tr**: Musée Départemental Breton, Quimper. **158tl**: Musée Départemental Breton, Quimper. **161t**: RMN/M. Bellot. *Le Génie à la Guirlande*, Charles Filiger. **164cl, cr, c**: Musée Départemental Breton, Quimper. **167br**: Josse. Musée du Château, Versailles. **168b**: Le Gonidec canning factory. **169b**: Josse. *La Belle Angèle*, P. Gauguin. Musée d'Orsay, Paris. **177t**: Keystone Illustration. **181tl**: Gamma/T. Rannou. **194b**: Pontivy town hall. **205t**: RMN/ M. Bellot. *Louis XII and Anne of Brittany at Prayer*. Musée Dobrée, Nantes. **206tl**: Musée du Château des Ducs de Bretagne. **206b**: G. Dagli Orti. Musée Dobrée, Nantes. **207al**: ADAGP, Paris 2002/RMN/C. Jean. *Le Gaulage des Pommes*, Émile Bernard. Musée des Beaux-Arts, Nantes. **207ar**: Hachette. **208bl**: Musée de Chantilly. *Duc de Mercoeur*. **211b**: Josse/Anonyme. *D'Elbée Libérant les Prisonniers Bleus*, Cholet. **213**: J. L. Charmet. *L'Hôtel de France à St-Malo*. Musée Carnavalet, Paris. **217t**: Logis de France. **228t**: Coreff. Brasserie des Deux Rivières, Morlaix. **230**: L. Bianquis except **al**: A. Chopin. **231**: L. Bianquis except **br**: A. Chopin. **242a**: Conserverie Le Gonidec. **242cl**: CRTB/J.P.Gratien. **243t**: CRTB/Martin Schulte-Kellinghaus. **243b**: G. Fisher. **244**: A. Chopin except *Almanach du Marin Breton*: Œuvre du Marin Breton, and nautilus shells: Verreries de Bréhat. **245**: A. Chopin. **246t**: A.-L. Gac. **246b**: G. Saliou. **253**: Hachette. View of Brest harbour. **255cl**: TV Breizh. **255 cr**: *Armen*; *Bretagne Magazine*. **255b**: A. Chopin. **258c**: Dorling Kindersley/ M. Alexander. **259**: Banque de France. **260**: Dorling Kindersley/ M. Alexander. **261t**: Andia Presse/Bigot. **262t**: press office, Air France. **262c**: Dorling Kindersley/P. Kenward. **264t**: Dorling Kindersley/M. Alexander. **264b**: SNCF-CAV/Fabro & Levêque. **266tl**: Dorling Kindersley/M. Alexander. **267**: Dorling Kindersley/M. Alexander.

Jacket: Front – DK PICTURE LIBRARY: Philippe Giraud bc and bl; Neil Mersh c; THE IMAGE BANK/GETTY IMAGES: Michael Pasdzior main image. Back – DK PICTURE LIBRARY: Philippe Giraud tl and br. Spine – THE IMAGE BANK/GETTY IMAGES: Michael Pasdzior.

Phrase Book

IN EMERGENCY

Help!	Au secours!	oh se**koor**
Stop!	Arrêtez!	aret-**ay**
Call a	Appelez un	apuh-**lay** uñ
doctor!	médecin!	med**sañ**
Call an	Appelez une	apuh-**lay** oon
ambulance!	ambulance!	oñboo-**loñs**
Call the	Appelez la	apuh-**lay** lah
police!	police!	poh-**lees**
Call the fire	Appelez les	apuh-lay leh
department!	pompiers!	poñ-**peeyay**
Where is the	Où est le téléphone	oo ay luh tehleh**fon**
nearest telephone?	le plus proche?	luh ploo **prosh**
Where is the	Où est l'hôpital	oo ay l'**opee**tal luh
nearest hospital?	le plus proche?	ploo **prosh**

COMMUNICATION ESSENTIALS

Yes	Oui	wee
No	Non	noñ
Please	S'il vous plaît	seel voo **play**
Thank you	Merci	mer-**see**
Excuse me	Excusez-moi	exkoo-**zay** mwah
Hello	Bonjour	boñ**zhoor**
Goodbye	Au revoir	oh ruh-**vwar**
Good night	Bonsoir	boñ-**swar**
Morning	Le matin	ma**tañ**
Afternoon	L'après-midi	l'apreh-**meedee**
Evening	Le soir	swar
Yesterday	Hier	ee**yehr**
Today	Aujourd'hui	oh-zhoor-**dwee**
Tomorrow	Demain	duh**mañ**
Here	Ici	ee-**see**
There	Là	lah
What?	Quel, quelle?	kel, kel
When?	Quand?	koñ
Why?	Pourquoi?	poor-**kwah**
Where?	Où?	oo

USEFUL PHRASES

How are you?	Comment allez-vous?	kom-moñ tal**ay** voo
Very well,	Très bien,	treh byañ,
thank you.	merci.	mer-**see**
Pleased to	Enchanté de faire	oñshoñ-**tay** duh fehr
meet you.	votre connaissance.	votr kon-ay-**sans**
See you soon.	À bientôt.	byañ-**toh**
That's fine	Voilà qui est parfait	vwalah kee ay par**fay**
Where is/are...?	Où est/sont...?	oo ay/soñ
How far	Combien de	kom-**byañ** duh keelo-
is it to...?	kilomètres d'ici à...?	metr d'ee-**see** ah
Which	Quelle est la	kel ay lah **deer**-
way to...?	direction pour...?	ek-**syoñ** poor
Do you speak	Parlez-vous	par-**lay** voo
English?	anglais?	oñg-**lay**
I don't	Je ne	zhuh nuh kom-
understand.	comprends pas.	**proñ** pah
Could you	Pouvez-vous parler	poo-**vay** voo par-**lay**
speak slowly	moins vite s'il	mwañ veet seel
please?	vous plaît?	voo play
I'm sorry.	Excusez-moi.	exkoo-**zay** mwah

USEFUL WORDS

big	grand	groñ
small	petit	puh-**tee**
hot	chaud	show
cold	froid	frwah
good	bon	boñ
bad	mauvais	moh-**veh**
enough	assez	assay
well	bien	byañ
open	ouvert	oo-**ver**
closed	fermé	fer-**meh**
left	gauche	gohsh
right	droit	drwah
straight ahead	tout droit	too drwah
near	près	preh
far	loin	lwañ
up	en haut	oñ oh
down	en bas	oñ bah
early	de bonne heure	duh bon **urr**
late	en retard	oñ ruh-**tar**
entrance	l'entrée	l'on-**tray**
exit	la sortie	sor-**tee**
toilet	les toilettes, les WC	twah-let, vay-**see**
free, unoccupied	libre	leebr
free, no charge	gratuit	grah-**twee**

MAKING A TELEPHONE CALL

I'd like to place a	Je voudrais faire	zhuh voo-dreh fehr
long-distance call.	un interurbain.	uñ añter-oorbañ
I'd like to make	Je voudrais faire une	zhuh voo**dreh** fehr
a collect call.	communication	oon komoonikah-
	PCV.	**syoñ** peh-seh-veh
I'll try again	Je rappelerai	zhuh rapel-
later.	plus tard.	**eray** ploo tar
Can I leave a	Est-ce que je peux	es-**keh** zhuh puh
message?	laisser un message?	leh-**say** uñ mehsazh
Hold on.	Ne quittez pas,	nuh kee-**tay** pah
	s'il vous plaît.	seel voo play
Could you speak	Pouvez-vous parler	poo-**vay** voo par-
up a little please?	un peu plus fort?	**lay** uñ puh ploo for
local call	la communication	komoonikah-
	locale	**syoñ** low-**kal**

SHOPPING

How much	C'est combien	say kom-**byañ**
does this cost?	s'il vous plaît?	seel voo play
I would like ...	je voudrais...	zhuh voo-**dray**
Do you have?	Est-ce que vous avez?	es-**kuh** voo zav**ay**
I'm just	Je regarde	zhuh ruh**gar**
looking.	seulement.	suhl**moñ**
Do you take	Est-ce que vous	es-**kuh** voo
credit cards?	acceptez les cartes	zaksept-**ay** leh kart
	de crédit?	duh kreh-**dee**
Do you take	Est-ce que vous	es-**kuh** voo
traveler's	acceptez les	zaksept-**ay** leh
checks?	chèques de voyage?	shek duh vwa**yazh**
What time	A quelle heure	ah kel urr
do you open?	vous êtes ouvert?	voo zet oo-**ver**
What time	A quelle heure	ah kel urr
do you close?	vous êtes fermé?	voo zet fer-**may**
This one.	Celui-ci.	suhl-wee-**see**
That one.	Celui-là.	suhl-wee-**lah**
expensive	cher	shehr
cheap	pas cher,	pah shehr,
	bon marché	boñ mar-**shay**
size, clothes	la taille	tye
size, shoes	la pointure	pwañ-**tur**
white	blanc	bloñ
black	noir	nwahr
red	rouge	roozh
yellow	jaune	zhohwn
green	vert	vehr
blue	bleu	bluh

TYPES OF SHOPS

antiques	le magasin	maga-**zañ**
shop	d'antiquités	d'oñteekee-**tay**
bakery	la boulangerie	booloñ-**zhuree**
bank	la banque	boñk
book store	la librairie	lee-**brehree**
butcher	la boucherie	boo-**shehree**
cake shop	la pâtisserie	patee-**sree**
cheese shop	la fromagerie	fromazh-**ree**
dairy	la crémerie	krem-**ree**
department store	le grand magasin	groñ maga-**zañ**
delicatessen	la charcuterie	sharkoot-**ree**
drugstore	la pharmacie	farmah-**see**
fish seller	la poissonnerie	pwasson-**ree**
gift shop	le magasin de	maga-**zañ** duh
	cadeaux	ka**doh**
greengrocer	le marchand	mar-**shoñ** duh
	de légumes	lay-**goom**
grocery	l'alimentation	alee-moñta-**syoñ**
hairdresser	le coiffeur	kwa**fuhr**
market	le marché	marsh-**ay**
newsstand	le magasin de	maga-**zañ** duh
	journaux	zhoor-**no**
post office	la poste,	pohst,
	le bureau de poste,	booroh duh pohst,
	le PTT	peh-teh-teh
shoe store	le magasin	maga-**zañ**
	de chaussures	duh show-**soor**
supermarket	le supermarché	soo pehr-**marshay**
tobacconist	le tabac	tabah
travel agent	l'agence	l'azhoñs
	de voyages	duh vwayazh

SIGHTSEEING

abbey	l'abbaye	l'abay-**ee**
art gallery	la galerie d'art	galer-**ree** dart
bus station	la gare routière	gahr roo-tee-**yehr**

cathedral	la cathédrale	katay-**dral**
church	l'église	l'ayg**leez**
garden	le jardin	zhar-**dañ**
library	la bibliothèque	beeble**leeo**-tek
museum	le musée	moo-**zay**
tourist information office	les renseignements touristiques, le syndicat d'initiative	roñsayn-**moñ** too-rees-**teek**, sandee-ka d'eenee-syat**eev**
town hall	l'hôtel de ville	l'**ohtel** duh veel
train station	la gare (SNCF)	gahr (es-en-say-ef)
private mansion	l'hôtel particulier	l'**ohtel** partikoo-**lyay**
closed for public holiday	fermeture jour férié	fehrmeh-**tur** zhoor fehree-**ay**

STAYING IN A HOTEL

Do you have a vacant room?	Est-ce que vous avez une chambre?	es-kuh voo-**zavay** oon shambr
double room, with double bed	la chambre à deux personnes, avec un grand lit	shambr ah duh pehr-son avek un groñn lee
twin room	la chambre à deux lits	shambr ah duh lee
single room	la chambre à une personne	shambr ah oon pehr-**son**
room with a bath, shower	la chambre avec salle de bains, une douche	shambr avek sal duh bañ, oon doosh
porter	le garçon	gar-**soñ**
key	la clef	klay
I have a reservation.	J'ai fait une réservation.	zhay fay oon rayzehrva-**syoñ**

EATING OUT

Have you got a table?	Avez-vous une table libre?	avay-**voo** oon tahbl leebr
I want to reserve a table.	Je voudrais réserver une table.	zhuh voo-**dray** rayzehr-**vay** oon tahbl
The check please.	L'addition s'il vous plaît.	l'adee-**syoñ** seel voo **play**
I am a vegetarian.	Je suis végétarien.	zhuh swee vezhay-**tehryañ**
Waitress/ waiter	Madame, Mademoiselle/ Monsieur	mah-**dam**, mah-demwah**zel**/ muh-**syuh**
menu	le menu, la carte	men-**oo**, kart
fixed-price menu	le menu à prix fixe	men-**oo** ah pree feeks
cover charge	le couvert	koo-**vehr**
wine list	la carte des vins	**kart**-deh vañ
glass	le verre	vehr
bottle	la bouteille	boo-**tay**
knife	le couteau	koo-**toh**
fork	la fourchette	for-**shet**
spoon	la cuillère	kwee-**yehr**
breakfast	le petit déjeuner	puh-**tee** deh-**zhuh-nay**
lunch	le déjeuner	deh-**zhuh-nay**
dinner	le dîner	dee-**nay**
main course	le plat principal	plah prañsee-**pal**
appetizer, first course	l'entrée, le hors d'oeuvre	l'oñ-**tray**, or-duhvr
dish of the day	le plat du jour	plah doo zhoor
wine bar	le bar à vin	bar ah vañ
café	le café	ka-**fay**
rare	saignant	say-**noñ**
medium	à point	ah **pwañ**
well-done	bien cuit	byañ **kwee**

MENU DECODER

l'agneau	l'an**yoh**	lamb
l'ail	l'eye	garlic
la banane	ba**nan**	banana
le beurre	burr	butter
la bière, bière	bee-**yehr**, bee-**yehr**	beer, draft
à la pression	ah lah pres-**syoñ**	beer
le bifteck, le steack	beef-**tek**, stek	steak
le boeuf	buhf	beef
bouilli	boo-**yee**	boiled
le café	kah-**fay**	coffee
le canard	kanar	duck
le chocolat	shoko-lah	chocolate
le citron	see-**troñ**	lemon
le citron pressé	see-**troñ** press-**eh**	fresh lemon juice
les crevettes	kruh-**vet**	prawns
les crustacés	**kroos**-ta-say	shellfish
cuit au four	kweet oh foor	baked
le dessert	deh-**ser**	dessert

l'eau minérale	l'oh **meeney**-ral	mineral water
les escargots	leh zes-kar-**goh**	snails
les frites	freet	chips
le fromage	from-**azh**	cheese
le fruit frais	frwee freh	fresh fruit
les fruits de mer	frwee duh mer	seafood
le gâteau	gah-**toh**	cake
la glace	glas	ice, ice cream
grillé	gree-**yay**	grilled
le homard	omahr	lobster
l'huile	l'weel	oil
le jambon	zhoñ-**boñ**	ham
le lait	leh	milk
les légumes	lay-**goom**	vegetables
la moutarde	moo-**tard**	mustard
l'oeuf	l'uf	egg
les oignons	leh zon**yoñ**	onions
les olives	leh zol**eev**	olives
l'orange	l'oroñzh	orange
l'orange pressée	l'oroñzh press-**eh**	fresh orange juice
le pain	pan	bread
le petit pain	puh-**tee** pañ	roll
poché	posh-**ay**	poached
le poisson	pwah-**ssoñ**	fish
le poivre	pwavr	pepper
la pomme	pom	apple
les pommes de terre	pom-duh **tehr**	potatoes
le porc	por	pork
le potage	poh-**tazh**	soup
le poulet	poo-**lay**	chicken
le riz	ree	rice
rôti	row-**tee**	roast
la sauce	sohs	sauce
la saucisse	soh**sees**	sausage, fresh
sec	sek	dry
le sel	sel	salt
la soupe	soop	soup
le sucre	sookr	sugar
le thé	tay	tea
le toast	toast	toast
la viande	vee-**yand**	meat
le vin blanc	vañ **bloñ**	white wine
le vin rouge	vañ **roozh**	red wine
le vinaigre	vee**naygr**	vinegar

NUMBERS

0	zéro	zeh-**roh**
1	un, une	uñ, oon
2	deux	duh
3	trois	trwah
4	quatre	katr
5	cinq	sañk
6	six	sees
7	sept	set
8	huit	weet
9	neuf	nerf
10	dix	dees
11	onze	oñz
12	douze	dooz
13	treize	trehz
14	quatorze	ka**torz**
15	quinze	kañz
16	seize	sehz
17	dix-sept	dees-**set**
18	dix-huit	dees-**weet**
19	dix-neuf	dees-**nerf**
20	vingt	vañ
30	trente	tront
40	quarante	karo**ñt**
50	cinquante	sañko**ñt**
60	soixante	swaso**ñt**
70	soixante-dix	swaso**ñt**-dees
80	quatre-vingts	katr-**vañ**
90	quatre-vingt-dix	katr-vañ-**dees**
100	cent	soñ
1,000	mille	meel

TIME

one minute	une minute	oon mee-**noot**
one hour	une heure	oon urr
half an hour	une demi-heure	oon **duh-mee** urr
Monday	lundi	luñ-**dee**
Tuesday	mardi	mar-**dee**
Wednesday	mercredi	mehrkruh-**dee**
Thursday	jeudi	zhuh-**dee**
Friday	vendredi	voñdruh-**dee**
Saturday	samedi	sam-**dee**
Sunday	dimanche	dee-**moñsh**